ADOBE
CREATIVE SUITE 2
WORKFLOW

BY

Jennifer Alspach

Shari Nakano

Steve Samson

ADOBE CREATIVE SUITE 2 WORKFLOW

O'REILLY®

Beijing, Cambridge, Farnham,

Köln, Paris, Sebastopol,

Taipei, and Tokyo

Adobe Creative Suite 2 Workflow
by Jennifer Alspach, Shari Nakano,
and Steve Samson

Published by O'Reilly Media, Inc., 1005 Gravenstein
Highway North, Sebastopol, CA 95472.

O'Reilly books may be purchased for educational,
business, or sales promotional use. Online editions
are also available for most titles (*safari.oreilly.com*).
For more information, contact our corporate/
institutional sales department: (800) 998-9938 or
corporate@oreilly.com.

Editors: Steve Weiss and Jennifer Eberhardt
Technical Editor: Sheila Julien
Production Editor: Genevieve d'Entremont
Cover Designer: Mike Kohnke
Interior Designer: NOON
Production Services: Specialized Composition, Inc.

Printing History:
December 2005: First Edition.

 This book uses RepKover, a durable
and flexible lay-flat binding.

ISBN: 0-596-10236-4

[F]

ABOUT THE AUTHORS

Jennifer Alspach

Jennifer is an expert on Adobe technologies and has written or coauthored many books, including *Acrobat 7 Visual QuickStart Guide* (Peachpit Press), *Illustrator CS Bible* (John Wiley & Sons), *Teach Yourself Photoshop 5.0/5.5* and *Photoshop and Illustrator Synergy Studio Secrets* (IDG Books), and *Illustrator 7 Complete* (Hayden Books). She is a world-renowned artist and has spoken at many conferences and trade shows.

Other works by Jennifer include *PhotoDeluxe Home Edition for Windows Visual QuickStart Guide*, *PhotoDeluxe for Windows, Macintosh Visual QuickStart Guide* (Peachpit Press); *Illustrator Filter Finesse* (Random House); *Microsoft BOB* (Que); and chapters from *Adobe Photoshop 5.5 Classroom in a Book* and *Illustrator 8.0 Advanced Classroom in a Book* (Adobe Press).

Shari Nakano

Shari Nakano is a web and graphics designer who has been in the computer industry for more than 10 years. She uses a variety of applications in her work, including most of the Adobe Creative Suite products (Acrobat, Photoshop, GoLive, and Illustrator); Macromedia Dreamweaver, Flash, and Fireworks; and various Microsoft Office products. A longtime user of Adobe Acrobat for both personal and business uses, she recently completed her first book, *Adobe Acrobat 7: In a Snap* (Sams Publishing).

Shari is currently the webmaster for a large agricultural firm in California's Central Valley, where she uses GoLive to create and maintain the company's internal web site. She also does web design and consulting for other Central Valley customers.

Steve Samson

Steve has 16 years of experience teaching about computer software. During that time he has conducted more than 1,000 classes and seminars on Adobe creative software, Microsoft Office software, and other productivity applications. Past clients include Adobe Systems, Bank of America, McDonnel-Douglas, Aetna, ExecuTrain, and the Los Angeles County Office of Education. For the past three years, Steve has served as a consultant for Adobe Systems's annual Tech Summit, a gathering of more than 200 engineers and other technical personnel from all over the world.

Steve's past work experience includes being a Senior Technical Writer and Senior Training Specialist for Adobe Systems, a Senior Instructor for Catapult Software Training, and a Manager of Technical Documentation for MetaTools (developers of plug-ins and companion software for Adobe creative applications).

In addition to his training experience, Steve has eight years of experience as an author. His published writing includes: *Teach Yourself Adobe Creative Suite All-in-One* (Sams Publishing); *PhotoDeluxe 2 Visual QuickStart Guide, ACT! 2.0 Visual QuickStart Guide*, and *The Macintosh Bible*, Fifth Edition (Peachpit Press); *Illustrator 7 Complete* and *Photoshop 4 Complete* (Hayden Books); and *Kai's Power Tools Studio Secrets* (IDG Books).

Steve has also served as a lead tech writer for Adobe Systems's Acrobat Messenger online help and as a technical editor for the Photoshop 5.5 software manual (Adobe Systems), *Photoshop 5.5 Classroom in a Book* (Adobe Press), and *Illustrator 8 Bible* (IDG Books).

ABOUT THE TECHNICAL EDITOR

Sheila Julien has more than five years of experience as a copywriter, editor, and technical editor. She has served as editor of the *SBS Digital Design* newsletter, which offers features and tutorials on a wide variety of software applications (particularly Adobe products). She also launched the *Photoshop Fix* newsletter. In addition to working with digital design publications, Sheila is currently an editor for an independent book publisher. Before entering the publishing industry, she taught English and journalism for six years.

COLOPHON

Our look is the result of reader comments, our own experimentation, and feedback from distribution channels. Distinctive covers complement our distinctive approach to technical topics, breathing personality and life into potentially dry subjects.

Genevieve d'Entremont was the production editor for *Adobe Creative Suite 2 Workflow*. Rachel Wheeler was the copyeditor. Jennifer Eberhardt, Phil Dangler, and Claire Cloutier provided quality control. Specialized Composition, Inc. provided production services.

Mike Kohnke designed the cover of this book using Adobe InDesign CS. Linda Palo produced the cover layout with InDesign CS, using the Adobe Univers font.

NOON (*www.designatnoon.com*) designed the interior layout. The text and heading fonts are Univers and Gotham Book. The illustrations and screenshots that appear in the book were produced by Robert Romano, Jessamyn Read, and Lesley Borash, using Macromedia FreeHand MX and Adobe Photoshop CS.

ACKNOWLEDGMENTS FROM JENNIFER ALSPACH

First and foremost, I want to thank Steve Weiss for taking an idea and bringing it to life. Huge thanks to Jennifer Eberhardt, who turned this jumble of words into an amazing book. Thanks as well goes to Sheila Julien for her great job of tech editing. Thanks to my husband Ted, for his unwavering support, and to Gage and Dakota, who have learned such patience and my mantra…just one more chapter. Also thanks to my wonderful support group of friends and family. You all are the true meaning of life.

ACKNOWLEDEGMENTS FROM SHARI NAKANO

A special thanks to Jennifer Eberhardt for all her support, hard work, and keeping me on track on this book. I couldn't have done it without my own personal cheering section! Another very special thanks to Sheila Julien for making sure I made sense!

A big thanks to Steve Weiss and O'Reilly for giving me the chance to write this book!

I would still be pounding my head against the wall if it weren't for help from the folks at Adobe. A special thanks to Devin Fernandez, Sonja Brix, and Whitney McCleary, whose input and expertise helped fill these pages.

A very big, special thanks to Steve Samson. His support and talent have been an inspiration to me.

And last but not least, a huge thanks to Jen Alspach for spearheading this book project. Without her, none of this would have been possible! Jen is an amazing woman, and I consider myself very lucky to have her not only as a colleague, but as a friend.

ACKNOWLEDGMENTS FROM STEVE SAMSON

Thanks to Jen Alspach for the opportunity to participate in this project in the first place and for "taking point" during the long trek towards its completion. (And also for her and Ted's many years of friendship.)

Thanks to Jennifer and Steve at O'Reilly, for their hard work and patience throughout the writing process, and to Jennifer and Sheila, for their great editing work.

And finally, thanks and much love to Shari for her love, support, and encouragement when I needed it most.

CONTRIBUTORS

Sonja Brix
Keith Bungo
Rick Cooper
Thomas DeMeo
Devin Fernandez
Lonn Lorenz
Whitney McCleary
Scott Sawyer
Bob Scheffel

TABLE OF CONTENTS

TABLE OF CONTENTS

Preface

Congratulations on picking up this book (if you're standing in a bookstore now, congratulations on *literally* picking up this book), as it's the only book you'll find that truly provides insights on using all of Adobe's Creative Suite products together.

It's pretty difficult to be an expert in any one product within the Creative Suite, let alone all five products—six if you're counting Bridge, and you probably should. This book isn't meant as a substitute for any or all of the thousand-page tomes out there about the intricacies of each product (which may or may not provide you with answers you're looking for). Instead, this book is designed to get you thinking about how the Creative Suite products interact with each other. You'll learn which products to use in certain situations, and how to shift your focus from the product you know best to the entire Suite (and become much more productive in the process). The focus of this book is on learning about optimal workflows:

- How to move between the products and when

- Why sometimes it's better to use Photoshop for certain tasks

- Why sometimes those tasks are better done in Illustrator

- How to take advantage of the powerful integration capabilities between the products (such as keeping files in their native formats when transferring them from one application to another)

- When creating a PDF is the right choice, and when to use Acrobat for the task rather than the application you're working in

The Creative Suite isn't just a bundle of Adobe creative products; it's a product in and of itself. Once you start using it that way, you'll become immensely more efficient and realize all sorts of capabilities you never knew were there.

This is the book that treats the Creative Suite as what it is: the ultimate creative product.

Comments and Questions

Please address comments and questions concerning this book to the publisher:

O'Reilly Media, Inc.
1005 Gravenstein Highway North
Sebastopol, CA 95472
(800) 998-9938 (in the United States or Canada)
(707) 829-0515 (international or local)
(707) 829-0104 (fax)

We have a web page for this book, where we list errata, examples, and any additional information. You can access this page at:

http://www.oreilly.com/catalog/adobecs2work

To comment or ask technical questions about this book, send email to:

bookquestions@oreilly.com

For more information about our books, conferences, Resource Centers, and the O'Reilly Network, see our web site at:

http://www.oreilly.com

Safari Enabled

When you see a Safari® Enabled icon on the cover of your favorite technology book, that means it's available online through the O'Reilly Network Safari Bookshelf.

Safari offers a solution that's better than e-books: it's a virtual library that lets you easily search thousands of top tech books, cut and paste code samples, download chapters, and find quick answers when you need the most accurate, current information. Try it for free at *http://safari.oreilly.com*.

01

Bridge and Version Cue:
The Hub for Creative Suite 2

Just when you thought you knew it all about Creative Suite, Adobe has gone and given you much more to work with—and the power to connect all your Creative Suite 2 applications via the new Bridge and manage your files with Version Cue CS2.

EXPLORING BRIDGE AND VERSION CUE

Adobe Bridge is a built-in browser that replaces the File Browser present in earlier versions of Photoshop. This control center lets you browse for files, view thumbnails, and organize files in all of the Creative Suite 2 formats (and many others as well). Bridge also enables you to do extensive file searches, even down to specific attributes that you've entered in a file's description area. And if you can't find what you're looking for in your own collection, within the Bridge Center you can view and buy images from an extensive stock photo library.

Version Cue CS2 brings an all-powerful file manager to the Creative Suite 2 product line, ending versioning headaches. Version Cue CS2 allows you to access all your files, using its powerful search engine to find what you're looking for—including any and all versions you've created of a particular file. Many creative professionals create multiple versions of a file, to show their clients a variety of ideas. Version Cue CS2 lets you organize and track all the current and historical versions of the files in a project. You can use Version Cue CS2 to track a file through the workflow process, and to send out PDFs of selected versions for comment and review.

Figure 1-1 shows the icons for Bridge (left) and Version Cue CS2 (right). Get used to these icons—you're going to be seeing them a lot!

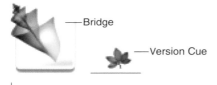
——Bridge

——Version Cue

FIGURE 1-1

USING AND VIEWING ADOBE BRIDGE

Just as Captain Kirk was able to command the U.S.S. Enterprise from his captain's chair on the bridge, you can use Adobe Bridge to browse and manipulate all your CS2 files from one central location. Gone are the days of manually searching your hard drive or file server for an image you thought was in a particular folder but wasn't, or opening numerous applications to view a group of selected images that are in different file formats.

Adobe Bridge provides a centralized location from which you can view all the files and images in a project or projects, browse and organize your collection, and even purchase stock photos. Just think what you'll be able to do with all the time you'll save now that you no longer have to spend hours looking for those files!

How to Access Bridge

You can access Bridge from Illustrator CS2, Photoshop CS2, or any of the other Creative Suite 2 applications, or you can use it as a standalone product. Feel free to choose any of these ways to open Bridge:

- In Windows, to start Bridge, go to the taskbar and choose Start→All Programs→Adobe Bridge. (If you are working with Adobe Bridge on a regular basis, you might consider adding a shortcut to it on your desktop. That way, Bridge is just a double-click away.)

- In Mac OS, on your hard drive, choose Applications→Adobe Bridge and double-click on the Bridge icon.

- From within Photoshop CS2, Illustrator CS2, InDesign CS2, or GoLive CS2, choose File→Browse.

tip	Bridge has a set of scripts that it loads automatically each time it starts. You can save startup time by disabling these startup scripts. To do so, simply hold down the Shift key while Bridge is starting up.

What You Can Do with Bridge

There's plenty you can do with Bridge. Here are just a few of the many features it offers, to whet your appetite:

BROWSING FOR FILES: With Bridge, you are not limited to searching for just native Adobe files, such as *.psd* documents; you can also search for non-Adobe files, such as Microsoft Word documents or files created in Macromedia Flash. To search for a specific file, select Edit→Find from the Bridge menu bar. This will open the Find dialog box, shown in Figure 1-2. Select where you want Bridge to look, indicate whether you want to search for past versions of Version Cue files, choose the Criteria (including all or part of the filename), and then click Find. The results will display in the content section of the Bridge work area. You can also save the search results as a collection with the Save as

Collection button. That way, you'll be able to access the same files again without having to redo the search. (For more on file searching, see "Searching for Files" later in this
chapter.)

FIGURE 1-2

RATING FILES: You can assign labels and ratings to your files in either Bridge or Version Cue. You can choose to apply any of the star ratings (1–5) to indicate the quality of a
file—for example, to mark which versions the client liked or disliked—or you can apply
a label to indicate its status (in progress, waiting for approval, finished, at printer, etc.).
Once you've applied ratings to your files, you can use those ratings to sort the files. For
instance, you may want to see only the images with the best quality ratings, or all images
at a particular stage in the workflow. To apply a rating to a file, select the file in the Version
Cue/Bridge window, choose Label, and then choose any of the star ratings or other labels.

BROWSING AND PURCHASING STOCK PHOTOS: You can browse through a wide variety of royalty-free images in the Adobe Stock Photos collection right from Adobe Bridge.
To access the Adobe Stock Photos, select Adobe Stock Photos in the Favorites panel. If
you find an image you like, you can add it to your shopping cart and purchase it, without
ever leaving Bridge (see Figure 1-3).

tip
Adobe Bridge lets you view images and other files in a slideshow presentation format. While in Bridge, navigate to the
folder containing the files and images you wish to view. Then
choose View→Slide Show from the Bridge menu bar.

FIGURE 1-3

THE BRIDGE CENTER: The Adobe Bridge Center, available only if you purchase Creative Suite 2, displays a Favorites panel, Recent Files and Recent Folders lists, an RSS Reader, and Tips and Tricks for all Adobe CS2 applications and other Adobe products, as shown in Figure 1-4. You can also synchronize the color format for all your Creative Suite 2 applications with the link to the Color Management tool at the bottom of the Bridge Center. If you need quick access to the online Adobe Help Center, click on the Open Help link in the lower-right corner.

---

tip

If you press Command-Shift-Option (Ctrl-Shift-Alt on Windows) when Bridge starts up, a troubleshooting dialog will open a display that allows you to clear the cache and reset preferences.

FIGURE 1-4

Supported and Unsupported File Formats

Because Bridge was designed and developed by Adobe, you probably won't be surprised to learn that Bridge supports all the native formats of each of the Creative Suite 2 applications. Any Creative Suite files, such as *.ai* or *.psd* documents, will render into gorgeous, large thumbnails in Bridge (if you give it a bit of time to generate them, that is). Figure 1-5 shows Illustrator files, JPEGs, and PNGs. (Note that the *.doc* file doesn't show a preview.)

Bridge supports the organization and management of pretty much all file types, but it doesn't provide previews for all file types. Table 1-1 lists some common file formats for which it won't generate thumbnail previews.

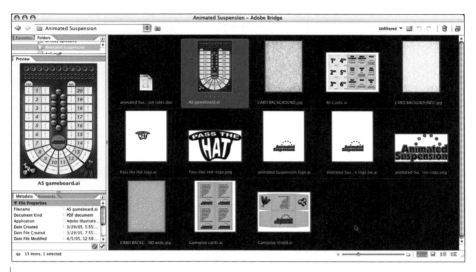

FIGURE 1-5

TABLE 1-1. FORMATS NOT SUPPORTED BY BRIDGE

PROGRAM	EXTENSION
Adobe Illustrator Version 9 and older	*.ai*
Aladdin StuffIt	*.sit* or *.sitx*
Macromedia Flash	*.fla*
Microsoft Excel	*.xls*
Microsoft PowerPoint	*.ppt*
Microsoft Word	*.doc*
QuarkXPress (Quark, Inc.)	*.qxd*
WinZip (WinZip Computing, Inc.)	*.zip*

Table 1-2 lists all the formats for which Bridge can generate previews—these are also the formats you'll probably have the most call for.

TABLE 1-2. FORMATS SUPPORTED BY BRIDGE

PROGRAM/FILE TYPE	EXTENSION
Adobe Acrobat	*.pdf*
Adobe Illustrator CS and CS2	*.ai*
Adobe InDesign CS and CS2	*.indd*
Adobe Photoshop (all versions)	*.psd*
EPS	*.eps*
GIF	*.gif*
HTML	*.htm* or *.html*
JPEG	*.jpg* or *.jpeg*
PNG	*.png*
RAW	*.raw*
SVG	*.svg*
SWF	*.swf*

To have the best Bridge experience, you might need to go through some of your older files and "update" them so that Bridge can create thumbnails for them.

One great feature of Bridge is how it supports multipage documents such as InDesign and PDF files. By default, the first page of a multipage document will be displayed as a thumbnail. However, you can set Bridge to display a thumbnail of a different page—just click the document, and you'll be able to choose any page in the file, as shown in Figure 1-6. Double-click any page in the document to open that page in the application in which it was created.

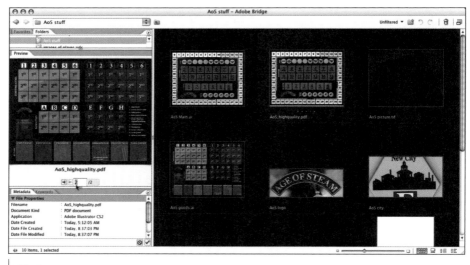

FIGURE 1-6

USING AND VIEWING VERSION CUE CS2

After you launch Bridge, you can select Version Cue CS2 from the Favorites list on the left side of the Bridge window. Version Cue CS2 was created to fix a file-management productivity issue. A lot of time can be wasted looking for files, organizing files within projects, and opening files to work on a project. However, from within Version Cue CS2, you can quickly and easily set up projects, access files, and launch all the necessary applications. With Version Cue, you can also choose whether or not to share your project: you can keep your files private or allow multiple people to access them. If you choose to share your project, you can make certain folders accessible and keep others off-limits. Using Version Cue improves productivity and enables everyone involved in a shared project to work at his or her peak.

Starting Projects

When you work in Version Cue, you create projects so that all persons working on a project can access the necessary files. You can use Version Cue for projects that involve only a single program, such as Illustrator, or for projects that involve the use of many programs together. For example, if you create a new project for an advertising piece, you might use Photoshop to touch up or tweak the image, add text and graphics in Illustrator, combine the Photoshop and Illustrator files in InDesign to do the layout, include web information using GoLive (so you can later create a web page), and finally turn the project into a PDF for review directly in Version Cue. Just like in real life, projects are kept in file folders in a virtual filing cabinet (Version Cue/Bridge).

To create a new project:

1. In the Version Cue pane, choose Tools→Version Cue→New Project (Figure 1-7).

FIGURE 1-7

2. In the New Project dialog box that displays, enter a Location for storing the project (either on your computer or on a server), the Project Name and Project Info, and whether on not you are sharing the project with others.

3. Click OK. Your project folder will now display in the Version Cue/Bridge browser.

Now that you have created your project (and shared it, if desired), you can add files or save files directly to the project folder.

Working with Files

You can drag and drop files directly into a project folder, or you can save a file into Version Cue from whatever application you're using. (For more on saving files, see "Saving Files to Version Cue Folders," below.)

If you're accessing files from a Version Cue project, it's best to use the Version Cue pane to access them, rather than jumping around on the hard drive to find the files. Version Cue can keep track of who's working on which files, which is very handy for shared projects. From the Version Cue pane, select the file that you want to work on, and double-click it to launch the application that it was created in. To find out who's working on a particular file, rest your mouse pointer over the file's page icon (Figure 1-8).

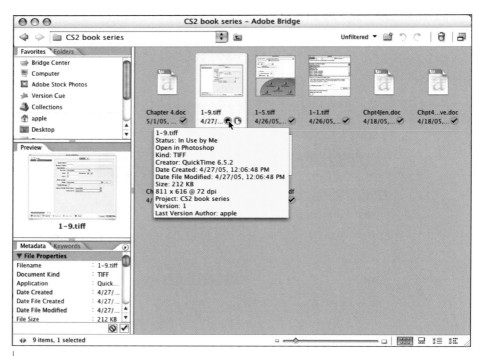

FIGURE 1-8

Viewing in Version Cue

Within the Version Cue pane, you can arrange the files as you like for better viewing and organizing. There are four views to choose from, which you can select via the View menu or the icons in the bottom-right corner of the screen:

THUMBNAILS VIEW: This view (the default) displays thumbnails of all the files within a project. Use the slider bar at the bottom of the Version Cue pane to make the thumbnails larger or smaller.

FILMSTRIP VIEW: This view shows the selected file in a large pane, with the other files displayed below it like frames in a filmstrip. Click on a different file to see that one in the large pane.

DETAILS VIEW: This view shows a small thumbnail and file information for the selected file. This information includes the filename, whether the file is synchronized, the date created, the date modified, the file size, the file type (.*pdf*, .*tiff*, .*doc*, etc.), and a list of any versions.

VERSIONS AND ALTERNATES VIEW: This view splits the pane into two vertical panes. If you select the Versions View button at the top right, the original file is shown on the left and any version names associated with that file are shown on the right. If you choose Alternates View, the original file is shown on the right and any alternates are displayed on the left (Figure 1-9).

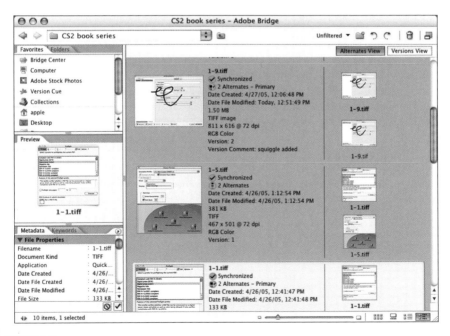

FIGURE 1-9

There's also a preview area in the Version Cue pane—click on a specific file to see a preview in the middle pane on the left. If the file happens to be a PDF with multiple pages, you can page through the file thumbnails.

Saving Files to Version Cue Folders

In Version Cue, as in any of the Creative Suite applications, you can save any file to the chosen directory on your computer using the File→Save or File→Save As commands. However, if you want to save a file in a Version Cue CS2 project folder, you'll need to choose the Save a Version command.

To save a file to a Version Cue project:

1. In any of the Creative Suite 2 programs, choose File→Save As.

2. In the Save As dialog box, choose the Use Adobe Dialog button. This will bring up the Adobe dialog, from which you can access more options and the Version Cue folders.

3. Enter a filename, and save the file in the proper Version Cue project folder (choose Version Cue from the listing on the left).

The Adobe dialog (Figure 1-10) is a super-enhanced box that offers more features than the basic Save As dialog box (Figure 1-11). Within the Adobe dialog, you can create a new project and folders within a project. Click the View icon at the top right to choose whether to view the listed files as thumbnails, details, icons, or tiles. To create a new project, click the Project Tools icon. All of the options found on the regular Save As dialog box—the format drop-down, Save options, and Color options—are also available on the Adobe dialog. There's also a Version Comments area, where you can enter comments (e.g., "original file") that you can view later in the Version Cue/Bridge browser.

[NOTE]

Adobe Acrobat 7.0 Professional and Adobe GoLive handle Version Cue in a different manner than the other Creative Suite applications and don't use the Adobe dialog box.

In Adobe Acrobat 7.0 Professional, turn on Version Cue by checking the Enable Version Cue Workgroup File Management button on the General tab of the Preferences panel. Once you've done this, you can save files to and open files from Version Cue projects, but instead of clicking the Use Adobe Dialog button to access the projects in the Save As dialog, you'll click the Version Cue button.

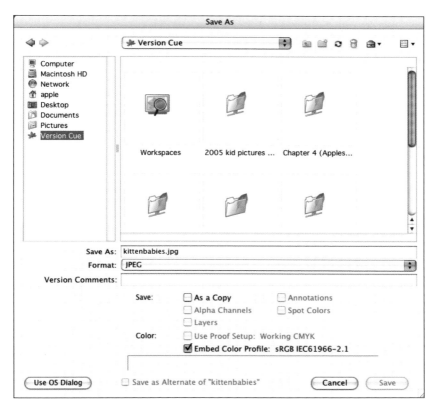

FIGURE 1-10

FIGURE 1-11

To access Version Cue from GoLive, choose File→Connect to Version Cue. Then choose the project or projects you want to work with using GoLive.

[NOTE]

In the Version Cue/Bridge browser pane, you can select an item by typing the first few letters of its name. The first item that begins with the letters you typed will be selected. If no filename begins with the letters you typed, the first item name that contains the string will be selected. This is useful for selecting files from a digital camera, which often begin with a prefix (e.g., *IMG_*). To select one of these files, simply type its unique ID.

Choosing File→Save in a CS2 application will save your local copy of the file. Choosing File→Save a Version will save the file as a version in Version Cue CS2, preserving a "snapshot" of the file as it stands. For example, say you're working on a logo design. Each time you edit the logo, you could save the new design to a new file, but a much neater solution would be to save the original file and all the subsequent versions together in Version Cue. That way, you'll be able to keep track of the progression of your work through all phases, and you won't wind up with a bunch of awkwardly named files floating around on your hard drive. (For more on versions, see "Using Versions and Alternates," later in this chapter.)

Searching for Files

You probably know from experience that searching for files sucks up a lot of production time. Often, when you've worked on many versions of a file, you'll find that you've forgotten the name of the specific version you want to return to. When you're juggling several projects, keeping track of the various files can be a nightmare. Fortunately, Version Cue comes with an extensive search engine that will help you refine the search process. The Find dialog box offers several ways to find a file:

SOURCE: You can search for files within a particular project, within Version Cue, within specific folders, within your Favorites, and more. You can also check the Include All Subfolders, Search Past Versions of Version Cue Files, and Find All Files options.

CRITERIA: Here is where you can really be specific about what you are looking for. You can choose from 11 options (Filename, File Size, Date Created, Date Modified, Document Kind, Label, Rating, Keywords, Description, Comments, and All Metadata) and specify whether the field contains, does not contain, matches exactly, starts with, or ends with the text you enter. You may specify up to 13 criteria settings.

MATCH: You can choose whether to display results that meet any of the specified criteria or all the criteria.

If it isn't already checked, you can also check the "Show find results in a new browser window" box to display the search results in a new window.

WORKING WITH VERSION CUE PDF REVIEW

Another great feature that Version Cue brings to Creative Suite 2 is its capability to start and manage web-based PDF reviews of your projects. The Version Cue Administration Utility is an essential tool for setting up and managing PDF reviews, projects, and user accounts. This utility is particularly useful because it allows you to send PDFs of your projects for review to clients and colleagues at offsite locations. Participants are able to view the PDF documents in a browser window and work with the usual commenting tools, such as the Note, Highlight, and Stamp tools. After completing the review of the project, the reviewer's comments are sent back, and Version Cue updates the original PDF review documents with the comments.

Starting the Version Cue 2 Administration Utility

The Version Cue 2 Administration Utility can be used to start and manage the PDF review process, view comments, search for PDF reviews in which you are a participant, stop reviews, and even reopen previously completed PDF reviews. Let's take a quick look at how it works.

To log onto the Version Cue 2 Administration Utility:

1. On Mac OS, click on the Version Cue icon at the top of the screen, and select Advanced Administration.

2. On Windows, double-click the Version Cue icon in the system tray (found on the far right side of the taskbar), and, in the Edit Project Properties dialog box, select Advanced Administration.

3. From a web browser, log directly onto the Version Cue Administration Utility by typing the IP or DNS address of the computer on which the Version Cue Workspace is installed.

4. From any CS2 application, choose File→Open, click the Use Adobe Dialog button, and choose the Version Cue workspace you want to administer. Then choose Tools→Edit Properties, and click Advanced Administration.

To participate in a Version Cue PDF review, reviewers must have Internet access and all of the following:

A LOGIN NAME: Each reviewer must have a Version Cue login name. You can assign a login name by clicking the Add a User link on the Home tab in the Version Cue CS2 Administration Utility browser window (Figure 1-12). You can also click Edit Users on the Home tab to add a user.

FIGURE 1-12

REVIEWER PRIVILEGES: You must provide reviewers with access to the Version Cue workspace that is hosting the review.

ADOBE ACROBAT 7.0 PROFESSIONAL: Reviewers need the Acrobat software to view and add comments to the PDF.

Assigning User Preferences

Before anyone can review a project, you must assign him a login name, as directed above, and then assign preferences.

To assign user preferences:

1. From the Home tab in the Version Cue CS2 Administration Utility browser window, select the Admin Access Level for all reviewers that you want to be able to comment. If the user will only be reviewing a PDF, set the access to User.

2. Next to Project Creation, uncheck the Allowed checkbox. Then enter the new user login name and assign a password.

3. If desired, enter the optional phone number, email address, and any comments.

4. Click Save.

Starting a New PDF Review

When your PDF document is ready for review and your reviewers have been set up with usernames and passwords, you can start the PDF review process. You can use any version of your PDF document to start a review, but only one version of that document can be used in an active review.

To begin a PDF review:

1. Log onto the Version Cue Administration Utility.

2. Click on the Version Cue PDF Review link to start the PDF review process.

3. Click Start a Review, as shown in Figure 1-13.

4. Under the Document List, select the PDF for review. If there are multiple versions of the PDF, select the version to be used for the review.

5. Click the Start a Review link.

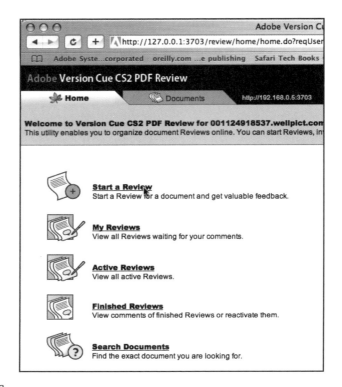

FIGURE 1-13

---

6. On the Documents tab, you can set a deadline, specify whether the reviewer comments will be Open (all comments are viewable by all reviewers) or Private (each reviewer can only see his/her own comments), add a description, and finally select the reviewers for the Version Cue PDF review (Figure 1-14). When you're finished, click the Next button.

---

7. Make changes to the Mail Subject and Mail Message, if desired.

---

8. Click the Start Review button to begin the PDF review process.

---

9. Version Cue starts your email program and displays the email message to the reviewers. The email message includes a link to the document. Send the email.

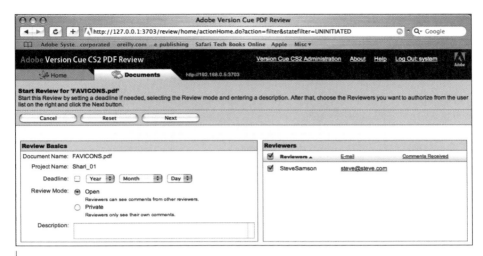

FIGURE 1-14

- -

Viewing PDF Review Comments

When the review process is complete and all comments have been submitted, it's time to take a look at what the reviewers wrote. You can view comments from a PDF review directly in the document or by using the Version Cue Administration Utility.

To view comments directly in the document, click on the version name in the Version Cue Administration Utility to open the document. To view comments with the Administration Utility, go to the Document History list, select the version of the PDF document used in the review, and then click View Comments.

KEEPING TRACK OF CHANGES

One of the highly touted features of Version Cue is that it enables you to easily keep track of the changes made throughout the life of a file, without resorting to a complex file-naming scheme. Version Cue offers the ultimate in file management capabilities, and its tracking system makes it impossible to overwrite or lose important versions of your work. You can keep track of variations of both Adobe and non-Adobe files with Version Cue, and you can view your versions and alternates from Bridge. (For more on versions and alternates, see the next section, "Using Versions and Alternates.")

Accessing Files

When you open a file to work on it in Version Cue, you are not actually working on the original; rather, you are working on a copy, so the original is not altered. Each time you save the file, you save the copy you are working on. If you choose Save a Version, the active copy is saved, and a new version is saved in the Version Cue project. This means that at any point you can return to the original, untouched version of the file, to any of the versions that you've saved along the way, or to the copy of the file that contains your most recent edits (which may or may not have been saved as a version).

Making Sense of File Status

Version Cue displays icons that clue you in on the status of your files. A variety of icons may be displayed in the Version Cue Workspace:

OPEN: Indicates that the file is open on your computer.

STATUS: Lets you know who is currently working on the file, or the status of the file (outdated, etc.).

SYNCHRONIZED: Indicates that your working copy is the latest known version of the file. This status is assigned when you save a version or manually synchronize a project.

NO WORKING COPY: Indicates that there is no original/local copy of the file on your computer. Version Cue will create a copy.

IN USE BY <USERNAME>: Lets you know a different user is working on the file.

CONFLICTED COPIES: Shows you that there is a version conflict because more than one person is trying to edit the file.

ONLY COPY: Indicates that this file is the only copy Version Cue has and that the file needs to be synchronized with the project.

OFFLINE COPY: Lets you know that Version Cue is offline and that if you work on your local copy of the file, you'll need to synchronize it in the project workspace.

OUTDATED COPY: Indicates that the local copy of the file is outdated—that is, that there is an updated copy in the project.

UNAVAILABLE: Indicates that Version Cue is offline or that you don't have access privileges for the file.

DELETED: Shows you that the file has been deleted, but not permanently erased.

Naming Files

Before Version Cue, naming files and trying to remember which file was which was one of the most difficult and time-consuming aspects of project management. Naming conventions were often quite complex, and comprehensible only to the person who had created them. There was also a constant danger of making a mistake and overwriting one version with another. Version Cue tackles the file-naming dilemma for you and makes it virtually impossible to accidentally overwrite a file.

In the Version Cue Workspace, you can actually view thumbnail images of the files and data about them, so that you can quickly and easily see which file you need to work on. If you change a file and save a new version, you simply write what you did in the Version Comments area so others can see what's changed.

USING VERSIONS AND ALTERNATES

A *version* is created to keep track of changes to a file—versions are essentially snapshots that you take along the way, to be referred back to later if necessary. Each time you change a file, you can save it as a new "version" of the original file. An *alternate* is a variation of your design, or an element of that design. For example, if you're using a photo in your design but you're torn between three different choices, you can save each photo as an alternate and quickly change them around when showing the design to your client.

Working with Versions

Versions allow you to save and track the history of a file in a Version Cue project. You can save your work at each stage of the design process, with a note about which stage the file is in or what changes have been made in that version (initial sketch, enhanced areas, added text, layout pages, and so on). Version Cue has built-in security and a series of alert warnings that prevent you from overwriting any of the versions. You can save versions of both Adobe and non-Adobe files.

1. Choose File→Save a Version.

2. In the Save a Version of <filename> dialog box, enter a comment for the version. This will usually involve a description of what you did (e.g., changed the file to black and white), so that anyone using the project can quickly identify which version is which (Figure 1-15).

Save A Version of purrandcassie.jpg

Version 3 comment:

Freaky kittens--Liquify and Levels

Saving will always save your changes locally. However, saving a version is how you define a series of edits as important or ready for sharing with others. You can also add comments to help clarify what changes have been made.

▼ Metadata for "purrandcassie.jpg"

Name	purrandcassie.jpg
Created	5/8/05 12:56 PM
Modified	5/8/05 1:16 PM
Size	555.97 KB
Type	JPEG image

Cancel   Save

FIGURE 1-15

3. Click Save.

The version is now saved in Bridge under Version Cue CS2 in the project folder that you have assigned to it.

tip

To update a version in GoLive, choose File→Connect to Version Cue. As GoLive is synchronizing the files with Version Cue, a Save a Version dialog box will come up. In this dialog box, you can enter a description for the version you're saving.

1. Choose Version Cue from the Bridge browser and double-click the file that you want to save a version of. The file will open in the application in which it was created.

2. Edit the file and then save it as you normally would.

3. From Bridge, choose Tools→Version Cue→Save a Version.

4. In the Save a Version dialog box, add a description of what was done in this version in the Version Comments area.

5. Click Save.

The version is now saved in Bridge under Version Cue CS2 in the project folder that you have assigned to it.

To view the versions of a file in Version Cue, open the project in the Version Cue/Bridge workspace and choose View→View as Versions and Alternates. The window will display the file and each version that has been created of it (Figure 1-16).

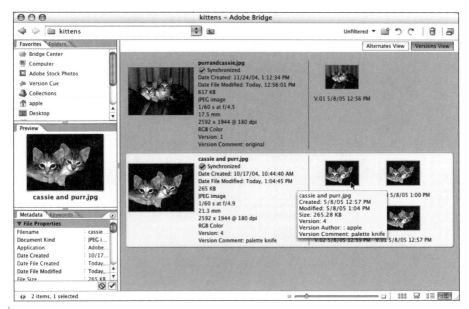

FIGURE 1-16

If you rest your cursor over one of the thumbnail images, a ScreenTip will pop up. This ScreenTip contains a description of the file, including the comment you added when you saved the version. The active version will be the last version you saved. You can make any of the versions active by promoting that version.

Promoting a version refers to making the selected version the active version. Make sure you have Versions and Alternates View chosen as your view, so you can see thumbnails of all the versions.

To promote a version:

1. Navigate to the file in the Version Cue/Bridge window.

2. Right-click (Windows) or Ctrl-click (Mac) the version you want to promote.

3. From the contextual menu, choose Promote Version.

4. In the Save a Version of <filename> dialog box that displays, enter a comment for the version you're promoting. (In the example in Figure 1-17, the comment was "Back to the drawing board").

5. Click Save to save this version and promote it to the active version.

FIGURE 1-17

Not only can you promote versions, but you can open any and all of the versions in the applications that created them so you can determine which versions you want to keep and which versions you want to delete.

After you have decided that a version is no longer needed, you can delete the version right in Version Cue.

To delete a version:

1. Navigate to the file in the Version Cue/Bridge window.

2. Right-click (Windows) or Ctrl-click (Mac) the version you want to delete.

3. From the contextual menu, choose Delete Version. You'll see a warning dialog box with the prompt "Are you sure you want to delete version <version number> of the file <filename>?" Deleted versions are unrecoverable. If you're sure you won't need it, click OK.

The version will be removed from the Version Cue project.

[NOTE]

You can also delete versions from the Administrative Utility in Version Cue, as long as you have the access permission.

Working with Alternates

Another way to create variations of a file with Version Cue is to use alternates. Let's say you have a publication that will be sent to all of the states in the United States. To customize the publication, you will create 50 different covers, each displaying a photo of the state that the publication will be sent to. With InDesign, you can lay out the entire publication and use alternates for each of the state graphics. You can then quickly switch between these alternates for publication. Version Cue lists all the available alternates in the project folder.

You may want to save one or many alternates of a file in your project folder. That way, you can quickly access the other files to show the client a different look.

1. Open the file you want to make an alternate in the program that you created it in.

2. Choose File→Save As.

3. Check the Save as Alternate <filename> box at the bottom of the Save As dialog box to save the file as an alternate (Figure 1-18).

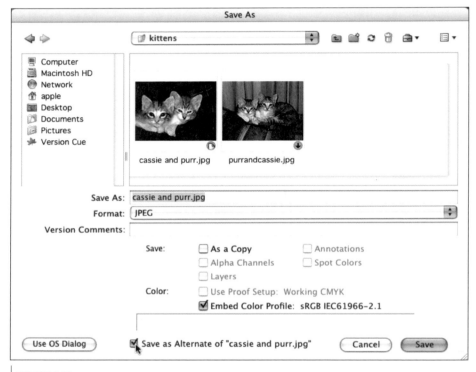

FIGURE 1-18

4. If you are saving to the same folder, enter a new name for the file. If you are saving to a different folder, you can keep the same filename.

5. Click Save.

Now you can view the alternate in the Version Cue/Bridge window.

To view an alternate in the Version Cue/Bridge window, click Alternates View at the bottom of the window. The primary file will be displayed in the left pane, and the alternates will be shown in the right pane (Figure 1-19). Here, you can see a thumbnail of the alternate as well as details on the alternate.

FIGURE 1-19

At any time, you can change the primary (the original file used in the project/design) to a different alternate.

To change an alternate to a primary:

1. Right-click (Windows) or Ctrl-click (Mac) the image in the right pane.

2. Select Alternates from the contextual menu.

3. In the Alternates for <filename> dialog box, select the alternate that you want to make primary.

4. Click Make Primary (Figure 1-20).

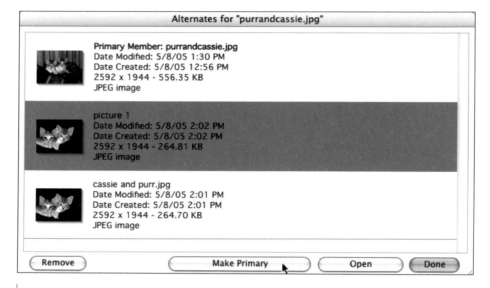

Alternates for "purrandcassie.jpg"

Primary Member: purrandcassie.jpg
Date Modified: 5/8/05 1:30 PM
Date Created: 5/8/05 12:56 PM
2592 x 1944 - 556.35 KB
JPEG image

picture 1
Date Modified: 5/8/05 2:02 PM
Date Created: 5/8/05 2:02 PM
2592 x 1944 - 264.81 KB
JPEG image

cassie and purr.jpg
Date Modified: 5/8/05 2:01 PM
Date Created: 5/8/05 2:01 PM
2592 x 1944 - 264.70 KB
JPEG image

Remove   Make Primary   Open   Done

FIGURE 1-20

5. Click Done.

The image you've selected will now be the primary file used in the project. This feature lets you flip between the alternates quickly to show the various choices to your client.

In the Alternates dialog box, you can also choose to remove or open an alternate.

The alternates for a file do not have to reside in the same folder as the file (or as each other).

1. In Bridge, open a second window.

2. Navigate to the folder containing the alternate file.

3. Select the alternate file—you *must* be in Alternates View to do this.

4. Drag the alternate file to the first Bridge window, to the right of the separator. The file in Version Cue updates immediately with the information that there are alternates.

5. Place the file in InDesign by choosing File→Place. Within InDesign, you can switch between alternates, and you can see all the alternates in one directory and as thumbnails, rather than having to look through a bunch of folders.

ADDING AND VIEWING METADATA

Though it sounds like a term straight out of X-Men, *metadata* is really just a funky name for something we all work with on a regular basis—information about a file. Operating systems (OSs) track information using metadata all the time. Although no one calls them that, things as basic as a file's name, type, date created and modified, and size are all types of metadata. Depending on your OS, you can search on all or some of these bits of metadata to locate a specific file.

In addition to the more familiar metadata, Adobe includes dozens of other text-based information fields that help to further define the characteristics of a file. As of this writing, you can enter some of this metadata manually into a file, but all sorts of metadata fields are populated automatically. To get an idea of how rich your documents are in terms of metadata, click on an image in Bridge and then click the Metadata palette in the lower-left corner (Figure 1-21).

You'll see all sorts of neat information (resolution, physical size, and more) near the top of the Metadata palette. But scroll down... and down... and down. You'll be amazed at the amount of information present. If the image is an original digital camera capture, you'll see everything that's stored in a standard JPEG file, including the exposure mode used for the shot and even the camera make and model (Figure 1-22). Photoshop native files can contain even more information. You can set what metadata you want to view—as well as other preferences—by choosing Bridge→Preferences.

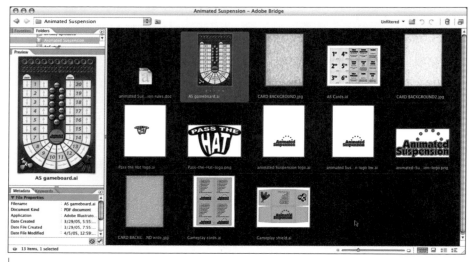

FIGURE 1-21

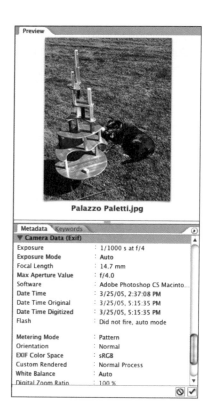

FIGURE 1-22

In the future, it isn't hard to imagine software (hopefully from Adobe) that populates even more snazzy and intelligent types of information into a file's metadata. For example, snippets of text from your files, such as the headings in a long document, might be included, or deep, rich details about images in a web page. When it comes to the Adobe Creative Suite file formats, text is cheap. Additional metadata information is so tiny relative to the original file size that adding a bit more of it is never an issue. A fully metadata-stocked image might be less than 1K larger than one with no metadata. Figure 1-23 shows two images side by side: one contains metadata and one doesn't. Can you tell the difference?

FIGURE 1-23

Using Metadata

Ignoring metadata, as you've probably done in the past, won't cause you to suddenly become unproductive and disorganized—but being aware of the rich metadata that already exists in your files will definitely benefit you. Here's an example to give you an idea of some of the information that lies at your fingertips. I have a folder full of imagery that I like to use for desktop backgrounds, shown in Figure 1-24.

FIGURE 1-24

Some of the images are incredibly clear, are a reasonable size for my 1600 x 1200 desktop (so that they aren't scaled up or down too much), and have good tonal values. An example of such an image (a close-up of the game Tongiaki) is shown in Figure 1-25. However, the tonal values of images made with digital cameras tend to vary with the brand and model of the camera (unless the images have been adjusted in Photoshop, which requires a certain level of skill). I was curious to know whether any one camera was better than another for these types of images, so I pulled out a few of the better images and checked to see what cameras they'd been made with. As it turns out, for my purposes there's a certain Olympus SLR with a macro lens that takes excellent pictures.

FIGURE 1-25

To really take advantage of metadata in your Adobe Creative Suite files, you should be thinking about how you'd like to organize and access your files in the future. Even if you're already über-organized, metadata will make your life much easier. And if you're a little messy or cluttered, the metadata that's already in your files should help you to organize and keep track of them.

Either way, adding just a bit more information manually—for instance, including the project name in all files related to a particular project—can net you a huge time savings in the future. Even if you keep all the files for a project together, there's a good chance that you'll have used at least one common or generic file in the project that you grabbed from some other location. Let's say you have to use a dinner menu over and over again in a project. To update the menu, you might want to grab some images that you've used before in a totally different context, and it'll be a lot easier to mark each of those images with the current project name than it would be to manually move or copy them into a common folder. Identifying the projects files belong to in their metadata can also save your hide if at some point you move one of the project files from the original project folder.

Adding Metadata in Photoshop, Illustrator, InDesign, Acrobat, GoLive, and Bridge

Each of the Creative Suite applications automatically saves metadata with files, but you can manually update the metadata as well. Choose File→File Info, and you'll see a dialog box that looks something like the one in Figure 1-26.

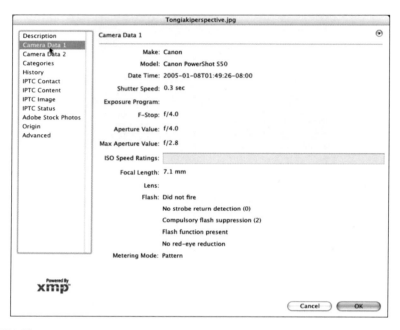

FIGURE 1-26

You can use this dialog box to add all sorts of information to your file that will help you identify it in the future. Enter whatever info you'd like, click OK, and then simply save the file—the metadata will be part of the file from that point forward.

Searching Metadata in Bridge

Bridge allows you to search for an image based on metadata contents.

To search for an image:

1. Choose Edit→Find.

2. In the Find dialog box (Figure 1-27), choose All Metadata from the Criteria pop-up menu, specify the text you want the metadata to contain (or not contain), and click Find.

FIGURE 1-27

You can search any and all metadata in the images in the current Bridge folder.

COLOR PROFILES

One of the big challenges for all but the most casual Creative Suite user is how to ensure consistent color throughout the creative process. Having one or more pieces of hardware without accurate color profiles can lead to lost time trying to fix apparent color problems during the preparation of an image, or to unpleasant surprises when it comes time to pick up a full-color print job. Three components have an impact on creating an accurate color profile: the monitor, the input device (such as a scanner or digital camera), and the output device (usually a color printer). Thus, you'll need to consider three types of color profile:

MONITOR PROFILES: An accurate monitor profile is critical because you will make decisions regarding the colors in your files based on what is displayed on your monitor. If your monitor is not accurately color calibrated, you have no chance of making good decisions.

INPUT DEVICE PROFILES: These profiles describe what colors your scanner or digital camera is capable of capturing.

OUTPUT DEVICE PROFILES: These profiles describe the color space of desktop and commercial printers.

For most situations and device combinations, it is highly recommended that you use one of the global color settings that ship with Creative Suite 2. Don't change advanced settings unless you know what you are doing or are specifically instructed to do so by your service bureau or a commercial printing professional.

Setting Global Color Settings

Setting global color settings has never been easier, thanks to Bridge. You can now specify global color settings with just a few mouse clicks.

To set global color settings:

1. In Bridge, select Edit→Creative Suite Color Settings (Figure 1-28).

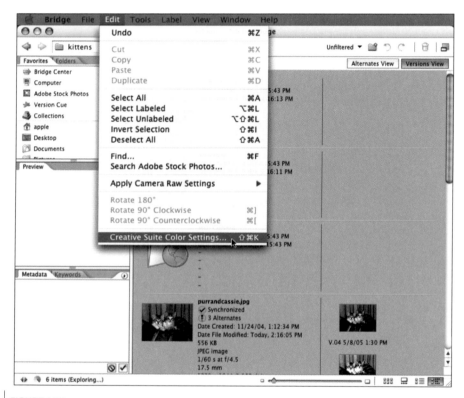

FIGURE 1-28

2. Select the desired setting from the list of available settings, and click the Apply button. (To see more settings, check the Show Expanded List of Color Setting Files box at the bottom of the dialog box, as shown in Figure 1-29.)

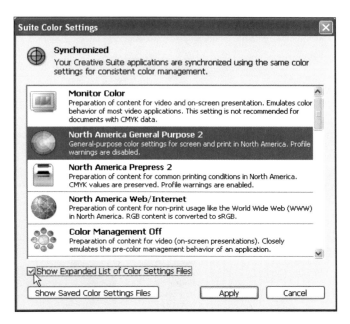

FIGURE 1-29

You can also open this dialog from the bottom of the Bridge Center window, by clicking "Open Color Settings." The Bridge Center will also indicate whether your Color Management setting is synchronized throughout your CS2 applications.

AUTOMATING TASKS WITH ACTIONS

Although it is incredibly useful to be able to make sophisticated changes to files (such as rotating or cropping a scanned image, adjusting the brightness and contrast, or correcting an unwanted color cast), making these changes manually to a large number of files can be incredibly time-consuming. This is where task automation comes to the rescue. Bridge allows you to select a file or a folder and then apply an *action*—a series of commands from a specific application—to the selected file or to all files within the selected folder.

Applying an Action

Applying an action is a simple matter of locating the file or folder you want to work with and then selecting the desired action from the Tools menu.

To apply an action:

1. In Bridge, navigate to the file or folder to which you want to apply the action.

2. From the Tools menu, choose the application and action that you want to apply (Figure 1-30). You can use a preset action, or you can record and save your own actions.

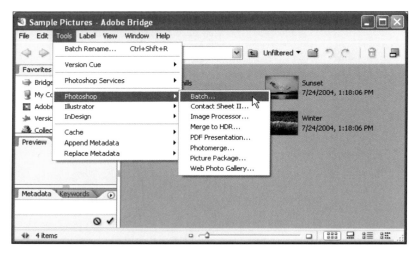

FIGURE 1-30

3. If the necessary application is not already open, it will open and a dialog box will appear with various settings specific to the action that you have chosen. Specify the settings that you want to use, and click the OK or Apply button.

TOP 5 THINGS TO TAKE AWAY FROM THIS CHAPTER

Here are the most important things to take away from this chapter:

1. The Adobe Bridge browser is the command center of the Creative Suite 2 products, from which you can browse, view, and organize all your Adobe (and non-Adobe) files.

2. Version Cue CS2 lets you manage and organize files, create projects, make versions of a file, and create alternates for any project from an easy-to-access, central location for all of the Creative Suite programs.

3. You can use Version Cue CS2 to conduct web-based PDF reviews of a project.

4. Metadata is a rich set of information about your files, accessible via the Metadata tab in the lower-left corner of the Bridge window.

5. You can set global color settings (so that all of your Creative Suite 2 products use the same color space) and use actions to automate tasks in Bridge.

Photoshop as Part of the Creative Suite

What do you think of when you think of Photoshop? Outrageous graphics? Doctored imagery? Complex and powerful tools? A true digital darkroom? Photoshop is all of this. And when Photoshop is used in the context of the Creative Suite, it becomes even more powerful.

The odd thing is, if you've used Photoshop on its own before, you'll probably find yourself using it a little less once you have access to the other Creative Suite applications. However, the impact Photoshop will have on your work will be even more significant than it was before.

AN OVERVIEW OF PHOTOSHOP

Photoshop is so ubiquitous that in many circles, it's used as a verb. And it's so mainstream that people who have never used the product know of it and have a basic grasp of its capabilities. On *The Daily Show*, Jon Stewart often mentions the application with tones of great admiration. After showing an (obviously) doctored photo, he quips, "Oh, Photoshop, how we love you."

Photoshop is used worldwide, by everyone in the design industry. To get a job in a creative professional industry, you need to know Photoshop at some level—knowing a competing product (even the techniques that could easily be transferred to Photoshop) has no real value in the job market. And a true "Photoshop Wizard" is valued quite highly by ad agencies, printers, and other companies whose primary business centers on rich visual communication.

Who Uses Photoshop

Partially because of its popularity, partially because of its initial accessibility, and partially because of its incredible, comprehensive, and varied toolset, Photoshop is used today for many more things than it was originally intended for. To its users, Photoshop isn't just an image editor; it's a graphics creation powerhouse, a file conversion machine, a production tool for web graphics, a large-format document creation and editing tool, and much, much more (Figure 2-1).

Photoshop isn't just a tool for professional photographers and graphic designers. Here are just some of the myriad of people who use Photoshop:

- The guy who creates the graphics for the Chicago White Sox scoreboard uses Photoshop to crop player images, create elements of motion graphics for animated sequences, and prepare background imagery for various types of information graphics.

- A designer at Hallmark uses Photoshop to enhance graphics created in Illustrator, create specialized text effects, and enhance photographs to be used in greeting cards and related materials.

- A creative director at Fossil uses Photoshop to help bring product imagery to life and enhance photographs of products so they're shown in their best light.

- A podiatrist in Santa Clara, California uses Photoshop to enhance X-rays of patients' feet, to help clarify issues ranging from bone spurs to fractures to unexpected foreign objects in a notoriously hard-to-image part of the body.

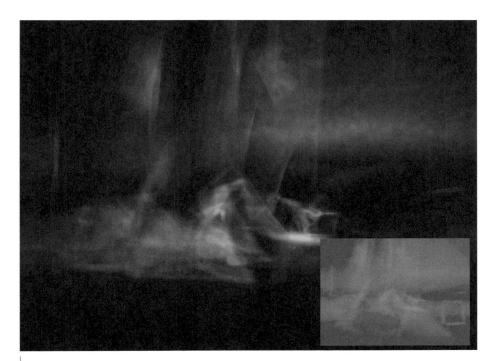

FIGURE 2-1

How People Use Photoshop

Although Photoshop has many uses, its primary use is as an image editing tool. *Image editing* is the process of taking a pixel-based image (typically a photograph, although it could be another type of graphic) and modifying it in some way. The different ways images can be modified fall into several categories:

COLOR CORRECTION: You can change the color of the overall image or specific portions of the image. Usually this means "fixing" the color of an image that is tinted or discolored in some way, although many color correction techniques are used to enhance images so that they look better than the original—not just better than the original image, but better than the original object, landscape, or whatever it was that was photographed in the first place!

IMAGE ENHANCEMENT: Images often are too dark or too light, don't show enough detail, are too grainy, appear out of focus, or have any number of other problems. Photoshop can be used to enhance various components of an image so that it looks better.

RETOUCHING: Stray hairs, bugs, telephone poles, people, and any other unwanted elements can all be removed from imagery. Photoshop can remove with ease moles that would otherwise require outpatient surgery to cut out. And the opposite is true as well: you can add a third eye to a family pet, give your brother-in-law green teeth, or drop a lion into a backyard barbeque.

GRAPHICS CREATION AND EDITING: Although the drawing tools in Photoshop are limited, they do allow you to create all sorts of graphics, from buttons and backgrounds to highly stylized text. And if you bring in graphics from Illustrator, the possibilities increase tenfold.

IMAGE PRODUCTION: Photoshop has an incredible arsenal of tools for modifying, transforming, and optimizing images. You can easily crop an image to a certain size, rotate it, or optimize its file size.

PREPARE IMAGES FOR THE WEB: Photoshop contains an entire second application specifically designed for web graphics and imagery: ImageReady. ImageReady feels an awful lot like Photoshop, but it has many tools and functions that are designed specifically for Web graphics. For straightforward tasks, such as creating JPEGs, GIFs, and PNGs, Photoshop includes a special mode just for exporting these formats for the Web, allowing complete control over appearance and optimization.

ORGANIZE YOUR IMAGES: Adobe Bridge, which was called the File Browser in previous versions of Photoshop, ships as part of Photoshop CS2—but Bridge isn't just for Photoshop imagery. Bridge lets you view and manage all your Creative Suite files visually. Think of the program as an, erm, "bridge" to the other Creative Suite 2 applications. While in Photoshop, you can grab an Illustrator document, and you can access a Photoshop image in any other application.

WHY GET THE CREATIVE SUITE INSTEAD OF JUST PHOTOSHOP?

You may be asking yourself whether you should purchase Photoshop as part of the Creative Suite or as a standalone product. That answer depends on the type of work that you do. In most cases, you'll benefit from having the other tools in the Creative Suite. However, it's easier to list the reasons why you might *not* need those extra tools. Buy the standalone version of Photoshop if:

- You are an amateur photographer, and you'll be using Photoshop primarily for basic image editing and color correction only.

- You are a cog in a giant creative production machine, and you have specific tasks that can be completed optimally in Photoshop.

- You never need to create anything complex that will go onto a web page.

- You don't need multiple pages.

- You won't need to size up or down your imagery in the future.

- You don't need to do deep edits of anything you're creating—once through, and you're done.

- You don't need to create any artwork from scratch.

Otherwise, you'll benefit greatly by using the entire Creative Suite.

Photoshop's Place in the Creative Suite

Although it can be put to a wide range of uses on its own, Photoshop becomes much more specialized when combined with the other Creative Suite 2 applications. In this context, Photoshop is:

- An image editing and correction tool, to be used on photos prior to placing them into InDesign, Illustrator, or GoLive.

- A graphics enhancement tool, to be used to enhance graphics created in Illustrator.

Although Photoshop can certainly do more than this, these are the tasks it excels at in the world of the Creative Suite, and these are the areas you'll want to master.

Although you may be tempted to do "as much as you can" in Photoshop before moving to another Creative Suite application, especially if you have experience with Photoshop or like using it more than the other applications, your productivity and the quality of your work will eventually suffer if you don't take advantage of the benefits the other Creative Suite products offer.

How the Other Creative Suite 2 Apps Add to Photoshop's Capabilities

InDesign, Illustrator, and GoLive are aggregator applications in regards to Photoshop— that is, the typical workflow is to edit an image in Photoshop and then place the image into one of the other three applications. However, because of the flexibility of pixel-based imagery, another workflow option is to take Illustrator graphics into Photoshop for post-production work.

You can also save Photoshop files as PDFs to be opened in Acrobat, and you can view PDFs in Photoshop (although they'll be rasterized).

The following section briefly discusses how the other Creative Suite applications work and offers a few more glimpses into how they combine with Photoshop's functionality to complete the total graphics and design picture. We'll return to the subject of using the Creative Suite applications together in Chapter 4.

LEARNING THE OTHER CREATIVE SUITE 2 TOOLS

To fully optimize your Photoshop usage, you'll need to become comfortable with the other tools in the Creative Suite—especially in those areas that are critical to a well-rounded
creative workflow. Although learning five different programs may seem overwhelming,
Adobe has made your job much easier by making the interfaces, terminology, and workflow between the applications as consistent and smooth as possible. Bridge is a great
example of how Adobe has worked to make this happen.

The following sections discuss the areas in each application that you should focus on to
get the most out of the entire Creative Suite. Your particular needs may vary slightly, but
learning the concepts and areas listed here will provide you with a solid foundation from
which to create your digital masterpieces.

Illustrator: Photoshop's Best Friend

Although Illustrator was lumped in earlier with InDesign and GoLive as an aggregator
tool, it's a dessert topping *and* a floor wax. Illustrator by itself is a creative tool used for
creating and editing graphics of almost any type imaginable: logos, fancy text, illustrations, diagrams, and more. At the same time, Illustrator documents often contain all sorts
of imagery and graphics themselves—for example, single-page advertisements, posters, cards, calendars, web page mockups, and complex designs incorporating dozens of
components.

In general, people tend to err on the side of using Photoshop for too much when instead
they could be doing things in Illustrator. Why choose one over the other? The primary
reasons are editability and scalability. Illustrator graphics are much more editable (meaning you can make changes without having to redo the graphics) than those you can create
in Photoshop, and Illustrator graphics are scalable to virtually any size. Graphics created
in Photoshop can usually be scaled down (made smaller) easily, but the images start to
decrease in quality when they're enlarged.

InDesign: Laying Out Imagery

There shouldn't be much confusion when determining whether to use InDesign or
Photoshop. These two applications live on opposite sides of the publishing process and
workflow. InDesign (like GoLive) tends to be the last stop in a workflow, with Photoshop
revisited during the late stages only to make changes to existing imagery. InDesign has
a bit of overlap with Illustrator and GoLive, but its use can be boiled down to a simple
three-word directive: multipage print layout.

InDesign is the product of choice for magazine and newspaper publishers, and many other short and long documents are produced in InDesign as well. Because InDesign accepts native Photoshop (and Illustrator) files, you can quickly place any Photoshop file into InDesign.

GoLive: Putting Photoshop Images on the Web

Photoshop is often used to create imagery, graphics, and user interface elements for use in GoLive. Those items are placed in GoLive using the *Smart Objects* technology, which allows for items to be dynamically updated from the source Photoshop file if the file is changed in either Photoshop or GoLive.

Acrobat Pro: The Finishing Touches

Photoshop can export PDF files directly and can include "sticky" notes (comments) in both a Photoshop file and the resulting PDF. Acrobat can be used to crop imagery created in Photoshop as full-page images (for late-stage formatting for various types of output needs), as well as to add additional PDF functionality.

Of course, the PDF file format is readable by pretty much everyone on the planet with a computer, so it's a great way to share your images with anyone, anywhere—all the while knowing that the viewing experience will be consistent across platforms.

WHAT YOU SHOULD AND SHOULDN'T DO IN PHOTOSHOP IF YOU HAVE THE CREATIVE SUITE

In many ways, Photoshop is the Swiss Army knife of graphics tools. But just as you wouldn't use the fork and spoon on your Swiss Army knife if you had a full-size fork and spoon at hand, there are many tools in Photoshop that you shouldn't use if you have access to the other Creative Suite applications. The biggest overlap occurs with Illustrator— as stated earlier, if you can do the same thing in Illustrator or Photoshop, you'll generally be better off doing it in Illustrator.

Imagery Versus Graphics: Understand the Difference

Photoshop excels at creating and editing imagery. Not so much with graphics. But what's the difference between the two?

Imagery includes photographs, drawings, and "art for the sake of art." *Graphics* are more structured in nature. They include logos, buttons (artwork intended for onscreen use), and iconic artwork (shapes and typographical artwork). You can use Photoshop for all of these purposes, but it really shines with photographs, art for the sake of art, and buttons.

Illustrator tends to be the choice of designers when it comes to graphics (drawings, logos and iconic artwork). Of course, this isn't an absolute; your computer won't explode (hopefully) if you create logos in Photoshop. Still, you can run into limitations very quickly. The worst scenario is that you end up designing to accommodate the limitations of your software of choice.

For imagery, Photoshop excels because it can do what Illustrator can't: easily simulate detail and complexity. Here's a great example of what we mean by simulating detail. Figure 2-2 shows an image of a face at the startlingly low resolution of about 72 pixels per inch (ppi). Yet your brain doesn't think of this image as low resolution at all, and it happily fills in details for you that really aren't there. Before you study the image for too long, turn the page and look at Figure 2-4, which is the same image at much higher resolution. Flipping back and forth between the two pages, you'll immediately notice that the first image isn't all that clear after all—your brain initially fooled you, because it looked pretty nice all by itself.

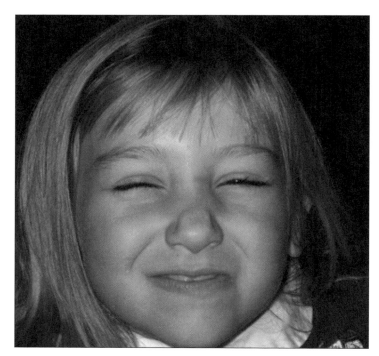

FIGURE 2-2

When it comes to graphics with hard edges, the difference is much more apparent. Figure 2-3 shows a Photoshop version of a graphic. The Photoshop version is a little choppy-looking. Now turn the page and look at the original Illustrator graphic in Figure 2-5. That's how this graphic should look, all smooth and crisp. When you flip between these two pages, the difference is even more startling than between the two images in Figures 2-2 and 2-4.

FIGURE 2-3

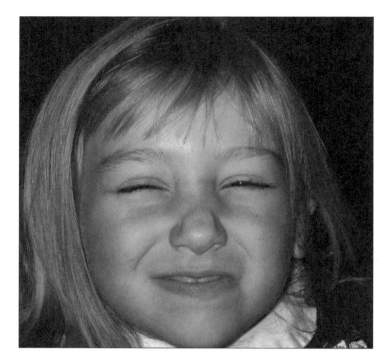

FIGURE 2-4

FIGURE 2-5

Typography

When you're deciding whether to create text elements in Photoshop or Illustrator/InDesign, the size of the text is the first thing you should consider. When it comes to typography, bigger is always better in Photoshop. Figure 2-6 shows text from Photoshop next to text from Illustrator. Note that as the size decreases, the legibility of the Photoshop text dramatically decreases as well. These examples are obvious ones, with the resolution of the Photoshop text set to 72 ppi; at higher resolutions, the difference won't be as noticeable.

Text from Photoshop   Text from Illustrator or InDesign

FIGURE 2-6

The second thing to consider when deciding whether to create type in Photoshop is how "stylish" it will be. Text that needs all sorts of bevels, highlights, and textures tends to be more successful when done in Photoshop, as shown in Figure 2-7.

FIGURE 2-7

Stretching, distorting, extruding, or adding basic drop shadows to text should probably be done in Illustrator, as shown in Figure 2-8. The clarity of text tends to rely on a higher resolution—the resolution is as high as possible in Illustrator, but often the text is rasterized in Photoshop, making the formerly crisp edges appear rough.

FIGURE 2-8

Comps

It's easy to do quick mock-ups (comps) in Photoshop, such as laying out a web page, a print ad, or some other quick visual. The biggest drawback to comping in Photoshop is that the work will need to be entirely redone afterward. Because you aren't going to use full-resolution imagery, final type, or exact positioning, the elements of a comp can't easily be adjusted for the final piece. Instead, you'll end up re-creating the piece "for real" in Photoshop or another application. If you know you're going to be creating the final piece in Photoshop (by itself) anyway, this isn't a bad thing—it's just a cost of the design process.

If your final product is going to be created in another of the Creative Suite applications, however, you're better off doing the comping there, even if it takes you a little longer than it would in Photoshop. Why? Because the extra time you might spend in InDesign, for example, will be subtracted from the overall time spent on the project. It's much easier to update existing elements and layouts than to start over from scratch, which is often what you have to do when you create comps in Photoshop.

Image Editing

Image editing runs the gamut from basic color correction to complex retouching and photo-illustration. Figure 2-9 shows a "before" image, and Figure 2-10 shows the "after" image.

FIGURE 2-9

FIGURE 2-10

For all your image editing needs, Photoshop is the place to be. Illustrator, InDesign, and GoLive all have limited image editing tools, but with few exceptions, Photoshop is where you'll want to do these tasks. You can crop images in InDesign and Illustrator, but it's awkward at best. Illustrator's Appearance palette and Effects are fine for making a select few enhancements to graphics you're creating (and will probably ultimately use) in Illustrator, but for heavy lifting with filters, you want Photoshop's snappy response and complex masking capabilities.

Graphical Enhancements

Graphics drawn in Illustrator often appear flat and lifeless, but you can use Photoshop to add depth, texture, and a naturalistic feel. Figure 2-11 shows an original Illustrator document, while Figure 2-12 shows a Photoshop-enhanced version. With a few quick adjustments, the artwork is given perspective and life.

FIGURE 2-11

FIGURE 2-12

**Here are the most important things to take away
from this chapter:**

1. Photoshop is more focused and powerful when used in the context of the Creative
   Suite.

2. Although Photoshop can do pretty much anything you need it to, understanding
   when to use it versus when to use the other Creative Suite applications will greatly
   benefit you.

3. Photoshop's primary function in the Creative Suite is for image editing, *not* for
   graphics creation.

4. Adobe Bridge is the "in-between place" for imagery that is en route to other Adobe
   applications.

5. Adobe Illustrator and Adobe Photoshop can be used together to create virtually any
   kind of graphics and imagery. Understanding each product fully is critical to optimizing what you can create and edit.

Image Preparation and Enhancement

At its core, Photoshop is all about making images look better. It won't make the events captured in that picture of Uncle Abernathy strangling Aunt Clara at last year's Thanksgiving "encounter" any less ugly, but it will help you ensure that both of the subjects are shown in their best light!

EXPLORING IMAGE AND PIXEL BASICS

Images are made of pixels. If you rolled your eyes when reading that last sentence, skip ahead to the "Sizing Images" section. If not, read on: the following section describes what pixels are and how they form images.

Pixels Up Close

Pixels are individual squares of color—any color—on a grid of thousands of squares that, together, form an image. Nowadays, even the smallest files can contain one or two million pixels. Digital camera manufacturers use the term "megapixels" (MP), where one megapixel equals about a million pixels.

Although one or two million pixels may seem like a lot, the resulting image isn't all that large. A typical 2-MP image is 1600 x 1200 pixels, or about the size of a 21-inch monitor. An 8-MP image is about 3500 x 2300 pixels, or about twice the width and height of a 2-MP image.

The interesting thing about pixels and megapixels is that the relative density of pixels is what creates more or less detail in an image. Look at the image shown in Figure 3-1, where one screen pixel is equal to one image pixel. If you look really, really closely, you can see the pixels.

FIGURE 3-1

Now look at the image shown in Figure 3-2, where *four* screen pixels are equal to one image pixel. No need to look closely here; the pixels are quite easy to spot.

FIGURE 3-2

Transparent Pixels

In Photoshop, in addition to being a specific color, pixels can also be partially transparent. If a pixel is transparent, you can see part or all of the pixel underneath it. If there's no image pixel behind the transparent pixel, Photoshop substitutes white.

Figure 3-3 shows a partially transparent image on top of another image. This example is offset to the left, so that you can see the original image for comparison purposes. All of the pixels in the "top" image are set to 50% transparency (via the Layers palette). You can easily see through the top image to the image beneath, although the result is actually not all that pleasing.

FIGURE 3-3

In this case, a better result might be gained from using transparency only on the background of the original poker chip image, as shown in Figure 3-4. Now—depending on your point of view—you have either giant poker chips or a grass-like tabletop. I like the giant chips myself.

FIGURE 3-4

To clarify the size of the poker chips, I'll add a dog to the image, as shown in Figure 3-5.

FIGURE 3-5

SIZING IMAGES

Image size is measured in three factors: dimensional size in pixels, physical size in inches (or another "real-world" measurement system), and storage size. You can always view the current image size in both pixels and physical size by choosing Image→Image Size. Unless you have storage issues or need to transfer your images remotely, you can usually ignore storage size and just focus on the pixels and inches. If you're concerned about storage size, consider cropping unwanted areas of your images, which removes pixels.

Dimensional Size

Images in Photoshop are always rectangular, with no exceptions. Each image is a specific number of pixels wide and a specific number tall. You can find the total number of pixels in the image by multiplying the width by the height. You'll get a true feeling for the pixel size of your image when you view it at 100%. Figure 3-6 shows an image of a stunning cloud-filled sunset at 100%; note that "100%" displays in the titlebar next to the image name.

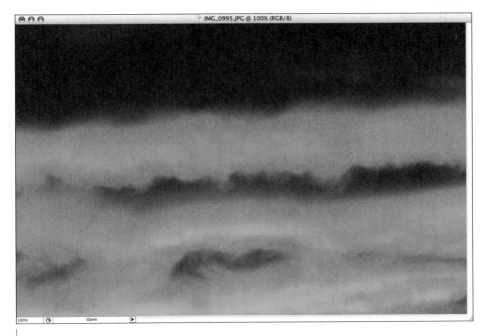

FIGURE 3-6

Physical Size

The physical size of an image—its dimensions in inches, pixels, cm, or some other physical measure—is fixed. However, two images with the same physical size can have very different dimensional sizes. For example, two 3" x 3" images can contain a very different number of pixels, depending on how many pixels per inch each image has. For example, in Figure 3-7, both images are 3" x 3". However, the image on the left has a grand total of 1,369 pixels (37 across and 37 down), whereas the image on the right has a total of 202,500 pixels (450 across and 450 down).

FIGURE 3-7

Storage Size

Each image will take up a certain amount of space on your hard drive. The storage size will be based partly on the dimensional (pixel) size of your image, and partly on the format you use when saving it. JPEGs tend to be the smallest, whereas TIFFs or PDFs embedded with Photoshop layer information are the largest.

Cropping

Cropping is the process of reducing the dimensional size of an image by removing rows and columns of pixels. Of course, when you crop an image you're changing its physical size as well, but the most important thing you're doing is getting rid of extra pixels. To crop an image, either choose the Crop tool, drag out the area you wish to crop, and then press Return (Mac) or Enter (Windows), or make a rectangular selection and choose Image→Crop.

INCREASING THE CLARITY OF AN IMAGE

What exactly is clarity? Most people will probably instantly equate clarity with sharpness and detail, but it's more than that. Clarity has to do with the color balance, the "feel" of an image, and how the image is cropped.

Proper cropping almost guarantees an improvement in image clarity, as Figure 3-8 shows rather well. On the left is the original, uncropped image; on the right is a cropped version of the same image. To be fair, the image on the right was scaled up so that it wouldn't look awkward, but to prove the point, use your hand to cover up the right image and then slide it over to the left image. The image on the right looks way better, thanks to proper cropping.

FIGURE 3-8

That's just one example—bringing up the detail level and enhancing edges that are too soft are other ways of increasing the clarity of an image. Before going into detail on those, however, it's important to note that such techniques for enhancing your images are rarely optimal when applied to an entire image. Selecting individual portions of an image (i.e., the subject or the background) and applying the necessary changes only to those areas will result in the best possible outcomes.

What to Avoid

Your first thought in approaching the issue of image clarity might be to use Brightness and Contrast, which sounds easy and friendly and works amazingly quickly—but you should absolutely never use this function for improving clarity. Doing so destroys data and quickly removes detail from highlights and shadows. Watch the darkest and lightest areas as you experiment with this function, and you'll see what I mean (experiment, but never use it for real!). Instead of Brightness and Contrast, use selections and masks to work on specific portions of your images, use Curves and Levels to adjust colors and brightness, and use Unsharp Mask and Gaussian Blur to heighten clarity.

Selections and Masks

Proper selecting of portions of imagery is essential to getting the best result. For example, when dealing with a specific subject, enhancing the subject separately from the background results in a much better end result. And whenever you spend a lot of time selecting a portion of your image, it's always a good idea to save the selection as a mask. This will allow you to access the selection in the future, if you have any additional enhancement work to do after you've saved and closed the image file.

Curves and Levels

Curves and Levels are the most powerful tools in your image-enhancement arsenal. Jump into the Curves dialog box (by choosing Image→Adjust→Curves), shown in Figure 3-9, to quickly set the white, black, and gray points of your image. This can result in a better-looking image pretty much instantly. When working in the Curves dialog box, be sure to click the box in the lower-right corner to see more detail in the curve display.

For a quick spectral glow effect, play with the Pencil control in the Curves dialog box on each of the channels, as shown in Figure 3-10.

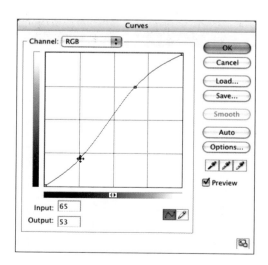

FIGURE 3-9

FIGURE 3-10

The Levels dialog box can be useful for quickly enhancing clarity by "stretching" and "squeezing" the image across a wider range of lightness to darkness. Figure 3-11 shows an image with the original Levels settings (left) and the adjusted image with "better" settings (right).

FIGURE 3-11

You can access all of the color adjustment controls, including Curves and Levels, through the Image→Adjust submenu, but a better option is to use adjustment layers (Layer→New Adjustment Layer). If you apply your color changes as adjustment layers, you'll be able to alter them at any time, even after you've saved and closed the file.

Unsharp Mask and Gaussian Blur

Unsharp Mask, when used on the subject of an image, can further distinguish the subject from the background. Gaussian Blur can be used on the background to make the subject stand out even more. Figure 3-12 shows an image as it appeared originally (left), as well as the resulting image when the foreground was sharpened and the background blurred (right). In order to do this, I made a selection of the background, applied the Gaussian Blur, and then chose Selection→Invert Selection so that the foreground was selected, allowing me to sharpen just the foreground.

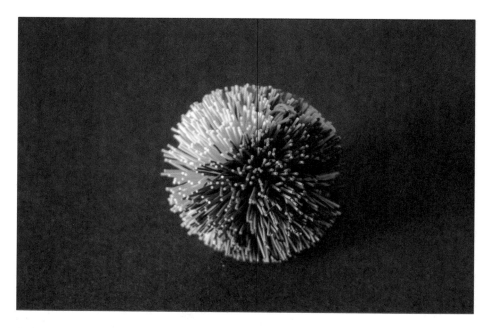

FIGURE 3-12.

CHAPTER 3

**Here are the most important things to take away
from this chapter:**

1. Images are created from a large number of pixels, each of which has a specified color.

2. In addition to controlling the color of the pixels in an image, Photoshop allows you to adjust the transparency of individual pixels.

3. Image size is based on pixels (dimensional size), inches or other units of real-world measurement (physical size), and the amount of space an image takes up when stored (storage size).

4. Use Levels and Curves to retain the most control and achieve the best results when adjusting the brightness and contrast of your image. Do not use Brightness and Contrast.

5. Selecting the subject and background prior to manipulating the image results in clearer images and better results.

How to Use Photoshop with the Other Creative Suite Applications

You have Photoshop, and you have the rest of the Creative Suite. Even if you're a longtime Photoshop user, things are different now. As we discussed briefly in Chapter 2, you'll find that there are a lot of things you may have done in Photoshop in the past that can be handled much better by one of the other CS2 applications.

For example, although Photoshop has had a Pen tool forever, you'll find that Illustrator's Pen tool and related features are much more powerful; likewise, InDesign's typographic tools are much easier to use. If you use all the applications in the Creative Suite together, playing to the strengths of each, you'll be much more productive.

TAKING ILLUSTRATOR GRAPHICS INTO PHOTOSHOP

Illustrator and Photoshop have a great symbiotic relationship, further enhanced by each application's capability to import files from and export files to the other. Although Illustrator purists might scoff at the idea of taking their infinitely scalable and editable files into Photoshop, where traditionally those two Illustratoresque aspects are sacrificed, the truth is that sometimes that's exactly the right thing to do... in fact, those files will then be much more editable and scalable than ever before. It all depends on your intent.

Although there are numerous ways to take Illustrator art into Photoshop, the most common method is to copy from Illustrator and paste into Photoshop. Photoshop CS2's new Smart Objects technology (discussed later in this chapter) works by copying and pasting, and Photoshop offers a lot of pasting options.

Pasting from Illustrator into Photoshop

You expect Photoshop to know what to do with Illustrator artwork that contains pixels, but what about paths? It turns out Photoshop is exceedingly smart in this area. When you paste your copied Illustrator artwork into Photoshop, you can choose for it to be handled in one of four different ways, as shown in Figure 4-1.

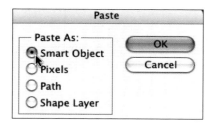

FIGURE 4-1

The Paste dialog box provides these options:

SMART OBJECT: Keeps a copy of the original Illustrator artwork available as long as the original artwork remains a Smart Object. Benefits of this option include the ability to edit the object in Illustrator and to scale the object without any loss of quality. Drawbacks include limited Photoshop functionality, such as the inability to apply filters to the Smart Object (without changing into "dumb" pixels, or pixels that are simply colored squares in an image). Smart Objects are discussed further in the next section.

PIXELS: Places the Illustrator artwork directly into Photoshop on a new layer. The artwork then acts similarly to any other Photoshop layer—except, of course, that it's probably more "designy" than a typical Photoshop layer. Figure 4-2 shows Illustrator artwork pasted into Photoshop as Pixels. Initially, pasted artwork results in an anti-aliased look; until you press the Return (Mac) or Enter (Windows) key, you can scale the artwork up or down freely with no loss in quality. Figure 4-3 shows the same artwork after the Return/Enter key has been pressed, which completes the rasterization process and removes the ugly little jaggies.

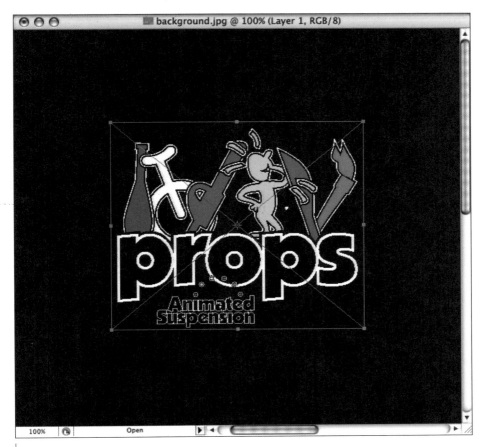

FIGURE 4-2

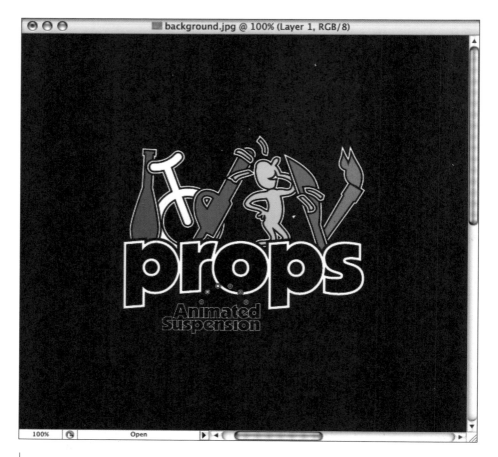

100%   Open

FIGURE 4-3

PATH: Places uncolored paths (no fill or stroke) from original Illustrator artwork into Photoshop. Those paths are then treated as if they were created directly in Photoshop, which means they can be used for masking or for selections. Figure 4-4 shows the same artwork from Figure 4-2 pasted into Photoshop as Paths instead of Pixels. Note that the text is not placed in this mode. The text elements "Props," "The," and "Card Game" are missing because they were created as text, not paths. However, the text "Animated Suspension" appears because it was created as a path in Illustrator.

FIGURE 4-4

SHAPE LAYER: Treats the Illustrator object as a Photoshop Shape Layer. Whereas this feature was somewhat valuable prior to CS2's Smart Objects, its usefulness is quite limited now. Suffice it to say that you can safely ignore this option without missing out on much. Figure 4-5 shows the artwork from Figure 4-2 again, this time pasted into Photoshop as a Shape Layer. Again, no text is placed in this mode.

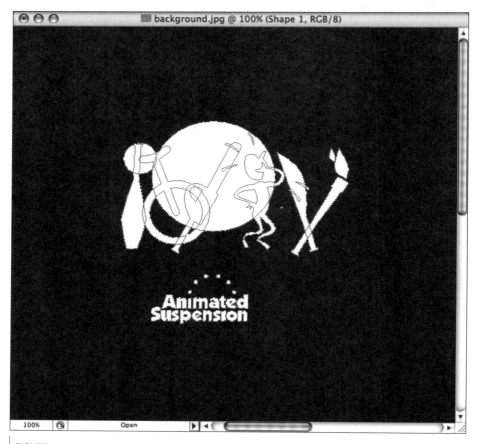

FIGURE 4-5

Note that if you've changed Illustrator's preferences, the Paste dialog box may not include the four options described above. If you find that this is the case, choose Preferences from the Illustrator menu, click on the File Handling & Clipboard option, and be sure that the PDF and AICB boxes are both checked, as shown in Figure 4-6. (Yes, it says "Clipboard on Quit," and no, I don't know why—it affects the clipboard any time you copy, not just on quit.)

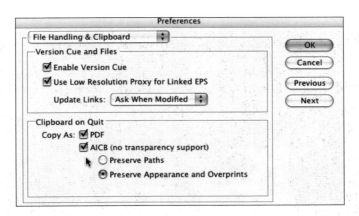

FIGURE 4-6

Using Smart Objects

One of the best new features in Photoshop CS2 is the capability to embed Illustrator CS2 artwork within a Photoshop file. All of the information about the Illustrator file is retained, allowing you to return to Illustrator to edit the file even after you have placed the art in Photoshop. To be clear, a Smart Object is not a link to an Illustrator file. Photoshop does not refer to a saved Illustrator document; instead, it maintains all of the Illustrator information in the Photoshop file. If you edit the Smart Object, you'll be editing a new instance of that art, not the original Illustrator file from which it came.

Figure 4-7 shows how Illustrator art looks after being placed into Photoshop as a Smart Object. Note that even though the result is path-based, the text comes in correctly and looks exactly like the result in Figure 4-2.

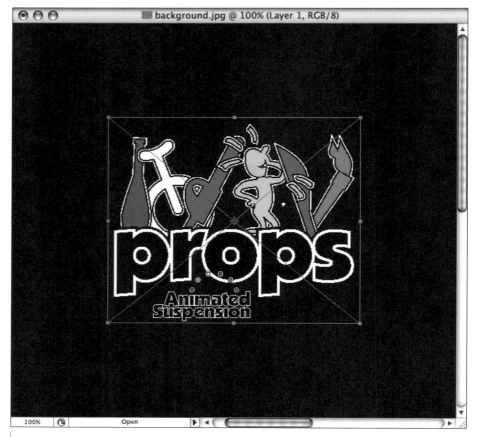

FIGURE 4-7

But whereas an object pasted as Pixels loses all of its vector attributes, an object pasted as a Smart Object keeps them, even after you press Return/Enter to remove the jaggies. Note that the paths are accessible only in Illustrator (if you choose to edit the Smart Object). Figure 4-8 shows how this Smart Object appears in the Layers palette.

After the Illustrator artwork is embedded in Photoshop as a Smart Object, the real fun begins. You can do all sorts of things to the Vector Smart Object layer, and still go back at any time and resize or edit the vector artwork.

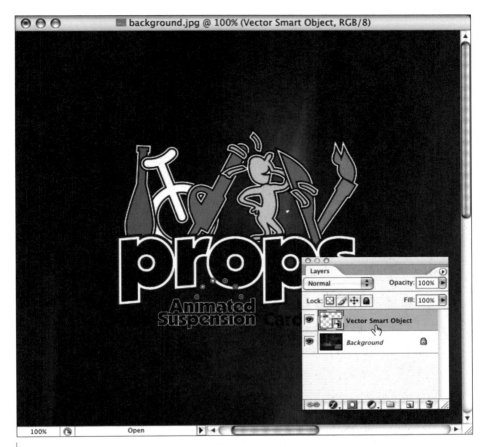

FIGURE 4-8

One thing you'll find exceedingly useful is the ability to apply adjustment layers to Smart Objects (Illustrator lacks the capability to make most of these adjustments, such as curves and levels adjustments). To affect just the Smart Object layer, be sure to check the Use Previous Layer to Create Clipping Mask checkbox in the New Layer dialog box that appears when you create your adjustment layer, as shown in Figure 4-9.

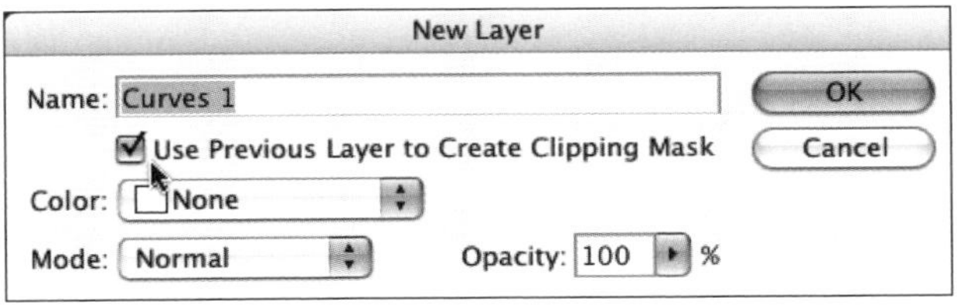

FIGURE 4-9

Figure 4-10 shows the "props" artwork after different layer effects and adjustment layers have been applied.

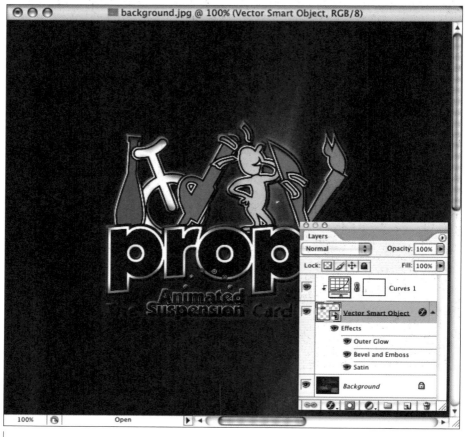

FIGURE 4-10

So far, the result isn't any different from what you'd get if you applied the same layer effects and adjustment layers to a pixel-based layer. But watch what happens when we scale up the artwork by 200% using Edit→Transform (Figure 4-11).

FIGURE 4-11

The artwork gets bigger, and the quality looks as good or better than when it was smaller! Even when we make an extreme jump in scale (to 500% of the original size), as shown in Figure 4-12, the quality is perfect. Keep in mind, though, that some of Photoshop's layer effects do not scale with the artwork (unlike Illustrator's effects), so you might need to edit the layer effects to compensate for your scaled artwork.

FIGURE 4-12

Another benefit of Smart Objects is that you can edit them while keeping scaling, layer effects, and adjustment layers intact. Let's look at an example. If we double-click on the document icon in the Vector Smart Object layer, the artwork is opened as a new Illustrator file, as shown in Figure 4-13. (Even if you did a "Select All" in Illustrator before you copied and pasted, Photoshop will create a new file for you to edit.)

FIGURE 4-13

In Illustrator, let's modify the file slightly, making the prop images smaller and changing the color of the word "Props" so that it contains green stripes (Figure 4-14). These changes would have been impossible in Photoshop, but they take just a few seconds to do in Illustrator.

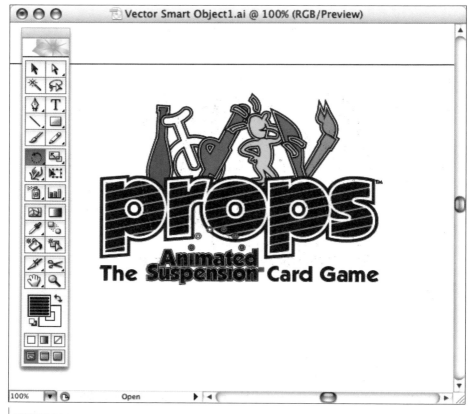

FIGURE 4-14

After we've made these changes, we must save and close the Vector Smart Object file. When we return to Photoshop, the file is updated with the changes, yet the scaling, layer effects, and adjustment layers remain as they were before we edited the file. The file does look a little different, though, as shown in Figure 4-15.

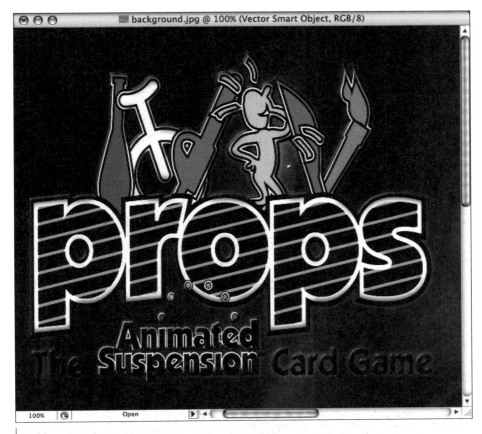

FIGURE 4-15

If you make changes to the overall dimensions of the artwork in Illustrator, when you return to Photoshop the art will stretch or shrink to fill the original dimensions. To fix this, choose the Move tool and select Show Transform Controls in the Transform bar. Then, begin to adjust the image by using transform boxes around the artwork. As you move a transform box handle, watch the numbers along the Transform bar until the Width and Height % values match (or just enter matching numbers). Press the Return/Enter key to accept the transformation. The result is a perfectly updated image, as shown in Figure 4-16.

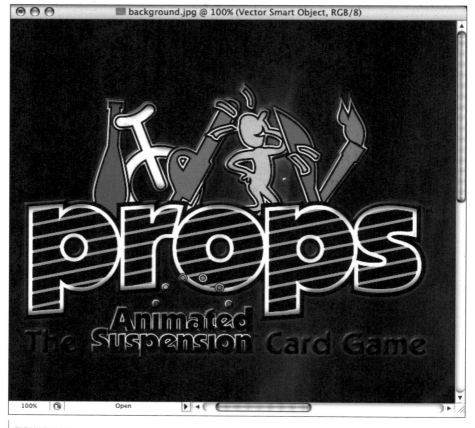

FIGURE 4-16

As you're working with Smart Objects, be acutely aware of dialog boxes popping up and telling you that the object will be converted (or rasterized) from a Smart Object to pixels when you do certain activities or choose certain tools. Clicking OK in these dialog boxes removes the ability to edit these files in Illustrator or to scale them without any loss in quality.

Exporting Illustrator Files to Photoshop Layers

In certain instances where you want to control individual objects from Illustrator within Photoshop, you might consider exporting layered Illustrator files into Photoshop layers, essentially turning your top-level Illustrator layers into Photoshop layers. Figure 4-17 shows an Illustrator document with several layers.

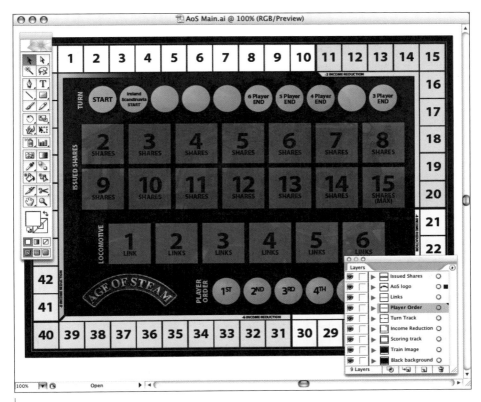

FIGURE 4-17

**To create a Photoshop document where each
Illustrator layer is a Photoshop layer:**

1. Open the art in Illustrator.

2. Choose Export from the File menu. Then choose Photoshop (*.psd*) as the Format.

3. Name the file and click Export.

4. In the Photoshop Export Options dialog box that appears (Figure 4-18), make sure the Write Layers option is selected and click OK.

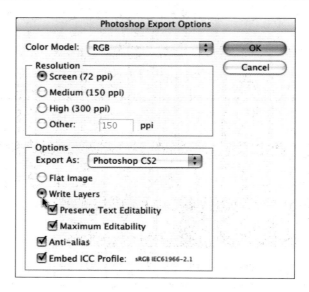

FIGURE 4-18

When you open the file in Photoshop, you'll see that there are now Photoshop layers for each of the Illustrator layers. You'll also find additional Photoshop layers for each of the distinct objects, such as type objects and placed images (Figure 4-19). Each of these Photoshop layers can be moved and treated just as if it were a native Photoshop layer, and the type layers can be edited directly in Photoshop.

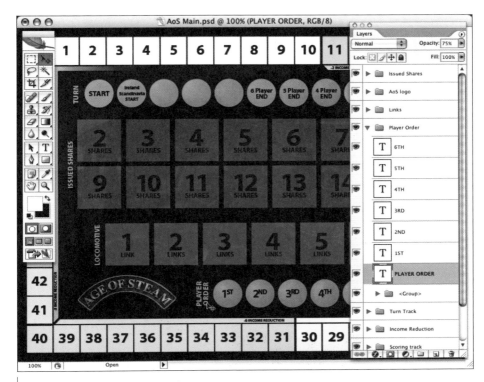

FIGURE 4-19

TAKING PHOTOSHOP IMAGES INTO ILLUSTRATOR

Although there are all sorts of ways you can take Illustrator art into Photoshop, the reality is that you'll find yourself going the other way most of the time: taking Photoshop images into Illustrator documents. There aren't as many options in this direction, but there are a few that you'll use time and time again. Copying and pasting is a favorite for quick moves between the applications, but savvy Illustrator users import saved native Photoshop files for the best results and highest quality.

Copying and Pasting

Pasting into Illustrator from Photoshop is straightforward, at least in terms of what you do: make a selection in Photoshop, choose Copy, go to Illustrator, and then click Paste. But what actually results might surprise you.

When you select in Photoshop, you select one layer at a time. That means you'll be pasting in only one layer of info, which typically isn't what you'll want. The workaround is to flatten your image in Photoshop, then copy it, and then undo the flattening before you go to Illustrator and paste it in. (You could use the Copy Merged command, but the results aren't always predictable.) Beware, though—forgetting to undo that flatten can be catastrophic if you happen to close the file (and save it) after going to Illustrator.

Illustrator is smart enough to keep the physical size of whatever you're pasting, so art that seems nice and big at 100% in Photoshop might paste into Illustrator much smaller if the ppi (in the Image Size dialog box) is set to anything less than 72. You can always check the ppi of a placed image in Illustrator by selecting the image and then choosing the Document Info palette's Embedded Images option (Figure 4-20).

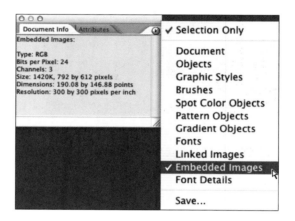

FIGURE 4-20

Opening and Placing Photoshop Images in Illustrator

The better way to work with Photoshop images is to open or place a saved Photoshop file in Illustrator. Doing so gives you the ability to link to the original file, so if you make changes to the Photoshop image, your Illustrator file will be updated immediately. You can also edit linked Photoshop images directly from Illustrator, popping out to Photoshop to make the changes and then back into Illustrator fairly quickly.

The differences between *opening* and *placing* Photoshop images are important. Only the Open command allows you to convert Photoshop layers to Illustrator layers (objects, actually, but it results in the same thing), and only the Place command allows you to link to the original image. Both methods allow you to embed a composite (single-layer) Photoshop file.

CHAPTER 4

Using Photoshop Layers in Illustrator

This section might be more appropriately entitled "stuff that doesn't work in Illustrator when you import layers from a Photoshop file," but nevertheless there are many reasons to use the functionality that's in place. Whenever you open a Photoshop file in Illustrator, you have the option to convert the Photoshop layers to Illustrator objects. If you choose this option (Figure 4-21), each Photoshop layer will appear as a separate object in your Illustrator file's Layers palette (Figure 4-22).

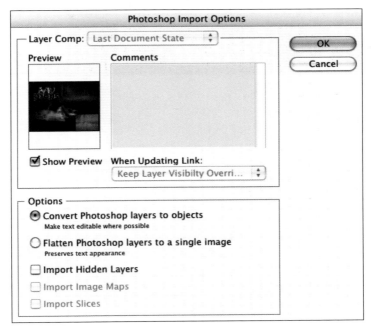

FIGURE 4-21

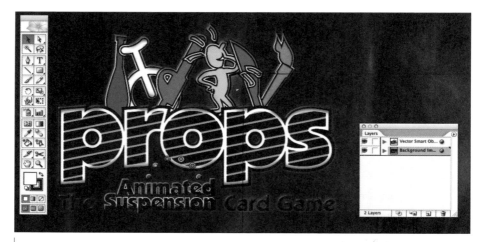

FIGURE 4-22

Here are a few important caveats when opening Photoshop images as layered files in Illustrator:

- Layers with layer effects will not be imported as separate layers. To get the result shown in Figure 4-22, I had to rasterize the Vector Smart Object layer and use Merge Visible in Photoshop to apply and remove the effects.

- Smart Objects are pixel-based when they are brought into Illustrator from Photoshop. This seems counterintuitive, but that's the way it works. (Of course, you could just as easily paste in the original Illustrator objects, either from Illustrator directly or from the "temporary" Illustrator document that is created when you edit a Vector Smart Object.)

- Blending modes and most transparency options are lost.

USING PHOTOSHOP IMAGES IN INDESIGN

Although the relationship between Photoshop and InDesign is entirely one-way (Photoshop is always giving, and InDesign is always taking), it works pretty smoothly from each side. InDesign users can paste or place native Photoshop files directly into InDesign documents, and unlike with Illustrator, layer information can be included in placed images. Also, you can easily edit one of those images in Photoshop by selecting it and choosing Edit→Edit Original.

The ability to manipulate layers from Photoshop in InDesign is less useful than it is in Illustrator, though, because imagery in InDesign tends to interact much less with other page elements. The big choice really comes down to whether or not you need to link to the original image. If you do, you need to use the Place command. If not, pasting is acceptable, but you'll run into the same issues that Illustrator users face — in particular, the inability to copy multiple layers easily.

Of course, with Photoshop you also have the ability to export the file in a variety of other file formats that InDesign can consume, but that requires an extra step and may result in loss of editability or an increase in file size.

As a final note, when placing Photoshop images into InDesign, as a rule the images should be in CMYK mode, because the majority of InDesign documents will be headed for print. Be aware, though, that Photoshop blend modes change based on the image mode they're in. Be careful to inspect your image when moving between RGB and CMYK, especially if you've been using blend modes on layers. Take a look at Figures 4-23 and 4-24. Figure 4-23 shows the original image with a Difference blend mode applied to the logo RGB mode. Figure 4-24 shows the result of converting the image from Figure 4-23 into CMYK mode.

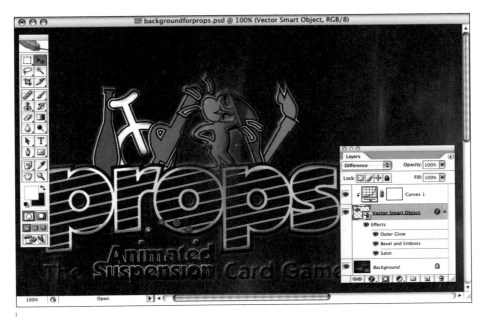

FIGURE 4-23

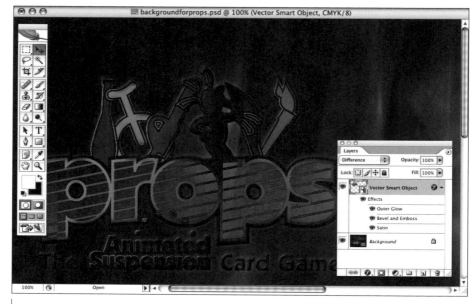

FIGURE 4-24

To prevent changing the image, flatten it entirely before making the switch to CMYK.

USING PHOTOSHOP IMAGES IN GOLIVE

GoLive's Smart Objects feature is quite similar to Photoshop's Smart Objects feature, with one exception: instead of storing the original artwork or image in the GoLive file (which is just HTML), GoLive references a "source object" from which the resulting web-ready object is created.

Web pages can use only web-friendly formats, which typically include JPEG, GIF, and PNG (SVG and SWF are also common, but they tend to require plug-ins and have more benefits from being vector-based than pixel-based). You can't include a Photoshop native (PSD) file on a web page. GoLive, however, can open a Photoshop native file and export it in the web-ready format of your choice.

1. Click the Smart button on the Objects palette (Figure 4-25).

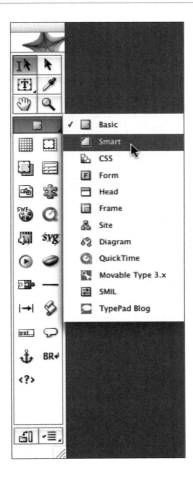

FIGURE 4-25

2. Drag the Smart Photoshop icon onto your page, and click the Source folder in the Inspector palette (Figure 4-26).

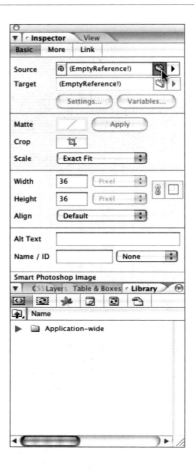

FIGURE 4-26

3. Locate and open the file you want to use. The Save For Web dialog box will appear (Figure 4-27). This is pretty much the exact same dialog box you'd get if you chose File→Save For Web in Photoshop, ImageReady, or Illustrator. However, instead of creating a separate, independent file, you're creating a linked file that will update automatically if you change the source (native) Photoshop file.

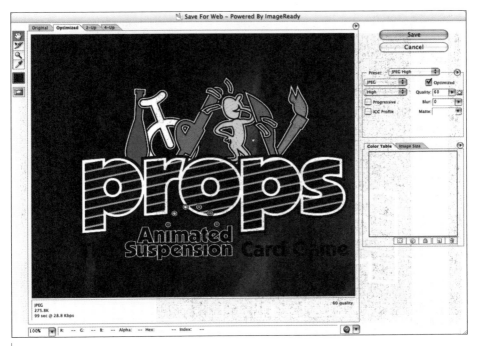

FIGURE 4-27

Figure 4-28 shows the Smart Object image placed in GoLive. All Smart Objects in GoLive are indicated by the "ying-yang" circle in the upper left of the object. Selecting and clicking one of these objects in GoLive will show you both the original source image and the resulting target image created in GoLive.

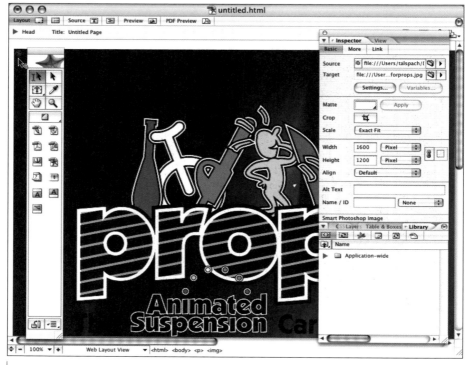

FIGURE 4-28

Here are the most important things to take away from this chapter:

1. There are myriad ways to place/open Photoshop files in Illustrator, InDesign, and Go-Live. Choose the one that fits each situation the best.

2. You can take Illustrator artwork into Photoshop by copying and pasting or by opening an Illustrator object in Photoshop.

3. Photoshop CS2's new Smart Objects feature allows Illustrator art to "live" in Photoshop. From Photoshop, you can edit the art in Illustrator at any time, even with various Photoshop layer effects, adjustment layers, and transformations applied to the art.

4. Placing Photoshop images in Illustrator and InDesign provides an option to link back to the original Photoshop file, which means that you can update the file in Photoshop, and the updates will be shown in Illustrator/InDesign.

5. Using GoLive's Smart Objects allows the original Photoshop document to remain intact, while creating a new, linked, web-ready file for the GoLive document.

Top 15 How Do I...? Photoshop Questions

In this chapter, you will find the answers to the top 15 questions designers ask about Photoshop, with special emphasis on Creative Suite-related workflows. These most commonly asked questions were compiled from questions asked in the Photoshop forums and posed to the Photoshop product team. If you have a specific problem or are looking to improve your skills, the step-by-step solutions included here should help. You'll find tips that will save you time, strengthen your creativity, and much more.

HOW DO I REMOVE COLOR CASTS FROM AN IMAGE?

If you have a photo that has a bit of a yellow, red, or other-colored tinge to it, or if it looks completely washed out (with a certain color predominant), you'll want to "normalize" that image so that it accurately represents the true color of the depicted objects. *Color casts*, where the lack or abundance of a certain color overwhelms the entire image, tend to be caused by a number of different lighting conditions. Color casts appear in both Camera RAW files and JPEG files from a digital camera. You can address them in a similar manner, but with Camera RAW files you'll be able to adjust the image before any pixel modification takes place, ensuring the best possible results.

> To remove color casts from a Camera RAW image:

1. In Photoshop, choose File→Open. In the Open dialog box, choose Camera Raw and then select the file you want to open. Click the Open button, and the image will open in the Camera Raw dialog box, as shown in Figure 5-1.

FIGURE 5-1

2. Because this image has a bluish cast to it, you might be inclined to jump directly to the Calibrate tab and decrease the blue saturation. Instead, try to ignore the color cast on the image for a moment and set the exposure properly. This photo was taken at dusk, a time when light plays all sorts of tricks. Setting the exposure properly is the most important thing you can do to get the image into a presentable form quickly. In Figure 5-2, I've unchecked the Auto checkbox by the Exposure slider and dragged the slider slightly to the left, which has a dramatic effect on the image.

FIGURE 5-2

3. After changing the exposure, play around with the Tint slider, moving it slightly to the right to remove bluish tints or to the left to remove yellowish tints. You also might want to adjust the remaining sliders (Shadows, Contrast, Brightness, and Saturation) at this point, but only slightly. Figure 5-3 shows the image after adjustments. As you can see, the bluish tint has been removed completely.

☑ Preview ☐ Shadows ☐ Highlights   R: --- G: --- B: ---

Settings: Custom

Adjust Detail Lens Curve Calibrate

White Balance: Custom

Temperature   7500

Tint   -34

Exposure   ☐ Auto   +2.70

Shadows   ☐ Auto   5

Brightness ☐ Auto   45

Contrast   ☐ Auto   +22

Saturation   +19

18.9%

☑ Show Workflow Options

Space: Adobe RGB (1998)   Size: 3504 by 2336 (8.2 MP)

Depth: 8 Bits/Channel   Resolution: 240 pixels/inch

Save...   Cancel

Open   Done

FIGURE 5-3

To remove color casts from a JPEG or other Photoshop image:

1. Open the image you want to edit. Change the Mode to Lab by choosing Image→ Mode→Lab Color. Lab color provides better control for color adjustment than the RGB or CMYK color spaces, both in terms of the types of controls available for adjustment and in terms of the (larger) size of the color space. In Figure 5-4, note the yellowish cast (caused by the brightness of a partially overcast day, not jaundice).

2. Because the entire image is affected with the yellow cast, you can work on the entire image instead of a specific selection. Choose Image→Adjustments→Color Balance. If you wish to make adjustments that you might want to change later, you can choose Layers→New Adjustment Layer→Color Balance instead.

tip

To remove casts completely, it's best to adjust highlights, then shadows, then midtones. A midtone adjustment can be overwhelming and might mask problems in the highlights and shadows. Adjusting highlights and shadows first prevents you from missing these problems.

FIGURE 5-4

3. In the Color Balance dialog box, click the Highlights radio button, and drag the slider away from the color of the cast (in this case, toward blue and away from yellow). In this particular image, the blond hair shouldn't be yellowed at all. Figure 5-5 shows the result of fixing the highlight color balance (look at the bright sections of hair in the image).

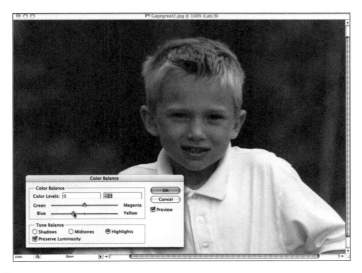

FIGURE 5-5

4. Next, select the Shadows radio button and adjust the shadows, taking care not to overdo your adjustments. In this image, note that the background and the color of the eyes are impacted by sliding the yellow/blue slider to the left. Figure 5-6 shows the result of shifting the shadows toward blue, away from yellow.

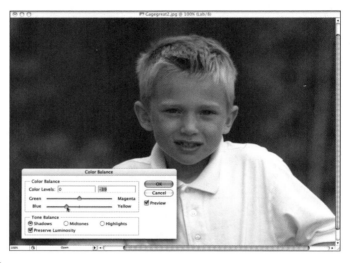

FIGURE 5-6

5. Finally, adjust the midtones. This will probably be a much finer adjustment than was needed for the highlights and shadows. At this time, you may wish to switch the color mode to RGB or CMYK (via Image→Mode), depending on what you'll be doing with it after Photoshop. The final image is shown in Figure 5-7.

FIGURE 5-7

HOW DO I PREPARE IMAGES FOR THE WEB?

Photoshop provides a multitude of controls, settings, and options for preparing images for the Web.

Broadband is becoming increasingly prevalent, and bandwidth limitation regarding compression of images is slowly becoming a thing of the past. With that said, there's still a noticeable difference in the time it takes to load a page with "uncompressed" images compared to dramatically compressed images. This is the surefire, always-works method to use for images destined for the Web.

To prepare an image for the Web:

1. In Photoshop, open the image you want to use and choose File→Save for Web. The image will appear in the Save For Web – Powered By ImageReady dialog box with the compression settings that were last used in the dialog box, as shown in Figure 5-8.

FIGURE 5-8

2. In most cases, you'll want to choose JPEG. (There are few benefits to the GIF and PNG formats that aren't outweighed by the universal acceptance of JPEG files in web software.)

3. Note that the size you're seeing the image at is the size it will appear on the web page. Sometimes, especially with digital camera images, images can appear quite large in the Save For Web dialog box. If you want to change the size of the image, click the Image Size tab, shown in Figure 5-9. Enter a different number in either the Width or Height field (the other field will update automatically), and click the Apply button. The image will be displayed at the new size.

FIGURE 5-9

4. To compare the current "compressed" image with the original, click the 2-Up tab at the top of the dialog box. This will allow you to see the original image compared to the compressed image. The compression in Figure 5-10 is set to JPEG Low, so that you can easily tell the difference between the original and the compressed image. Depending on the image, high levels of compression might not make much of a visible difference.

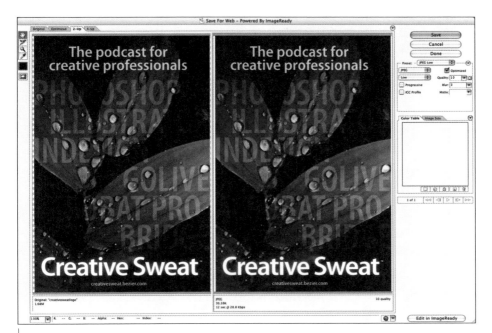

FIGURE 5-10

5. Once you're happy with the compression settings, click the Save button.

6. In the Save Optimized As dialog box, set the location and the name. Be sure the file-name has a .jpg extension if you've chosen JPEG as the file type.

When you save the original Photoshop file, it remembers the settings, location, and name of the Save for Web file you've saved, so if you update the file, you can hop into Save for Web and click Save to quickly update your web-ready image.

HOW DO I SET UP IMAGES FOR PRINT?

As a Creative Suite user, it's unlikely that you'll print very often directly from Photoshop. If you're a long-time Photoshop user who's used to doing everything in Photoshop, you'll want to get used to setting your image mode to CMYK (Image→Mode→CMYK Color) and then placing the image inside Illustrator or InDesign for printing. However, if you are go-ing to print directly from Photoshop, follow the steps below.

1. With your image open, choose File→Page Setup and make sure your printer is select-ed in the Page Setup dialog box (Figure 5-11). Verify that the page size shown matches the paper to which you'll be printing, and click OK.

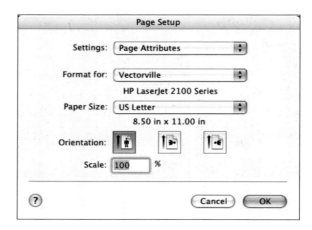

FIGURE 5-11

2. In the lower left of the document, you'll see a wide area that gives some information about the document, such as "Open," the document storage size or dimensions, and so on. Click and hold on the displayed text, and you'll see how the image will appear on the page you're printing. The page is shown as a big white rectangle. The image is a black box with an X through it. If you can't see all four of the edges of the box (Figure 5-12), you'll need to resize your image, as discussed in the following step.

3. If necessary, change the size of your image. Choose Image→Image Size, and make sure that the Resample Image checkbox in the Image Size dialog box is *not* checked (Figure 5-13). Then change the document width and height so that they're both slightly smaller than your page size. Most printers can't print to the edge of a page, so making your image a little smaller than the page avoids any of the edges being chopped off. Changing the size of an image without resampling it changes the print resolution, but not the image resolution.

4. Choose File→Print.

FIGURE 5-12

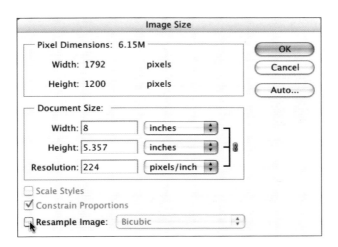

FIGURE 5-13

HOW DO I GET PHOTOSHOP LAYERS TO APPEAR IN ILLUSTRATOR?

Because both Photoshop and Illustrator have layers, it makes sense that you'll some-times want to use layers from one product in the other. It's nice to be able to manipulate individual layers from a Photoshop image in Illustrator, so you can make adjustments to a portion of the image. Before you embark on this, however, keep in mind that a few things in Photoshop won't work properly when you open a Photoshop layered file in Illustrator, including layer effects, adjustment layers, and blend modes. If your Photoshop file has these, you'll want to flatten the image—or at least those effects—before bringing the file into Illustrator.

To open layers of a Photoshop image in Illustrator:

1. In Illustrator, open your Photoshop file by using File→Open. Note that you cannot place a Photoshop file with layers into Illustrator; you can only open it.

2. In the Photoshop Import Options dialog box that appears, choose the "Convert Photoshop layers to objects" option (Figure 5-14).

FIGURE 5-14

3. In Illustrator's Layers palette, each Photoshop layer will be a different object (Figure 5-15).

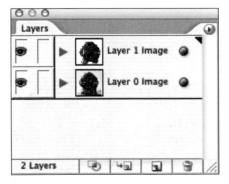

FIGURE 5-15

4. After you have the image in Illustrator in separate layers, you can do all sorts of interesting things with it. Our sample image as it initially appears in Illustrator is shown in Figure 5-16.

FIGURE 5-16

5. The image in Figure 5-17 was created by tracing the top layer (which contained just the clock), colorizing it slightly, and adding a stroke to the traced pieces.

FIGURE 5-17

HOW DO I MAKE TEXT ON A PATH?

If you choose to make text on a path in Photoshop, you'd better have a really good reason for it. There's almost no benefit to using Photoshop for text on a path if you have the Creative Suite, because both Illustrator and InDesign provide much more comprehensive Path Type tools. Although you *can* put type on a path in Photoshop, owning Illustrator and InDesign means you never have to. And you never should. But if you must...

To put type on a path over an image:

1. Place the Photoshop image you're working on in Illustrator (File→Place). The image should appear in Illustrator, as shown in Figure 5-18.

FIGURE 5-18

2. Using the Pen or Pencil tool, draw the path that you'd like the type to appear on (Figure 5-19).

FIGURE 5-19

3. With the Type on a Path tool (found in the Type tool slot to the right of the Type tool) selected, click on the middle of the path and type your text (Figure 5-20).

FIGURE 5-20

4. To adjust the text, choose the Selection tool (black arrow) to automatically select the path. Click the "Center text" button on the Control palette at the top of the screen to center your text (Figure 5-21).

FIGURE 5-21

5. Click the vertical bar in the middle of your text, and drag it so that it is centered on the path you drew (Figure 5-22).

FIGURE 5-22

6. Change your text options until the text appears the way you'd like (Figure 5-23).

FIGURE 5-23

The great thing about doing your text in Illustrator is that the text not only remains editable (as it does in Photoshop), but its resolution is independent of the image. This means that if you print from Illustrator the text will be super crisp, as opposed to printing from Photoshop, where the text will have to be anti-aliased (fuzzy) just so that it doesn't appear jagged.

HOW DO I REMOVE RED EYE?

Anyone who has futzed around with a camera's red-eye reduction flash functionality will tell you it's not worth it. Digital camera red-eye options work by faking out the eyes of the subjects: a preliminary flash is set off that causes the pupils of the subjects' eyes to contract, reducing or eliminating the red-eye effect that is caused by the reflection of the flash in dilated pupils. However, the initial flash tends to confuse the subjects, and many of them blink, move, or stop smiling before the shutter fires, resulting in a totally unusable picture. Photoshop's new Red Eye tool is a great, super-fast way to correct red-eye problems. It's incredibly easy to use, too—the only trick is finding it.

To remove red eye from an image:

1. In Photoshop, open the image that has red eye, like the one shown in Figure 5-24.

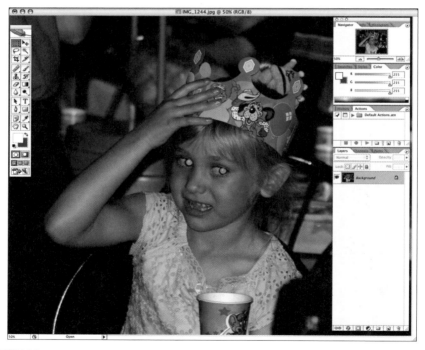

FIGURE 5-24

2. Choose the Red Eye tool, which is hidden away in the Healing Brush tool slot (Figure 5-25).

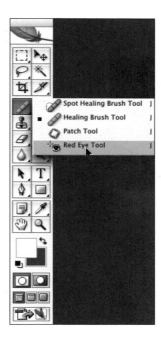

FIGURE 5-25

3. Drag the tool across the area where the eyes are and release the mouse button. Photoshop will find the red eyes (Figure 5-26).

FIGURE 5-26

The eyes will change to mostly black (to represent pupils), as shown in Figure 5-27. If you don't get the result you wanted (for example, part of the eye might still be red), you can use the tool again, or you can undo the action, change the settings in the Control palette at the top of the screen, and then try it again.

FIGURE 5-27

HOW DO I TURN MY IMAGE INTO A PDF?

To make an image more secure and readable on virtually any device, you can turn it into a PDF document.

To turn an image into a PDF document:

1. Choose File→Save As. The Save As dialog box will appear. Choose Photoshop PDF from the list of Formats, and click Save (Figure 5-28).

2. The Save Adobe PDF dialog appears. Be sure to check the Preserve Photoshop Editing Capabilities checkbox, which allows you to open the file in Photoshop and still have access to the image's layers and other Photoshop-specific image attributes (Figure 5-29). Click Save PDF.

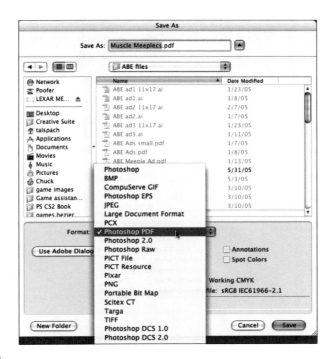

FIGURE 5-28

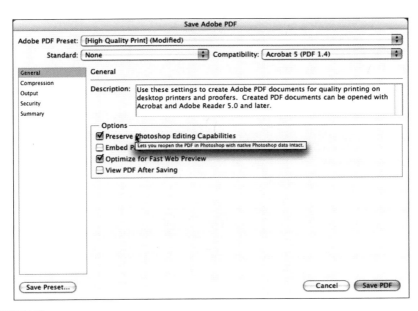

FIGURE 5-29

You can now open the file in Acrobat and view your image as it will appear to anyone else who has Acrobat or the Adobe Reader (Figure 5-30). This image was originally an Illustrator file, but you can save any type of image as a PDF—from photos to artwork you've created yourself.

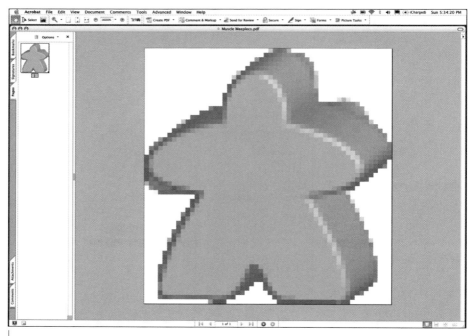

FIGURE 5-30

HOW DO I INCREASE PHOTOSHOP'S PERFORMANCE?

Tired of waiting for images to open and save, and for operations to process?

To get the fastest possible Photoshop performance:

INCREASE YOUR RAM: RAM is the single most important factor when dealing with large images. Photoshop uses RAM to temporarily store information and changes; when it runs out of RAM, it starts using your hard drive, which is dramatically slower than RAM. You should have at least 1 GB of RAM on your computer for optimal results (although if you only work with small files, having a lot of RAM is much less important).

USE THE FASTEST PROCESSOR AVAILABLE: Whether you're on a PC or a Mac, using the latest and fastest processor is a surefire way to see an improvement in performance for most operations. While you're at it, if you have the option of getting a dual-processor machine, do so. Photoshop takes advantage of dual processors more than any other Creative Suite application.

USE A FASTER HARD DRIVE: The faster your hard drive is, the faster Photoshop will launch, open, and save files—all tasks that you'll be doing time and time again.

RESAMPLE (DOWN) YOUR IMAGES FIRST: Instead of color correcting, editing, and working on original files, resize your images before doing those activities to the size you want to end up with. Of course, if you plan on resampling up via the Image Size dialog box (making the image bigger), you should wait until after you've done all your editing to change the size. Note, however, that resampling up is almost always a bad idea.

HOW DO I CREATE AN IMAGE WITH A TRANSPARENT BACKGROUND?

By default, most images in Photoshop open up with a solid (usually white) background color. When you "delete" pixels, you'll be changing them to white. In order to create an empty background, you'll need to use layers.

To make the background of an image transparent:

1. Open the image for which you want to change the background. Figure 5-31 shows a typical digital camera image opened in Photoshop. Note that the Layers palette has a single layer, "Background."

FIGURE 5-31

2. In the Layers palette, press Option/Alt and double-click the Background layer. This will change that layer into a "real" Photoshop layer that can deal with transparency. This change is shown in Figure 5-32. Note that the italicized word "Background" has been replaced by the non-italic "Layer 0." If you don't press Option/Alt when double-clicking, you'll get a dialog box that allows you to change the name of the layer when creating it.

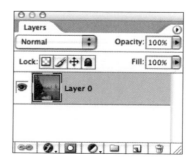

FIGURE 5-32

3. Using any combination of selection tools (the Magic Wand/Lasso combination tends to work the best), select the background of the image, as shown in Figure 5-33.

FIGURE 5-33

4. If you want to add a semi-soft edge to the image, choose Select→Inverse to choose the image, choose Select→Feather, and then enter a value such as 1 or 2 pixels in the Feather Selection dialog box. This will soften the edge of the image so that there won't be jaggies between the background and the image. After feathering, choose Select→ Inverse again so that the background, and not the image, is selected.

5. Press the Delete (or Backspace) key on your keyboard. The background will be re-moved (Figure 5-34). When you save the image for placing in another Creative Suite application, be sure to save it as a *.psd* image so that the transparency is preserved.

FIGURE 5-34

HOW DO I EXPORT LAYERS TO INDIVIDUAL FILES?

You might come across or create a Photoshop file that has several layers that you want to separate. You can extract a single layer or many layers to use as individual images.

To export layers to files:

1. Open the Photoshop file that has images on different layers that you'd like as individual files.

2. Choose File→Scripts→Export Layers To Files (Figure 5-35).

3. In the Export Layers To Files dialog box (Figure 5-36) that appears, enter a name in the File Name Prefix text box. This name will be the prefix for each of the files.

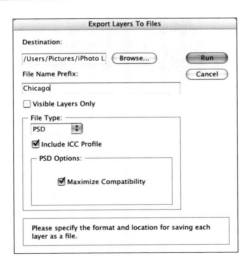

4. Click the Run button, and each layer will be exported as an individual file.

HOW DO I CREATE ANIMATIONS FOR THE WEB?

If you're using the Creative Suite, you have all the tools you need to make great animations. The steps below walk you through the creation of a spinning 3D animation, using Illustrator, ImageReady, and GoLive. Although Photoshop layers are required, you can do this without ever opening Photoshop!

To create a spinning 3D animation for the Web:

1. Create a 3D extruded object in Illustrator. I've created a 3D "meeple," as shown in Figure 5-37. To do this, I took a basic 2D shape in Illustrator, chose Effect→3D→Extrude & Bevel, and set the Extrude Depth to 192 points and the Tall-Round Bevel to a Height of 4 points.

FIGURE 5-37

GIF-type animations consist of several *frames* of images, or entire images repeated again and again with slight differences between them. The next set of steps shows how to create each step in the animation.

2. While holding down the Option/Alt key, drag a copy of the object to the right of the original object. The Option/Alt key creates a copy of whatever you're dragging, so you should now have two objects, like the two meeples shown in Figure 5-38.

CHAPTER 5

FIGURE 5-38

3. With the second object selected, double-click the 3D Extrude & Bevel line in the Appearance palette, which opens the 3D Extrude & Bevel Options dialog box (Figure 5-39).

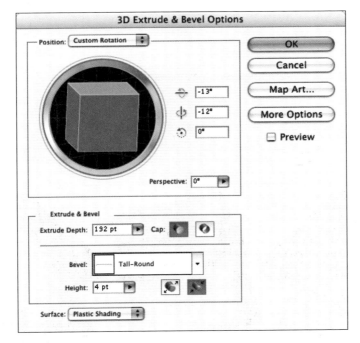

FIGURE 5-39

4. Change the second (green arrow) value by 180. In my example, I started at –12, so I changed the value to 168 (Figure 5-40). Click OK.

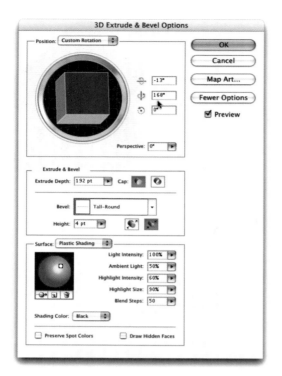

FIGURE 5-40

---

5. Select both objects, and then choose Object→Blend→Make. A "middle" object will appear, like the one shown in Figure 5-41.

FIGURE 5-41

In order to get a smooth animation, you need more than just one step between the two ends.

---

6. Choose Object→Blend→Blend Options. Change the Spacing to Specified Steps, enter a number to represent the number of "in-between" animations you'd like (Figure 5-42), and then click OK.

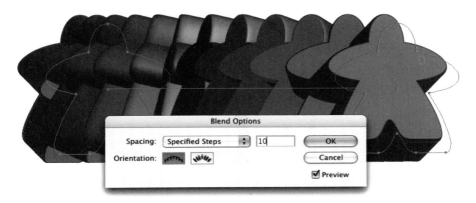

FIGURE 5-42

7. In the Layers palette, click on the Blend entry, as shown in Figure 5-43.

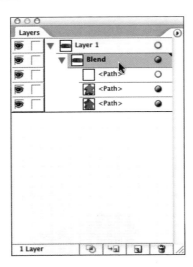

FIGURE 5-43

8. Choose Release to Layers (Sequence) from the Layers palette pop-up menu (accessed in the upper-right corner of the Layers palette). The result will be several additional layers, as shown in Figure 5-44.

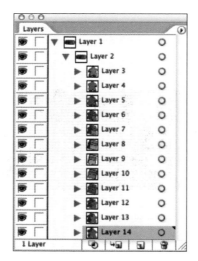

FIGURE 5-44

9. Select all the objects and then click the Horizontal Align Center button in the Align palette so that the objects overlap (and don't move to the right when animated), as shown in Figure 5-45.

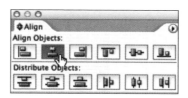

FIGURE 5-45

The result will be pretty ugly (Figure 5-46), because all the objects are stacked on top of each other.

FIGURE 5-46

10. Choose File→Export, and choose Photoshop (*.psd*) as the Format. Click the Export button. The Photoshop Export Options dialog box appears, as shown in Figure 5-47. Be sure that Write Layers is selected, and click OK.

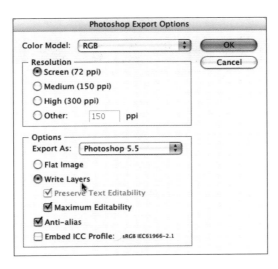

FIGURE 5-47

You need to use ImageReady for the next step, because Photoshop doesn't have an Animation palette.

11. In ImageReady, open the *.psd* file you just exported from Illustrator. The file will appear in the same "stacked" form you saw in Illustrator (Figure 5-48).

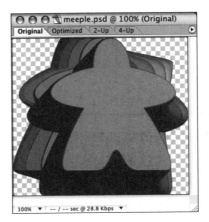

FIGURE 5-48

12. In the Animation palette pop-up menu, choose Make Frames From Layers. Each layer will be turned into a frame and displayed separately in the Animation palette, like the ones in Figure 5-49.

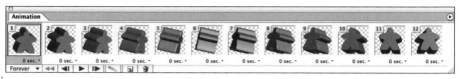

FIGURE 5-49

If you want to preview your animation, click the Play arrow at the bottom of the Animation palette.

13. Choose File→Save Optimized, and pick a location for your file. By default, the file type will be *.gif*, and the name of the file will be the name you used when you exported it from Illustrator.

14. In GoLive, open the web page on which you'd like the animation to appear. Drag the Image icon from the Objects palette to the web page (Figure 5-50).

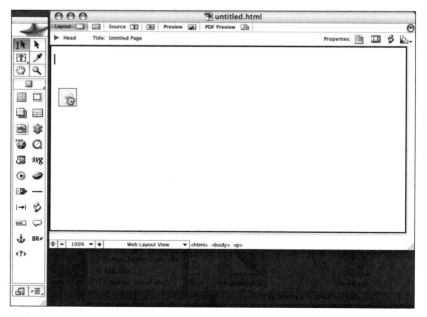

FIGURE 5-50

15. In the Inspector palette, choose the *.gif* file you saved. The first frame of the *.gif* file should appear in your page (Figure 5-51).

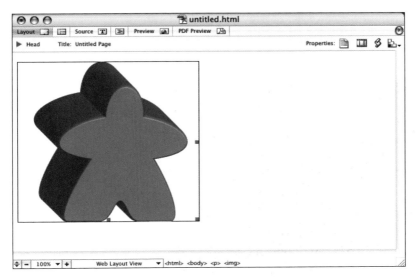

FIGURE 5-51

16. Click the Preview tab to see your animation in action (Figure 5-52).

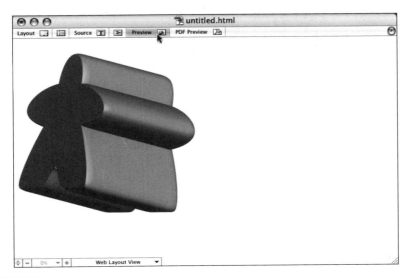

FIGURE 5-52

HOW DO I CLEAR THE SCREEN OF PALETTES AND THE TOOLBAR?

Photoshop palettes can easily obscure your work area, as shown in Figure 5-53. However, you can use shortcuts to hide palettes and the toolbar.

FIGURE 5-53

1. Press the Tab key, and all your palettes and the toolbar will vanish temporarily (Figure 5-54). You can get them back by pressing Tab once more.

FIGURE 5-54

1. Press Shift-Tab, and all your palettes will vanish, but your toolbar will remain, as shown in Figure 5-55. You can get them back by pressing Shift-Tab once more. If you've moved your palettes around and want to put them back where they were, choose Window→Workspace→Default Workspace.

FIGURE 5-55

HOW DO I CREATE A CONTACT SHEET?

Although you can use Photoshop to create a contact sheet, it's awkward and confusing. Instead, select your images in Bridge and use its built-in Contact Sheet feature.

To create a contact sheet:

1. In Bridge, select the images you'd like to be on the contact sheet (Figure 5-56).

FIGURE 5-56

2. Choose Tools→Photoshop→Contact Sheet II, and the Contact Sheet II dialog box will appear (Figure 5-57).

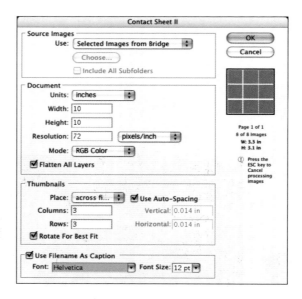

3. Make any changes as necessary in the Contact Sheet II dialog box, and then click OK.

The Contact Sheet function is actually a complex script that runs in Photoshop (even if you started in Bridge), putting all the images you selected in place as you specified in the Contact Sheet dialog box. Do not interrupt the process while the script is running. The final contact sheet I created from the selected images in Figure 5-56 is shown in Figure 5-58.

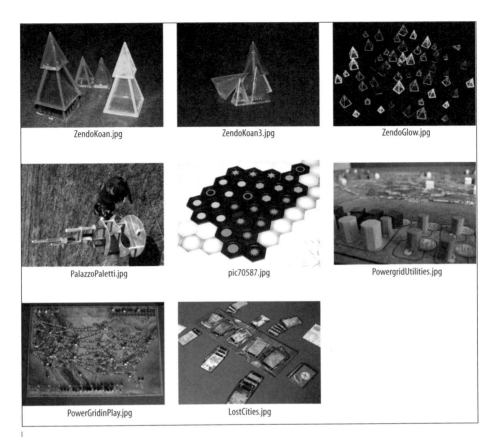

ZendoKoan.jpg ZendoKoan3.jpg ZendoGlow.jpg

PalazzoPaletti.jpg pic70587.jpg PowergridUtilities.jpg

PowerGridinPlay.jpg LostCities.jpg

FIGURE 5-58

HOW DO I PRINT TO AN INKJET PRINTER?

Although inkjet printers are more commonly used for printing imagery than other types
of printers, you can apply this method to other types of printers as well.

To print to an inkjet printer:

1. Choose File→Print with Preview. The Print dialog box will appear with a preview of
   how your image will look on the page, as shown in Figure 5-59. You'll be able to
   see whether what you want to print will fit on the page properly, and correct it if
   necessary.

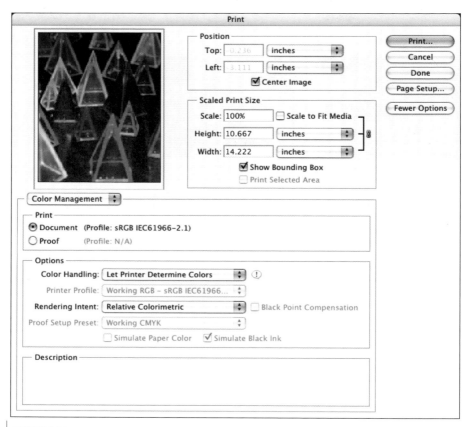

FIGURE 5-59

2. Figure 5-59 shows no border around the edge of the image, and I know that the entire image isn't shown. If this happens to you, you can quickly fix it by clicking the Scale to Fit Media checkbox (Figure 5-60).

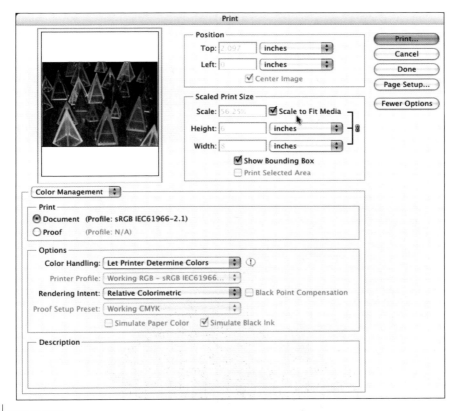

FIGURE 5-60

3. Click the Print button, and the image will print to your printer with the content scaled to fit on the paper size you have chosen.

HOW DO I CREATE A BORDER AROUND AN IMAGE?

If you'd like to create a solid-color border around the outside of an image, without losing any of the contents of the image, you can do it quickly right in Photoshop. If you want to create anything more ornate than a simple solid-line border, you should place your image into Illustrator and use the extensive stroke and path tools there. This example shows how to create a border using Photoshop only.

To create a border around an image in Photoshop:

1. Change the "background" color to the color you'd like your border to be. The background color is the color of the swatch on the toolbar that is partially obscured by the foreground color. In Figure 5-61, the background color is red.

FIGURE 5-61

2. Choose Image→Canvas Size and check the Relative checkbox. Enter the Width and Height you'd like the frame to be (I used 20 pixels). The "Canvas extension color" drop-down will be set to Background by default, and is available only if you have a Background layer in your document. Figure 5-62 shows the Canvas Size dialog box for a document that has a Background layer. Click OK.

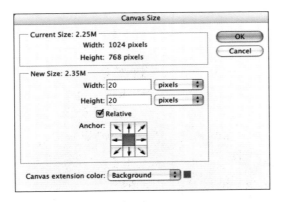

FIGURE 5-62

[NOTE]

If the bottommost layer is the Background layer (it should say "Background" in italics), the border will appear automatically after step 2. If not, you'll need to complete steps 3 and 4.

3. If your document doesn't have a Background layer, create a new layer by clicking the "Create a new layer" icon at the bottom of the Layers palette, and move it below the other layers in the document, as shown in Figure 5-63.

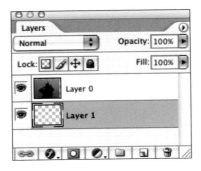

FIGURE 5-63

4. Press Command-Delete (Mac) or Control-Delete (Windows), and the background will be filled with the background color. Figure 5-64 shows the framed image (which looks the same whether you had a Background layer or not).

FIGURE 5-64

THE END

This ends the answers to the top 15 How Do I...? questions. Should you find yourself with more questions that you need answers to, check out the Adobe Photoshop forums at Adobe's web site: *http://www.Adobe.com/support/forums/main.html*.

Illustrator as Part of the Creative Suite

When you think of Illustrator, what do you think of? Logo design? Fabulous print ads? Amazing invitations? A toolbox of ideas and tools to let your "inner" go "outer"? Yep, Illustrator is all this and more. Add to Illustrator the other amazing programs that come with the Creative Suite, and there's no telling what you can do.

You've probably used Illustrator alone, without the other Creative Suite 2 programs, and thought you were doin' just fine. But once you see how powerful your graphics can be with the Creative Suite, Illustrator will never be alone again.

AN OVERVIEW OF ILLUSTRATOR

When you ask anyone in the know what program they'd use to do graphics, the answer is always Illustrator. Graphics can be sketches, line art, maps, cartoons, logos, and more. No other program offers the variety of tools and ease of use that Illustrator does. From basic logo design to high-end realistic graphics and all the stops in between, Illustrator can handle any load. You can take a rough sketch, use Live Trace, add text, color, and shadows, and in no time at all have a finished product ready for printing, video, or the Web.

Who Uses Illustrator

Illustrator is a major tool for pretty much any and every graphic design professional, and even fledgling designers. The variety of graphics you can create with Illustrator is astounding: from comic book scenes to complex logos, ads for magazines, fully detailed airplane schematics, and intricate medical illustrations. So who does what with Illustrator? Here are just a few examples of how the program is used today:

• One amazing, versatile artist I know uses Illustrator to design intricate logos (Figure 6-1).

• Highly recognized playing-card creators use Illustrator to create the front and back card designs.

• An amazingly realistic EAA Fly-In poster was created using Illustrator as its base (Figure 6-2).

• Freelance artists use Illustrator to create everything from greeting cards to technical art used in college reference books.

FIGURE 6-1

ROCKY MOUNTAIN
EAA REGIONAL FLY-IN

FRONT RANGE AIRPORT
JUNE 25TH - 26TH, 2005 • DENVER, COLORADO

FORUMS • WINGS SAFETY SEMINARS • BUILDING WORKSHOPS • AIRCRAFT MANUFACTURERS • PANCAKE BREAKFAST
AIRCRAFT MODELERS • AVIATION VENDORS • AIRSHOW DAILY • YOUNG EAGLE RALLY
Hosted by the Rocky Mountain Region EAA Chapters

For more information about the 2005 Rocky Mountain EAA Regional Fly-In visit us at: www.rmrfi.org

Although Illustrator is widely known as a graphics creation tool, its capabilities go way beyond the mundane. Illustrator has a variety of features that you can use for many diverse projects:

DRAWING TOOLS: Illustrator provides a plethora of tools to create any line style you want. From the toolbar, choose from the Pen, Pencil, Paintbrush, Line Segment, Rectangle, and Ellipse tools, or choose from a variety of polygons. Each tool creates a different line effect. The Paintbrush tool can create a natural, sketchy effect with thick and thin lines, whereas the Pen, Line Segment, and Pencil tools create lines of equal thickness.

TURNING SKETCHES AND PHOTOS INTO VECTORS: In the past, many designers have relied on the Pen and other drawing tools to trace over a sketch or photo that has been scanned and then opened in Illustrator. New to Illustrator CS2 is the *Live Trace* feature, which allows you to manipulate the settings from sketchy to super tech. Figure 6-3 shows a photo on the left and a version that's been Live Traced as an illustration on the right.

FIGURE 6-3

EASY CREATION OF REPETITIVE SYMBOLS: Using the Symbol tools and graphic styles, you can create and enhance repetitive objects quickly. With the Symbol Sprayer and other Symbol tools, you can apply symbols and alter the sizes, location, color, and relation between the symbols in no time at all (Figure 6-4).

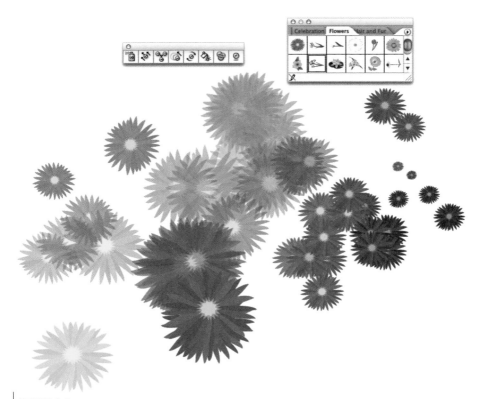

FIGURE 6-4

AMAZING TEXT EFFECTS: Take your text or text-based logo to the next level by apply-ing graphic styles. What's even cooler is that after applying these amazing effects to your type, you can still edit the type!

3D EFFECTS: Add a third dimension with the use of the 3D effects. Use the Revolve fea-ture, found under the 3D area of the Effect menu, to revolve a line around an axis in order to create 3D images such as chess pieces, lamps, balusters, and much, much more.

LIVE PAINT: Instantly drop in color, add transparency, and fix any color gaps in an image that remains fully editable. This feature lets you play around with "painting" your colors and intuitively follows how you naturally want to draw.

WHY GET THE CREATIVE SUITE INSTEAD OF JUST ILLUSTRATOR?

You may be wondering why you need more than just Illustrator to create killer graphics. Although Illustrator is an amazing program on its own, you can combine it with the power of Photoshop, InDesign, GoLive, and Acrobat Professional to bring your projects to completion. All of these programs directly relate to each other. You may not use all five for one project, but I guarantee that you'll use combinations of the programs to complete various projects required by your employer.

For example, say you use Illustrator to create comic book graphics, including text. You could then use InDesign to create the pages and layout, and finally use Acrobat to preflight the complete comic book and send it to a printer. Or you might create a print ad in Illustrator; open the graphic in Photoshop to add lighting, atmosphere, and realistic touches; and again take the project into Acrobat to preflight the file before sending it to a printer. You also can take any of your projects into GoLive to complete them with a web design.

Illustrator is the starting point, the tool you use to jump-start the creative process. Use Illustrator to "sketch out" ideas, thoughts, and graphics for your current project. Add lines, text, color, gradients, 3D effects, and other graphic effects. Then continue the creative workflow process by using Photoshop to add the realistic touches, InDesign to create multiple-page layouts, Acrobat to review the files, and GoLive to create a web site to display your work.

What Illustrator offers is the editability and scalability of vector graphics, which retain the quality that pixel-based images lack when scaled or edited. Add to that the benefits of layering, using masks, blends, and beautiful editable text, and you'll see where Illustrator fits in the scheme of things. (For more about vectors and pixels, see "Photoshop: Imagery" and "Vectors Versus Pixels," later in this chapter.)

The Illustrator CS2 interface is almost identical to that of Photoshop and the other Creative Suite 2 products, so using them together is easy and intuitive. The following sections discuss how the Creative Suite applications work together and combine with Illustrator to make a grand finale of your presentation.

LEARNING THE OTHER CREATIVE SUITE 2 TOOLS

To truly get the full grasp of Illustrator, maximize your creativity, and focus your energies, you need to be able to use the other Creative Suite 2 applications. Using these applications together makes for a smooth creative workflow.

A common workflow practice is bringing Photoshop images into Illustrator and taking Illustrator images out to Photoshop. One of the more common uses of a Photoshop image is to place the image in Illustrator and use Live Trace and Live Paint to make an easy, quick graphic from the photo or sketch.

You can create PDF files from Illustrator (or any of the other Creative Suite 2 applications), or you can use Acrobat to combine and create multiple PDF files. The following sections provide specifics on how the other Creative Suite applications work with Illustrator.

Photoshop: Imagery

Many Illustrator users also use Photoshop for their graphic creations. With Illustrator's Place command, you can import raster-based (pixel-based) images from Photoshop into Illustrator. So, what's the difference between Photoshop and Illustrator images? The answer is: pixels versus vectors.

Photoshop images consist of tiny little squares, or *pixels*, of color. The combination of the color blocks makes up the photo or image. All pixels are square, and all Photoshop images are square; even spaces that appear to be "empty" and contain no color are actually made up of white pixels. If you zoom in close on a Photoshop image, you'll see the squares that make up the image. And if you enlarge a pixel-based photo and print it, you'll see that the image is wrecked—you cannot scale (enlarge) a wallet-sized photo of your child up to 24 x 36 poster size and have it still look good. Whenever you enlarge a pixel-based image, you lose quality.

Vector images, on the other hand, consist of paths with points that can be sized, rotated, and manipulated and still retain their quality at any size. Vectors are based on curves, or, more appropriately, a Bezier curve.

Despite this difference, Photoshop and Illustrator can actually work very well together. For example, you can use Photoshop to tweak and enhance a photo, and then use Illustrator to place the image and add text, graphics, borders, and so on to complete the package. If you place a photo from Photoshop in Illustrator, you can also use Live Trace to convert the pixels to vectors and then use Live Paint to quickly add color. Illustrator also contains Photoshop filters, so if you find you want to apply a Photoshop effect, you can just stay in Illustrator rather than going back and forth. Plus, you can export layered Illustrator files into Photoshop with the layers intact.

Many designers either place photos in Illustrator to add elements, or use Photoshop to clean up hand-drawn sketches and place them in Illustrator to be redrawn. Figure 6-5 shows an advertisement created using Illustrator and Photoshop together.

Got all your eggs in one basket?

It's time to think of diversifying your investments

Gage Alspach

Making investing easy

FIGURE 6-5

InDesign: Layout

InDesign is the page layout program in the creation workflow process. Although Illustrator offers some page layout capabilities, it has its limitations. Most notably, Illustrator is limited to one page, whereas in InDesign you can do as many pages as you'd like. If you are looking for a multiple-page layout, InDesign is the program of choice.

InDesign is used to lay out the text and images for newsletters, menus, newspapers, magazines, in-house publications, and more. O'Reilly Media, in fact, greatly reduces the publishing time of a book by using InDesign. The text comes in the form of Microsoft Word documents, the art as Illustrator *.eps* files, and screenshots as *.tiff* files. InDesign combines all of these elements, and then PDFs are created for the reviewing process. After the review and correction passes are complete, the files are sent off to preflight and, finally, to the printer.

GoLive: Web Site Creation

You can use Illustrator to design the look of the amazing web pages you can create in GoLive. One of the coolest integrations is that if you plan your layers in Illustrator carefully, the layers can be translated into variables in GoLive. Designers and illustrators mock up entire web sites in Illustrator, and production web designers take the elements of those mock-ups into GoLive. Illustrator files are placed in GoLive as Smart Objects, which means that if you update the files in Illustrator, the artwork will automatically update in GoLive.

Acrobat Pro: Review and Preflight

Wow—Acrobat and Illustrator. Nice pair, don't you think? Okay, so you may be wondering how these two programs go together. Once again, one reason stands out above the rest. Say it with me... multiple pages. Yep, in Illustrator you can create only one-page files. Let's say you're working on a highly illustrated children's picture book, and you want to get it press-ready. In Illustrator, you create each page as a separate file and save each file in PDF or EPS format. In Acrobat, you can then use the Create PDF→From Multiple Files command, select all of the individual Illustrator files that make up the book, and combine them into one PDF document. Then, you can set up the book for review, create bookmarks, and finally run preflight to have it ready for the printer in no time.

Another great feature is that the PDF presets available in Illustrator are shared across the Creative Suite applications, ensuring consistency and adding to the ease of workflow.

WHAT YOU SHOULD AND SHOULDN'T DO IN ILLUSTRATOR IF YOU HAVE THE CREATIVE SUITE

Let's face it, there are some things that other programs do better than Illustrator. For example, Illustrator can't select only the background of a photo and create a blur (just as Photoshop can't add columns of text). If you have all the Creative Suite 2 programs at your fingertips, it is more productive to use the programs for what they were designed for than it is to try to make one program do it all.

In this section, we'll briefly revisit the question of when to use Illustrator versus Photoshop, and then we'll step through the workflow of a sample project to illustrate how you can use the CS2 applications together to achieve a goal.

Vectors Versus Pixels

The age-old discussion rears its ugly head. Which is better, pixels or vectors? The answer is simple: both. Each has its own merits and uses, and they can actually coexist quite peacefully. As discussed earlier, pixels are little squares and vectors are curved lines. Photoshop uses pixels, and Illustrator uses vectors.

Photoshop manipulates pixels amazingly and can use those pixels to simulate detail and realism. To see the actual squares, you have to really zoom in. For example, Figure 6-6 shows a beautifully enhanced photo in Photoshop. Now take that same beautiful photo and zoom in drastically (Figure 6-7). The image looks radically different when you can see all the individual squares, compared to the scaled-out version that puts them all together.

FIGURE 6-6

FIGURE 6-7

Illustrator, on the other hand, bases its objects on curves and outlines. The same image in Illustrator zoomed in or scaled up looks the same (see Figure 6-8 and Figure 6-9).

FIGURE 6-8

FIGURE 6-9

Each program has its benefits and drawbacks, but used together, you have the best of both worlds. For example, vectors (lines) can be crisp and can often show fine illustration details better than rasters, but rasters can represent continuous tones (as in photos) more realistically and naturally than vectors.

Beginning the Creative Process

So you're ready to begin a new project. Once you set up the project in Version Cue (see Chapter 1 for more on using Version Cue and Bridge), you can get started.

Let's step through the workflow of a sample project, designing a CD cover for a client. We'll start with Illustrator, which is the best tool to use when beginning a design project. Use Illustrator (in combination with Photoshop if you want) to create your key elements, such as imagery and text. Then, use InDesign to combine those key elements and create a multiple-page layout.

Color and Image Editing

For the CD design, an actual painting was scanned in. We could have used Illustrator to place the images and tweaked the color using the Photoshop filters available in Illustrator, but the file would have been large, and the job is much easier to do in Photoshop. In Photoshop, we duplicated the painting three more times and tweaked the color in each one. We used this beautiful piece of art to depict the four women in the group Opposite Sax, and then placed the art in the Illustrator file.

Text

The placed art was moved around, and then text was added over the top. Some of the text was turned into outlines so that the letters could be moved individually. Hands down, Illustrator still has the best text features of any of the Creative Suite programs.

Graphic Elements

Still in Illustrator, the Brush tool was used to create the saxophone. The Scissors tool was then used to cut away part of the sax, to show that the word *sax* is coming from the saxophone. Figure 6-10 shows the CD front cover.

Layout

Finally, the inside of the CD was laid out using InDesign. The design incorporated the music info, acknowledgments, and other text, all of which was put together with InDesign. The art elements were also combined using InDesign. Although you might think of using Illustrator to do the whole layout, the CD insert has multiple pages, and because Illustrator can't do multiple-page layouts, the natural choice is to use InDesign to create the pages.

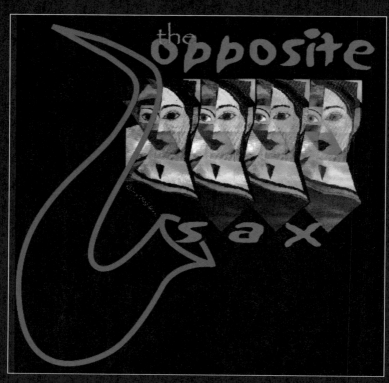

FIGURE 6-5

Here are the most important things to take away from this chapter:

1. You can best take advantage of Illustrator as a powerhouse program when it's combined with the other Creative Suite products. Although you may feel more comfortable using Illustrator for all of your needs, taking advantage of the strengths of the other products will increase your productivity.

2. Illustrator and Photoshop naturally go together to make beautiful music.

3. Photoshop images consist of pixels, whereas Illustrator images consist of vectors. Each has its own strengths, so before you design, decide which program meets your needs.

4. Illustrator can create amazing web page mock-ups that can then be used in GoLive.

5. Multiple pages are best handled in InDesign and even Acrobat.

What Makes Illustrator the Creation Tool

You are ready to embark on the beautiful journey of creativity. Maybe you started with crayons, finger paints, or peanut butter, but you are yearning to do more with better tools. You also may have gone the artistic route via charcoal, pastels, and paints, but you want to try those techniques in a medium where you can "undo" your work without having to get a new piece of paper or start a new canvas.

Naturally, the first program in the chain of the creative workflow process is Illustrator. With Illustrator, you can take a rough sketch and turn it into something amazing. Illustrator has a vast number of tools to create with. This chapter describes how you can use those tools—from the Pen, Pencil, and Paintbrush drawing tools to the more advanced tools such as Live Trace, Live Paint, and 3D—to create amazing graphics.

EDITING TEXT OR VECTOR IMAGES

One of the greatest things about using Illustrator to create art of any kind is the infinite editability of your work. No longer do you have to wreck an expensive sheet of paper by erasing or trying to cover up an idea gone awry. Illustrator lets you erase and edit—and even start over—without a single tree ever having to give its life. You can use a variety of tools to create, fix, or enhance any design, whether it involves text or vectors.

Type Tools

Illustrator has an impressive array of Type tools, which include Type, Area Type, Type on a Path, Vertical Type, Vertical Area Type, and Vertical Type on a Path. Pretty much anything you want to do with type, you can do by using one or more of these tools. Just as you use the tools to create your text, you also can use them to edit text. What is pretty amazing with Illustrator text is that you can apply a variety of effects (such as warping, adding 3D effects, or applying graphic styles), and the text remains editable.

Long ago, if you wanted to add special effects to type, you had to turn the type into outlines—that is, change the type to paths in the shape of the letters—which removed the ability to edit them. Today, you no longer have to convert type to outlines to apply Illustrator effects. However, if you do decide to convert to outlines (for example, to apply Photoshop effects), the type still won't be editable, just as before.

Figure 7-1 shows a variety of fully editable text examples. Figure 7-2 shows text that has been converted to outlines. This text has some really cool effects, but it can no longer be edited.

FIGURE 7-1

FIGURE 7-2

Live Effects

Live effects in Illustrator can take a drawing from drab to fab in no time—without affecting the original artwork. Illustrator comes with a wide variety of live effects that you can apply to vectors or to a placed image. "Live" means that once you've selected the item to be changed, BOOM, it happens, and you see the effect immediately. All of the live effects are found under the Effect menu. The live effects for vectors include:

3D: Includes Extrude & Bevel, Revolve, and Rotate.

CONVERT TO SHAPE: Convert to Rectangle, Rounded Rectangle, or Ellipse.

DISTORT AND TRANSFORM: Houses Free Distort, Pucker & Bloat, Roughen, Transform, Tweak, Twist, and Zig Zag.

PATH: Choose from Offset Path, Outline Object, and Outline Stroke.

PATHFINDER: Includes Add, Intersect, Exclude, Subtract, Minus Back, Divide, Trim, Merge, Crop, Outline, Hard Mix, Soft Mix, and Trap.

RASTERIZE: Convert vectors into pixels by choosing the resolution, background, and other options. Use this option if you want to convert the vectors into pixels so that you can apply the Photoshop effects from the Effect menu.

STYLIZE: Includes Add Arrowheads, Drop Shadow, Feather, Inner Glow, Outer Glow, Round Corners, and Scribble. Scribble creates amazing sketch-like effects.

SVG FILTERS: Apply any of the standard SVG filters or import your own SVG filters. SVG is a graphics file format and web development language.

WARP: Choose from Arc, Arc Lower, Arc Upper, Arch, Bulge, Shell Lower, Shell Upper, Flag, Wave, Fish, Rise, Fisheye, Inflate, Squeeze, and Twist.

These live effects let you turn text into a banner, give a technical drawing a more organic flair, quickly apply arrowheads to point out specifics in a schematic layout, add a drop shadow to give the illusion of depth, and much, much more. Figure 7-3 shows a few examples of live effects.

FIGURE 7-3

SCALING GRAPHICS

If I were to say, "Take a teeny tiny flower and make it eight feet tall," could you do it? Yes, you could—and the flower would be just as finely detailed at the gigantic size as it was at the small size. This is the power of Illustrator. Making vectors large or small isn't the only thing that Illustrator can do, however. You can apply several transformations, all at once or individually. The transformation tools are:

SCALE: Resizes an object uniformly or non-uniformly by setting an origin point to scale the object from.

ROTATE: Rotates an object around a set origin. Rotate 0–180 degrees, or apply a negative to rotate counter-clockwise around the origin.

SHEAR: Creates a flattened-perspective image of the object.

REFLECT: Using an axis, mirrors an object across the axis horizontally or vertically.

WARP: Mushes objects, like pushing them with your finger. The object moves in the direction you move your cursor. Figure 7-4 shows a house before warping (left) and after (right).

FIGURE 7-4

You can access all of the above transformation commands under the Object→Transform menu, as well as the Transform Each command. Transform Each lets you transform each object independently of the others, or apply a random transformation. You also can find a variety of other transformation tools, such as the Reshape and Warp tools, under the Effect menu.

USING LIVE TRACE FOR CONVERTING PHOTOS AND SCANS

Ever wanted to use a photo as a graphic? Live Trace is the solution to all of your tracing problems. Live Trace lets you trace in color, grayscale, or black and white. You can choose from a variety of presets or create your own. The Preview checkbox lets you see what the result will be before applying the trace. Figure 7-5 shows a placed image that had Live Trace applied, using the Detailed Illustration setting. The placed image on the left was traced in black and white, the center image was traced in grayscale, and the image on the right was traced in color. You can then take the traced vector image and change the color, add pizzazz, resize it, and more.

FIGURE 7-5

The presets available for Live Trace are Default, Color 6, Color 16, Photo Low Fidelity, Photo High Fidelity, Grayscale, Hand Drawn Sketch, Detailed Illustration, Comic Art, Technical Illustration, Black and White Logo, Inked Drawing, and Type. Figure 7-6 shows each of the standard presets applied to one image.

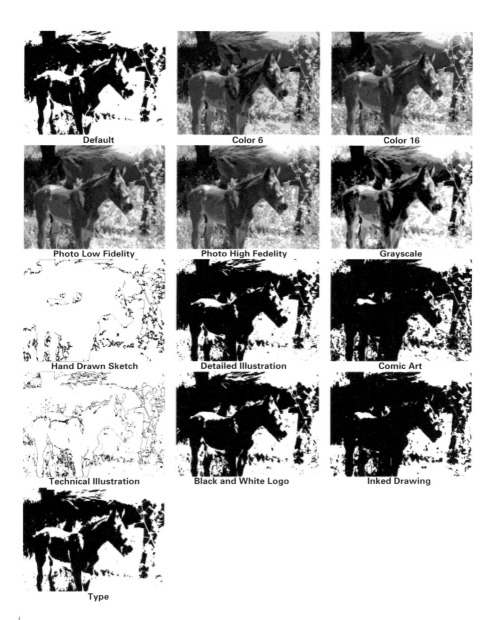

Default   Color 6   Color 16

Photo Low Fidelity   Photo High Fedelity   Grayscale

Hand Drawn Sketch   Detailed Illustration   Comic Art

Technical Illustration   Black and White Logo   Inked Drawing

Type

FIGURE 7-6

You also can set your own options to create the look you want, by choosing Object→Live Trace→Tracing Options. If you want to use one of the available presets or a preset that you've saved (not customized), just select the object and choose a preset from the Control palette. After tracing, you can use the Control palette to adjust the options, click an icon to reopen the dialog box, or go to Live Paint. The tracing options are:

PRESET: Lists the preset tracing options that Illustrator provides, plus any that you've created.

MODE: Allows you to choose the color mode for your tracing.

THRESHOLD: Lets you choose the value setting for Black and White mode.

PALETTE: Lists the preset palette settings.

MAX COLORS: Lets you choose the maximum colors used in tracing.

OUTPUT TO SWATCHES: Generates swatches for each color used in the tracing and places them in the Swatches palette.

BLUR: Blurs the placed image before you trace, which smoothes out any jaggies.

RESAMPLE: Lets you resample the image to a specified resolution. Use this for really large images, to make the tracing go faster.

FILLS: Creates a filled area in the traced image (available only in Black and White mode).

STROKES: Lets you put a stroke on the paths of the traced image (available only in Black and White mode).

MAX STROKE WEIGHT: Lets you choose the maximum pixilated area that will have a stroke; larger areas will be outlined and filled.

MIN STROKE LENGTH: Lets you choose the minimum length of a pixilated area to be traced.

PATH FITTING: Enables you to pick the distance between the trace and the pixel image.

MINIMUM AREA: Lets you choose how small of a pixilated area will be traced.

CORNER ANGLE: Allows you to pick how sharp the turn is drawn between a corner anchor point and a smooth anchor point.

RASTER: Lets you choose from a pop-up how you want to view the original raster.

VECTOR: Lets you choose from a pop-up how you want to display the final tracing.

Color Trace and Grayscale Trace

The Color and Grayscale Traces take a bit longer to apply, but the effect is magnificent. Choose from a preset, then set the number of colors or grays in the Max Colors field.

1. Choose Object→Live Trace→Tracing Options. (If you just choose Make from the Live Trace menu, it will use the default trace options.) I chose Color from the Mode pull-down menu instead of choosing a preset. You also can edit, import, or export presets by choosing Edit→Tracing Presets.

2. Pick a tracing preset or alter a preset to suit your desired result. For Figure 7-7, I chose 24 colors for the image on the left and 90 for the image on the right, to show that more color means more detail.

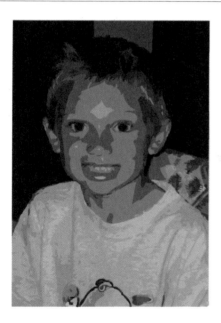 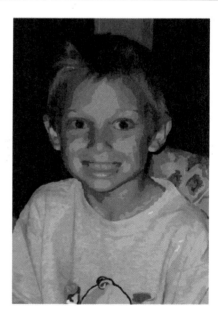

FIGURE 7-7

3. Click Trace to see the traced results.

The higher the Max Color number is, the more detail you'll see. However, you will find that more detail takes longer and results in a larger file. Experiment with the settings. For example, for a more graphic feel, use fewer colors.

Black and White Trace

The Black and White option for tracing creates a strong graphic image (Figure 7-8). Many of the preset trace options are set for black and white. If you want to spice things up a bit and add color, use Live Paint.

FIGURE 7-8

USING LIVE PAINT TO ADD COLOR TO OBJECTS

With the addition of Live Paint in Illustrator CS2, adding color has never been easier. After you apply Live Trace, you need to turn the object into a Live Paint group before you can paint. To do this, select the object, choose the Live Paint Bucket tool, and either click in the object or click the Live Paint button in the Control palette.

Live Paint divides the image into different areas to which you can apply color. It determines faces (center fill areas) and edges (dividing paths) by the color differences in the traced object. Then, you simply use the Live Paint Selection tool to select an area. After the area is selected, you can add a color, a pattern, or a gradient to the area (you can't apply transparency, brushes, gradient meshes, effects, flares, or symbols to Live Paint objects).

Think of Live Paint as the tool that creates the coloring book outlines for you to color in. The Live Paint Selection tool lets you select all the areas that share a similar color, even if the areas don't touch—if you triple-click on a color, all colors like that one are selected (similar to how the Magic Wand tool works). You can then fill in all of the like colors at the same time.

To apply color to a Live Paint object:

1. Use the Live Paint Selection tool to choose the area you want to change. (Or, if you are painting a single area, you can use the Live Paint Bucket tool.) The area will outline in red (by default) so you can see what area the tool selected. Also, while selecting an area with the Live Paint Selection tool, notice that placing the tool on the edge of an area creates a thin red outline and designates the stroke to be filled instead of the fill (thicker red outline).

2. With the area selected, choose a color from the Swatches palette, or create your own color by using the Color palette. The new color fills in the selected area (Figure 7-9).

FIGURE 7-9

If you use the Live Paint Bucket tool (instead of the Live Paint Selection tool), you should first select a color from the Swatches palette. Then, click the desired area with the Live Paint Selection tool to fill it with color (or change the color in the case of a color trace).

USING OTHER ENHANCING TOOLS

Illustrator comes with a bunch of creation tools in addition to the ones previously mentioned. Once you have a graphic drawn, you can enhance it by using gradients, gradient meshes, envelopes, brushes, graphic styles, and symbols. These amazing features can help you take your graphic to the next level with little to no effort.

Gradients

Ever seen a beautiful, smooth background that goes from dark to light (or vice versa), and wondered how you can create this effect? Gradients are the answer. Gradients are quick and easy to use, and the results can be stunning. You choose the gradient from the Type pull-down menu in the Gradient palette. A Linear gradient results in a smooth, blended look. A Radial gradient adds a nice three-dimensional look to a circle. Figure 7-10 shows a Radial gradient (left) and a Linear gradient (right).

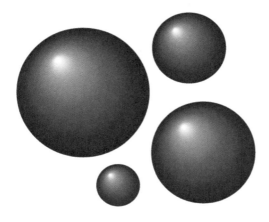

FIGURE 7-10

CHAPTER 7

The Gradient tool also allows you to change the highlight of the Radial gradient or the angle of the Linear gradient. If you double-click on the Gradient tool, the Gradient palette displays. In the Gradient palette, you can change the color, the closeness of the colors to each other, and the angle.

Although you can find gradients in the Swatches palette, there aren't many to choose from there. To access more gradients, choose Window→Swatch Libraries→Other Library. From the Presets folder, open the Gradient folder, and take your pick from a bunch of gradients.

Gradient Meshes

To create realistic, smooth gradients that follow any flowing shape, use the Gradient Mesh tool, which allows you to set various lines and points to define how the gradient is applied. The Gradient Mesh tool can create a dimensional feel by using different colors for depth. You can create a Mesh object with a regular pattern of lines and points by choosing Object→Create Gradient Mesh and then entering the number of rows and columns you want, and the direction of the highlight. To create a gradient mesh with a varied pattern, use the Gradient Mesh tool to click the points where you want to add the highlights or shadows. You can click with the Gradient Mesh tool to add points, but you need to choose a color swatch (or black or white) while clicking to add something like a highlight or shadow. Alternatively, click to add a point and then click a color swatch. Figure 7-11 shows a tank top before the gradient mesh was applied (left) and after (right).

FIGURE 7-11

Envelopes and Warp Effects

If you're looking for an easy way to turn your text into a banner, envelopes are for you. Look for the Warp effects under the Effect menu, or choose Object→Envelope Distort, which allows you to make an envelope with a mesh or top object, too (as well as Envelope Options). Remember that you have to select the type with the Direct Selection tool and not the Type tool to make this work.

The Warp effects are envelopes that are applied to the selected object or text. They include Arc, Arc Lower, Arc Upper, Arch, Bulge, Shell Lower, Shell Upper, Flag, Wave, Fish, Rise, Inflate, Squeeze, and Twist. What's really cool is that you can select any of the Warp effects, and check the Preview box to see what the effect will look like. You can cycle through all the options to see how they'll affect your object, and then select one to apply. Figure 7-12 shows the word *bezier* with each of the warp affects applied.

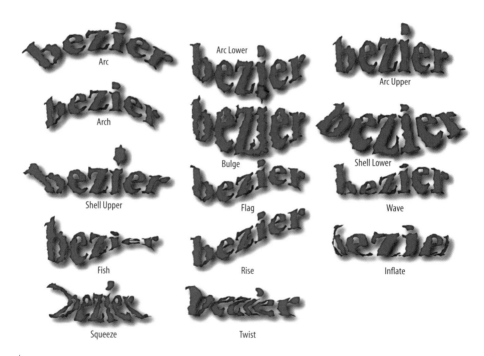

Arc

Arc Lower

Arc Upper

Arch

Bulge

Shell Lower

Shell Upper

Flag

Wave

Fish

Rise

Inflate

Squeeze

Twist

FIGURE 7-12

[NOTE]

For more on using envelopes and Warp effects, see "How Do I Put Text in a Shape (Envelope)?" in Chapter 9.

Brushes

Wow, Illustrator has "got it goin' on" with its choice of brushes. Choose from calligraphic or hand-drawn brush effects, but don't stop there. Under Window→ Brush Libraries (or the Brushes palette's menu), you'll find Artistic, Decorative, and Border brush styles, too. Figure 7-13 shows a basic painted flower in the upper left without any brush applied; the other three flowers have different brush styles applied. To apply a different brush, select the painted object first, and then click a different brush in the Brushes palette. To top all this off, Illustrator also enables you to create your own brushes and save them with the other brush presets.

FIGURE 7-13

Graphic Styles

Graphic styles are a quick way to apply cool effects from a choice of presets. Illustrator has a ton of presets to choose from, and you can create your own graphic style. Figure 7-14 shows a bunch of graphic styles applied to text—and yes, the text is still fully editable.

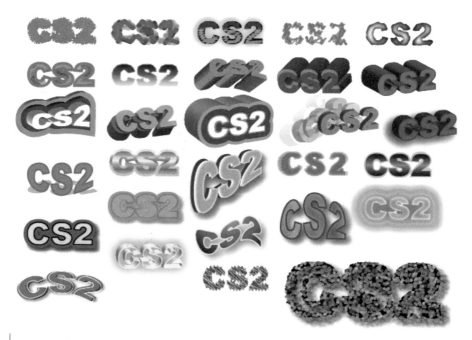

FIGURE 7-14

If you want to change a color or another part of a graphic style, use the Appearance palette to customize it. You also can use the Appearance palette to select and change a specific action done to the object. After you select the action in the Appearance palette, the corresponding palette will usually pop up so you can make changes. Alternatively, you can often just make changes from the Control palette.

The graphic styles available in the Graphic Style Libraries (accessible under the Window menu) include 3D Effects, Artistic Effects, Buttons and Rollovers, Default CMYK, Default RGB, Image Effects, Neon Effects, Scribble Effects, Textures, and Type Effects.

[NOTE]

For more on changing a preset graphic style or creating one of your own, see "How Do I Change a Graphic Style?" in Chapter 9.

Symbols

Ever spent time looking for one of those graphics that you have to use over and over, like a bouquet of flowers, or a field full of airplanes, or maybe even a box of bugs? The Symbols feature has it all. Choose from a variety of symbols (with more found under Window→Symbol Libraries), and then customize them to change the sizes, color, positioning, and more.

To apply a symbol, use the Symbol Sprayer tool found in the Toolbox. Double-clicking a symbol tool opens the Symbolism Tools Options dialog box. After you spray out a bunch of bugs, flowers, commuters, etc., use the other Symbol tools to tweak the graphic. The Symbol Sprayer tools are:

SYMBOL SPRAYER: Places the symbols on your page.

SYMBOL SHIFTER: Changes the position or location of symbols.

SYMBOL SCRUNCHER: Moves the symbols closer together or, if you hold down the Option (Mac) or Alt (Windows) key, farther apart.

SYMBOL SIZER: Makes symbols larger or, if you hold down the Option/Alt key, smaller.

SYMBOL SPINNER: Spins the symbols around a central axis.

SYMBOL STAINER: Lets you apply different colors to the symbols so they don't all look exactly alike.

SYMBOL SCREENER: Applies transparency to add depth.

SYMBOL STYLER: Lets you apply a graphic style to a symbol.

[NOTE]

For more on creating symbols and using the Symbol tools, see "How Do I Create a Symbol?" in Chapter 9.

The Symbol Sprayer tool is by far the most fun tool you'll ever play with and still get really amazing results. Figure 7-15 shows an aquarium full of fish created using the Symbol tools. You can turn almost any object you create into a symbol—just select the object, and then choose New Symbol from the Symbols palette. The only objects that you can't turn into symbols are gradient mesh and raster objects.

FIGURE 7-15

**Here are the most important things to take away
from this chapter:**

1. With the editability and scalability it offers, Illustrator is the ultimate creation tool.

2. Live Trace is the best and quickest way to convert a pixel image to a vector image.

3. Live Paint lets you quickly select and apply colors, gradients, and patterns to a graphic.

4. Envelopes/Warp effects let you push a graphic into a shape.

5. The Symbol Sprayer tool is a quick way to apply a lot of a certain object. The other Symbol tools let you change the size, location, color, transparency, and more, to add variety to the symbols.

How to Use Illustrator with the
Other Creative Suite Applications

In this chapter, you'll see how one artist starts a project in Illustrator and then uses each of the other Creative Suite programs to complete the piece. You'll also see how naturally the Creative Suite 2 products flow together to create a smooth workflow for any project. Although you may not use all five Suite products each time you work on a project, I can guarantee that you'll use at least two or more programs. Starting a project in Illustrator seems to be the natural flow. For example, you can scan that hand-drawn sketch you threw together on a scrap of paper into Illustrator, and take it from there.

FIGURE 8-1

USING THE SUITE FROM BEGINNING TO END

Joe Jones of Artworks Studio created the *Wings Over the Rockies Air Space Museum* poster by using all five of the Creative Suite 2 applications. Figure 8-1 shows the finished project in all of its glory.

Joe used Illustrator to start this project. He then used Photoshop, InDesign, and Acrobat to create the final piece. Finally, he used GoLive for pieces of the web site, which incorporated elements from the poster.

Creating in Illustrator

The initial layout of the poster was done in Illustrator. Joe used Illustrator to establish the design and colors of the project. The logo at the bottom of the page was created completely in Illustrator, and the amazing shadows and highlights were created with the Gradient Mesh tool (Figure 8-2).

FIGURE 8-2

After the layout, color, and logo were established, Joe used photos to add more elements to the poster. He tweaked and adjusted the photos in Photoshop.

Adding Depth and Realism in Photoshop

Joe took photographs of people, the front end of an airplane, and clouds to incorporate into the poster design. He managed to convince some of the museum volunteers to be a part of the photo shoot and donate their images to the poster.

Figure 8-3 shows the original photo. His thought process was to show different ages and genders, as well as using a classic war-era propaganda design that depicted the figures in the signature "hero" pose. Joe used Photoshop to rearrange the people in the photograph, and he added painterly effects to the figures to create the look of an oil painting (Figure 8-4).

FIGURE 8-3

FIGURE 8-4

For the airplane, Joe took a picture of the B-18 Bolo, an early-war medium bomber housed at the air museum (Figure 8-5). Then he used various Photoshop tools to make the photo of the bomber look like a painting. Photoshop brushes are a great way to create painterly effects. You also can use the Effects commands, but with this method your changes are applied to the entire area or selection. By using a brush, you can control exactly where you want to apply the painterly look.

FIGURE 8-5

Another item that would become part of the final composite was a photo of a hangar to go behind the plane. (Interestingly enough, just inside the hangar doors, Glenn Miller and his orchestra performed during the war!) The hangar, plane, and people were combined by using separate Photoshop layers, so that Joe could add shadows and give depth to the poster.

For the background, Joe used additional airplanes and a photo of clouds. Joe has been taking cloud pictures for approximately three years and now has an impressive collection. From this collection of clouds, he pulled Figure 8-6 to use for the poster. Finally, he combined the elements in Photoshop to make one flattened file.

FIGURE 8-6

Using InDesign to Lay Out the Poster

After Joe finished combining the photo elements in Photoshop, it was time to use InDesign to combine the Photoshop and Illustrator files and complete the layout of the poster project. Figure 8-7 shows the poster with the text added.

You can import text from programs such as Microsoft Word by using InDesign's Place function. If you choose File→Place to insert your text, InDesign displays a cursor that you can then use to drag out the text box. Alternatively, you can create the text box first and then choose File→Place.

JOIN THE AIR MUSEUM NOW!

IT'S
YOUR DUTY, *TOO*...

Help protect our heritage!

ARTWORK VOLUNTEERED BY JOE JONES

**– ENLIST TODAY –
IN A VOLUNTEER
ASSIGNMENT**

**– CONTACT –
Your Volunteer
Coordinator–NOW–
303–360–5360 • Ext.111**
Visit us on the Web at: www.wingsmuseum.org

FIGURE 8-7

Joe put in his text boxes and moved them around to get the right look for the layout of the poster. Then, by using the Place function, he placed all of the other Photoshop and Illustrator elements and arranged them in the poster design.

After the poster was completed, Joe exported the file as a PDF file so that he could send it to his client for approval.

Sending PDFs for Review and Commenting with Acrobat

Once a design is complete, the next step in the workflow process is to send the file to the client for review, commenting, and approval. To begin, open the PDF in Acrobat 7.0 Professional. In Acrobat, choose Comments→Send for Review→Send by Email for Review. Acrobat walks you through how to send the PDF file for review. In the steps for setting up the email review, click the Customize Review Options button and select "Display Drawing Markup Tools for this review." Additionally, you can choose to allow users of the free Adobe Reader 7.0 to participate in the review. The client can add notes, comments, and more, and then send the file back to you.

After final approval, use Acrobat to preflight the file for printing (Advanced→Preflight). *Preflighting* is used to check a document for errors before sending it to a printer. Acrobat's preflight tools include many of the industry standards for printing—from PostScript to the PDF/Xa standards—which you can use to be sure your document will process properly.

Creating a Professional Web Site with GoLive

One of the final steps in a project is often to create a web site with GoLive. Not every client requires this, but there's been a shift in the mindset of many companies, who now like to have complete web sites available for clients (and potential clients) to view.

Joe Jones, the designer of the *Wings Over the Rockies Air Space Museum* poster, also created the War Eagles Air Museum's home page, shown in Figure 8-8. For this web site, Joe used GoLive's Smart Objects to convert the instrument panel from the poster for incorporation into the web site (Figure 8-9).

Smart Objects are found in GoLive's Objects palette. Under this palette, they are known as Smart Illustrator Objects. A *Smart Object* is an object that has a specified source file. The source file is in the format in which the object was originally created, such as a native Illustrator or Photoshop format. When you double-click a Smart Object, the original application launches so that you can edit the original, which will update automatically in GoLive.

As with other Smart Objects in GoLive, you can place a Smart Illustrator Object into a web page, and GoLive will convert the Adobe Illustrator source file into a web-friendly format (primarily SVG, using Illustrator). You also can place any EPS file created in Illustrator as a Smart Illustrator Object into a web page, and GoLive will use the ImageReady engine to convert the file to a GIF, JPEG, or PNG. If you choose to scale the image, GoLive automatically leverages the source file to scale without degradation.

GoLive and Illustrator also support a unique mobile workflow. SVG (Scalable Vector Graphics) files created in Illustrator can be animated using any of the third-party animation tools, such as Ikivo Animator. Then, you can use GoLive to add interactivity, such as links, play/pause buttons, and so on. This Creative Suite workflow allows you to produce high-quality mobile content with rich user experiences that can be used by the majority of the smart/feature phones, which include SVG player support.

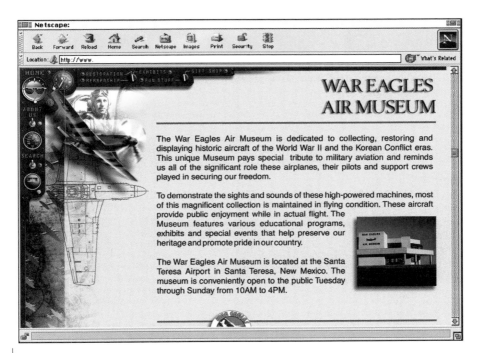

FIGURE 8-8

FIGURE 8-9

Another workflow feature is the ability to save color swatches to the "Exchange" and share them across the different Suite applications, including Illustrator and GoLive. You can save a set of swatches as an Adobe Swatch Exchange file, then simply choose an easily accessible location, such as a Version Cue project folder, where you want the Exchange file to go.

ILLUSTRATIONS CREATED BY INTEGRATING CREATIVE SUITE 2 PROGRAMS

Many artists use multiple programs to create amazing illustrations. Figure 8-10 is another such piece by artist Joe Jones. This piece, called "Aviation Nation," was the first all-digital work to make it into The Smithsonian. This was an important accomplishment for Joe and other artists whose works have followed. Joe often uses Illustrator and Photoshop to create beautiful artwork.

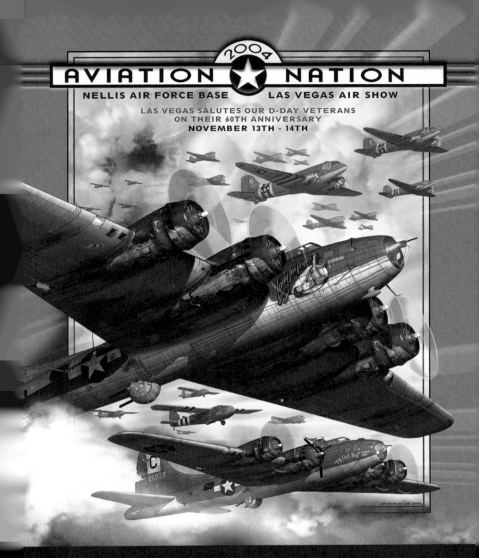

FIGURE 8-10

In Figures 8-11 and 8-12, Dr. Thomas Ravin has combined actual photographs and Illustrator elements to show the muscles and tendons in the shoulder and foot. He created these amazing medical illustrations by using Photoshop to seamlessly blend the photos with the areas created in Illustrator. To blend the photos with the illustrations, Tom used the Transparency feature. Another way would be to use a drop shadow and manipulate the transparency there to blend out to the photographs.

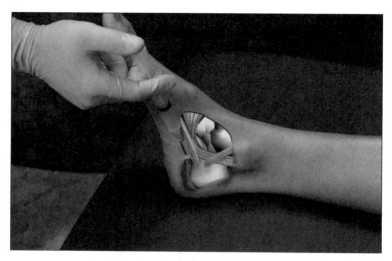

FIGURE 8-11

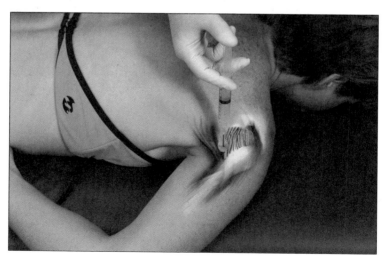

FIGURE 8-12

Artist Brian Warchesik also uses Illustrator and Photoshop together, to creates tunning fantasy illustrations. He starts each illustration with hand-drawn sketches. He then scans these sketches and firms them up using Illustrator's drawing tools. The Pen tool is Brian's friend when it comes to tracing over his sketches. He adds the color in Illustrator and enhances the realism (for example, adding highlights and shadows) with Photoshop tools. Brian also uses paths to create bump maps for texture maps in Photoshop. Figures 8-13 and 8-14 show some examples of his work. To see more amazing artwork from Joe Jones and Brian Warchesik, visit *http://www.artworksstudio.com*.

FIGURE 8-13

FIGURE 8-14

Here are the most important things to take away from this chapter:

1. Illustrator is a starting point for turning sketches into logos and for creating incredible type effects and amazing illustrations.

2. Use Photoshop to add texture, shadows, and realistic artistic effects to your illustrations.

3. InDesign is perfect for combining your Illustrator elements, Photoshop creations, and text to create layouts for posters, advertisements, articles, and more.

4. Acrobat is the perfect tool to use for sending a file for review and for preflighting a file before sending it to the printer.

5. GoLive is the tool to use for web site creation. You can effortlessly combine Illustrator and GoLive, adding Smart Illustrator Objects to your web pages.

Top 15 How Do I...? Illustrator Questions

In this chapter, you will find the answers to the top 15 questions designers ask about Illustrator. These most commonly asked questions were compiled from questions asked in the Illustrator forums and posed to the Illustrator product team. If you have a specific problem or are looking to improve your skills, the step-by-step solutions included here should help. You'll find tips that will save you time, strengthen your creativity, and much more.

HOW DO I TURN A BITMAP IMAGE INTO A VECTOR IMAGE?

If you have a photo that you want to turn into a vector (line-based) image, what do you do? The answer is, "It depends." What do you want the end result to be? With Illustrator's Live Trace, you can create a replica of the photograph based on the photo. Or, if you are looking to use the photo as a guide, you can use Illustrator's powerful drawing tools, such as the Pen tool, to trace the image for a creative logo or graphic.

To create a vector image using Live Trace:

1. In a new Illustrator document, choose File→Place. Select the file you want to use, and click the Place button.

2. With the placed image selected, choose Object→Live Trace→Tracing Options. Here, you can set the type of tracing. Figure 9-1 shows a color trace using 170 colors.

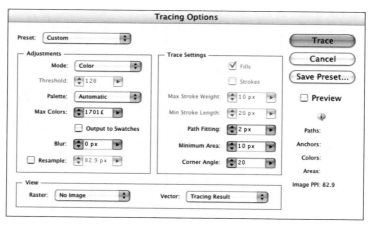

FIGURE 9-1

3. Click the Trace button to start the trace. The status bar displays the progress of the trace (Figure 9-2).

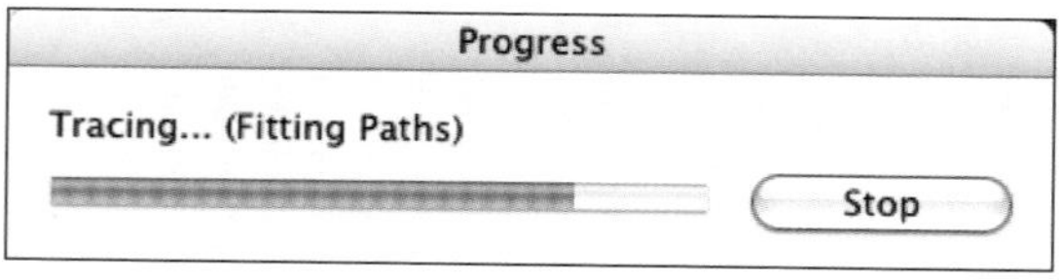

FIGURE 9-2

Figure 9-3 shows the final piece, rendered in vectors. The figure on the left shows the Preview (color) view, and the figure on the right shows the image that was expanded to show the individual vectors in outline view.

FIGURE 9-3

To create a vector image using the Pen tool:

1. Open a new Illustrator document, and choose File→Place. Select the file you want to use, and click the Place button.

2. With the placed image selected, choose Object→Lock→Selection. This will prevent you from accidentally moving the image as you trace.

3. Select the Pen tool.

4. Choose No Fill and a black stroke from the toolbar.

5. Start tracing the image. I like to work in a clockwise direction (Figure 9-4), but this is purely a matter of personal preference. The Pen tool can be tricky, so one thing to keep in mind is to just keep going—you can edit the lines later.

FIGURE 9-4

The left side of Figure 9-5 shows the traced image. The right side of Figure 9-5 shows the image after applying a brush stroke from the Brushes palette to add flair.

FIGURE 9-5

How you draw or trace a photo image depends on what you plan to do with the image later. I like to use the Pen tool if I want to be able to edit it easily and add my own creative edge. If you are looking to re-create the original and possibly use various effects on the image, opt for one of the Live Trace options to get what you are looking for. In Figure 9-6, the Grayscale Live Trace option was used with 15 levels of grays. Then, a Scribble effect (Effect Stylize Scribble) was applied with a Sharp setting from the Settings pop-up menu. There is no end to what you can do with Live Trace and the Pen tool.

FIGURE 9-6

HOW DO I EXTRUDE TEXT (MAKE IT 3D)?

You can create a 3D image in Illustrator by using the Blend tool, but did you know that you can get a realistic 3D effect revolving around three axes? Long ago, the program Dimensions was incorporated into Illustrator to enable you to apply 3D effects to 2D objects. In addition to creating editable 3D text, you can take a line and revolve it around an axis to create something like a baluster or a chess piece. You can also create a bottle by extruding a line and then mapping artwork such as a label to the outside of the bottle. The examples below will show you how to create 3D text by using the Blend tool and the 3D command.

To make 3D text using the Blend tool:

1. Create a line of type using the Type tool. Give the type a color.

2. Press the Option/Alt key and drag a copy of the text slightly below and a tad off center from the original text.

3. Add a different color to the copied text and send the art to the back (Object→Arrange→ Send to Back), as shown in Figure 9-7.

FIGURE 9-7

4. Using the Blend tool, click on the endpoint of the original line of type and then the opposite endpoint of the copied line of type. The default is to do a one-step blend (Figure 9-8).

FIGURE 9-8

5. Add more steps to make a smoother blend by choosing Object→Blend→Blend Options to launch the Blend Options dialog box.

6. Choose Specified Steps from the Spacing pop-up menu. This example uses 10 steps to create a nice, smooth 3D type effect. Click OK.

7. To add to the effect, apply a drop shadow (Effect→Stylize→Drop Shadow).

8. Finally, apply a Warp effect, which essentially puts the text in an envelope (Figure 9-9).

FIGURE 9-9

The best thing about these type effects is that they are still fully editable. Even if you discover a mistake after you have applied the 3D effect to the text, don't worry. You can use the Text tool to select the letter or letters you need to fix and then enter the correct spelling (Figures 9-10 and 9-11). Because you started this project in Illustrator—the "creation" program—you can easily go back in and edit the 3D text. This is something you cannot do in any of the other Creative Suite products.

FIGURE 9-10

FIGURE 9-11

To extrude text:

1. Using any of the text tools, create the text you want to extrude (Figure 9-12). This example uses the Type on a Path tool on a circle. For extruding text, any font will work, but for adding a bevel, a wide, thick font produces the best results. This example uses 90-point Copperplate Gothic Bold.

FIGURE 9-12

2. Choose Effect→3D→Extrude & Bevel. In the 3D Extrude & Bevel Options dialog box, click the Preview box to see how the text looks with the default settings applied (Figure 9-13).

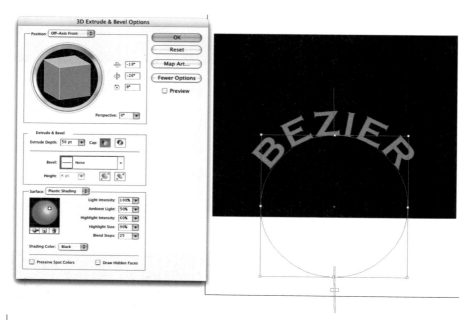

FIGURE 9-13

3. Add a bevel by choosing a Bevel option from the pop-up menu in the 3D Extrude & Bevel Options dialog box. You can preview the applied bevel as well. Some of the more complex bevels will mangle the serifs on the fonts, so when you choose your font, try to choose one with thick serifs or use a sans-serif typeface.

4. Change any of the Position or Extrude & Bevel settings, or click More Options to change the Surface settings. Click OK to apply the 3D effect to your type (Figure 9-14).

In Illustrator, you can create eye-catching logos in no time. Illustrator's type capabilities are phenomenal. In addition to 3D effects, you can create many other cool effects with type that remains editable.

FIGURE 9-14

To access any of the graphic style libraries, choose Window→Graphic Style Libraries, and then choose a library. To begin, create your type and either apply or click on a graphic style from the Graphic Styles palette. Try out a variety of graphic styles to see some really cool effects (Figure 9-15).

Scribble 1

Scribble 4

Scribble 9

Raised Edge

RGB Cartographic-Foothills

RGB Concrete

Crusty

Emergence

Triple Stack

FIGURE 9-15

HOW DO I RETAIN MY LAYERS IN PHOTOSHOP?

Many Illustrator users are familiar with developing their entire designs using layers, only to lose them in Photoshop—but not anymore. You can now retain all of those layers you created so painstakingly in Illustrator and use them in Photoshop.

To retain your Illustrator layers in Photoshop:

1. Open the layered Illustrator file. Figure 9-16 shows an illustration of a house layout in RGB mode. This illustration contains 18 separate layers.

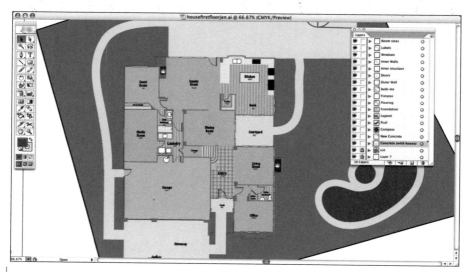

FIGURE 9-16

2. Choose File→Export to launch the Export dialog box.

3. In the Export dialog box, choose Photoshop (.*psd*) from the Format pop-up menu. Then, enter a Version Comment so that you know what the file is about, choose the save location, and click the Export button (Figure 9-17). This launches the Photoshop Export Options dialog box.

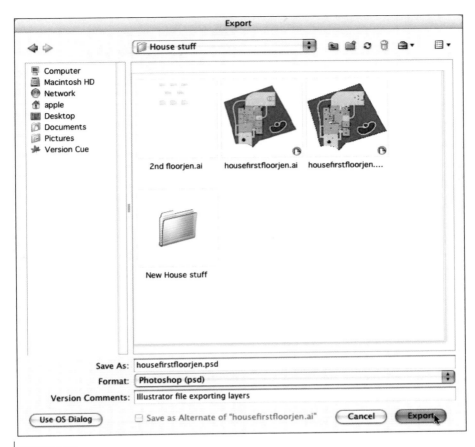

FIGURE 9-17

4. In the Photoshop Export Options dialog box, check that the Write Layers checkbox under Options is selected, as in Figure 9-18 (by default, it is). Enter the Resolution and Color Model, and then click OK to start the export.

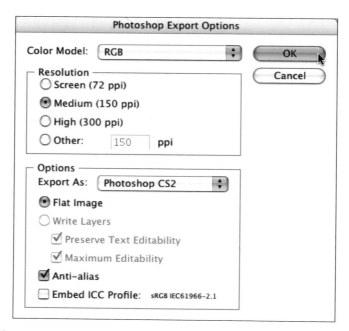

FIGURE 9-18

5. In Photoshop, choose File→Open. Locate the exported .psd file you just created and click Open.

6. When the update message displays, click Update to retain your layers (Figure 9-19).

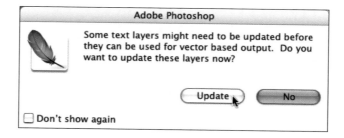

FIGURE 9-19

In Photoshop, you'll see that the layers have been retained (Figure 9-20). Now you can apply your favorite Photoshop effects to specific layers of your Illustrator document.

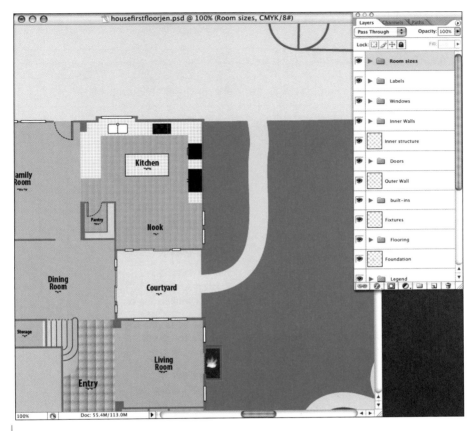

FIGURE 9-20

HOW DO I APPLY A DROP SHADOW TO AN ENTIRE LAYER?

As you can imagine, applying a drop shadow to several different items can be quite tedious. Fortunately, there is an alternative: you can place all of the objects on the same layer and apply a drop shadow to the entire layer in a single step.

1. Make sure that all of the objects to which you want to apply a drop shadow are on the same layer—and that any objects you don't want a drop shadow applied to are on a different layer.

2. Create a new layer by choosing New Layer from the Layers palette pop-up menu.

3. Give the new layer a name, such as "drop shadow layer" (Figure 9-21).

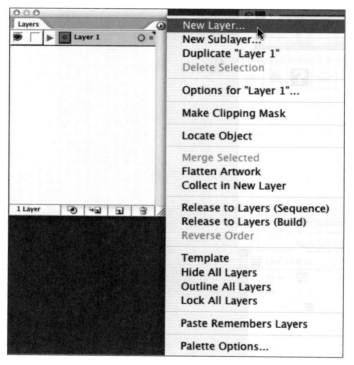

FIGURE 9-21

4. Select all of the objects you want to have a drop shadow.

5. In the Layers palette, drag the tiny colored square that indicates your selected objects to the new layer you created (Figure 9-22).

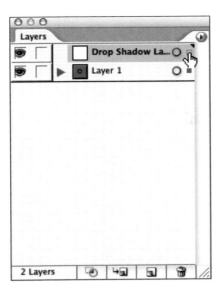

FIGURE 9-22

6. Select the entire layer by clicking on the circle next to the layer name in the Layers palette (Figure 9-23).

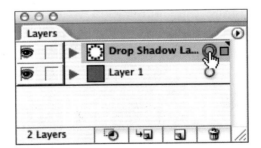

FIGURE 9-23

7. Choose Effect→Stylize→Drop Shadow to launch the Drop Shadow dialog box.

8. Choose the Mode (this example uses Normal), Opacity, X and Y Offsets, Blur, and shadow color (this example uses dark green instead of black, to create a more realistic shadow on the green board). You can also click Preview to see how it will look before you apply the effect (Figure 9-24).

Drop Shadow

Options

Mode:	Normal
Opacity:	75 %
X Offset:	7 pt
Y Offset:	7 pt
Blur:	5 pt
⦿ Color: ■	○ Darkness: 100 %

OK

Cancel

☑ Preview

FIGURE 9-24

9. Click OK to set the shadow for all of the objects (in this case, trees).

The example used here for applying the drop shadow is a game board. The trees were created from green circles, to which I applied various types of Roughen effect (Effect→ Distort & Transform→Roughen). Figure 9-25 shows the finished game board, trees and all.

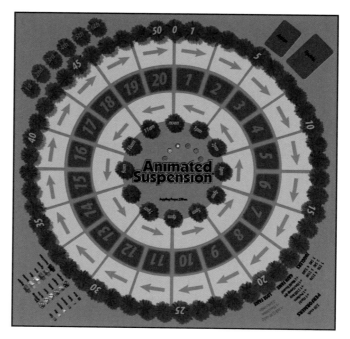

FIGURE 9-25

HOW DO I CREATE A REALISTIC-LOOKING FLARE?

Because Illustrator's Flare tool simulates the reflection from a camera lens, you can use it to create cool effects such as the reflection in an eye. Photographers tend to only like the actual reflection if it enhances the photo, like the perfect sparkle on the hood of a car. Illustrator gives you the power to put that reflection exactly where you want it to be.

To add a flare to an object (in this case, an eye):

1. Zoom in to the area to which you want to add a reflection or flare. In Figure 9-26, the painterly cat's eye is dull and black.

FIGURE 9-26

2. Using the Flare tool (housed in the Toolbox, with the Rectangle tool), click and drag out a flare in the area where you want to see the reflection (Figure 9-27).

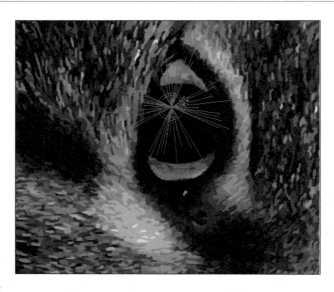

FIGURE 9-27

3. If you like what you see using the default settings, you're finished. Figure 9-28 shows a flare that's been added to give a reflection in both eyes.

FIGURE 9-28

4. If you are unsatisfied with the flare, you can change it by selecting the flare and double-clicking on the Flare tool to launch the Flare Tool Options dialog box (Figure 9-29). You can also do this *before* creating a flare, so that you create a new flare with your customizations.

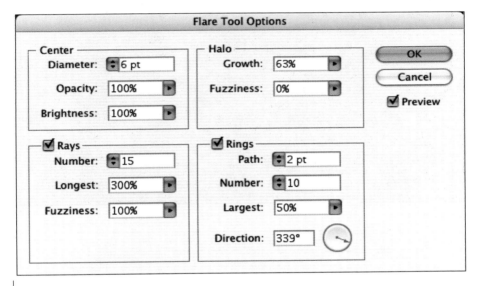

FIGURE 9-29

5. In the Flare Tool Options dialog box, change the settings and check the Preview box to see what the flare will look like before applying it.

The Flare tool can create nice bright spots or reflections and blend them out to the colors in your object. For instance, the Flare tool creates beautiful stars on a dark night sky (Figure 9-30).

FIGURE 9-30

For an even faster and easier starry sky, drag out only one flare (star) and, with that star selected, make it a symbol by choosing New Symbol from the Symbols palette menu. Name your symbol, and then use the Symbol Sprayer tool to spray out the rest of the sky. Then use the other Symbol tools to change the sizes, add transparency, move the stars around, and more. (For more on this topic, see "How Do I Make a Symbol?".)

Another use of the Flare tool is beautifully displayed in Figure 9-31. This horror movie poster has incorporated the Flare tool to emphasize the mystery of the movie.

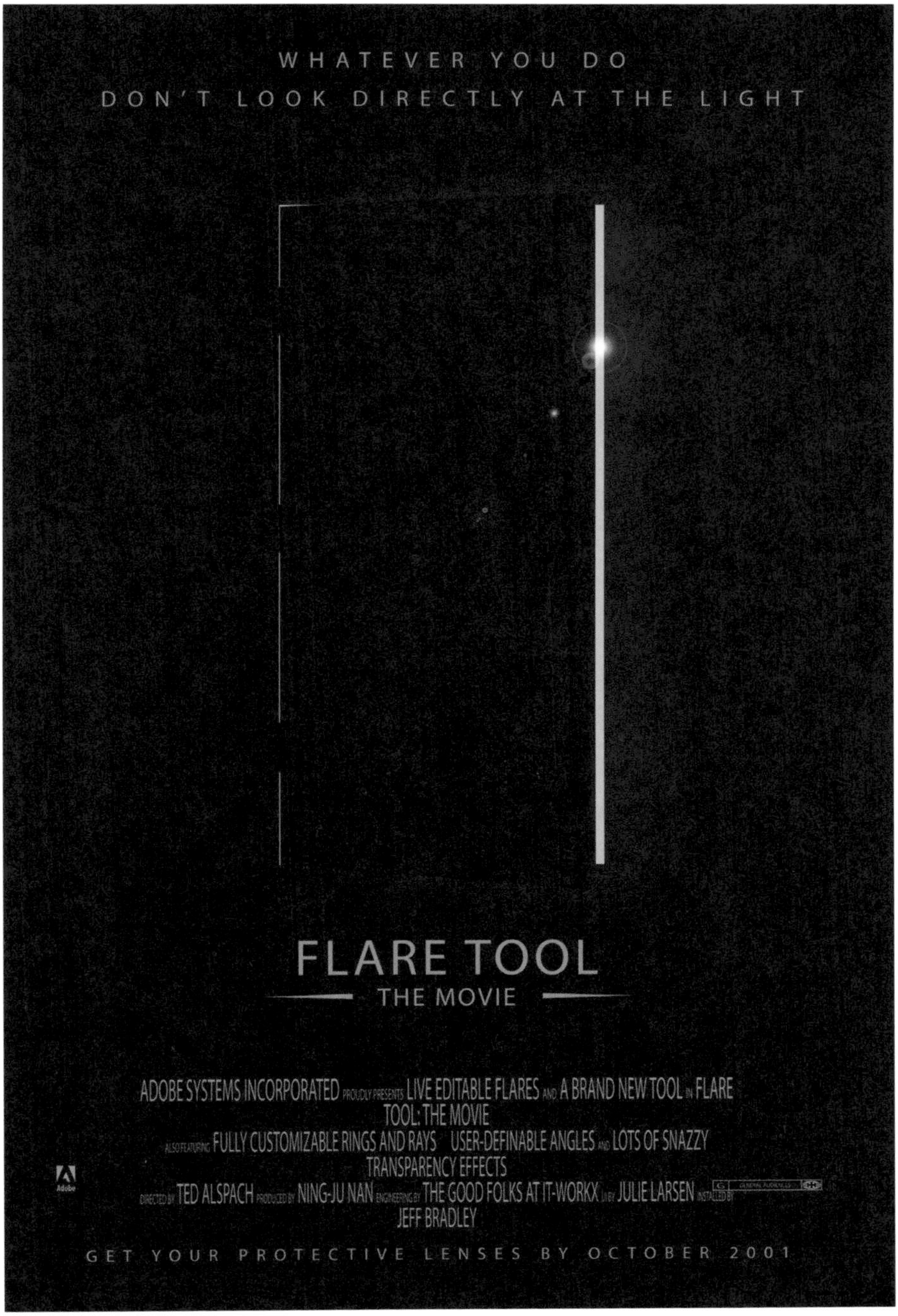
WHATEVER YOU DO
DON'T LOOK DIRECTLY AT THE LIGHT
FLARE TOOL
THE MOVIE
ADOBE SYSTEMS INCORPORATED PROUDLY PRESENTS LIVE EDITABLE FLARES AND A BRAND NEW TOOL IN FLARE TOOL: THE MOVIE
ALSO FEATURING FULLY CUSTOMIZABLE RINGS AND RAYS USER-DEFINABLE ANGLES AND LOTS OF SNAZZY TRANSPARENCY EFFECTS
DIRECTED BY TED ALSPACH PRODUCED BY NING-JU NAN ENGINEERING BY THE GOOD FOLKS AT IT-WORKX UI BY JULIE LARSEN INSTALLED BY JEFF BRADLEY
G
Adobe
GET YOUR PROTECTIVE LENSES BY OCTOBER 2001

FIGURE 9-31

HOW DO I CHANGE A GRAPHIC STYLE?

Since graphic styles were added to Illustrator, they have saved designers a ton of time, enabling us to create cool effects with no effort. *Styles* are multiple effects applied to an object that are saved in a palette so that you can quickly apply the styles to any object. Illustrator comes with many preset graphic styles, which you can modify or add to at will—for example, you may want to change the color or another aspect of an existing style, or you may feel that none of them quite suits your purpose and decide to create your own. The first set of steps below shows you how to customize a style; the next set shows you how to create a style from scratch.

To change an existing style:

1. Apply a style to change the color of an object or text. Then choose the style from the Graphic Styles palette.

2. Choose the Appearance tab of the Graphic Styles palette to see the graphic style's makeup (Figure 9-32).

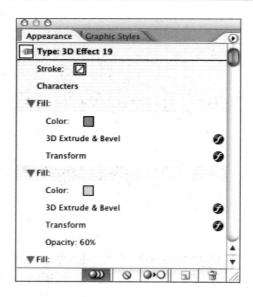

FIGURE 9-32

3. To change the color, click on the Fill color swatch in the Appearance tab, and then click on a color swatch or drag the color sliders to create a new color. The color of your selected object will change immediately (Figure 9-33).

FIGURE 9-33

4. Continue to do this until you have all the colors as you want.

5. Click on the Graphic Styles tab.

6. Choose New Graphic Style from the Graphic Styles palette pop-up menu (Figure 9-34).

New Graphic Style...
Duplicate Graphic Style
Merge Graphic Styles
Delete Graphic Style

Break Link to Graphic Style

Select All Unused

Sort by Name

✓ Thumbnail View
Small List View
Large List View

✓ Override Character Color
Graphic Style Options...

Open Graphic Style Library ▶
Save Graphic Style Library...

FIGURE 9-34

7. Enter the new name for your graphic style.

Changing a graphic style is pretty straightforward. But what if you want to create your own graphic style instead of using a default? First create the look you want for the object (in this example, we'll create a tree), and then you can follow some of the previous steps. Although you could look in the Symbol library for trees, for this tree we need an aerial view (as in doing a landscape drawing), which you won't find in the Symbol library.

1. Create an object, such as a simple green circle (Figure 9-35).

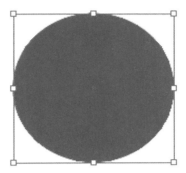

FIGURE 9-35

2. Apply the various effects and color changes to make the object as you want it. To create the trees shown in Figure 9-36, I applied Roughen (Effect→Distort & Transform→ Roughen) and then Scribble (Effect→Stylize→Scribble) effects.

FIGURE 9-36

3. To make this your tree style, choose New Graphic Style from the Graphic Styles palette pop-up menu.

4. Enter a name for your new style. This example uses "tree."

5. Click OK, and your new graphic style will appear in the Graphic Styles palette (Figure 9-37). To use it on any object you want to have that look, select the object and click your style in the palette.

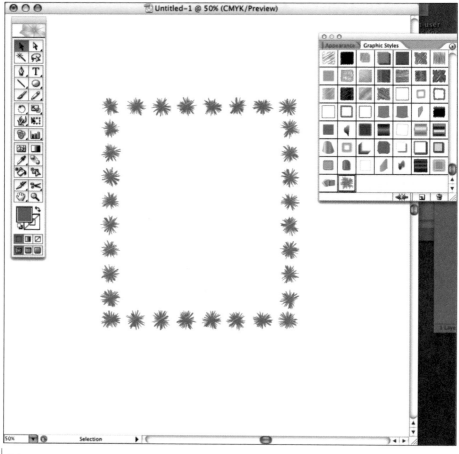

FIGURE 9-37

HOW DO I MAKE A SYMBOL?

Why would you want to use a symbol instead of copying an image repeatedly? Well, the power of the symbol is the file size. When you copy a detailed object multiple times, the information for that object is stored in the file for each and every instance of the object.

With symbols, however, you can repeat the object as many times as you'd like, and Illustrator records the file information for only one instance instead of every instance. This results in huge file size savings. Plus, symbols are just plain old fun!

Illustrator comes with quite a variety of symbols (for more symbol libraries, see Window→Symbol Libraries), and if you can't find what you're looking for, you can easily create your own symbol. The Symbol tool is used to create both print and web graphics. Not only are they repeatable and reusable, but you can customize them with the other Symbol tools.

To create a custom symbol:

1. Create an object for a symbol. You can include text, mesh objects, raster images, and grouped objects to create your object. Figure 9-38 shows a sheep that was created for a symbol. Here, the sheep is included on a green background so that you can see it.

FIGURE 9-38

2. Select the object, and then choose New Symbol from the Symbols palette. (You can also drag the object onto the Symbols palette or click the New Symbol button at the bottom of the Symbols palette.)

3. Enter a name for the symbol, and click OK. (If you dragged the object into the Symbols palette or clicked the New Symbol icon, you'll have to double-click the symbol to enter a new name.) The new symbol will now appear in the Symbols palette (Figure 9-39).

Symbol Options		
Name: Sheep|	OK	
		Cancel

FIGURE 9-39

The next step is to use the Symbol Sprayer tool to create a bunch of your object (in this case, sheep). Then, using the other Symbol tools, you can vary their size, location, color, transparency, and more.

To use the Symbol tools:

1. Choose the Symbol Sprayer tool from the toolbar.

2. Click and drag around your page to "spray" the symbols, just as you would with a can of spray paint. You now have lots of sheep (Figure 9-40). Note that if you spray several symbols, they will all be together in one bounding box.

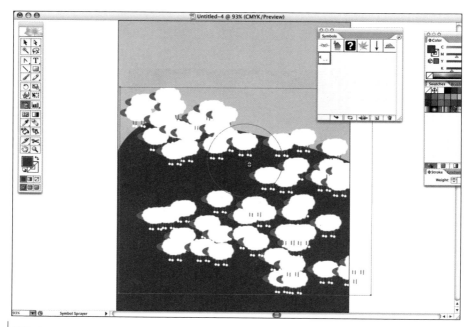

FIGURE 9-40

3. Choose the Symbol Shifter tool, and click and drag to move the sheep around. You can also use the Symbol Scruncher tool to pull the symbols together or (if you hold down the Option/Alt key) push them apart.

4. Use the Symbol Sizer tool to make the symbols larger or (if you press the Option/Alt key) smaller, so you have some bigger sheep and some smaller sheep. Click once or click and hold to make the objects even smaller/larger.

5. The Symbol Spinner tool rotates the symbols around an axis. Click and drag in a direction and the symbols will rotate around that center click point (Figure 9-41).

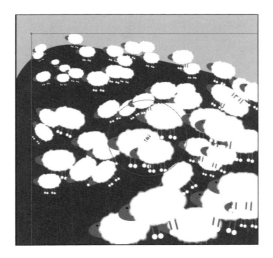

FIGURE 9-41

6. Use the Symbol Stainer tool to add different colors to the symbols. Choose the Symbol Stainer tool, then click on a color swatch or create your own color. Click once to apply the color to a single symbol or click and drag to apply the color to multiple symbols (Figure 9-42). Note that in this figure, the sheep's noses are the only things to change color, because the bodies are rasterized objects.

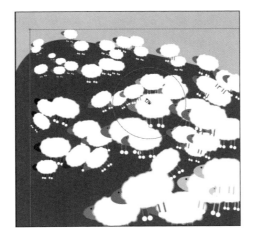

FIGURE 9-42

7. If you want some of the symbols to be transparent, use the Symbol Screener tool. Click a single symbol to add transparency to that symbol, or click and drag to add transparency to multiple symbols. The longer you hold down the mouse button, the more see-through the symbols will be (Figure 9-43).

FIGURE 9-43

8. The last tool is the Symbol Styler tool. Use this to apply any of the graphic styles to your symbols. Select the Symbol Styler tool, select a graphic style from the Graphic Styles palette, then click or click and drag to apply that style to one or more symbols (Figure 9-44).

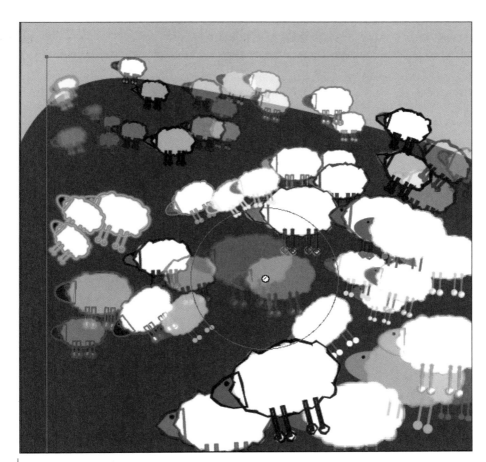

FIGURE 9-44

<table>
<tr><td>**tip**</td><td>If you are using a graphic style from a library other than the default, you'll have to drag and drop the style into the default palette to use it with the Symbol Styler tool. If you don't select a style, the Symbol Styler tool uses the last style chosen.</td></tr>
</table>

HOW DO I PUT TEXT ON A CIRCLE?

Text on a circle makes for eye-catching logo design. The key to creating text on a circle is using the right Type tool. After you create the type, you can apply many different effects to it. You can even use regular type and apply an effect or graphic style to give the illusion of type on a circle.

To create type on a circle:

1. Create a circle using the Ellipse tool. Hold down the Shift key to get a perfect circle. (To draw a perfect circle from a center point, press the Option/Alt key.)

2. Choose the Type on a Path tool from the Toolbox (found housed with the Type tool).

3. Click on the top of the circle, and type the text that you want to appear (Figure 9-45). Next comes the adjusting.

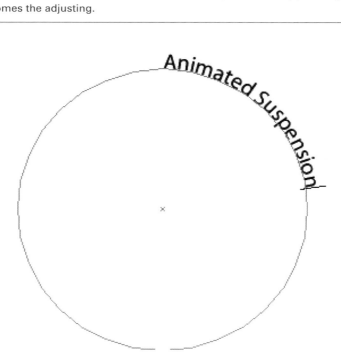

FIGURE 9-45

4. While the type is still selected, go to the Paragraph tab of the Type palette (or choose Window→Type→Paragraph), and choose "Align center." The type will move to the bottom of the circle. Don't worry; you'll pull it back to the top.

5. Click on the Direct Selection tool (or press V). Locate the vertical bar in the middle of the text, and then drag the bar up to the top of the circle (Figure 9-46).

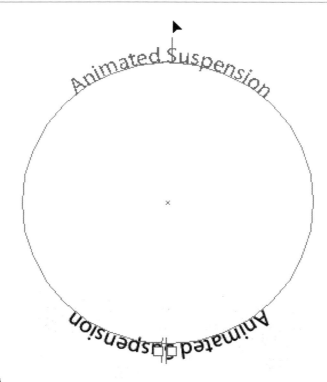

FIGURE 9-46

6. With the type selected, choose Type→Font and choose a typeface. You can also choose a different typeface from the font pop-up menu on the Character palette.

7. Choose a font size by entering a number or choosing a size from the pop-up menu on the Character palette. You can also choose Type→Size and then pick a size from the list.

8. Pick a different color from the Color palette or from the Swatches palette (Figure 9-47).

9. With your text on the circle, you can now apply any graphic style. In this case, the type was changed to 3D to create a three-dimensional logo, as shown in Figure 9-48.

HOW DO I PUT TEXT IN A SHAPE (ENVELOPE)?

Type can be so much fun when you think outside the box—or shall I say, the envelope? You can make any type much more exciting by applying the Warp (envelope) command and other effects. And no matter how many effects and commands you apply right on top of each other, your type will always be editable.

To create circular type using the Warp effects:

1. Create the type you want to use.

2. Choose Effect→Warp and choose an effect (at 100% Bend).

Figure 9-49 has an Arc applied at 100% Bend. This is a fast way to create type on a circle. Figure 9-50 has Shell Upper applied at 100% Bend, and Figure 9-51 has Bulge applied at 100% Bend.

FIGURE 9-49

FIGURE 9-50

FIGURE 9-51

1. Create the type you want to stuff in an envelope.

2. Choose Effect→Warp→Flag.

3. Check the Preview box so that you can see how the type changes as you alter the sliders (Figure 9-52).

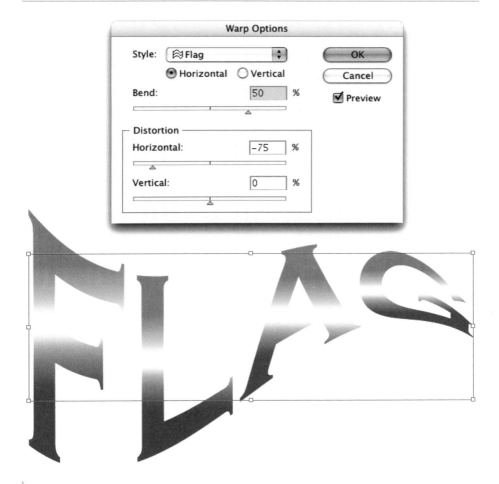

FIGURE 9-52

4. Click OK to fit your type in that envelope.

1. Create the type you want to distort.

2. Choose a graphic style to apply to the text from the Graphic Styles palette. This example uses Harmony Collage.

3. Choose Effect→Distort & Transform→Roughen (Figure 9-53). Enter your settings and click OK.

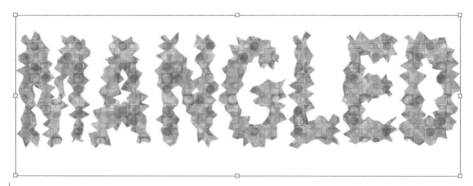

FIGURE 9-53

4. Choose Effect→Warp→Shell Upper. Here, the Horizontal button is checked, with a Bend of 35% (Figure 9-54).

FIGURE 9-54

5. Choose Effect→Stylize→Drop Shadow. In this example, Multiply Mode was applied, with an Opacity of 75%, X and Y Offsets of 10 points, and a Blur of 5 points.

The final text shown in Figure 9-55 has four different effects applied and is still fully editable.

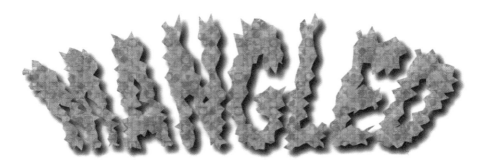

FIGURE 9-55

HOW DO I CREATE A MECHANICAL GEAR?

This issue has plagued designers since the beginning of Illustrator. As is often the case, there are several ways to do the same thing. This section shows you one fast and easy way.

To create a mechanical gear:

1. Using the Star tool (housed with the Rectangle tool in the Toolbox), create a star. To add more points to your star as you are drawing, press the up arrow (or press the down arrow to remove points).

2. Draw a circle on top of the star, cutting through the star points (Figure 9-56). The figure should look like a big sun. Make sure the circle and star have no stroke and no fill applied.

FIGURE 9-56

3. Select both the star and the circle, and then choose Crop from the Pathfinder palette to cut off the edges of the star (Figure 9-57).

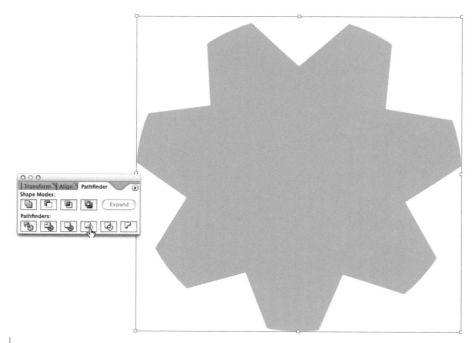

FIGURE 9-57

4. Go to Outline mode (View→Outline), and remove the extra pieces from the crop with the Direct Selection tool. Make sure you pay close attention when getting rid of the extra pieces.

5. Return to Preview mode (View→Preview).

6. Draw a circle in the center of the "gear."

7. Select both the circle and the gear shape, and choose Object→Compound Path→ Make. You could just place a white circle inside the gear to look like a hole, but if you put anything behind it, it will be obvious that it isn't a hole. Compound Path actually makes a hole in the object (Figure 9-58).

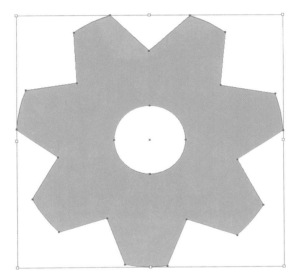

FIGURE 9-58

8. Select Effect→3D→Extrude & Bevel.

9. Increase the Default Bevel to a larger amount, or alter the Extrude Depth. Check the Preview box to see how thick you want the gear to be.

10. Click More Options and move the lighting highlight around in the Surface Preview to make the gear look the way you want.

11. Click OK to see the 3D gear (Figure 9-59).

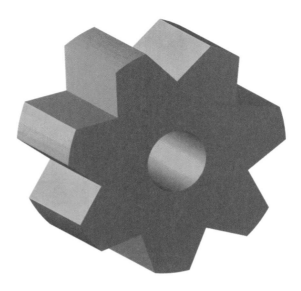

FIGURE 9-59

HOW DO I TURN A SYMBOL INTO AN ART BRUSH?

Brushes are a quick, easy way to make a strong statement in a single brush stroke. Illustrator has a plethora of default brush strokes, as well as an entire library of brushes to explore. If that isn't enough for you, then this little tip might catch your eye. Although you can use clip art, you may be able to create the effect you're after right within Illustrator—you can turn any of the symbols from the Symbol libraries into a brush, and paint in what you need. For example, say you want to create a party invitation, but you have only two people. Well, that's all you need to create a crowd of people and get them to dance! Let's see how it works.

To make an art brush from a symbol:

1. Create a new file, choose Window→Symbol Libraries, and choose a library. Drag a symbol onto the file. This example uses Male Figure and Female Figure from the Tiki library—we'll start with the Male Figure.

2. Choose Object→Expand. Here, the default Object and Fill settings are used (Figure 9-60). Click OK to expand the symbol.

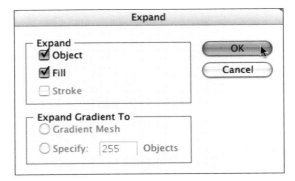

FIGURE 9-60

3. After the object has expanded, you can change the colors of the symbol by using the Direct Selection tool. I've left them as they were (Figure 9-61).

FIGURE 9-61

4. Select the figure and choose New Brush from the Brushes palette.

5. Choose New Art Brush from the New Brush dialog box (Figure 9-62). This launches the Art Brush Options dialog box, where you can set the Name, Direction, Size, Flip, and Colorization settings. The direction you choose is how you'll draw: Right to Left, Left to Right, Bottom to Top, or Top to Bottom. I chose Top to Bottom (the default). I also chose 100% for Size, chose to go without a Flip, and left the Colorization Method as None (Figure 9-63).

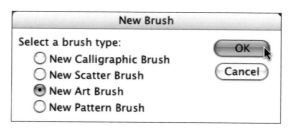

FIGURE 9-62

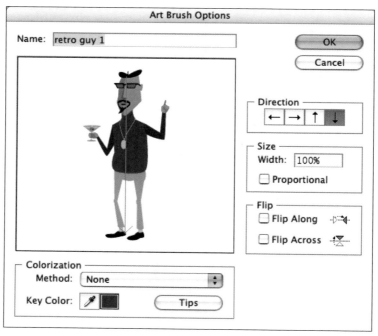

FIGURE 9-63

6. Enter a name for the brush, and click OK.

CHAPTER 9

7. Now that you have your Male Figure brush saved in the Brushes palette, you can reuse the same guy. You can reposition and recolor him to add more guys, and you can make more brushes with different people.

8. Repeat steps 1 through 7 for the Female Figure.

9. Make sure any symbols are deselected, and choose the Brush tool from the Toolbox.

10. Choose one of your new brushes from the Brushes palette.

11. Drag a brush stroke from top to bottom for your person. Varying the length of your lines results in taller and shorter people.

12. Pick another of your brushes, and repeat step 11 to create more people for your crowd (Figure 9-64).

FIGURE 9-64

13. At any time, you can use the Direct Selection tool to change the length of any of the lines. If you curve the brush stroke, the people will have a bend in them, which makes them look as if they're dancing.

HOW DO I MAKE A "HOLE" IN AN OBJECT?

Have you ever wondered how illustrators create a hole in an object that shows the background peeking though, or how to make a cool piece of text that has a picture inside of it? The answer to these design questions is the compound path. You can create a simple donut by drawing a smaller circle over a larger circle and then choosing the Object Compound Path→Make command. The hole will appear where the two objects overlap, and the hole will take on the attributes and effects of the backmost item in the stack. That is the simple explanation of the hole. To try something a bit more complex, in the first example below we'll create a chunk of Swiss cheese. We'll also look at another way to make holes in objects, and how to use type as a mask for an image.

To create a compound path:

1. Select the object and all the holes you want to punch out of it. Figure 9-65 shows a chunk of Swiss cheese.

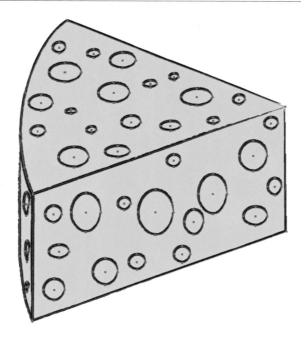

FIGURE 9-65

2. Choose Object→Compound Path→Make. If all of the circles didn't pop in a hole, don't worry (Figure 9-66). The fix is simple: you simply need to change the direction of the circles.

CHAPTER 9

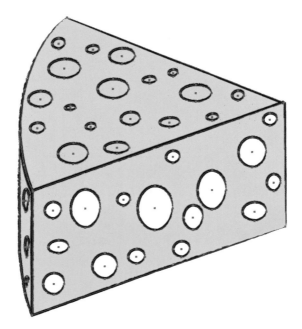

3. Use the Direct Selection tool to select the holes that didn't work, and choose Window→Attributes (Figure 9-67).

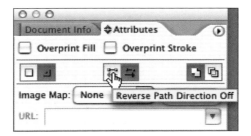

4. Click the Reverse Path Direction Off icon to fix the holes. Figure 9-68 shows the cheese with holes.

FIGURE 9-68

Another way to create a "hole" is to use the Pathfinder effect.

To create a hole using the Pathfinder command:

1. Select the object and the holes.

2. Choose Window→Pathfinder.

3. In the Pathfinder palette, click the Exclude icon in the Shape Modes row.

Voilà! You have holes, and no extra step changing the direction of the circles' paths.

Another really cool feature is to use type as a mask for an image. The only problem you'll run into is if you change the type to outlines so you can customize your text and then try to use a clipping mask. But there is a solution, again using a compound path.

To create masked type with outlined type:

1. Create your type and select it with the Selection tool.

2. Convert the type to outlines by choosing Type→Create Outlines.

3. Alter your type (Figure 9-69).

FIGURE 9-69

4. Select the text and choose Object→Compound Path→Make. Don't worry if the text becomes transparent—simply click the Fill button and choose a color for the text.

5. To place the image you want to flow in the text, choose File→Place, locate your image, and click the Place button.

6. Move the placed image behind the text by choosing Object→Arrange→Send to Back.

7. If necessary, Select All, and then choose Object→Compound Path→Make. Figure 9-70 shows the final image fitted inside the text.

FIGURE 9-70

HOW DO I COLORIZE A CARTOON?

Cartoon art is all the rage. You can take any cartoon you've created and turn it into a piece of art. Sharon Kenny creates the "Pepper" cartoon by hand. I took the cartoon and used Live Trace to create the comic art look; then, after activating Live Paint, I added color to the black and white comic strip.

1. To begin, you will need to convert your file using Live Trace. Place the image by choosing File→Place (Figure 9-71).

FIGURE 9-71

2. Choose Object→Live Trace→Tracing Options. This launches the Tracing Options dialog box.

3. Choose Comic Art from the presets (Figure 9-72).

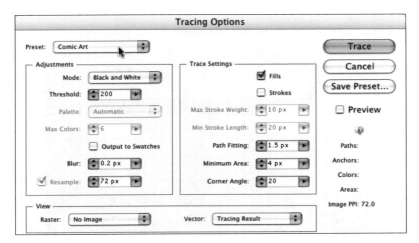

FIGURE 9-72

---

4. Click the Trace button.

---

5. Choose Object→Live Trace→Convert to Live Paint.

---

6. The cartoon is now comprised of filled areas. Click on a color you want to put in the cartoon from the Swatches or Color palettes.

---

7. Choose the Live Paint Bucket tool from the Toolbox.

---

8. Click with the Live Paint Bucket tool on the area you want to color. (If you see a message that prompts you to create a Live Paint Group, respond accordingly.) Illustrator fills the area with the color you chose (Figure 9-73).

FIGURE 9-73

9. Repeat Steps 6 through 8 to colorize your cartoon (Figure 9-74).

FIGURE 9-74

As long as you convert the traced objects to Live Paint, you can apply Live Paint to any object, black and white or otherwise. Figure 9-75 shows a grayscale file that was converted to Live Paint and had color applied.

FIGURE 9-75

HOW DO I DO MULTIPLE PAGES IN ILLUSTRATOR?

Illustrator users have long awaited the ability to create multipage documents. Illustrator can now take a tiled document, save it as a multipage PDF, and show the tiling overlay in the Print dialog. To do this, however, you must have Illustrator CS2, Acrobat Distiller 5.0 or higher, and a PostScript printer driver.

To create multiple pages in Illustrator:

1. When creating your document (File→New), be sure to set the Size as Custom. That way, you can specify the Width and Height to include all the pages you want in your new document. For this example, I created a 6-page document by entering 8.5 inches as the width and 66 inches as the length/height (Figure 9-76).

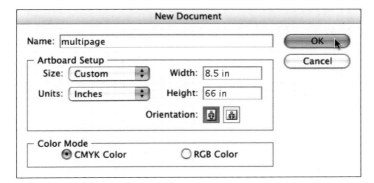

FIGURE 9-76

2. Create all of your pages. In this case, I created a rectangle and used it a guide for each of my pages.

3. Put or place all of your illustrations within the guides you made for your pages (Figure 9-77).

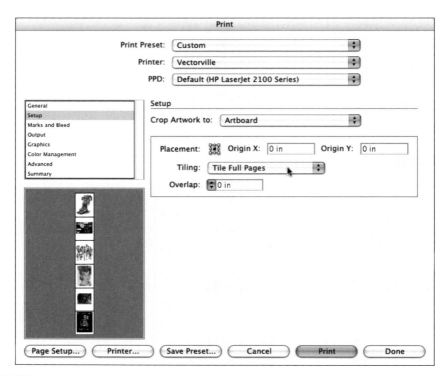

FIGURE 9-77

---

4. Choose File→Print.

---

5. In the Print dialog box, choose Setup from the list on the left.

---

6. Under the Tiling pop-up menu, choose Tile Full Pages. The pages will display in the preview box (Figure 9-78).

---

7. Click the Done button. Illustrator will number the pages for reference only, from left to right and top to bottom, on the bottom left of each page.

---

8. Choose File→Save As.

---

9. Pick Adobe PDF from the Format pull-down menu in the Save As dialog box.

---

10. Click the Save button. This launches the Save Adobe PDF dialog box.

FIGURE 9-78

11. In the Save Adobe PDF dialog box, check the Create Multi-page PDF from Page Tiles checkbox in the Options pane (Figure 9-79).

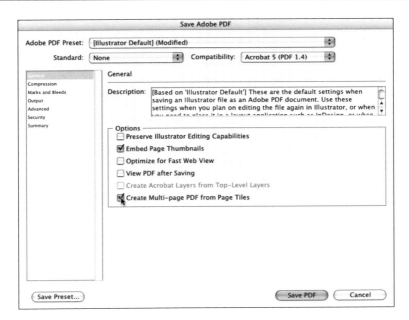

FIGURE 9-79

12. Click the Save PDF button to save the file as multiple pages. You'll get a warning that saving the document with "Preserve Illustrator Editing Capabilities" unchecked may disable some editing features when the document is read back in. Click OK to continue.

13. Open the PDF in Acrobat to see the multiple pages (Figure 9-80).

FIGURE 9-80

HOW DO I MAKE MY ILLUSTRATION SKETCHIER?

Originally, illustrators used computers to create technical, computer-like drawings. Nowadays, illustrators want the convenience and ease of the computer, but the free, loose feel of a hand-drawn sketch. Although you could purchase a pressure-sensitive tablet and do nice-looking sketchy drawings on that, you can also use Illustrator to take the stiff, perfect lines of your illustrations and set them free. Making an illustration sketchier works with vector images only; if you are using a raster image, use the Photoshop filters to achieve a similar effect.

1. Select the object you want to make sketchier.

2. Choose Effect→Stylize→Scribble.

3. From the Scribble presets in the Settings pop-up menu, choose one that makes your illustration sing.

4. Check the Preview box to see what it will look like (Figure 9-81).

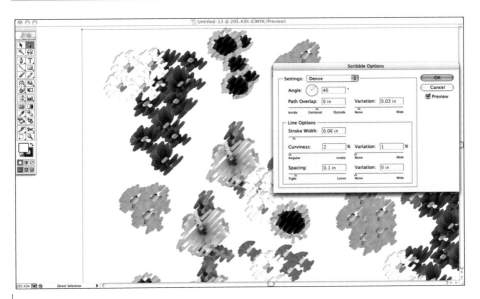

FIGURE 9-81

5. When you find the look you are going for, click OK.

Figure 9-82 shows a flower group with each of the Scribble presets applied. As with graphic styles, you can alter any of these presets or make your own custom scribble.

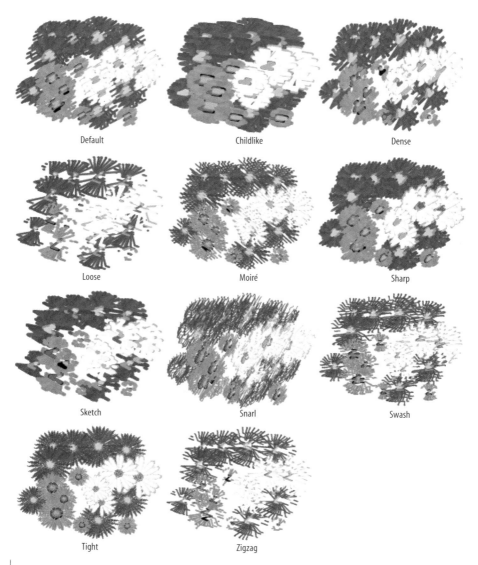

FIGURE 9-82

THE END

This ends the answers to the top 15 How Do I...? questions. Should you find yourself with more questions that you need answers to, check out the Adobe Illustrator forums at Adobe's web site: *http://www.Adobe.com/support/forums/main.html*.

10

Acrobat Professional as Part
of the Creative Suite

When you think of Acrobat, what comes to mind? Easy PDF distribution? Form creation? Commenting on files? Although it does all that with ease, when combined with the Creative Suite, Acrobat goes beyond your expectations.

Adobe Acrobat 7.0 Professional lets you control your PDF (Portable Document Format) files. You can use it to organize, distribute, review, and preflight a plethora of file types, from reports to advertisements. Acrobat is the base of the print production workflow. Use it to combine files, send them for review, distribute them via the Internet, add comments, create slideshows, and preflight files to send for printing.

AN OVERVIEW OF ACROBAT

Nowadays, Acrobat is used in a variety of ways because it is the easiest and most common way to share files. With the free Adobe Reader software (*http://www.adobe.com*), anyone can view the PDF file format. Encompassing uses from sharing photos among relatives to encrypting private documents in law firms, Acrobat is a truly versatile tool.

Whether you are a seasoned user or just starting out, you can use Acrobat to create PDFs for email distribution or uploading to the Web, send out PDFs for comment and markup reviews, develop forms, proof files and prepare for prepress, put together slideshows, and more.

Who Uses Acrobat

Acrobat is one of those few amazing programs that *everyone* uses. Any level of user can turn to Acrobat to create a PDF. For example, you might create a PDF of potential magazine covers from your InDesign files that you can then send to clients for approval. Acrobat is also commonly used for forms—from creating forms to filling in forms to posting forms on the Internet for online purchasing. (For more on creating forms with Acrobat, see "How Do I Create a Form with Designer?" in Chapter 13.) Law firms have turned to Acrobat for their secure forms, digital signatures, and email distribution. The Internal Revenue Service (IRS) and many financial institutions also have embraced the PDF workflow for their documents.

How People Use Acrobat

Acrobat PDF has become the industry standard for file distribution. Because of that standard, a wide variety of companies turn to Acrobat to fill their needs:

- High-tech companies use PDFs for creating their technical manuals for electronic publishing, saving tons of money by avoiding traditional publishing fees.

- Graphic designers save money and time during the review cycle by using Acrobat's online review features.

- Field engineers and tech people access forms and guides from PDF files housed on a central server.

- Real estate transactions are processed quickly using Acrobat's security and signing features.

- Law firms use large PDF documents online to quickly search out specifics, which is much quicker than the manual searches that had to be done before Acrobat.

CREATING PDFS

With Acrobat 7.0 Professional, there is a smooth workflow that makes PDF creation reliable, consistent, and user-friendly. Commenting features are available even to users of Adobe Reader, so everyone can comment on a file in the reviewing process. Comments are easily organized and trackable. The editing process can all be done on the PDF file, using Bridge and Version Cue to quickly go between the various applications.

Improved PDF creation lets you create print-quality PDFs directly from Acrobat. Adobe has made PDF creation consistent among all of the Creative Suite programs, created a common storage location for all of the PDF settings, made loading and customizing settings easy, and added the ability to load legacy settings.

Consistent PDF Creation Among Adobe Programs

Previous versions of Adobe products created PDF files independently of each other, but all of the Creative Suite 2 products now have the same user interface for PDF creation. The Creative Suite 2 products also share the PDF settings file among themselves. Each program includes the same five presets from which you can choose:

SMALLEST FILE SIZE: Use this preset for creating the smallest file size for Internet distribution. This file will not take long to upload or download, but it will not produce a high-quality print for output.

HIGH QUALITY PRINT: This preset creates a PDF that can be used in various ways, from creating a PDF for use within other programs (such as InDesign) to printing to desktop printers.

PRESS QUALITY: Use this option for creating a high-quality print or for a prepress workflow.

PDF/X-1A:2001: This preset is for high-end printing purposes. Files with this setting have embedded fonts, specified color settings (either CMYK or Spot), set page boundaries, and traps.

PDF/X-1A:2002: Use this preset as you would the PDF/X-1a:2001 preset. The added advantage of this preset is that it supports color management.

In addition to these presets, you can create custom PDF presets that can be used in all of your Creative Suite 2 products. The PDF settings files are saved in the same location for sharing among the programs. These custom presets also can be shared in-house and with clients. To create a preset in any of the Creative Suite 2 applications, click the Save Preset button after making changes in the Save Adobe PDF dialog box when you choose to save as a PDF.

Creating the Best PDFs

Use these tips to create the best PDFs:

- Identify what the final output of the PDF will be. If the file is intended for a printer, ask the printer for their method of PDF export.

- If your printer has a preset, get the preset from them and use it for your files. If not, use preset standards for creating your PDFs. These presets are developed from much research on the most common methods of creating PDFs.

- Make sure you don't mix your colors—for example, you don't want a file that contains both CMYK and spot colors.

- Embed your fonts to prevent any font conflicts or issues when printing.

- Make sure you run your preflight program in Acrobat. If your printer has a preflight program, get that from them as well.

- Preview your file before sending it to the printer to see what it will look like and to look for any problems before printing.

USING ACROBAT'S PRINT PRODUCTION TOOLS

Acrobat comes with a whole selection of tools for print production (Figure 10-1). You can use these print production tools to prepare your PDF for final printing output, preflighting the file, and fixing any problems that the Preflight command reveals.

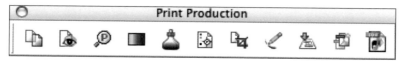

FIGURE 10-1

To access the Print Production toolbar, choose Tools→Print Production→Show Print Production Toolbar. Take a moment to review the Print Production toolbar buttons, described here (from left to right):

TRAP PRESETS: Lets you assign and save trap settings, or choose from presets.

OUTPUT PREVIEW: Lets you see the separations and individual plates in your file, and check overprinting, color warnings, and ink coverage.

PREFLIGHT: Enables you to analyze the PDF file to check for problems with resolution, transparency, compatibility, and more.

CONVERT COLORS: Converts your RGB colors to CMYK and embeds color profiles.

INK MANAGER: Lets you change the way inks are used, previewed, and output.

ADD PRINTER MARKS: Adds standard printer marks for positioning.

CROP PAGES: Enables you to define where to crop, trim, and bleed art on the page.

FIX HAIRLINES: Searches the document and replaces any hairline weights with a heavier line weight.

TRANSPARENCY FLATTENING: Allows you to control the amount that the file will be rasterized when flattening transparency.

PDF OPTIMIZER: Lets you analyze the file to create the smallest file size and set the saving version.

JDF JOB DEFINITIONS: Creates a JDF (Job Definition Format) file that includes the requirements of the printer as well as copies, media type, and other important information on printing a file.

In this chapter, we'll focus on the Preflight, Output Preview, and PDF Optimizer tools. We'll take a look at the full suite of print production tools in the next chapter.

Preflighting is used to check a document for errors before sending it to a printer. Acrobat 7.0 Professional has an amazing preflighting program built right in. Acrobat's preflighting tools include several industry standards for printing, from PostScript to checking for compliance with PDF/Xa standards to be sure your document will process properly. Use this preflight program to check for any potential problems with the content of your PDF, then use the other print production tools to fix any problems encountered. Then use the Output Preview option to see your file as it will print. Previewing will show you any additional problems, such as overprinting or font problems. When you're ready to send out your file, if you're uploading it to the Web or an FTP site, you'll want to use the PDF Optimizer to ensure you get a quality print without an excessive file size.

Preflighting a PDF

Preflighting a PDF has become much easier with Acrobat 7.0 Professional. The Preflight Profiles menu comes with a variety of presets to choose from. The profiles were created from the most common usages of preflighting, to make it easier to select the correct preflight. You can choose from Compliant with PDF/A (Draft), Digital press (B/W), Digital press (color), Magazine Ads, Newspaper Ads, PDF/X1a, various Sheetfed offset and Web offset options, and more.

1. Open the PDF you want to preflight.

2. Choose Advanced→Preflight, or press Command-Shift-X (Mac) or Ctrl-Shift-X (Windows).

3. From the Preflight dialog box, select a Profile. Figure 10-2 shows the Digital Press (Color) selection.

FIGURE 10-2

4. Click the Execute button to start the preflighting process. The Acrobat preflight program will analyze the file for any potential problems for the profile you have chosen.

5. The Results button displays any errors or warnings found after Acrobat has analyzed the PDF file (Figure 10-3). This allows you to fix outstanding issues before sending the file to a printer. You can jump between the various tabs at the top of the Preflight dialog box to see the Results, Profiles, Reports, and so on. Also, you can click on a checkbox in the Results area to see a detailed explanation of the error.

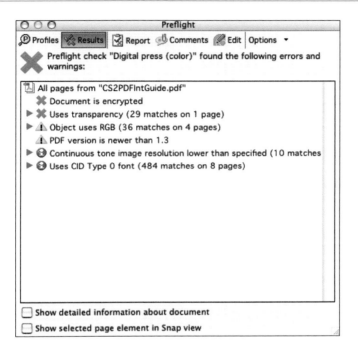

FIGURE 10-3

Before running Preflight, you can edit a preset profile or create your own custom profile. Many printers use a specific profile for preflighting their files; you'll want to get the profile directly from your printer to ensure a smooth printing workflow.

To add a profile to your preset folder, drag the file you received from your printer into the PDF preset shared folder. On a Mac, you can find this at \Library\Application Support\ Adobe PDF\Settings. On Windows, you can find it at C:\Documents and Settings\All Users\ Documents\Adobe PDF\Settings.

If you store your presets correctly, all of the Creative Suite 2 programs will be able to access your printer's preflight profile.

You also can preflight PDF files you have created in other programs using Acrobat 7.0 Professional. To preflight any PDF, simply open it in Acrobat and then run the Preflight command to check the file.

Fixing Errors Found During Preflight

Now that you've preflighted your PDF, it's time to fix any errors you've found. You can use Acrobat's print production tools to correct any problems you may have encountered with your PDF file in preflighting. For example, say you've found some conflicting color spaces and hairline rules. Open the Print Production toolbar, found under the Print Production submenu of the Tools menu, to make the changes to your PDF.

To fix the colors in your document:

1. Click the Convert Colors button in the Print Production toolbar. This opens the Convert Colors dialog box (Figure 10-4).

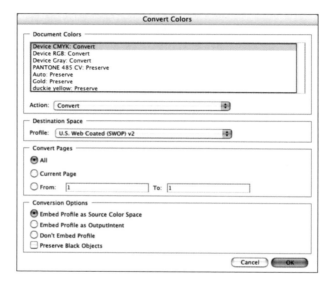

FIGURE 10-4

2. In the Convert Colors dialog box, you'll see all of the colors in the document. Here you can select a color space and choose an action to apply to the color space. In the Action pop-up menu, choose from Preserve, Convert, or Decalibrate, or use the option to map to one of the specified colors present in the current document.

3. Choose a Profile from the Destination Space pop-up menu.

4. Under Convert Pages, select how you want the pages converted: All, Current Page, or specific page ranges.

5. Select one of the Conversion Options from the radio buttons, select the Preserve Black Objects checkbox if you want, and choose OK. The file will now be converted according to your input.

To fix the hairline rules:

1. Click the Fix Hairlines button in the Print Production toolbar.

2. Enter values for the hairline width threshold and the replacement width.

3. Specify the pages to check, and click OK.

After you have corrected all of the issues, run Preflight again just to be sure nothing was missed or fixed incorrectly. Once you've run Preflight and fixed any reported errors, the next step is to preview the file to double-check that the file is now correct.

Previewing a PDF

Before you print a PDF, you should always preview it in Acrobat. Choose Advanced→Output Preview to see each plate separation, proof the colors in your file, and see combined plates of color. The Output Preview dialog box has two preview areas: Separations and Color Warnings.

Choosing Separations in the Preview box lets you view each plate alone or in any sequence you choose (Figure 10-5). The default Simulation Profile is U.S. Web Coated (SWOP) v2, but you can choose from a variety of presets as well. The Simulate Ink Black and Simulate Paper White options under the Simulation Profile drop-down provide you with a fairly accurate view of the printed product.

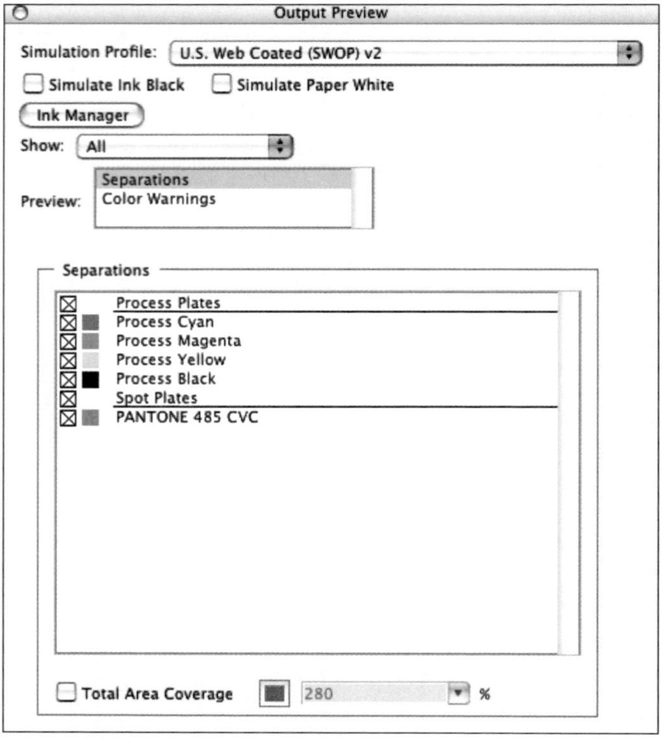

FIGURE 10-5

If you choose Color Warnings in the Preview box, you can see any warnings that might affect the printing. Checking the Show Overprinting box will display the overprinting colors in the default orange or another color of your choice (to select a different color, click the orange square and select one from the swatches or the color wheel). Figure 10-6 shows the text that has been made to overprint by displaying an orange outline around the text. Once you see this, you can rest assured that your text won't knock out the colors below and create a trapping nightmare.

Figure 10-7 shows the Rich Black text box checked to show which areas will print in Rich Black (100% cyan, 100% magenta, 100% yellow, and 100% black creates a Rich Black). In the PDF, the color cyan indicates which areas will print as Rich Black. To change this to a different color, click on the cyan swatch. These are great visuals to show you how your PDF will end up printing.

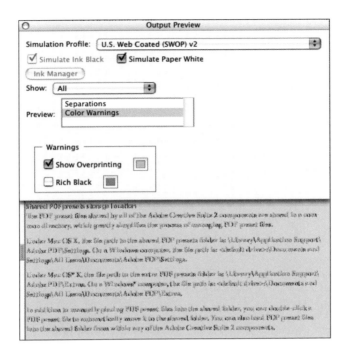

FIGURE 10-6

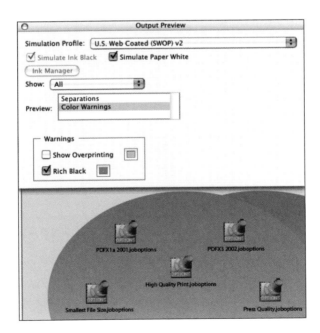

FIGURE 10-7

Optimizing Your PDF

If you are sending out your PDF via email or posting it to an FTP site for a printer or for reviewing purposes, you'll want to make sure the PDF is optimized to be the smallest file size and still have the requirements to be a quality print.

Acrobat's optimizing tool is found in the Print Production toolbar. Click the PDF Optimizer button to access the PDF Optimizer dialog box. If there are unsaved changes, you'll be prompted to save the file before continuing, and you'll have to save again when you're finished adjusting the PDF Optimizer settings to preserve the optimized file. On the left side of the dialog box are the areas you can select to optimize:

IMAGES: Under the Image Settings options, choose how you'll downsample and compress Color, Grayscale, and Monochrome Images, and, if you're using JPEG compression, pick the quality.

SCANNED PAGES: Choose the quality of compression and, if you compress based on color content, select the filters from the various pop-up menus. To access these choices, you need to first check the box that says "Optimize compression of page regions based on color content."

FONTS: Use this area to embed all or only selected fonts in the PDF file.

TRANSPARENCY: Here you can choose to flatten any transparent areas. Adjust the Raster/Vector Balance, Line Art and Text resolution, and Gradient and Mesh resolution settings, and select various text, stroke, and other options.

DISCARD OBJECTS: Choose from various checkboxes to discard comments and form widgets; form submission, import, and reset actions; JavaScript actions; external cross references; alternate images; embedded thumbnails; private data; document structure; and hidden layers. You also can convert smooth lines to curves, and detect and merge image fragments.

CLEAN UP: Select how you want to compress objects and encode streams, whether to remove invalid bookmarks/links and unreferenced named destinations, and whether to optimize the PDF for fast web view.

WORKING WITH PRINT PRODUCTION STANDARDS: PDF/X AND JDF SUPPORT

Acrobat supports two print production standards: PDF/X (and subsets) and JDF. The Portable Document Format X (PDF/X) subset for graphic arts file exchange is the standard format for any documents that go to high-quality/resolution printing output. The Committee for Graphic Arts Technologies (together with Adobe) created the PDF/X format to ensure an accurate exchange of files. This format also gets rid of any file errors such as color, trapping, and font issues.

The Job Definition Format (JDF) was created to give users direction on how to prepare a file for printing by the print service provider. The JDF format is based on the XML format, but it goes a step further in including information such as the number of copies, the preflight profile, and more.

PDF/X Support

The PDF/X standard was created for print-quality pages. This standard defines the file to prevent the occurrence of any of the font, color, or trapping issues that plague the printing process. Under the PDF/X format are other subsets, such as:

PDF/X-1A: This preset is used mainly for ads that follow a printing standard. This standard defines how CMYK (non-color-managed) files will be delivered to the printer.

PDF/X-3: This superset of PDF/X-1a has all of the benefits of PDF/X-1a, plus color-managed workflows. Here, you can use RGB files that are device-dependent.

PDF/X-1A:2001, PDF/X-3:2002, PDF/X-1A:2003, AND PDF/X-3:2003: These subsets were created from PDF 1.3 (from Acrobat 4) to support the older format. The 2003 versions support Acrobat 5's PDF 1.4 and handle JBIG compression.

PDF 1.4 supports transparency, but the results may not be consistent. If you are working with transparent graphics or objects, be sure to flatten the transparency before creating your PDF/X file.

To create a PDF/X file:

1. Open the Preflight dialog box (Advanced→Preflight).

2. Click the PDF/X icon found at the bottom left of the dialog box to convert the PDF to a PDF/X file.

3. In the Preflight: Convert to PDF/X dialog box, choose the type of PDF/X file to convert to, select the output condition, and set the Trapped key to true or false (Figure 10-8).

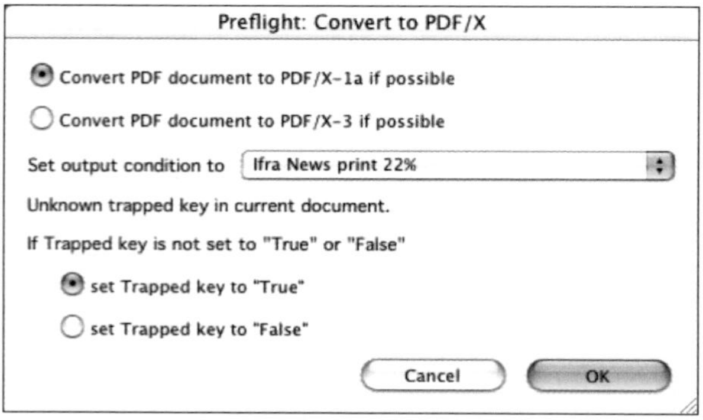

Preflight: Convert to PDF/X

⦿ Convert PDF document to PDF/X-1a if possible

◯ Convert PDF document to PDF/X-3 if possible

Set output condition to [Ifra News print 22% ⬍]

Unknown trapped key in current document.

If Trapped key is not set to "True" or "False"

    ⦿ set Trapped key to "True"

    ◯ set Trapped key to "False"

        (Cancel) (OK)

FIGURE 10-8

4. After you click OK, the file will show the progress of the conversion by analyzing the pages.

5. Once the pages are analyzed, you'll save the file as whatever type of PDF/X file you chose. If you haven't fixed any errors found during preflight, you will get a message saying the conversion has failed.

The standard PDF/X settings are meant for files that are going to be printed on a web offset press using a coated stock paper. If you are printing on a different type of press, you will need to customize your PDF/X file settings. To create a custom setting, use a standard one to get you started, and save it with a new name so you'll have it for the next time you print with that printer. When editing the settings, change only what you need and leave the standards where you can.

After you create your PDF/X file, use Preflight to ensure you have the best possible file to send to your printer. Once you've preflighted the file, the PDF/X icon at the bottom left of the Preflight dialog box will show a green checkmark, indicating that the file is PDF/X ready and good to go to the printer.

JDF Support

JDF files organize a print job's specifications, ensuring a better print workflow for your PDF files. Now, in Acrobat 7.0 Professional, you can create your own JDF files (linked to your PDFs) to send to your printer. The JDF file handles every aspect of the printing process, from the number of copies, binding, information on each section of the file, page size and orientation, scaling, and inks, right down to the last minute detail. If you want your file printed a certain way and not altered by the printer's preflighting information, you can embed your preflight information right in the file.

1. Click the JDF Job Definitions tool in the Print Production toolbar. (To access the Print Production toolbar, choose Tools→Print Production→Show Print Production Toolbar.)

2. Click the New button in the top-left corner of the JDF Job Definitions dialog box. This launches the Create New Job Definition dialog box.

3. Choose whether the JDF file will be based on a new file, on the document, or on another job definition.

4. Enter a filename, and click the Create and Edit button so that you can alter any of the areas you want (Figure 10-9).

5. In the Edit JDF Job Definition dialog box, enter general information such as the Product Name, Job ID, Embedded Preflight Profile, Binding Settings, and so on.

6. Click the Add Section button at the bottom of the dialog box to divide the file into sections, then specify more information, such as the Section Name, Number of Pages in the section, Page Size, and Media settings. Sections are used for distinguishing the pages in the PDF that have different page settings, different media settings, different inks (to add a different ink setting, click the ink tab next to the general tab), and Scaling Policy.

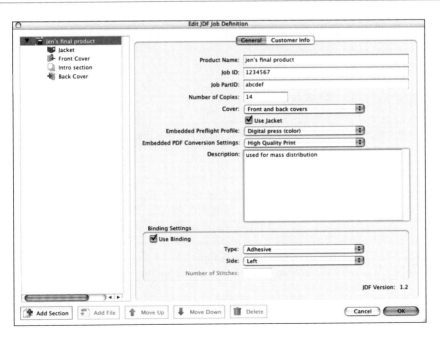

FIGURE 10-9

7. Click Product in the pane on the left, and then click the Customer Info tab to enter the Billing Code, Customer ID, Customer Job, Customer Order ID, and Contacts.

8. After you click OK, you'll see your new setting in the JDF Job Definitions dialog box (Figure 10-10).

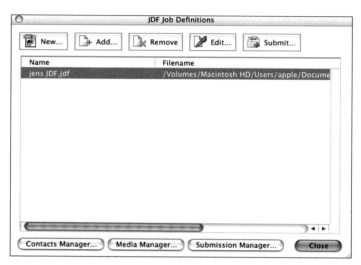

FIGURE 10-10

After you have created a JDF Job Definition and before you submit your JDF file, you must create a submission setup.

To create a submission setup:

1. Click the Submission Manager button at the bottom of the JDF Job Definitions dialog box and click the Add button.

2. In the Submission Setup dialog box, enter a Name and select your pre-submission options. In the Default PDF Conversion Settings drop-down, choose from High Quality Print, PDF/A:Draft, PDF/X-1a:2001, PDF/X-3:2002, Press Quality, Smallest File Size, or Standard. This will help you in creating a JDF Job Definition file that conforms to the industry standards. You also may opt to combine PDF files into a single PDF file, insert blank pages, include annotations, and preflight PDF files. If you choose to preflight the PDF files, you can choose from a specific preset of Preflight profiles.

3. In the Submission Options section, choose "Submit to a folder" and enter a Path (Figure 10-11).

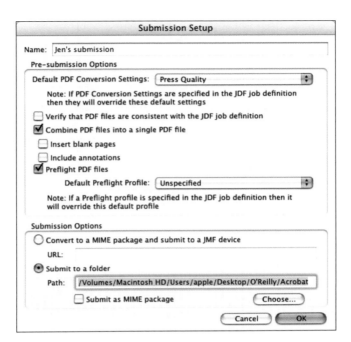

Submission Setup

Name: Jen's submission

Pre-submission Options

Default PDF Conversion Settings: Press Quality

Note: If PDF Conversion Settings are specified in the JDF job definition then they will override these default settings

☐ Verify that PDF files are consistent with the JDF job definition
☑ Combine PDF files into a single PDF file
☐ Insert blank pages
☐ Include annotations
☑ Preflight PDF files

Default Preflight Profile: Unspecified

Note: If a Preflight profile is specified in the JDF job definition then it will override this default profile

Submission Options

○ Convert to a MIME package and submit to a JMF device

URL:

⦿ Submit to a folder

Path: /Volumes/Macintosh HD/Users/apple/Desktop/O'Reilly/Acrobat

☐ Submit as MIME package   Choose...

Cancel   OK

FIGURE 10-11

4. After you have created a submission, you can click the Submit button in the JDF Job Definitions dialog box.

5. In the Submit dialog box, choose the Job Definition first, and then select Submit To from the pop-up.

6. Click the Start button. The file will now be combined in the submission location.

Next, click the Media Manager button at the bottom of the JDF Job Definitions dialog box to specify the paper quality and media (paper or transparency) for the print job.

To specify color and paper settings:

1. In the Media Manager dialog box (Figure 10-12), click Add. Then, in the Media dialog box, choose your Media Type, Grade, Weight, Thickness, Grain Direction, Opacity, Texture, Front and Back Coating, Stock Type and other settings.

2. Under the color settings, set the color and shade of paper you are using.

3. Don't forget to enter a description for your settings to be saved.

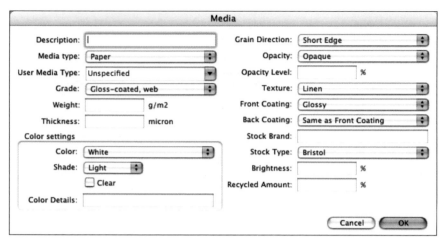

Media

Description:		Grain Direction:	Short Edge
Media type:	Paper	Opacity:	Opaque
User Media Type:	Unspecified	Opacity Level:	%
Grade:	Gloss–coated, web	Texture:	Linen
Weight:	g/m2	Front Coating:	Glossy
Thickness:	micron	Back Coating:	Same as Front Coating

Color settings

Color:	White	Stock Brand:	
Shade:	Light	Stock Type:	Bristol
	☐ Clear	Brightness:	%
Color Details:		Recycled Amount:	%

Cancel OK

FIGURE 10-12

You also can create a template of your JDF to send to your customer or printer. You can find more information about JDFs in Chapter 11.

Here are the most important things to take away from this chapter:

1. Check with your printer to determine how to create the best PDF. Use the printer's presets and any other files they may have to make your printing workflow go smoothly.

2. Always preflight your PDFs to ensure they are error-free and comply with the industry standards.

3. Preview your PDFs before sending them to the printer so you can see if there are any unresolved issues.

4. Optimize your PDFs so you can send the cleanest, smallest, best-quality files possible.

5. Use the print production standards (such as PDF/X and JDF support), which were created by the users in the industry to ensure ease of PDF workflow.

PDFs in a Print Workflow

When it comes to high-end printing, Acrobat 7.0 Professional has the tools to get your file printer-ready. From a Print Production toolbar to an actual preflighting command, you can easily get your file ready for top-quality printing on a digital press.

Acrobat's advanced features enable you to optimize and crop your files, add printer marks, preview the output, and more. New to Acrobat 7.0 is the ability to submit a job to your printer with a linked JDF Job Definition file.

UNDERSTANDING WHEN TO USE NATIVE FILES VERSUS PDFS

So, it's finally time to send that file to the printer. You have two choices for how to send it: as a native file or a PDF. A *native* file is an original file saved in the native format of the program in which it was created. One reason a printer might ask for a native file is so they can change an output-specific setting, such as creating a PostScript, in the original file. Many prepress people feel more comfortable creating the PostScript files themselves. A *Portable Document Format* (PDF) file is your other choice. PDF was invented by Adobe as a standard way to transfer files and is now accepted as the industry standard. PDFs are searchable, secure, and accessible. Nowadays, printers often ask specifically for PDF files. Printers also may send you the presets for preflighting your files, to make their lives—and yours—easier.

WORKING WITH THE PRINT PRODUCTION TOOLS

Acrobat makes the job of the print workflow user easy. The Print Production tools, found under the Tools menu, let you check for and correct a variety of printing issues. To access the Print Production toolbar, choose Tools→Print Production→Show Print Production toolbar. Each of the tools in the Print Production toolset has its use in the final printing process. Use one or all of the tools to prepare your PDF file for printing.

Trap Presets

Trapping refers to how much colors overlap to prevent white lines between colors when you print. Trapping also sets colors to overprint. When you need to change the default trapping preset, or when your printer sends you specifics on how they want the colors trapped, use the Trap Presets command to edit an existing preset or create a new one. When you choose the Trap Presets button in the Print Production toolbar, the Trap Presets dialog box launches. From this dialog box, you can choose from the default settings or create a new preset with your printer's specifications.

To create a new preset:

1. From the Print Production toolbar, choose the Trap Preset button.

2. Click the Create button in the Trap Preset dialog box.

3. In the New Trap Preset dialog box, enter a Name, Trap Width, Trap Appearance, Images, and Trap Thresholds (Figure 11-1). After you have filled in all of the information, click OK. Your new preset now appears in the Trap Presets dialog box.

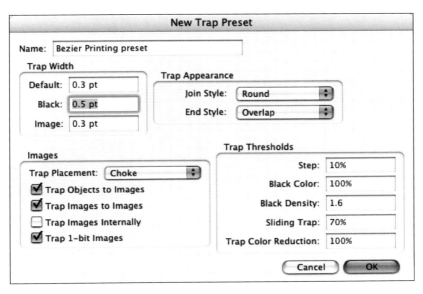

FIGURE 11-1

After you have created a new preset, you can assign that preset to your PDF document by choosing the Assign button in the Trap Presets dialog box. In the Assign Trap Presets dialog box, you can apply the preset to all pages of the PDF document or to a specific page range.

Output Preview and Ink Manager

Wanna see what your file will look like when you print it? Use Output Preview to get a gander at any issues that might come up at the printer. Output Preview lets you see separations, look at individual plates, check ink cover, and find any color warnings (by selecting the Color Warnings option in the Preview box), which will check for overprinting.

What's so cool about this feature is that you can click on one plate and view that separation only (after you uncheck the Process Plates box and a single plate displays in grayscale), or you can pick and choose which plates to view. With multiple plates, they display in their appropriate colors, as shown in Figure 11-2.

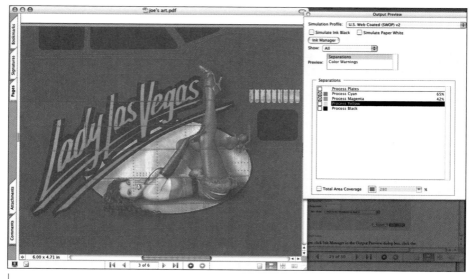

FIGURE 11-2

In addition to checking the plates, you also can manage your inks with the Ink Manager. You can access the Ink Manager from the Print Production toolbar or from within the Output Preview dialog box, by clicking the Ink Manager button. Ever wanted to convert spot colors or change a spot color to the CMYK values? You can use Acrobat's Ink Manager to do just that, as well as to control how the inks appear in Output Preview (Figure 11-3).

Ink Manager

	Name	Type	Density	Sequence
	Process Cyan	Normal	0.610	1
	Process Magenta	Normal	0.760	2
	Process Yellow	Normal	0.160	3
	Process Black	Normal	1.700	4
	PANTONE 485 CVC	Normal	0.938	5

Process Cyan

Type: Normal

Neutral Density: 0.61

Trapping Sequence: 1

Ink Alias: [No Alias]

☐ Convert All Spots to Process

Cancel   OK

FIGURE 11-3

Preflight

Preflighting—sounds like preparing to take off in an airplane, doesn't it? Indeed, *pre-flighting* is what you do to a file to prepare it to go winging off to a printer. Much like an airplane pilot goes through his checks before every flight to ensure safe air travel, you'll want to preflight your file to ensure that it arrives at the printer intact, and with all of its pieces working smoothly together.

Preflighting checks your document for any potential problems such as missing fonts, unlinked files, mismatched color spaces, and more. Preflighting a file will show you all of the problems in the file so that you can fix them instead of paying the printer extra money to do it for you. The Results pane of the Preflight dialog box (accessed via the Print Pro-duction toolbar or under the Advanced menu) goes so far as to tell you exactly what you need to fix by preflighting against a specific profile (Figure 11-4).

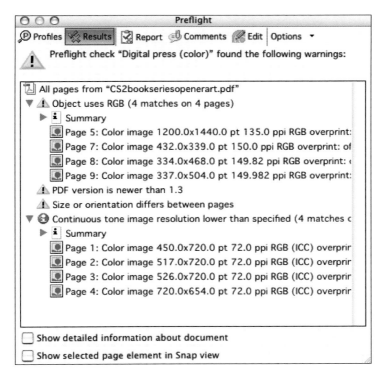

FIGURE 11-4

As shown in Figure 11-4, this file, which was preflighted with the Digital press (color) profile, uses RGB, and each page in the file that has an RGB image is listed along with the file size and resolution. Other errors show that the file is using an old version of PDF (1.3) and that the size or orientation of the pages differs from page to page. All of these issues need to be resolved before sending this file to the printer.

Convert Colors

Acrobat can convert a PDF document to a different color space. Maybe you have a document that has some objects in the RBG color space, but you want the entire document to be printed in the CMYK color space. Another really nice feature of Acrobat is that you can convert one page, or the entire document.

Add Printer Marks

You can quickly and easily add printer marks to any PDF document, opting to show the registration marks, color bars, trim and bleed marks, and page information. To add printer marks, choose the Add Printer Marks button from the Print Production toolbar. In the Add Printer Marks dialog box, select which marks to show and specify certain pages or all pages. Pick the Line Weight and Style of the marks as well.

Crop Pages

Crop pages does just that—from the Crop Pages dialog box, you can specify the right, left, top, and bottom margins to crop a page. Or you can choose Fixed Sizes and choose a specific size, such as Tabloid, from the Page Sizes drop-down menu (Figure 11-5). As with the other options, you can apply the crop settings to a single page or to the entire document.

Fix Hairlines

Hairlines are typically considered to be line weights of .25 point or less (you can set the threshold in the Fix Hairlines dialog box). These lines often print improperly because of their tiny weight. The Fix Hairlines option replaces these problem lines with lines of a heavier weight. You also can choose to apply a heavier line weight to certain fonts, PostScript patterns, and crop marks, so they print out nicely.

Transparency Flattening

Any document that has transparency involved will need to be flattened before going to the printer. You can flatten the transparency by using either the Transparency Flattening tool or the PDF Optimizer, both found in the Print Production toolbar. When choosing Flattener settings, pick low or medium resolutions for black and white desktop printers, pick medium resolutions for color desktop or PostScript printers, and pick high resolutions for high-end output devices. To access the Flattener Preview dialog box, choose the Transparency Flattening button from the Print Production toolbar.

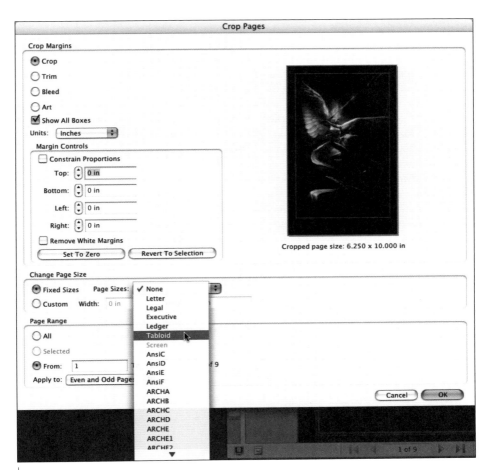

FIGURE 11-5

- -

PDF Optimizer

You can use the PDF Optimizer to flatten transparent objects and transparent areas in your file, but that's not all it does—it also reduces the file size of the PDF for faster print-ing. To achieve this, the PDF Optimizer removes everything unneeded (such as invalid links, invalid bookmarks, comments, external cross references, and more) from the file.

1. Choose PDF Optimizer from the Print Production toolbar. (You can also choose File→ Reduce File Size, but with this method the file will automatically be optimized with the default settings—you can't choose the settings this way.)

2. In the PDF Optimizer dialog box, adjust the Images, Scanned Pages, Fonts, Transparency, Discard Objects, and Clean Up settings to pare down the file size. In the Discard Objects Settings area, you can choose to discard comments and form widgets; form submission, import, and reset actions; all JavaScript actions; external cross references; alternate images; embedded thumbnails; private data of other applications; document structure; and hidden layer content. Also, you can set which version of Acrobat you want the file to be compatible with, convert smooth lines to curves, and detect and merge image fragments (Figure 11-6). Many files have a lot of extraneous information that should be removed, which will make for smaller file sizes in the end.

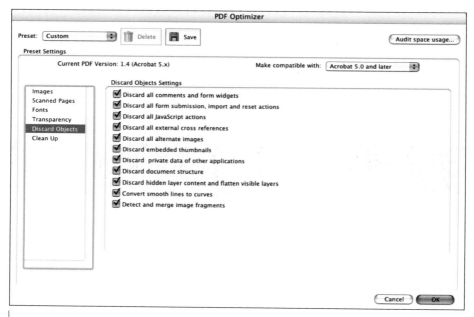

FIGURE 11-6

3. When you have all the settings as you want them, click OK.

4. The first thing you'll be asked to do is to save the file. Then the optimization will start. There is no need to save the file again after optimization.

JDF Job Descriptions

Ever have one of those complicated jobs that has to go to the printer, and you're worried there might be problems? Adobe has your answer in the JDF (Job Definition Format) file, available in Acrobat 7.0 Professional. JDF creates a job ticket file that is the control for the entire print production workflow. To create a JDF file, choose JDF Job Descriptions from the Print Production toolbar, and then choose Create or Edit. With the JDF file, you can add job information such as the number of pages, page size, inks used, scaling, orientation, and more. (For more on using JDF files in Acrobat, see Chapter 10.)

PRINTING PDFS AND POSTSCRIPT FILES

Whew—all done preparing your file. Now it's time to get it printed. Printing from Acrobat 7.0 Professional is pretty much the same as printing from other applications. The question is, are you printing to a desktop printer or sending the file out for high-end printing? Printing to your desktop printer is pretty straightforward, but printing to a PostScript printer can get more involved.

Adobe PDFs house settings for printing to a PostScript printer. These particular settings will end up overriding the printer's defaults.

To create a PostScript file:

1. Choose File→Save As, and pick PostScript from the Format pop-up menu.

2. Click the Settings button to set any of the advanced options (such as Download Asian Fonts if using a file with Asian fonts).

If you want control over the PostScript printing of your files (for halftone settings and more), you can use Acrobat to set your PostScript options. You'll find the PostScript settings by clicking the Advanced button in the Print dialog.

You can use Acrobat's Print dialog to adjust the settings for a PostScript file that you're going to send to your printer, but another option is to use Acrobat Distiller to turn the PostScript file into a PDF to send to the printer. Distiller comes packaged with Acrobat and can be launched alone (from the Acrobat Applications folder) or from within Acrobat (by choosing Advanced→Acrobat Distiller). Alternatively, if you want even more control over how your PDFs are made, you can use Acrobat's JDF Job Definitions dialog to convert your PostScript files.

However you create your PDFs, you'll want to ensure that they comply with the print production standards. If you use Distiller to convert your PostScript files to PDF, you should include specific settings for the files, such as PDF/X standards. If you use the JDF Job Definitions dialog, you'll be able to specify exactly how you want the file printed in the job ticket file and send that file along to the printer.

- -

To Distill or Not to Distill... That Is the Question

Let's say you've created a PostScript file in another application, such as Adobe Illustrator. If you want increased control over that file for printing, you can use Distiller to turn the file into a PDF. Sure, you can create a PDF directly from Illustrator, but when you use Distiller, you can include specific settings for the PDF file, such as PDF/X standards (as described in the next section).

Or maybe you receive PostScript files on a regular basis and need to change them into PDFs. Instead of opening and distilling each file individually, you can set a "watched" folder for all new files to be put into and have Distiller automatically convert them into PDFs. To set the watched folder, choose Settings→Watched Folder. This is where Distiller is quite powerful. You don't have to do the work—it's all done for you.

To distill a PostScript file:

1. From Acrobat, launch Distiller by choosing Advanced→Acrobat Distiller.

2. If you want to choose a setting other than the default, you must do this before opening the file. In Distiller, choose a different setting from the Default Settings pull-down menu (Figure 11-7).

3. Choose File→Open.

4. Locate the PostScript file and click Open. (You also can drag and drop a PostScript file onto the Distiller window.) The file will be converted.

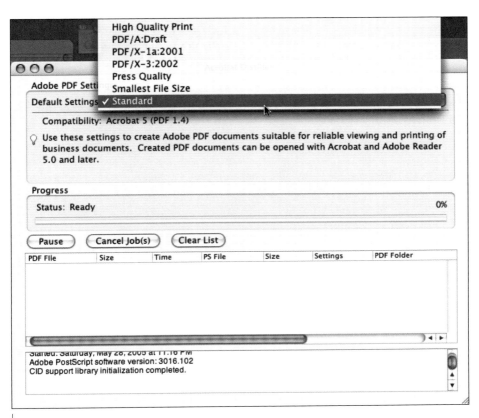

FIGURE 11-7

PDF Settings

If you use Distiller, you can ensure that your file prints just the way you want it to by creating a custom Adobe PDF setting. The PDF settings enable you to set how objects and images are compressed, whether fonts are embedded or not, the resolution, and more. To edit one of the predefined default settings or create your own PDF settings in Distiller, choose Settings→Edit Adobe PDF Settings or Add Adobe PDF Settings. The PDF settings you'll choose for your printed file are:

GENERAL: Enter values for Compatibility, Object Level Compression, Auto-Rotate Pages, Binding, Resolution, and Default Page Size; specify which pages to apply your settings to; and choose whether to Embed thumbnails and Optimize for fast web view.

IMAGES: For Color, Grayscale, and Monochrome images, choose a downsampling method and set the Compression/Image Quality.

FONTS: Choose values for Embed all fonts, Embed OpenType fonts, Subset embedded fonts when percent of characters used is less than (enter a value between 1 and 100%), and When embedding fails (choose Cancel job, Warn and Continue, or Ignore); and select which fonts to always and never embed.

COLOR: Enter information about your Adobe Color Settings, Color Management Policies, Working Spaces, and Device-Dependent Data.

ADVANCED: Select your desired Options and Document Structuring Conventions.

STANDARDS: Enter values for Standard Reporting and Compliance, If Neither TrimBox nor ArtBox are Specified, If BleedBox is Not Specified, and Default Values if Not Specified.

PDF/X Files

PDF/X standards were created for blind exchange of print-ready files. The PDF/X standard takes care of many common printing problems, such as font, color, and trapping issues. The many variations of the PDF/X standard are based on upgrades and changes to the PDF versions. The 2001 and 2002 standards are based on PDF 1.3, and 2003 standards are based on PDF 1.4. Before creating a PDF/X file, preflight the file; then fix any issues.

You can create a PDF/X file using the Preflight dialog box, as discussed in the "PDF/X Support" section in Chapter 10, or you can use Distiller. Distiller cannot process PDF or JDF files, so you'll have to start with a PostScript file (which you can create in Acrobat or any of the other Creative Suite applications). Before you open the file in Distiller, choose the appropriate PDF/X setting for conversion from the Default Settings pull-down menu.

JDF Files

As discussed in Chapter 10, the JDF file is the control for the entire print production work-flow. In the JDF Job Definitions dialog box, click the Submit button to convert all your PostScript files to PDF using the settings in your JDF file. Acrobat then either gives you a final file as a MIME, or uploads the file to the printer directly. (If you are a printer, you can create a JDF template to send to your customers to ensure problem-free printing.)

**Here are the most important things to take away
from this chapter:**

1. Understand the difference between native and PDF file formats: a native format is an original application file format; PDF is the industry standard format for file exchange.

2. Use Acrobat's Print Production tools to prepare your files to be sent to the printer.

3. Preflight, preflight, preflight... need I say more?

4. Use Distiller for better control over PDF creation and for converting PostScript files to PDF.

5. Use custom PDF settings or JDF files to ensure better control over your printed file.

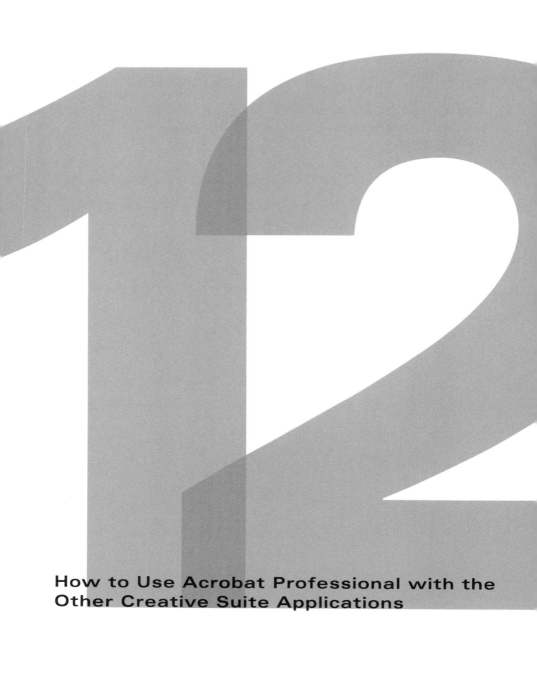

12

How to Use Acrobat Professional with the
Other Creative Suite Applications

Many people want one application to be the be-all, end-all program that will do everything they need. Can you imagine such a program, though? It would be way too overwhelming and hard to learn. That's why Adobe makes multiple products to fit everyone's needs. But when you use the products together, you have that be-all, end-all... Creative Suite 2.

Acrobat is where you bring together the work you've done in the other CS2 applications. Use Acrobat to create multipage documents, make slideshow presentations using Photoshop and Illustrator images, send files for review and commenting, and finally, preflight your PDF files to ensure a smooth printing workflow.

COMBINING MULTIPLE ILLUSTRATOR PAGES INTO A SINGLE DOCUMENT WITH ACROBAT

Extra! Extra! Read all about it! You can use Acrobat to achieve that often-desired goal of combining Illustrator files into a multipage document. Because Illustrator lacks the capability to create multipage documents (think newsletters, CD covers, and more), here is a perfect instance of how you can use the Adobe Creative Suite 2 products together.

Sure, you can use InDesign to create multiple-page layouts with your Illustrator files, but if you don't need to add anything in InDesign, why not use Acrobat instead? You can use Acrobat' s Create PDF→From Multiple Files option to create the PDF file in one step, instead of first placing the files in InDesign to create the PDF and then opening it in Acrobat. Acrobat is a powerful program that you can use for all your PDF needs.

To create a PDF from multiple files:

1. In Acrobat, choose File→Create PDF→From Multiple Files. (Alternatively, use the Create PDF tab in the menu bar at the top of the screen.) This launches the Create PDF from Multiple Documents dialog box.

2. In the Add Files area, click the Browse/Choose button to locate the files you want to add.

3. In the Open dialog box, choose a file and click the Add button. If you want to add multiple contiguous/adjacent files from the same folder, click the first item in the block, and then Shift-click the last item to select everything in between. To add non-contiguous files in a folder, hold down the Command (Mac) or Ctrl (Windows) key as you click each one. Each selected file will show up in the Create PDF from Multiple Documents dialog box (Figure 12-1).

4. Repeat the preceding step until you have selected all of the files you want to include in your new PDF document.

5. In the Arrange Files area, you can delete or rearrange the files. You can also rearrange and delete the files after the combined file is made.

6. Preview the file if desired, then click OK. Acrobat combines all of the files and launches the Save As dialog box so that you can give the new file a name.

You now have a multipage document containing all of your Illustrator files. Now that you have all the files in one document, you can use the Pages tab on the left side to rearrange the files—simply drag and drop one page above or below another page (Figure 12-2).

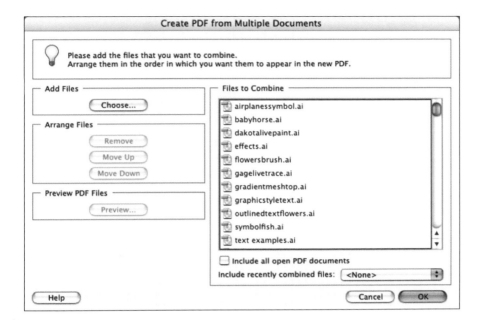

FIGURE 12-1

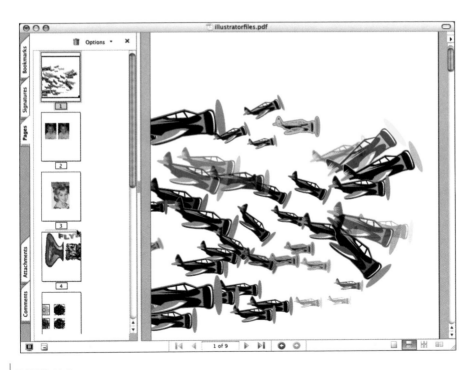

FIGURE 12-2

What else can you do with your new PDF? Well, by using Acrobat's Add Headers & Footers dialog box, you can add headers, footers, and page numbers to your project, all in one easy step.

To add headers, footers, and page numbers:

1. Choose Document→Add Headers & Footers.

2. Across the top of the Add Headers & Footers dialog box, locate the three panes that relate to where the header appears: flush left, center, or flush right. Enter the Header information directly in the area where you want it to appear. In Figure 12-3, I added my name as a Header in the center of the page. The font is Papyrus, and the size is 18 points.

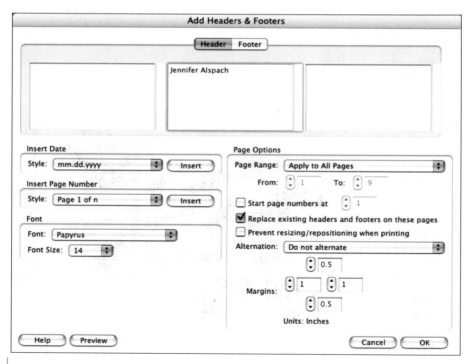

FIGURE 12-3

3. To add a footer, click on the Footer tab. Enter the footer information in the area where you want it to appear (flush left, center, or flush right). I entered "Portfolio" as a centered footer for this portfolio mailing.

4. To add the date to a header or footer, choose the Header or Footer tab, and then click in a pane to choose a location. If you already have text there, you can add the date beside the existing text or press the Return/Enter key to add the type below the initial text. Choose a date format from the pop-up menu under Insert Date.

5. Click the Insert button to insert the date.

6. To add page numbers to the footer, click the Footer tab. Click in a pane to choose the page number location, and then choose a page number format from the pop-up menu under Insert Page Number.

7. Click the Insert button to insert the page number. At any time while adding the headers and footers, you can click the Preview button at the bottom left of the Add Headers & Footers dialog box to see what the headers and footers will look like (Figure 12-4).

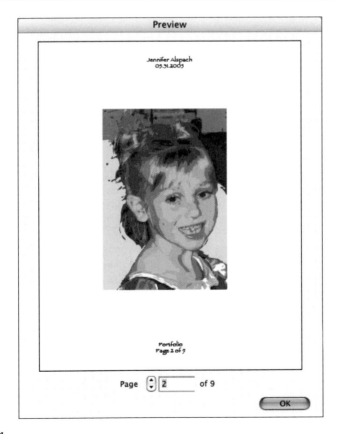

FIGURE 12-4

8. In the Page Options section, you can choose to apply the header and footer to all pages or pick a specific page range. Here, you also can set the starting page number, replace existing headers and footers on these pages, prevent resizing/repositioning when printing, set alternation (even or odd pages), and set margins. After you have entered all your information, click OK.

CREATING A SLIDESHOW IN ACROBAT WITH PHOTOSHOP IMAGES

One of the little-used features of Acrobat is the capability to create a slideshow presentation. This can be useful for displaying your work to clients or sending photos to your family. A slideshow is a great way to send a presentation, because the recipient can use the free Adobe Reader program to view it.

Acrobat can import many different types of files to change into PDFs: BMP, Compuserve GIF, HTML, JDF Job Description, JPEG, JPEG 2000, PCX, Pict, PNG, PostScript/EPS, Text, and TIFF files. You also can create a PDF directly from Microsoft Word.

To create a slideshow, first you need to create the PDF from multiple files. You can use this method of combining files even if they are already PDFs. After you have combined the files, you can set the preferences for the slideshow.

To set the slideshow preferences:

1. Open the Preferences dialog box by choosing Acrobat Preferences (Mac) or File Preferences (Windows). Alternatively, press Command-K (Mac) or Ctrl-K (Windows).

2. In the Preferences dialog box, choose Full Screen from the Categories listing on the left.

3. In the Full Screen Navigation section, indicate how long to display each slide (in seconds), whether to loop at the end of the slideshow, whether to allow viewers to press the Escape key to exit the slideshow and to left-click to go forward and right-click to go back, and whether to display the navigation bar.

4. In the Full Screen Appearance section, you can specify how to transition between slides, or to ignore all transitions. You also can set how the mouse cursor displays, and choose a background color for the slideshow (Figure 12-5).

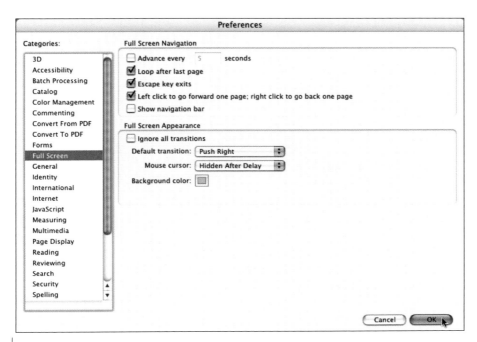

FIGURE 12-5

---

5. Click OK when you're finished.

6. Choose View→Full Screen or press Command-L (Mac) or Ctrl-L (Windows) to see the slideshow (Figure 12-6).

FIGURE 12-6

Use transitions wisely—you don't want them to take away from what you're present-ing. Flashier transitions such as the Blinds and Glitter options can distract viewers from the actual content of the presentation, and they're likely to wear thin after a while. Also, although random transitions can be fun to use, a cleaner presentation tends to use a consistent transition for all of the pages.

tip   You also can set transitions by choosing Document→Set Page Transitions.

SENDING AN INDESIGN FILE FOR COMMENTING AND REVIEWING WITH ACROBAT

Acrobat is the best application to use for sending out files for reviewing and commenting, as well as for final distribution. With Acrobat, you can turn a file (say, a magazine article that you created in InDesign) into a PDF, and then send the file to your client or another reviewer via email.

Sending a File for Review

So you need to send your InDesign file out for comments before finalizing the project for your client? With Acrobat, you can do just that. From InDesign, choose File→Print, and then choose Adobe PDF 7.0 from the Printer pop-up menu. This will create a PDF file from your InDesign file. Now the file is ready to bring into Acrobat to send for review. (Alterna-tively, in Acrobat, you can choose File→Create PDF→From File to create a PDF from the native Illustrator file.)

To send a PDF for review via email:

1. Choose Comments→Send for Review→Send by Email for Review. This launches the Send by Email for Review wizard, which takes you step by step through the emailing process.

2. The current PDF will show up as the default PDF file to send. If you don't want to use that file, click the Choose button to locate a different PDF.

3. Click the Next button. If the file is larger than 5 MB, you'll get a warning message that the file is large and may not email correctly.

4. Enter the email addresses of the reviewers. You also can access your Address Book to add reviewers.

5. Choose Customize Review Options to launch the Review Options dialog box.

6. In the Review Options dialog box, set the email address to which you want the review-ers to respond. Select the "Display Drawing Markup Tools for this review" and "Also allow users of Free Adobe Reader 7.0 to participate in this review" checkboxes. The latter option allows people with Adobe Reader to access the commenting tools. Click OK.

7. Click the Next button.

8. Preview the text or wording that will be sent with the invitation for review, and add to the Invitation Message. Click Send Invitation to launch your email program, so you can actually send the file for review (see Figure 12-7).

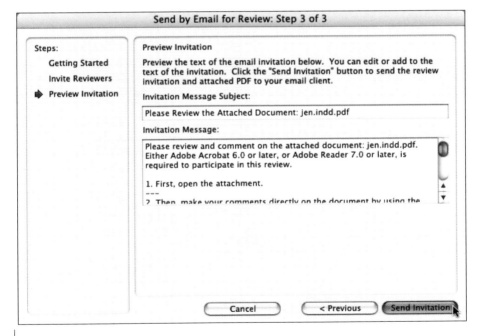

FIGURE 12-7

Commenting on a Document

Let's say you're the lucky reviewer of this PDF file. Now you need to comment on the file. In the Commenting toolbar, you'll find these tools:

NOTE: Adds collapsible boxes so that you can enter text notes in a specific document area.

TEXT EDITS: Allows you to enter comments right on the PDF, in the form of replacing, highlighting, or inserting text.

DRAWING MARKUPS: Used to add callouts, lines, shapes, rectangles, and circles (see below).

STAMPS: Used to imprint standard business, dynamic, and custom stamps to get your message across.

HIGHLIGHTS: Adds text effects such as underline, strikethrough, and highlight.

ATTACH FILE AS A COMMENT: Used to add a recorded sound or a specific file to a PDF.

SHOW: Lets you see a reviewer's comments on the PDF file you are reviewing.

All of this seems pretty straightforward—but wait, there's more. For the adventuresome reviewer, there are advanced commenting tools that you can use as well. To display the Drawing Markups toolbar, choose Tools→Drawing Markups→Show Drawing Markups Toolbar (or use the Comment & Markup tab in the menu bat at the top of the screen). The Drawing Markups tools are:

CALLOUT: Used to add a leader line attached to callout text that you enter.

CLOUD: Converts the lines you draw into a puffy cloud shape.

DRAWING TOOLS: Includes the Arrow, Pencil, Pencil Eraser, Rectangle, Oval, Line, and Polygon tools, which you can use for your comments.

DIMENSIONING: Lets you add dimension lines to a PDF.

TEXT BOX: Allows you to add comments directly on the PDF rather than with a collapsible note.

Now that you get the gist of the tools, you can add comments to the PDF you received for review.

1. From the Commenting toolbar (Comment & Markup→Show Commenting Toolbar), choose the Note tool.

2. Drag out a box in which to enter your text.

3. On the note, enter the information that you want to convey. As you enter your text, you can see how the note will look when fully expanded. You can drag the box to any size you want, as shown in Figure 12-8.

FIGURE 12-8

4. Click the close button (the X) in the upper-right corner of the box to collapse the note.

tip

You can change the color, icon, and opacity of the note by accessing the contextual menu and choosing Properties. To access the contextual menu, Ctrl-click (Mac) or right-click (Windows) in the note box. In the Note Properties dialog box, click the color swatch to change the color, choose a different icon from the list, and/or drag the Opacity slider to totally change the look of your note (Figure 12-9).

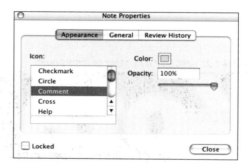

FIGURE 12-9

After you have commented on the file, you'll need to send it back to the reviewer. If you have Acrobat Professional or Standard, you can export your comments and then email the *.fdf* file (FDF stands for File Definition Format, which is used for sending comments and forms). If you are the initiator of the review, when you receive the *.fdf* file, you can choose Comments→Import Comments to incorporate the comments from all of your reviewers into your original PDF document. You also can choose to export comments from the Comments menu. Now you can make the appropriate changes before you present the file to your client.

PREFLIGHTING PDFS FROM ILLUSTRATOR AND PHOTOSHOP

Preflight is the powerful command that looks for potential problems in your PDF file so that you can fix any errors before you send your file to the printer. InDesign has a Preflight command included, but to preflight Illustrator or Photoshop files, you'll need to use Acrobat. This is a win-win situation, because many printers accept PDF files for printing. For more information on preflighting in Acrobat, see Chapter 10. (Because GoLive deals with web pages that are not bound for a printer, there is no need to preflight files created in GoLive.)

To access Acrobat's preflighting tools, choose Advanced→Preflight (or choose the Pre-flight button from the Print Production toolbar). The Preflight menu provides a variety of preset profiles to choose from. Some of the profiles include:

- Compliant with PDF/A (Draft)
- Digital press (B/W)
- Digital press (color)
- Magazine Ads
- Newspaper Ads
- PDF/X-1a:2001 compliant
- PDF/X-1a:2003 compliant
- PDF/X-3:2002 compliant
- PDF/X-3:2003 compliant
- Sheetfed offset (CMYK and spot colors)
- Sheetfed offset (CMYK and spot colors, medium res.)
- Sheetfed offset (CMYK)
- Web offset (cold set, CMYK, medium res.)
- Web offset (cold set, CMYK and spot colors)

If you don't see a preset profile that fits the bill, choose Edit from the Preflight dialog box and either click the New icon to create a new profile with all of the settings you want, or select a preset to base your settings on and click the Edit icon to modify it.

To preflight a file for a magazine ad:

1. If the file is a PDF, open the file in Acrobat. If the file is not a PDF, choose File→Create PDF→From File and then open the PDF.

2. Choose Advanced→Preflight. This launches the Preflight dialog box.

3. Choose Magazine Ads from the Profiles listing.

4. If you don't want to preflight the entire document, select the "Preflight only pages" box and enter a page range.

5. Click the Execute button to start. Once completed, the results display in the Results pane. To see more information about the results, click on the arrows (Figure 12-10).

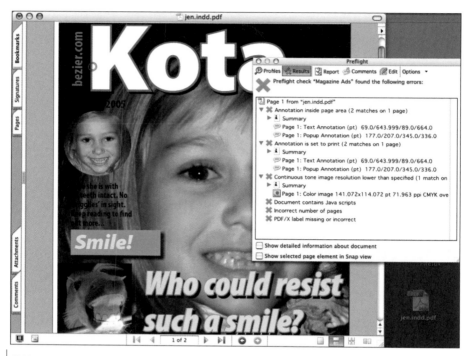

FIGURE 12-10

After you have preflighted the file, use Acrobat's print production tools to fix any errors. (For more on the print production tools, see Chapter 11.) After you have fixed all of the errors, it's a good idea to run Preflight again, just to be sure you fixed everything you needed to and didn't introduce any new problems.

Here are the most important things to take away from this chapter:

1. Acrobat brings together work done in the other Creative Suite 2 products.

2. Acrobat can be used to create multiple-page PDFs from Illustrator (and other) documents.

3. You can create an amazing slideshow presentation using Acrobat.

4. With Acrobat, you can send out a PDF created from any program for review and commenting.

5. Use Acrobat to preflight Illustrator and Photoshop documents.

Top 15 How Do I...? Acrobat Questions

In this chapter, you will find the answers to the top 15 questions designers ask about Acrobat. These most commonly asked questions were compiled from questions asked in the Acrobat forums and posed to the Acrobat product team. If you have a specific problem or are looking to improve your skills, the step-by-step solutions included here should help. You'll find tips that will save you time, strengthen your creativity, and much more.

HOW DO I CREATE A POSTSCRIPT FILE?

You may be wondering why you would want to create a PostScript file at all. Well, Post-Script has many benefits. As an example, let's say you've created a Photoshop image. Because Photoshop images are pixel-based, they can create a serious printing problem referred to as "jaggies"—if the image is printed at a larger scale, the individual pixels start to show, creating a jagged-edge effect. PostScript defines the image by a mathematical equation (or, in actuality, a programming language) instead of by the pixels, which creates a smoother edge and eliminates the jagged-edge problem.

To create a PostScript file:

1. In any application, choose File→Print, click the PDF button, and choose Save PDF as PostScript.

2. Under the Output Options pull-down menu, check "Print to file" (Figure 13-1).

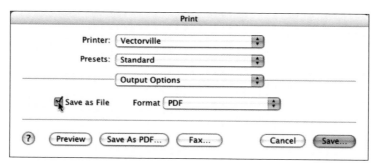

FIGURE 13-1

3. Select PostScript from the Format pull-down menu options (Figure 13-2).

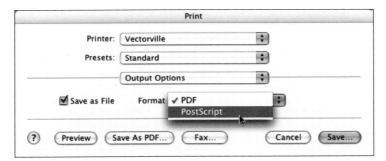

FIGURE 13-2

4. Click the Save button.

5. In the Save to File dialog box, enter a name and choose a location in which to save the PostScript file. Click Save.

6. The PostScript file is now saved in the location you have chosen. You can tell that the file is now a PostScript file by the "ps" that displays as part of the file icon (Figure 13-3).

FIGURE 13-3

HOW DO I DISTILL A POSTSCRIPT FILE SO I CAN OPEN IT IN ACROBAT?

After you have created a PostScript file, you need to distill the file so you can open it in Acrobat. The ability to distill PostScript files comes in handy when you have clients that don't have PDF drivers to create PDFs, or when you are printing to a PostScript printer. Because all applications have the Print command, you can always print a PostScript file and then use Distiller to convert the PostScript file into a PDF.

1. Launch Acrobat Distiller from Acrobat by choosing Advanced→Acrobat Distiller (or double-click the Acrobat Distiller icon found in the Adobe Acrobat 7.0 Professional folder on your computer). This launches the Acrobat Distiller window (Figure 13-4).

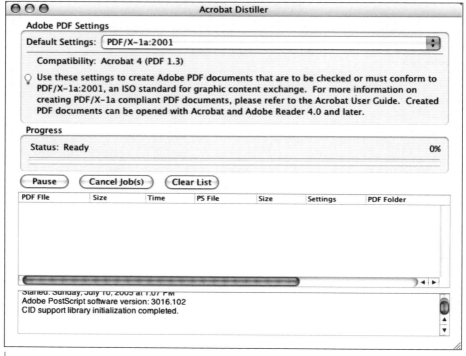

FIGURE 13-4

2. From the Default Settings pop-up, choose a setting for your file. When you select a setting, a description of that setting displays (Figure 13-5).

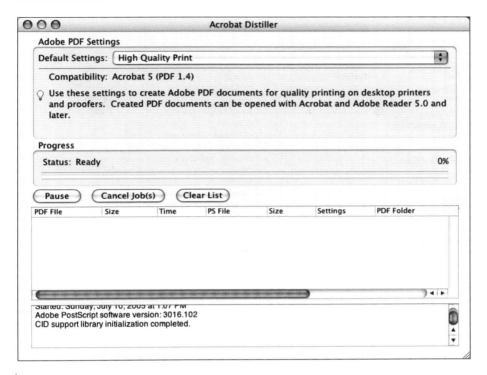

FIGURE 13-5

3. Choose File→Open and locate the PostScript file you want to convert. Notice that information about the file is listed in the right side of the Open dialog box (Figure 13-6).

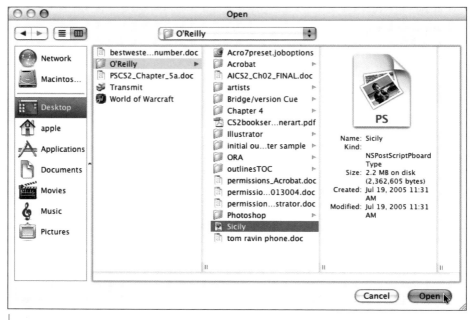

FIGURE 13-6

4. Click the Open button. The file will be converted immediately. The status will be displayed in the Progress area of the Acrobat Distiller window (Figure 13-7).

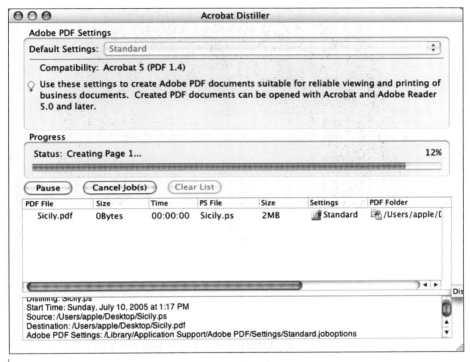

FIGURE 13-7

5. In Acrobat, choose File→Open. Locate your distilled file, which now has a *.pdf* extension.

6. Click Open to see your file. Notice that although the image in Figure 13-8 looks like a regular photograph, the extension in the titlebar indicates that the file is a PDF.

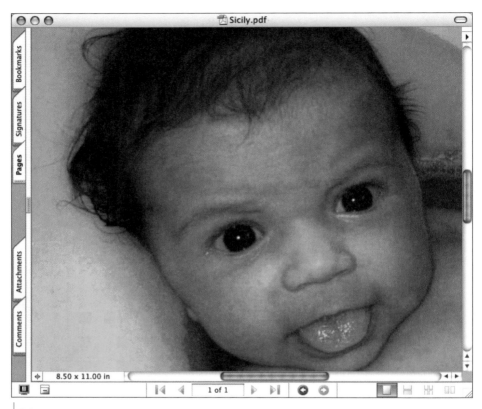

FIGURE 13-8

HOW DO I CREATE A JDF FILE?

A Job Definition Format (JDF) file describes how to prepare a file for printing. You may be wondering what is different about JDF and PDF/X files. JDF takes the printing preparation a step further by including the preflight profile, number of copies for the job, binding settings, section information, page size, page orientation, scaling, inks used, and so on. Additionally, the JDF file provides a job ticket for the project for which you are creating the file.

1. In Acrobat, open the PDF file that you are sending to print and choose Tools→Print Pro-
   duction→JDF Job Definitions. This launches the JDF Job Definitions dialog box (Figure
   13-9).

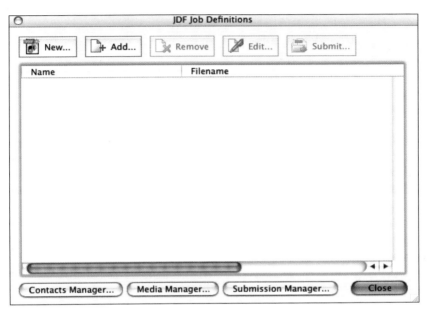

FIGURE 13-9

2. Click the New button to create a new JDF file. This launches the Create New Job Definition dialog box.

3. Specify whether the file is based on a new file, the current document, or a different job
   definition.

4. Enter a filename for the JDF file.

5. Click the Create and Edit button (Figure 13-10). This launches the Edit JDF Job Definition dialog box, which you can use to enter more information about the JDF file.

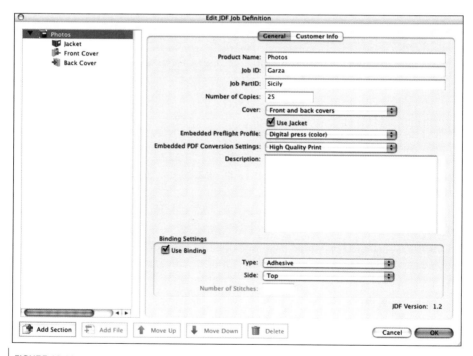

Create New Job Definition

Based on

- ⦿ New
- ○ Based on the document:
- ○ Based on the job definition:

JDF Version `1.2`

An empty job definition will be created

Filename

`Garza`   [Choose...]

Current Directory: /Users/apple/Documents

(Create and Edit...)   (Cancel) (**Create**)

FIGURE 13-10

6. Enter values in the Product Name, Job ID, Job PartID, Number of Copies, Cover, Embedded Preflight Profile, Embedded PDF Conversion Settings, Description, and Binding Settings areas (Figure 13-11).

Edit JDF Job Definition

▼ 🖭 Photos
  🔲 Jacket
  📑 Front Cover
  📑 Back Cover

[General] [Customer Info]

Product Name: `Photos`

Job ID: `Garza`

Job PartID: `Sicily`

Number of Copies: `25`

Cover: `Front and back covers`

☑ Use Jacket

Embedded Preflight Profile: `Digital press (color)`

Embedded PDF Conversion Settings: `High Quality Print`

Description:

Binding Settings

☑ Use Binding

Type: `Adhesive`

Side: `Top`

Number of Stitches:

JDF Version: 1.2

[📝 Add Section] [📄 Add File] [⬆ Move Up] [⬇ Move Down] [🗑 Delete]   (Cancel) (**OK**)

FIGURE 13-11

7. To divide the file into sections, choose the Add Section button at the bottom of the Edit JDF Job Definition dialog box. You'll want to do this if you have a file with different page settings, media, and inks, so that you can specify more information for the individual sections. The new section will appear on the left side of the Edit JDF Job Definition dialog box (Figure 13-12). On the right, you'll be able to include additional information such as the Section Name, Number of Pages, and Page and Media settings.

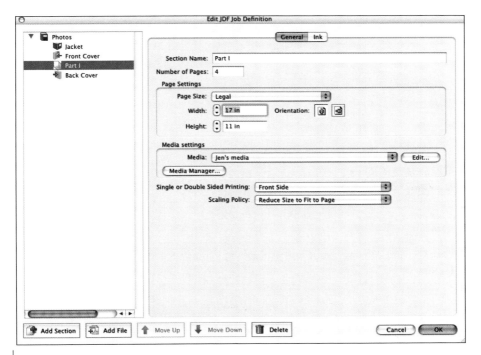

FIGURE 13-12

8. When you've entered the necessary information for any sections you've added, click Product at the top of the left pane, and then click the Customer Info tab to add customer information for this file (Figure 13-13). This includes such information as the Billing Code, Customer ID, Customer Job, Customer Order ID, and Contacts.

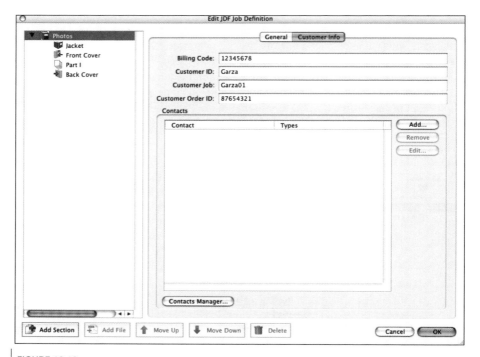

FIGURE 13-13

9. Click OK, and you'll see your new JDF setting in the JDF Job Definitions dialog box (Figure 13-14).

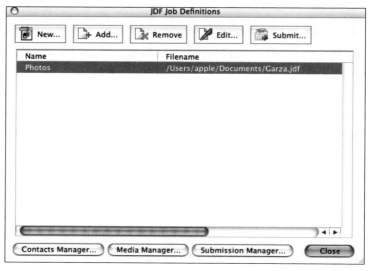

FIGURE 13-14

After you create a JDF file, you'll need to create a submission setup and then submit the file. For more information on creating a submission setup and submitting a file, see "JDF Support" in Chapter 10.

HOW DO I MODIFY A PDF PRESET?

Acrobat comes with a variety of PDF presets, but these won't always be exactly what you're looking for. Maybe the preset you need for a particular project is slightly different from one that's offered, or maybe you want to permanently change an existing preset. Let's say you've reviewed all of the presets that come with Acrobat 7.0 Professional and can't find one that's appropriate. In this case, you can simply modify one of the existing presets to create your own custom preset—using Distiller, you can choose your own PDF settings.

[NOTE]

On a Mac, you can find the preset files at \Library\Application Support\Adobe PDF\Settings. On Windows, you can find them at C:\Documents and Settings\All Users\Documents\Adobe PDF\Settings.

To edit a PDF preset:

1. Launch Distiller (Advanced→Acrobat Distiller).

2. From the Default Settings pop-up menu, choose a base setting from which to create your custom setting. In this example, I chose the Standard setting.

3. Choose Settings→Edit Adobe PDF Settings. This launches the Adobe PDF Settings: Standard dialog box (Figure 13-15).

4. Under the General tab, enter your file options (Figure 13-16). Also, choose your default page size.

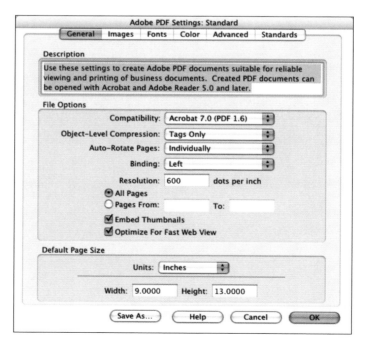

FIGURE 13-15

FIGURE 13-16

5. Under the Images tab, choose your settings for Color Images, Grayscale Images, and Monochrome Images (Figure 13-17).

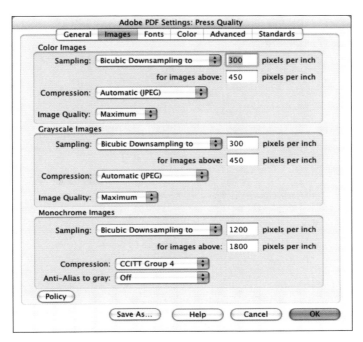

FIGURE 13-17

6. Clicking the Policy button (toward the bottom of the dialog box) brings up the default policies for color, grayscale, and monochrome images. Choose from Ignore, Warn and continue, or Cancel job for an image resolution below a specified pixels per inch setting (Figure 13-18). Click OK after entering the resolution to return to the Adobe PDF Settings: Standard dialog box.

7. Choose the Fonts tab to access options for embedding fonts (Figure 13-19). Set your embedding options and indicate what to do when embedding fails. You can select fonts in the Embedding area on the left to add to the Always Embed Font and Never Embed Font areas on the right.

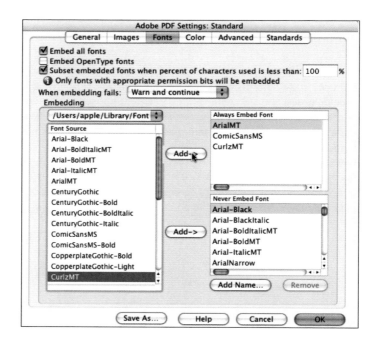

FIGURE 13-18

FIGURE 13-19

8. Click the Color tab to include your Adobe Color Settings and Device-Dependent Data settings (Figure 13-20).

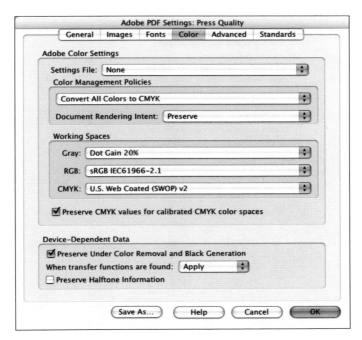

FIGURE 13-20

9. Click the Advanced tab to access the more advanced options. You can choose from a variety of Options and Document Structuring Conventions, as shown in Figure 13-21.

10. Finally, on the Standards tab, specify your preferred settings for the Standard Reporting and Compliance, If NeitherTrimBox nor ArtBox are Specified, If BleedBox is Not Specified, and DefaultValues if Not Specified in the Document areas (Figure 13-22).

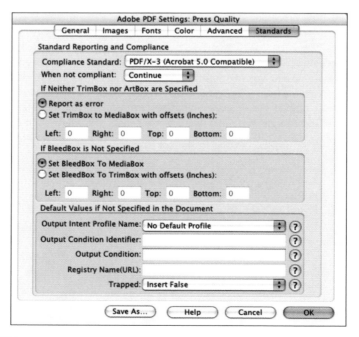

Adobe PDF Settings: Standard

General | Images | Fonts | Color | **Advanced** | Standards

Options

☑ Allow PostScript file to override Adobe PDF Settings
☑ Allow PostScript XObjects
☑ Convert gradients to smooth shades
☑ Convert smooth lines to curves
☑ Preserve Level 2 copypage semantics
☑ Preserve Overprint Settings
  ☑ Overprinting default is nonzero overprinting
☐ Save Adobe PDF Settings inside PDF file
☑ Save original JPEG images in PDF if possible
☐ Save Portable Job Ticket inside PDF file
☐ Use Prologue.ps and Epilogue.ps
☐ Create Job Definition Format (JDF) file

Document Structuring Conventions (DSC)

☑ Process DSC comments
  ☐ Log DSC warnings
  ☐ Preserve EPS information from DSC
  ☐ Preserve OPI comments
  ☑ Preserve document information from DSC
  ☑ Resize page and center artwork for EPS files

(Save As...)   (Help)   (Cancel)   (**OK**)

FIGURE 13-21

Adobe PDF Settings: Press Quality

General | Images | Fonts | Color | Advanced | **Standards**

Standard Reporting and Compliance

Compliance Standard: PDF/X-3 (Acrobat 5.0 Compatible) ▼
When not compliant: Continue ▼

If Neither TrimBox nor ArtBox are Specified

◉ Report as error
◯ Set TrimBox to MediaBox with offsets (Inches):

Left: 0   Right: 0   Top: 0   Bottom: 0

If BleedBox is Not Specified

◉ Set BleedBox To MediaBox
◯ Set BleedBox To TrimBox with offsets (Inches):

Left: 0   Right: 0   Top: 0   Bottom: 0

Default Values if Not Specified in the Document

Output Intent Profile Name: No Default Profile ▼ (?)
Output Condition Identifier: (?)
Output Condition: (?)
Registry Name(URL): (?)
Trapped: Insert False ▼ (?)

(Save As...)   (Help)   (Cancel)   (**OK**)

FIGURE 13-22

11. When you have all your settings as you want them, click the Save As button at the bottom of the Adobe PDF Settings: Standard dialog box. This launches the Save dialog box.

12. Enter a name for your new preset, and click Save.

You will now be able to access your new custom preset under the Acrobat Distiller Default Settings pop-up menu, as shown in Figure 13-23.

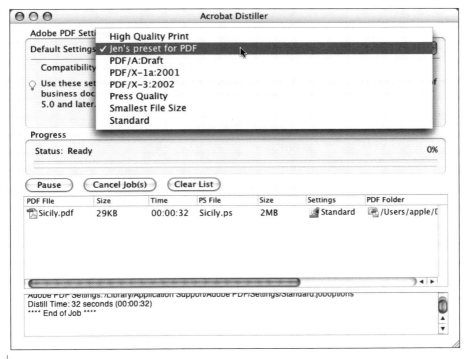

FIGURE 13-23

HOW DO I ADD OR REMOVE A PDF SETTING?

If you need to add a preset to your list, or you want to remove one that you no longer need from your already large list of presets, never fear—you can add and remove presets with relative ease.

To add a PDF setting:

1. In Distiller, choose Settings→Add Adobe PDF Settings. This launches the Add Adobe PDF Settings dialog box.

2. Locate the file you want to add—this file must include the *.joboptions* file extension— and click Open (Figure 13-24). The preset you added will now be available under the Default Settings pop-up.

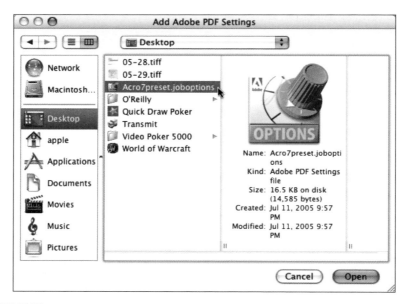

FIGURE 13-24

1. In Distiller, choose Settings→Remove Adobe PDF Settings. This launches the Select Adobe PDF Settings dialog box (Figure 13-25).

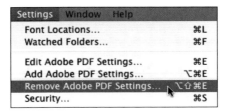

FIGURE 13-25

2. Select the PDF setting that you want to remove, and click the Remove button (Figure 13-26). There is no warning—the preset is removed immediately, so be sure you really want to remove the setting.

FIGURE 13-26

HOW DO I CREATE A FORM WITH DESIGNER?

Adobe LiveCycle Designer 7.0 is a program that lets you create a form—including both the design of the form and the actual form fields. Unfortunately, Designer is available only on Windows systems (it comes packaged with Adobe Acrobat 7.0 Professional). You can create your entire form from start to finish with Designer, but if you do so, you have to use

Designer to edit the form. You won't be able to use Acrobat for editing—when you design forms in Designer, you can only use Acrobat to create the form fields.

[NOTE]

Many people use Designer for the entire form creation process, but keep in mind that you can create the design of the form in any program and then save the file as a PDF. From Acrobat, you can create form fields to complete the process. This is an especially good option for Mac users.

To create a form with Designer:

1. Launch Adobe LiveCycle Designer, and choose New from Template in the Welcome screen. (Alternatively, you can click the close button in the Welcome screen and choose File→New.) This opens the New Form Assistant.

2. In the New Form Assistant, choose how you want to create the form (Figure 13-27). Pick New Blank Form, Based on a Template, Import a PDF Document, or Import a Word Document. I chose Based on a Template.

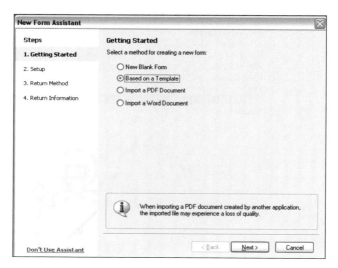

FIGURE 13-27

3. Click the Next button.

4. Choose from the large list of default templates, depending on the type of form you want to create. You can preview the form in the Preview window beside the list of default templates (Figure 13-28). I chose Customer Satisfaction Survey.

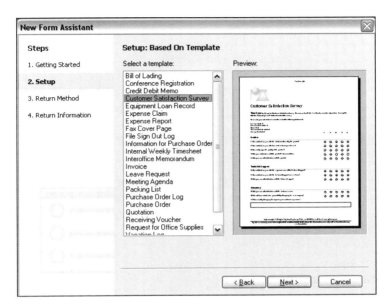

FIGURE 13-28

5. Click the Next button.

6. Choose how you want the form distributed and returned. Pick from Fill then Submit, Fill then Submit/Print, Fill then Print, or Print (Figure 13-29).

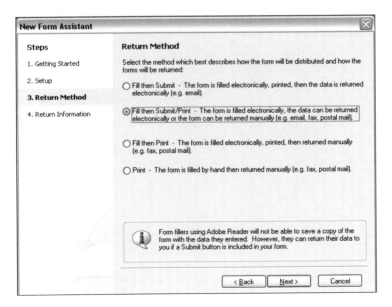

FIGURE 13-29

7. Click the Next button.

8. Enter the information for the return email address.

9. Click the Finish button to see your new form in the main window of Designer (Figure 13-30).

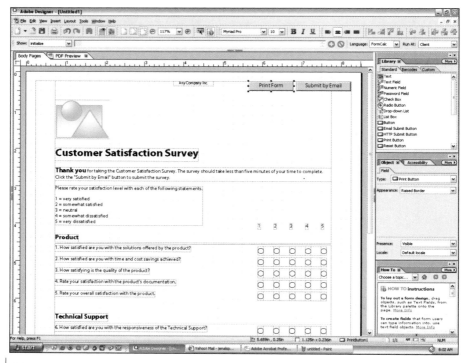

FIGURE 13-30

10. To save the file, choose File→Save As, enter the name and location, and click Save. Click the Print Preview tab in the Adobe Designer window to see the actual file without the coding (Figure 13-31).

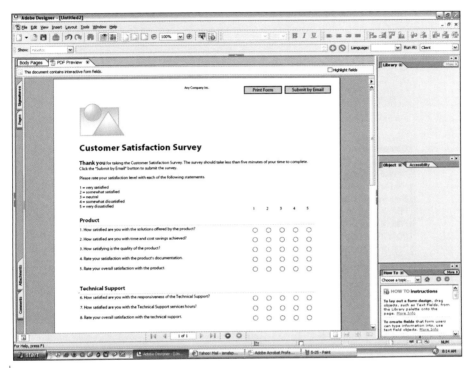

FIGURE 13-31

11. Open the file in Adobe Acrobat to enter the information for the form fields.

HOW DO I PREFLIGHT MY FILE FOR PRINTING?

Preflighting is a series of checks performed on a document to prepare it for printing. The Preflight commands were created based on the industry standards for PostScript printing. Acrobat provides a variety of preset profiles for you to choose from, depending on how you want your file printed. Preflighting is, at minimum, a three-part process: first you need to preflight the file to locate errors, then you need to correct any errors that are found (the PDF Optimizer is a great tool for this purpose), and then you need to run Preflight again to make sure that the corrections were successful and that no further errors have been introduced.

1. In Acrobat, open your document and choose Advanced→Preflight. This launches the Preflight dialog box.

2. Choose a Preflight profile from the list (Figure 13-32). I chose Digital press (color) for this example.

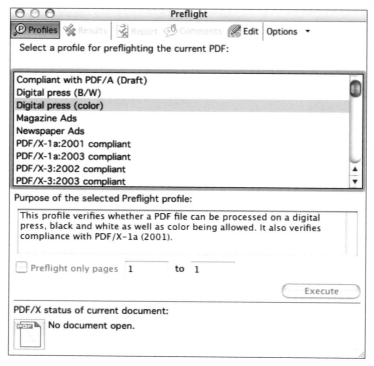

FIGURE 13-32

3. Click the Execute button to start the preflighting process. Figure 13-33 shows the progress as Preflight scans and checks the file for any potential errors for printing this file to a digital color printer.

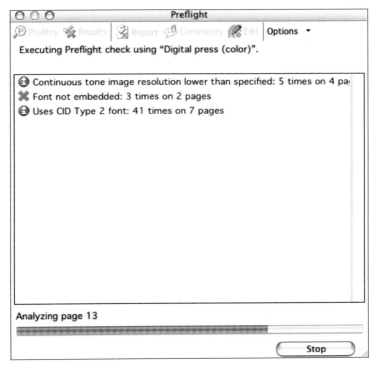

FIGURE 13-33

4. When the process is complete, any errors are displayed in the Results pane (Figure 13-34). Click Report at the top of the Preflight dialog box to create a printable report of the errors, or click Comments to see the errors displayed in the document as comments.

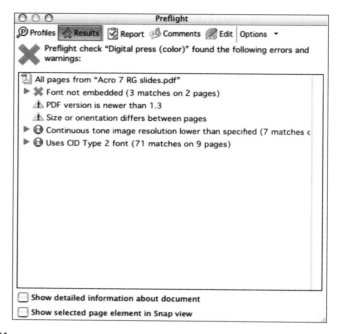

FIGURE 13-34

The next step is to correct any problems in the file, using Acrobat's print production tools (as discussed in Chapter 10). The PDF Optimizer (found under the Advanced menu or on the Print Production toolbar) is a great way to fix many of the problems you may encounter.

To optimize your PDF:

1. Choose Advanced→PDF Optimizer. This launches the PDF Optimizer dialog box.

2. Choose Images from the list on the left, and set your options for Color, Grayscale, and Monochrome images, as shown in Figure 13-35.

3. If you are using any scanned pages, set your options for Scanned Pages.

4. Under Fonts, you'll see a list of the document's embedded fonts (Figure 13-36). You can choose to Unembed certain fonts or to Retain fonts that were unembedded.

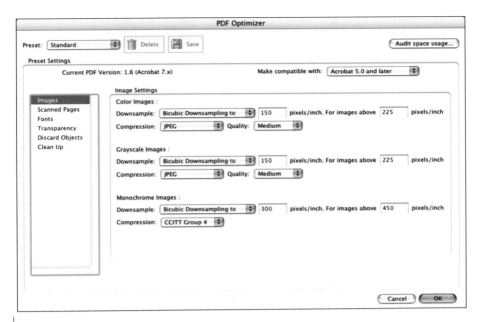

FIGURE 13-35

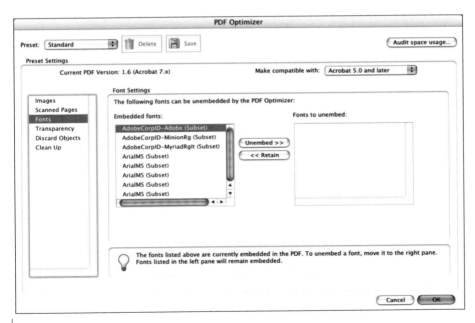

FIGURE 13-36

5. If the document uses any transparency, be sure to set the Transparency settings.

6. Under Discard Objects, choose the settings for removing unnecessary elements. This is a great way to reduce the file size.

7. Under Clean Up, choose a compression option, and then check or uncheck the various Clean Up options.

8. When you've customized your settings, click OK to run the PDF Optimizer on your document. This launches the Save Optimized As dialog box.

9. Enter a new name for the optimized file (or leave the original name if you want to overwrite the original), and then choose a location.

10. Click the Save button. You'll see the progress of the optimization at the bottom of the document (Figure 13-37).

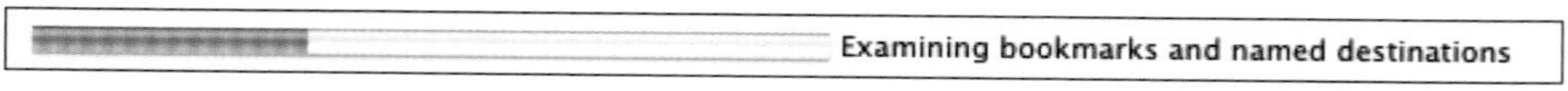

| ▓▓▓▓▓▓▓▓▓▓▓▓▓ | Examining bookmarks and named destinations |

FIGURE 13-37

Now, run Preflight again to make sure all of the errors have been fixed.

[NOTE]

For more on preflighting and optimizing your files, see Chapters 10 and 11.

HOW DO I SEND MY PDF FOR REVIEW VIA EMAIL?

Any file you create can be turned into a PDF, which you can then send to anyone for reviewing. It's true that not everyone has Acrobat 7.0 Professional, but anyone can download Acrobat Reader 7.0 for free from Adobe's web site (*http://www.Adobe.com*). When your file is ready to share with reviewers, convert the file into a PDF by choosing File→ Create PDF From File. You'll have to decide whether you want the reviewers to just look at the file or whether you want to enable them to make comments in the file.

1. Open your PDF and choose Comments→Send for Review→Send by Email for Review. This launches the Send by Email for Review Wizard (Figure 13-38).

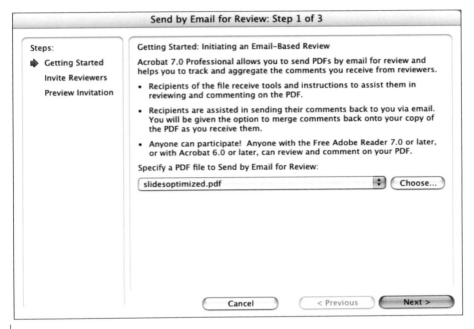

FIGURE 13-38

2. The current PDF will show up as the PDF to send. If that's the correct file, click the Next button. If not, click Choose, select the file you wish to send for review, and then click Next.

3. In the Invite Reviewers area, enter the reviewers' email addresses, or click the Address Book button to choose the reviewers from your address book.

4. If you want the reviewers to be able to add comments, click the Customize Review Options button. This launches the Review Options dialog box.

5. If you want to make the Drawing Markup tools available, check the "Display Drawing Markup Tools for this review" box (Figure 13-39). By default, the "Also allow users of Free Adobe Reader 7.0 to participate in this review" box is checked, which allows users of Adobe Reader 7.0 to comment and mark up the PDF file.

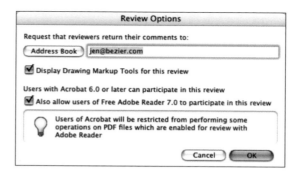

FIGURE 13-39

6. Click OK to exit the Review Options dialog box.

7. Click the Next button.

8. On the Preview Invitation screen, you can read the Invitation Message Subject and the Invitation Message (Figure 13-40). Feel free to edit either as you see fit.

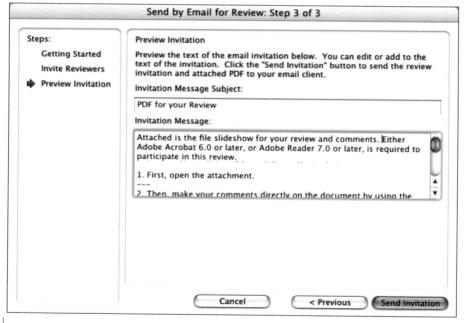

FIGURE 13-40

9. Click Send Invitation. Acrobat will automatically locate your email program, from which it will send the invitation (Figure 13-41).

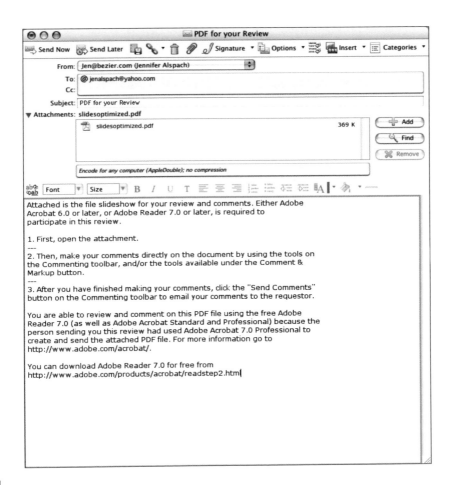

FIGURE 13-41

10. Acrobat will send you a message (Outgoing Message Notification) to notify you that a file was sent to your email program, and if your program is on a schedule, the email will be sent (Figure 13-42).

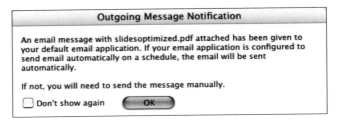

Outgoing Message Notification

An email message with slidesoptimized.pdf attached has been given to your default email application. If your email application is configured to send email automatically on a schedule, the email will be sent automatically.

If not, you will need to send the message manually.

☐ Don't show again   OK

FIGURE 13-42

11. Click OK.

After the reviewer receives the PDF, he or she can mark it up accordingly and email the file back to you. When you receive the marked-up file, you can incorporate the comments into your original PDF file (to do this, choose Comments→Import Comments and select the returned PDF).

[NOTE]

For more on sending files for commenting and review with Acrobat, see Chapter 12.

HOW DO I ADD COMMENTS TO MY PDF?

This is probably one of the most important tasks to tackle, because you can add many different types of comments to a PDF—from a simple note to a sound-recorded clip, Acrobat lets you do it all.

To add a note comment:

1. From the Comment and Markup button in the Tasks toolbar, choose Show Commenting Toolbar.

2. Click on the Note tool.

3. Click and drag a box out to the size you want the note to be (Figure 13-43).

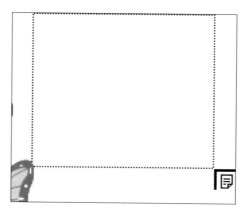

FIGURE 13-43

4. Enter the text in the note (Figure 13-44).

FIGURE 13-44

5. To collapse the note, click the X in its upper-right corner.

6. To open the note, double-click on the note icon with the Hand tool.

To change the note properties:

1. Click the Options arrow to activate the Note Options or Ctrl-click/right-click on the note to activate the context-sensitive menu.

2. Choose Properties from the context-sensitive menu (Figure 13-45). This launches the Note Properties dialog box.

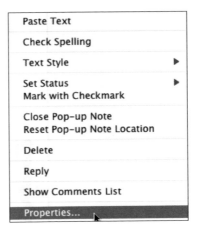

FIGURE 13-45

3. On the Appearance tab, you can change the note's color, icon, and opacity (Figure 13-46).

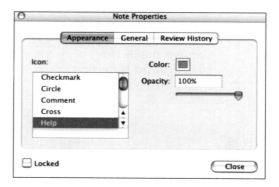

FIGURE 13-46

4. On the General tab, enter the author and subject information (Figure 13-47).

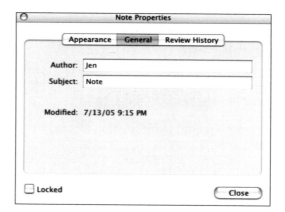

FIGURE 13-47

5. On the Review History tab, you can view any changes that have been made to this particular comment.

6. Click the Close button when you are done editing your note.

You can change the size of your note at any time, by dragging the lower-right corner diagonally to make it smaller or larger. You can also move the note by clicking on the top or bottom border and dragging it to another location.

1. Click the Text Edits button in the Commenting toolbar, and choose Indicate Text Edits Tool from the pop-up menu (Figure 13-48). This launches the Indicate Text Edits information box. Click OK to continue.

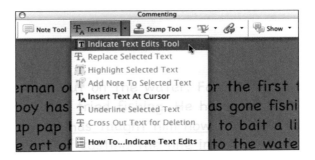

FIGURE 13-48

2. Click and drag a selection around the text you want to edit (Figure 13-49).

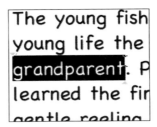

FIGURE 13-49

3. Choose a text edit from the Text Edits pop-up menu (Figure 13-50). I chose Replace Selected Text.

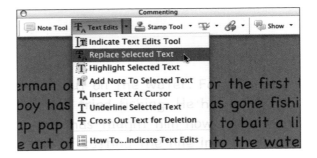

FIGURE 13-50

4. A note pops up for you to enter the replacement text, and you'll see that the selected text is now crossed out (Figure 13-51).

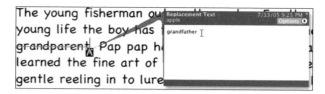

FIGURE 13-51

As if that weren't enough, you can make several other kinds of comments, too. You can add various stamps to a document; highlight, underline, or cross out text; and even add sound or movie clips or other files to your PDF—all of these options are available on the Commenting toolbar.

HOW DO I CREATE A PDF FROM A MICROSOFT WORD FILE?

You can't use Acrobat's Create PDF→From File command to convert a Microsoft Word document into a PDF, because .doc is not a supported file type—but amazingly, you *can* create a PDF directly from Word. When you install Adobe Acrobat 7.0 Professional, a plug-in is downloaded into Microsoft Word, enabling you to convert Word documents to PDF directly within the application. Keep in mind that you can't create a PDF from Microsoft 2001 or older versions, though.

To create a PDF from Microsoft Word:

1. Start Microsoft Word and open a document that you want to convert.

2. If the PDFMaker toolbar is not showing, choose View→Toolbars→Adobe Acrobat PDF-Maker.

3. Click the Convert to Adobe PDF button in the PDFMaker toolbar (Figure 13-52). If you haven't already saved the document, Acrobat PDFMaker will prompt you to save the document.

FIGURE 13-52

4. In the Save dialog box that displays, enter a name and location for your file (Figure 13-53).

FIGURE 13-53

5. Click Save to convert your file to a PDF.

Now you can open the file in Acrobat 7.

[NOTE]

The preceding steps can also be used to create a PDF from within Microsoft Excel and PowerPoint, as well as Internet Explorer. The PDFMaker plug-in that is installed with Acrobat 7.0 Professional supports Microsoft Word, Excel, PowerPoint, Visio, and Project; Internet Explorer for Windows; and Autodesk AutoCAD.

HOW DO I CONVERT A PDF BACK TO A MICROSOFT WORD FILE?

What do you do if you want to turn a PDF of a Microsoft Word file back into a Word document? Simple—use the Save As command in Acrobat 7.0 Professional. You can convert a PDF into any number of formats, including EPS, HTML, JPEG, Microsoft Word, PNG, PostScript, Rich Text Format, Text (Accessible), Text (Plain), TIFF, and XML 1.0.

To convert a PDF to a Microsoft Word document:

1. With the file open in Acrobat, choose File→Save As. This launches the Save As dialog box.

2. Select Microsoft Word Document from the Format pop-up menu (Figure 13-54).

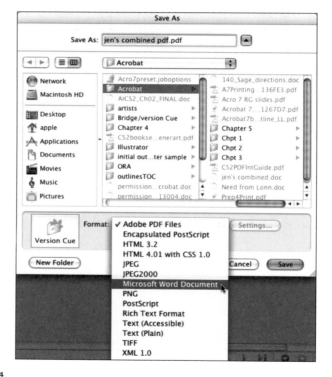

FIGURE 13-54

3. In Microsoft Word, open the document (Figure 13-55).

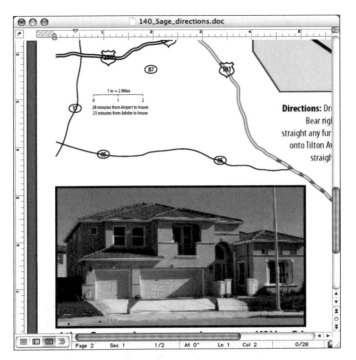

FIGURE 13-55

tip

You can also use the Save As command to convert a PDF into any of the other formats mentioned above—just select the desired format from the Format pop-up menu in the Save As dialog.

HOW DO I ADD A LINK TO MY PDF FILE?

With Acrobat 7.0 Professional, you can make your PDFs interactive by adding links and actions, such as opening a specified page when you click on a link. When it comes to adding content to your PDFs, you have many cool options—for example, you can add a link to another spot in the same PDF, to a different document, or to a web site, or you can include sound or video clips.

1. In Acrobat, open the PDF and go to the area of the document in which you want to place the link.

2. Choose Tools→Advanced Editing→Link Tool, or click on the Link tool in the Advanced Editing toolbar.

3. With the Link tool, drag out a rectangle the size of the area you want the users to click on to activate the link (Figure 13-56). When you let go of the mouse button, the Create Link dialog box is launched (Figure 13-57).

FIGURE 13-56

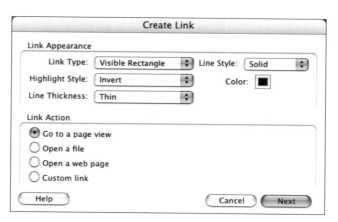

FIGURE 13-57

4. Choose the Link Type from the pop-up menu. This is how the link will appear (visible or invisible). If you choose Visible Rectangle, you can then set the Line Style, Highlight Style, Color, and Line Thickness.

5. Choose a Link Action (Go to a page view, Open a file, Open a web page, or Custom link). For this example, I chose Open a file.

6. Click the Next button.

7. This launches the Select File to Open dialog box. Locate the PDF you want to open when the link is clicked, and click Select.

8. This launches the Specify Open Preference dialog box. You can set windows to open in the existing window, to open in new window, or to use the preference that the user has set (Figure 13-58).

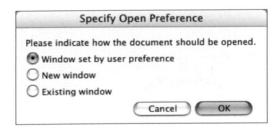

FIGURE 13-58

9. Click OK to set the link.

10. To activate the link, choose the Hand tool from the toolbar, and click on the rectangular link area (Figure 13-59). You are immediately taken to the linked file (Figure 13-60), which is set to open in a new window in this example.

FIGURE 13-59

FIGURE 13-60

To add a sound to a PDF:

1. Repeat steps 1–4 from the preceding section.

2. In the Create Link dialog box, set the options for how you want the link to look (Line Style, Highlight Style, Color, and Line Thickness).

3. Under Link Action, choose Custom link.

4. Click the Next button. This launches the Link Properties dialog box (Figure 13-61).

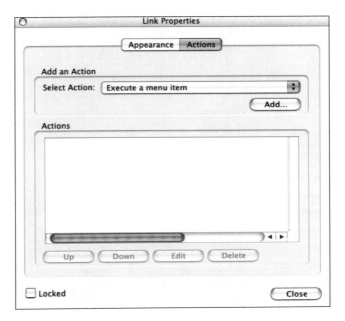

FIGURE 13-61

5. Click the Actions tab, and choose "Play a sound" from the Select Action pop-up (Figure 13-62).

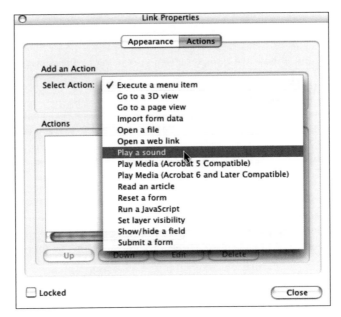

FIGURE 13-62

6. Click the Add button. This launches the Select Sound File dialog box.

7. Locate the sound you want to add, and click the Select button (Figure 13-63).

FIGURE 13-63

8. Click Close.

9. To play the sound, choose the Hand tool from the toolbar and click on the link.

HOW DO I SEE OVERPRINT AND OUTPUT PREVIEWS IN MY PDF?

When you proof your PDFs, one of the things you check for is overprinting. *Overprinting* is intentionally printing one layer of ink on top of another where two different colors overlap, eliminating any chance of a white gap appearing during printing. Overprinting offers trapping protection. Before sending any file to the printer, in addition to running Preflight and PDF Optimizer, you'll need to check for overprinting and preview your final file.

1. Choose Advanced→Overprint Preview (Figure 13-64). This turns on the Overprint Preview. Choosing it again turns off the Overprint Preview.

FIGURE 13-64

Output Preview, on the other hand, is a bit more involved. With Output Preview, you can
select which color plates you want to view and control the inks.

1. Choose Advanced→Output Preview (or choose Output Preview from the Print Production toolbar). This launches the Output Preview dialog box (Figure 13-65).

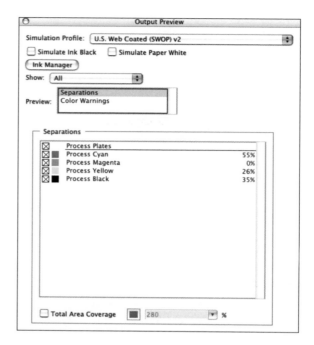

FIGURE 13-65

---

2. In the Preview box, select Separations.

---

3. To view only specific plates, click the X next to each of the plates you don't want to view. In Figure 13-66, I chose to view only Cyan and Magenta. You'll see the colors instantly in the PDF document.

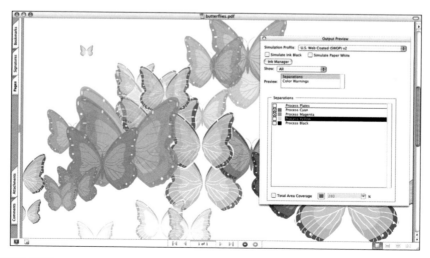

FIGURE 13-66

---

4. To see how the PDF will look printed on white paper, click the Simulate Paper White checkbox. You'll notice that the colors aren't quite as bright as you'd think (Figure 13-67).

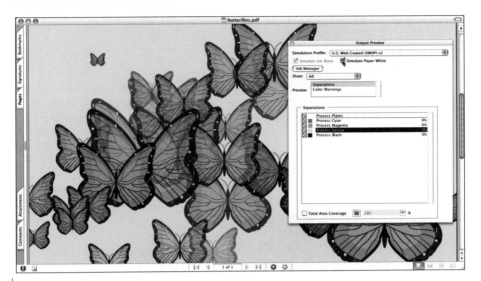

FIGURE 13-67

5. Click on the Ink Manager button to launch the Ink Manager dialog box (Figure 13-68).

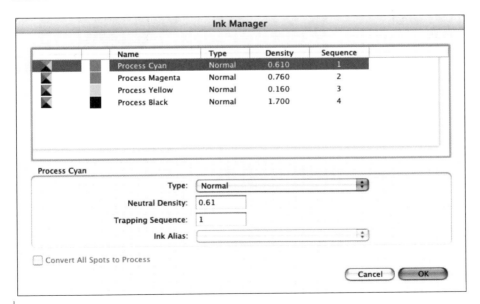

FIGURE 13-68

6. For each of the process colors, you can set the Type (Normal, Transparent, Opaque, or OpaqueIgnore), Neutral Density, Trapping Sequence, and Ink Alias. The trapping sequence is the order in which the colors are printed. The default sequence is Cyan 1, Magenta 2, Yellow 3, and Black 4, but you can change the order (you'll need to click a color box first). Also, if you have a spot color in your PDF, you can check the Convert All Spots to Process box.

7. Click OK to exit the Ink Manager.

8. To check the coverage of the colors, make sure Separations is selected in the Preview area, and rest the crosshairs of your cursor over your PDF. In the Separations area, you'll see the percentage of ink coverage for each color area you point to (Figure 13-69).

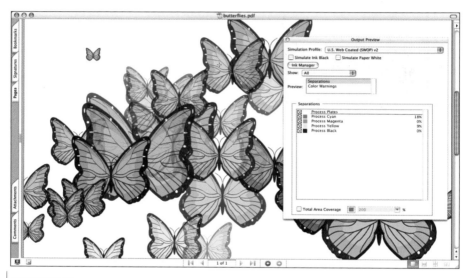

FIGURE 13-69

9. To exit the Output Preview dialog box, click the Close button.

HOW DO I CONVERT COLORS USING DISTILLER?

Acrobat Distiller, that useful tool for converting PostScript files to PDF, is also a powerful color converter for your documents. While you are converting a document to PDF, you can convert the colors as well.

To convert colors using Distiller:

1. In Distiller (Advanced→Acrobat Distiller), choose the PDF setting you want to use from the pop-up Default Settings menu (Figure 13-70). I chose High Quality Print.

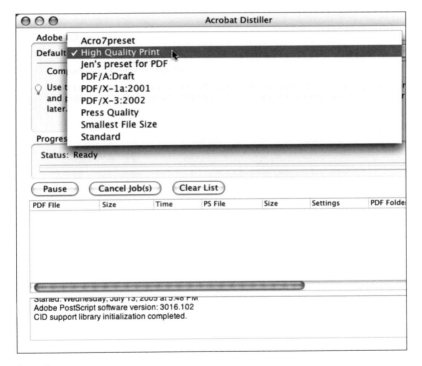

FIGURE 13-70

2. Choose Settings→Edit Adobe PDF Settings. This launches the Adobe PDF Settings: High Quality Print dialog box.

3. Click on the Color tab at the top of the dialog box, as shown in Figure 13-71.

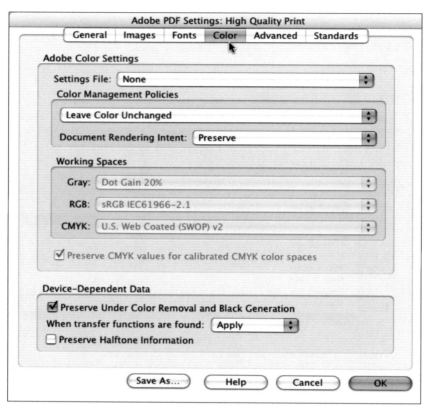

FIGURE 13-71

4. Under Color Management Policies, choose the color conversion you want from the pop-up menu (Figure 13-72). I chose Convert All Colors to CMYK.

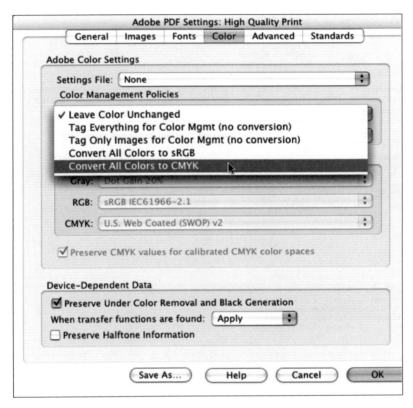

FIGURE 13-72

5. Click OK. This launches the Save dialog box so that you can give your PDF setting a new name.

6. Enter a name and click Save. Your saved PDF setting will now appear as the selected option in the Default Settings pop-up menu (Figure 13-73).

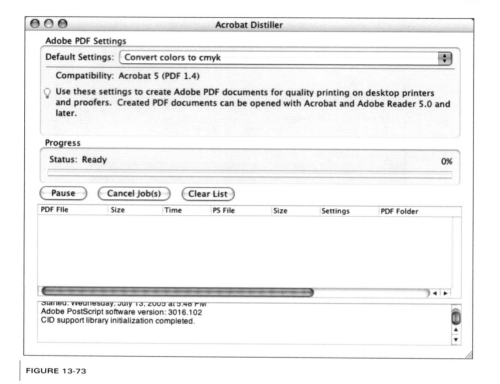

FIGURE 13-73

7. Choose File→Open.

8. Locate the file you want to convert, and click Open. The file will be converted according to your new settings.

HOW DO I CREATE A PRESENTATION IN ACROBAT?

With Acrobat, you can do oh so many amazing things! One of the most fun is creating a presentation. You can use Excel charts, photos, illustrations—anything at all—to make a stunning presentation with slide transitions. Anyone who can view a PDF will be able to view your presentation.

1. In Acrobat, choose File→Create PDF→From Multiple Files to launch the Create PDF from Multiple Documents dialog box.

2. Click the Choose button under Add Files.

3. Locate the file(s) you want to add, and click the Add button. The files will show up in the Files to Combine window (Figure 13-74). To select a block of contiguous files from one folder, click the first file and then Shift-click the last file in the block. To add non-contiguous files in the same folder, press the Command/Ctrl key as you click each file. If the files are in different folders, you'll have to repeat steps 2 and 3 for each folder.

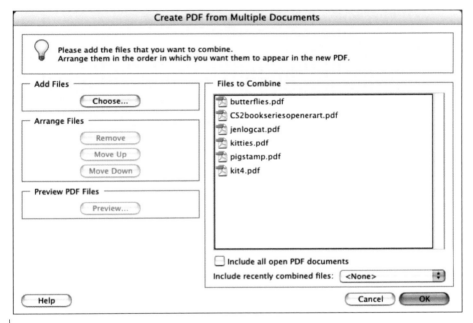

FIGURE 13-74

4. To change the order of the files, drag them above or below other files in the Files to Combine area (Figure 13-75). You can also rearrange them later, in the combined PDF file.

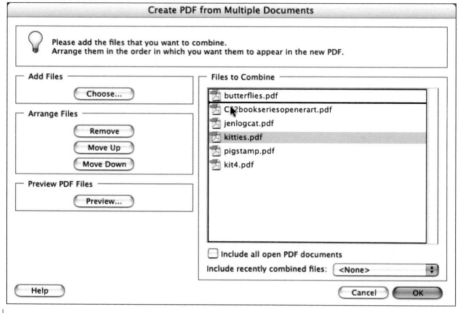

Create PDF from Multiple Documents

Please add the files that you want to combine.
Arrange them in the order in which you want them to appear in the new PDF.

Add Files
> Choose...

Arrange Files
> Remove
> Move Up
> Move Down

Preview PDF Files
> Preview...

Files to Combine
- butterflies.pdf
- C 2bookseriesopenerart.pdf
- jenlogcat.pdf
- kitties.pdf
- pigstamp.pdf
- kit4.pdf

☐ Include all open PDF documents
Include recently combined files: <None>

Help   Cancel   OK

FIGURE 13-75

5. Click OK. This will combine the files and launch the Save As dialog box.

6. Enter a name for the combined file/presentation, and click Save.

7. Open Acrobat Preferences (Command/Ctrl-K).

8. Choose the Full Screen option on the left side of the Preferences window.

9. Under Full Screen Navigation, set the Advance in seconds, and then set any other presentation options (Figure 13-76).

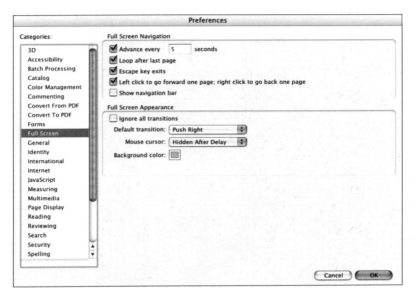

FIGURE 13-76

10. Under Full Screen Appearance, set the default transition you want to use (Figure 13-77).

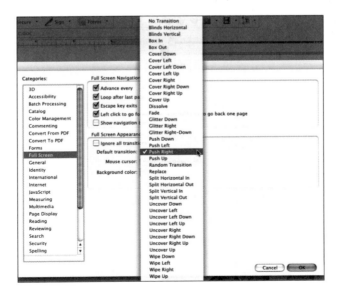

FIGURE 13-77

11. Set cursor options and the background color, and then click OK.

12. To start the presentation, choose View→Full Screen (or press Command/Ctrl-L). Figure 13-78 shows the first slide of the presentation.

FIGURE 13-78

13. To stop the presentation, press the Escape key or press Command/Ctrl-L.

You can use the presentation feature to send a portfolio to potential clients, send a job for review, or create something as simple as a family album of photographs.

[NOTE]

Another great feature of Acrobat is that when you use a photo in Acrobat, you can access the Picture Tasks menu, found in the upper-right menu bar. Under Picture Tasks, you can create your own photo layout for printing on your photo printer.

THE END

This ends the answers to the Top 15 How Do I...? questions. Should you find yourself with more questions that you need answers to, check out the Adobe Acrobat forums at Adobe's web site: *http://www.Adobe.com/support/forums/main.html.*

14

InDesign as Part of the Creative Suite

When InDesign was first announced in 1999, graphic design professionals waited eagerly to see if it would live up to its promise of delivering top-notch page layout power in a familiar Adobe interface. Indeed, the most promising aspect of a new high-end publishing program from Adobe was that design professionals would be able to apply their knowledge of Illustrator and Photoshop to learn this new application quickly and easily. Not only did InDesign meet the promise of being easy for Adobe customers to learn, but it also offered a level of integration with Adobe's other applications that competing page layout programs simply couldn't match.

In the years since its initial release, InDesign has seen several upgrades. With each upgrade, its feature set has become richer and its capability to collaborate with its Adobe siblings has grown stronger. With the release of Creative Suite 2, Adobe has brought all of the applications even closer together and has added a new piece, Bridge, to make file sharing and file management even easier.

AN OVERVIEW OF INDESIGN

Before looking at how InDesign fits into the Creative Suite, it's important to understand what InDesign is, how it's used, what you shouldn't try to do with it, and the relationship between InDesign, Acrobat, and the PDF file format.

When most people think of Adobe software, they think of manipulating photographic images with Photoshop or creating sophisticated illustrations with Illustrator. These two flagship products are *content creation* tools. That is, they are used to create the graphical content that is used in magazine ads, product packaging, web site interfaces, and a host of other design destinations. InDesign, like GoLive, is a layout tool. Both are used to combine content from other sources into a final form. InDesign is a page layout tool and GoLive is a web site layout tool, but both work the same way: they allow you to combine text and images into a final form for print or web distribution.

How People Use InDesign

Page layout is the process of combining text, graphics, and other elements together on a page. Page layout can be as simple as placing a couple of columns of text and a graphic or two together to create a one-page newsletter to photocopy and hand out at a local club meeting, a brochure (see Figure 14-1), or it can be as sophisticated as creating a full-color, high-gloss, multipage advertisement to be printed in a major magazine. The key factor in page layout is the focus on combining existing content, rather than creating new content.

For simple page layout, there are literally dozens of different applications that you can use, from word processors on up. For sophisticated page layout, however, there are really only a couple of products on the market, and Adobe InDesign is at the top of that short list. That isn't to say that you can't use InDesign for simple page layout as well, though— for all its power, InDesign is a remarkably easy application to learn and use.

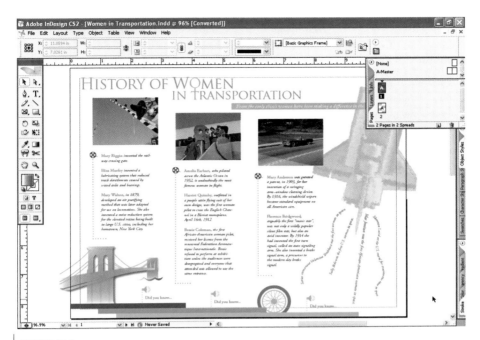

FIGURE 14-1

In a typical page layout scenario, text is written and revised in Microsoft Word, photographic images are prepared in Photoshop, and illustrations are created in Illustrator. These three different types of content are then brought into InDesign and positioned on the page (or pages, in a longer publication). Headings are often created directly in InDesign, as are additional simple graphic objects such as lines, boxes, and other border or background elements. After everything is laid out, final text formatting is applied and the document is checked for any potential problems. The file is then sent to a professional printing bureau—often in PDF format—for final printing and binding. PDFs can be created in InDesign or in Acrobat 7.0 Professional.

Who Uses InDesign

Because InDesign is both very powerful and very easy to work with, it is used by a wide range of people for all sorts of publishing needs. Here are a few examples:

- A business coach and consultant in Atlanta uses InDesign to create a quarterly newsletter that she sends out to clients and business associates. She composes all of the text in Microsoft Word, and then places it into an InDesign template file. She adds stock artwork and photographs from workshops she has conducted and other events.

- Two restaurant owners in Southern California use InDesign to create and update their menus. They rely heavily on InDesign's close integration with Photoshop to make it easy for them to keep their photo-intensive menus up to date. All of the titles and descriptions are done directly in InDesign.

- A technical writer in Philadelphia self-publishes a set of workbooks for custom database applications. He writes each section as a separate file in Microsoft Word and creates technical diagrams in Illustrator. He then combines everything in InDesign and emails his publication files to a service bureau for printing and binding.

- A production artist for a San Francisco design firm works closely with graphic designers on full-color print advertisements for high-profile clients. Her job is to take layouts that others have created and preflight them in InDesign to ensure that the final output matches the mock-ups that have been approved by the clients and the management team.

WHY GET THE CREATIVE SUITE INSTEAD OF JUST INDESIGN?

If you are already a Creative Suite 2 owner, congratulations! If you are not, you may be trying to decide between purchasing (or upgrading to) InDesign as a standalone application or getting the full Creative Suite. This is an important decision, and one that will greatly affect your creative potential.

Why Get Just InDesign?

The only advantage of getting just InDesign instead of the full Creative Suite is that it costs 40% less (according to the official Adobe web site—retail prices may vary). But considering that the Creative Suite contains Photoshop, Illustrator, GoLive, and Acrobat *in addition to* InDesign, *plus* the new Bridge file-management application, you get a lot of value for the additional 40% cost.

However, if all you will ever want to do is to combine existing text and graphics together on the page, with no additional graphics creation or modification, no sophisticated enhancements to any PDF files that you may create, no development of web sites or web content, and no management of different versions of your publications or source files, then purchasing InDesign by itself may be the best option for you.

Why Get the Full Creative Suite?

The full Creative Suite contains InDesign, Photoshop, Illustrator, GoLive, and Acrobat, plus Bridge (a new file- and version-management application). Depending on what you use InDesign for, chances are you will need at least one other of these applications and will probably be able to find good uses for most, if not all, of the rest. If you see yourself using at least one of the other CS2 products on a regular basis, you may want to consider purchasing the full Creative Suite. If you think you may use two or more of these products in addition to InDesign, the full Creative Suite is a must-have. Let's take a quick look at the uses to which InDesign users might be able to put the other CS2 applications:

PHOTOSHOP: Used for doing more to photographs and other images than basic adjustments such as cropping, rotating, or resizing. Photoshop allows you to retouch photographs, "airbrush" out unwanted elements, remove red-eye, darken or brighten an image, balance or shift colors, combine elements of different images, and much, much more. Photoshop is also ideal for repurposing images, because it allows you to save composite, multi-layered images and then go back and pull out pieces of the images at a later date.

ILLUSTRATOR: Used for creating line art or other drawings such as logos, diagrams, maps, or illustrations. InDesign has some drawing tools, but for anything other than simple shapes and line drawings, you will want access to the full set of vector-based drawing tools and features found in Illustrator. These will allow you (with a little skill and creativity on your part) to create rich, complex, and compelling illustrations.

GOLIVE: Used for creating web sites. If you are creating content for a purely printed method of distribution, you don't need GoLive at all. However, as ubiquitous as the Internet is, these days less and less content is being prepared for print distribution only.

ACROBAT: Used when you want to create PDF files that are more ambitious than simple online versions of printed documents. Acrobat allows you to combine, modify, and customize PDF files; secure PDF files; create sophisticated navigational structures; and add multimedia and interactivity to PDF files.

BRIDGE AND VERSION CUE: Used to track different versions of publications; source files such as text documents, photos, illustrations, and stock images; work collaboratively on a project without having to check files in or out; and host web-based PDF reviews for clients or colleagues.

LEARNING THE OTHER CREATIVE SUITE 2 TOOLS

Owning the full Creative Suite is a good start, but to get the most out of your purchase you'll need to learn to use all of these amazing applications together, playing to the strengths of each. Many excellent books are available for each of these products, but the following sections contain a brief snapshot of each application and how it works with InDesign.

Photoshop: The King of Image Editing

Photoshop is so well known as an image-manipulation application that its name has been turned into a verb—it's not uncommon to hear people say that they are going to "Photoshop" an image to remove an unwanted element or that an obviously manipulated image has been "Photoshopped."

The reason for Photoshop's popularity is a combination of ease of use and truly amazing results. For all of its power, Photoshop is a remarkably intuitive application to learn. You "paint" on an image using familiar tools such as a pencil or brush, you use an eraser tool to wipe away parts of an image, and all of the overall adjustments are done by dragging sliders while you watch the color, brightness, or saturation change before your eyes.

Photoshop uses *layers* to separate image elements, as shown in Figure 14-2. For example, you can have a background color or image on the bottom layer, more layers in the middle (each containing a different person, building, or other element), and a final top layer containing special text effects such as a drop-shadowed title.

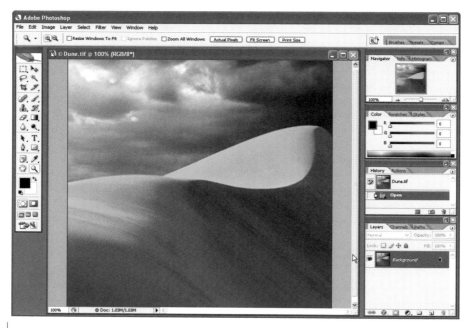

FIGURE 14-2

Photoshop is a pixel-based image editor, which means that the entire image is composed of thousands of tiny squares (pixels) of different colors. Usually, these pixels are so small that you can't make them out and the image looks like a regular photograph, but Photoshop lets you zoom in until you can easily see and work with individual pixels. This is also the reason why it's difficult to create smooth text in Photoshop.

Illustrator: The Ultimate Drawing Tool

Illustrator is the perfect complement to Photoshop's pixel-based photographic manipulation capabilities (Figure 14-3). Although every bit as powerful as Photoshop and capable of some amazing results of its own, Illustrator is not nearly as easy to learn or use. There are three reasons why Illustrator has a higher learning curve than Photoshop. The first is that most Illustrator images start with a blank page and require you to create everything yourself. The second is that Illustrator is a vector-based drawing program (where objects are made up of individual lines and independent shapes), and vectors are harder to understand and work with than pixels. The third reason is that many of Illustrator's tools are difficult to learn or use. Whereas Photoshop offers relatively straightforward Brush and Eraser tools, Illustrator has, among other things, a Pen tool that acts nothing like a real-world pen and a Gradient Mesh tool that simply has no real-world equivalent.

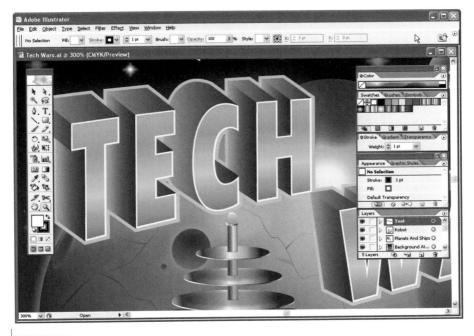

FIGURE 14-3

On the other hand, Illustrator offers two important advantages over Photoshop—editability and scalability. Because Illustrator graphics are vector-based, each object in the finished image is independent from every other object. This means that you can go back to a finished Illustrator file, select one object out of hundreds, and then rotate, resize, reshape, or recolor it without affecting the rest of the image. This type of post-production image editing is extremely difficult to do with Photoshop images.

The other big advantage of Illustrator files is that because the entire file is made up of mathematically defined line-based objects, you can resize an Illustrator graphic any amount with absolutely no distortion or loss of quality. Photoshop files can be sized down with no problems, but they cannot be enlarged without severe degradation of image quality.

GoLive: Powerful Web Site Authoring

Unlike Photoshop and Illustrator, which are graphics creation applications, GoLive is a layout application. Text and graphic content are brought into GoLive and placed on the page according to the logical and aesthetic needs of the user. In this respect, GoLive is very similar to InDesign. Where GoLive differs is that the pages in question are web pages, not printed pages (Figure 14-4).

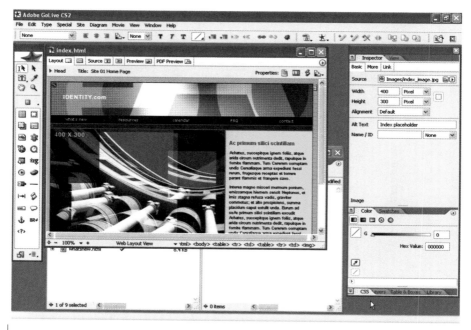

FIGURE 14-4

GoLive makes it easy to create professional-quality web sites with a layout grid for precise placement of page elements, as well as site templates that you can use as a foundation for creating your own web site. GoLive also has an incredible array of web objects that you can use to add tables, rollover buttons, floating boxes of text or images, special JavaScript actions, and much more. All of these objects can be daunting to beginning users, but GoLive is an application where you can get good results without touching 80% of the features that are available.

For the advanced user, GoLive also offers a full set of web site management features, making it ideal for both the design and administration sides of any web team.

- -

Acrobat: PDF Creation and Enhancement

Of all of the Creative Suite 2 applications, Acrobat is the least obviously appealing to Adobe's traditional customer base: graphic design professionals. Acrobat is not a content creation tool by any means. It has fewer graphics creation and text editing features than even InDesign and GoLive. But what Acrobat does offer users is the ability create and modify custom PDF files, something that no other application in the world can do.

In many ways, learning Acrobat feels more like learning a Microsoft Office product than an Adobe product. Instead of the familiar Adobe Toolbox, you have Office-like toolbars across the top of the document window, as shown in Figure 14-5. Instead of a plethora of palettes loaded with various controls, most of the Acrobat functionality is accessed through the application menus. This is intentional, because Acrobat, more than any other Adobe product, is geared toward business users rather than the graphic design community.

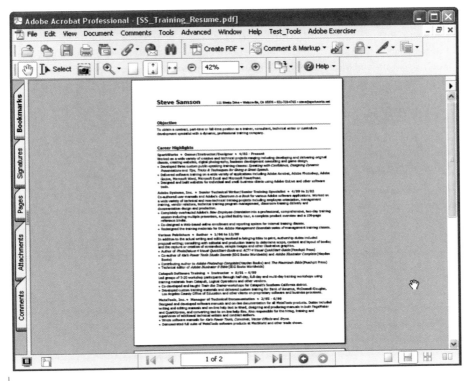

FIGURE 14-5

Whether you are creating a document for online viewing or traditional printing, PDF will probably be the final form your document takes, and Acrobat has no peer when it comes to creating and modifying PDFs.

UNDERSTANDING WHEN TO USE PHOTOSHOP OR ILLUSTRATOR INSTEAD OF INDESIGN

Before the Creative Suite, many Adobe customers—especially small business owners or independent graphic designers—owned only one or two Adobe products. This often left them in the situation of needing to perform tasks for which they didn't have the proper tools. The dilemma then was whether to purchase and learn a new application or try to figure out a way to do layout work in Photoshop, create a complex illustration in InDesign, or some other awkward workaround. One of the biggest advantages of using the Creative Suite is that you always have the right tools for the job, no matter what that job might be. So, when should you use InDesign, Photoshop, and Illustrator?

- InDesign is a destination for text and graphics and should not be your primary tool for text composition or graphics creation. You should create the majority of your text in Microsoft Word and your graphics in either Photoshop or Illustrator, before even launching InDesign. What InDesign excels at is layout of text and graphics together on the page. With InDesign, you can make subtle adjustments to text formatting and positioning, create and apply styles, place text in multiple columns, and wrap text around your Photoshop- or Illustrator-created graphics.

- Photoshop's primary function is as an image editing and composition tool. Most of the work done in Photoshop consists of manipulating existing photographic or other scanned images. Use Photoshop to clean up a scanned photograph, adjust color and brightness, crop or "airbrush" out unwanted elements, or combine elements from different photographs into a single image.

- Illustrator is a true graphics creation tool. Unlike with Photoshop, with Illustrator you typically start with a blank page and create an image from scratch, so a bit more skill and artistic talent is needed to get good results. Use Illustrator to create technical illustrations such as maps and diagrams or creative illustrations such as concept art and logos. With its precision and line-drawing abilities, Illustrator is also an excellent form creation tool.

INDESIGN AND ACROBAT: UNDERSTANDING THE PDF WORKFLOW

As a document layout application, InDesign is a crucial part of any publishing platform. But InDesign is only one piece of a larger picture: PostScript, Acrobat, and the PDF file format are also important parts of the publishing process. Understanding the basics of how documents are created and printed will help you to get the most out of InDesign.

PostScript and PDF

Way back in 1982, John Warnock and Chuck Geschke (Adobe's founders) came up with a new computer language, which they called *PostScript*. Unlike traditional computer languages such as FORTRAN and C, PostScript didn't allow you to write programs for a computer to execute. Instead, PostScript was a page description language that allowed computers to talk to printers and describe exactly how a document should look. With PostScript, every letter and line in a document is precisely and mathematically defined. Any printer that understands PostScript can output a PostScript document exactly as its author intended it to look. PostScript's capability to describe pages precisely was a perfect fit for Apple's new LaserWriter printer and a new page layout program called PageMaker (originally published by Aldus, but later acquired by Adobe). Together, these three technologies ushered in the desktop publishing revolution.

PostScript has seen several upgrades and enhancements, but its roots as a language solely intended to describe printed output left it unable to make the jump to the Internet and online document distribution. Enter Adobe's Portable Document Format (PDF). Adobe introduced PDF in June of 1993, and the impact it has had on the way documents are distributed has equaled, if not exceeded, the impact of its older sibling, PostScript.

PDF is also a page description language, but it is much more efficient and flexible than PostScript, and it was designed for the online world. In addition to simply displaying a document on the screen or outputting it to a printer, PDF has full support for sound and video, as well as user interaction in the form of buttons and clickable links. PDF also has sophisticated security features such as high-level password protection and digital signatures.

[NOTE]

Technically, PDF is really just an enhanced version of the PostScript language. In fact, the original name for the PDF file format was IPS, or Interchange PostScript. Because of the close relationship between PDF and PostScript, you can view and even edit PDF files in Illustrator. You can also open and view Illustrator files with Acrobat.

When to Use Acrobat Instead of InDesign

Before InDesign came into existence, PageMaker, FrameMaker, and QuarkXPress were the three main page layout applications. Each of these programs produced PostScript output for printing, and online document distribution was left to Acrobat and PDF. In time, the PDF file format expanded to include support for the CMYK color space (cyan, magenta, yellow, and black—the four inks used in commercial printing) and other factors necessary for traditional print applications. As it developed, PDF started to gain popularity with service bureaus and large commercial print shops due to its smaller file sizes, faster printing times, and more reliable performance than PostScript.

Because of PDF's growing popularity with the commercial print industry, when InDesign was being developed, it was designed with full support for PDF output. You can generate PDF files directly from InDesign, complete with sophisticated preflighting tools (tools for checking a document for potential printing problems).

What Acrobat has that InDesign lacks, however, is the capability to work with existing PDF files. InDesign can generate a PDF version of any document that it creates, but you need Acrobat if you want to combine multiple PDFs into a single file, insert or remove pages from a PDF, include sound or video, create a navigational structure with links, add password protection, or annotate a PDF with comments, instructions, or reviewer feedback.

TOP FIVE THINGS TO TAKE AWAY FROM THIS CHAPTER

Here are the most important things to take away from this chapter:

1. InDesign is a remarkably powerful but still easy-to-use professional page layout application. It is used to lay out everything from newsletters to technical manuals to full-color magazines.

2. InDesign is a destination for text and graphics, but it is not the best choice for creating either. Use Microsoft Word or some other word processing program to write your text, and use Photoshop and/or Illustrator to create your graphics.

3. Owning the full Creative Suite gives you access to everything you need to create compelling graphics for your InDesign publications, as well as tools for creating web sites and sophisticated PDF documents and the Bridge application for organizing and accessing text documents, images, and other resources.

4. Use Photoshop to modify and combine photographs and other pixel-based images. Use Illustrator to create vector-based line drawings such as maps, diagrams, and logos.

5. PostScript is a page-description language that tells printing devices how to output your computer-generated documents. PDF is a newer, more efficient and more flexible document description language that includes features for onscreen display and interactivity as well as printed output.

15

How to Create Publications in InDesign

In theory, the process of creating a publication in InDesign is fairly simple—you set up your document, add text and artwork, and make adjustments until you're happy with the results. Of course, if it were truly that easy, this would be a very short book. There are many things to consider when setting up your document. Also, the process of adding text often involves a lot of editing and formatting, and the artwork that you include often needs to be cropped, rotated, or otherwise adjusted. So how does all this work? Let's take a look.

SETTING UP THE DOCUMENT

One common mistake that many new InDesign users make is to try to jump immediately into placing text and graphics on the page. Although this works for simple documents such as flyers or announcements, more complex documents will quickly deteriorate without a plan and some sort of structure to the document. This is especially true for multipage documents and documents that use the same basic layout but have updated content, such as newsletters. When setting up your document, pay special attention to items such as page size, margins, and columns, and be sure to set up your guides and grids.

Document Options

The first step in creating a publication is to set up your document. Unlike in Photoshop or Illustrator, where you can simply start with a blank canvas and create something on it, in InDesign the size and shape of your "canvas" is critically important and must be decided upon before you do anything else. And although column and margin settings aren't as critical as page size, specifying the number of columns and the size of your page margins before you get started will make your layout work a lot easier.

To create a new InDesign document:

1. From the File menu, select New→Document.

2. In the New Document dialog box, specify the number of pages in your publication (Figure 15-1).

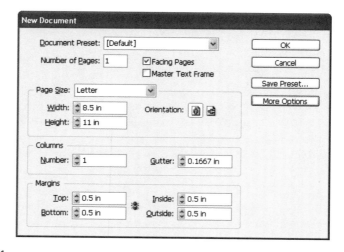

FIGURE 15-1

3. If you intend to print your document on both sides of each page, make sure the Facing Pages option is selected. (This is the default option.)

4. If you want to have a text frame automatically placed on every page of your document, select the Master Text Frame option.

5. Select a Page Size from the drop-down list or specify a custom page size in the Width and Height fields, and then choose either Portrait or Landscape orientation.

6. In the Columns section, specify the number of columns and the width of the gutter (the amount of space between columns).

7. In the Margins section, specify how much space should be left between the top, bottom, left, and right edges of the page and the content area. If the Facing Pages option is selected, the Left and Right fields will be replaced with Inside and Outside fields.

8. Click OK to create your new document.

tip

You can use several different units of measurement in InDesign. The default units are picas, which are used in traditional typesetting and professional publishing, but you can use whatever units you are most comfortable with. You can enter values in other units by typing the unit abbreviation along with the value (for example, .5 in or 2.5 cm), and InDesign will convert your measure to the default units. To change the default unit type, choose Edit→Preferences→Units and Increments (Windows) or InDesign→Preferences→Units and Increments (Mac), and select the desired unit type from the Ruler Units section.

Grids, Guides, and the Ruler

Although skill with InDesign is obviously needed to create a successful InDesign document, just knowing how to use the application isn't enough to create a professional-looking publication. A good balance of text and images is important, as is precise placement and careful alignment of objects on the page. InDesign provides three tools to help you structure your pages so that they have an aesthetically appealing and professional appearance: layout grids, user guides, and the document ruler.

A *layout grid* is exactly what it sounds like—a background grid that you can use to line up objects on the page. You can adjust the grid size to suit your needs and turn the display of the grid on or off. You also can turn on a snap-to feature so that as you move objects, they automatically jump, or snap, from one grid increment to the next.

1. Choose Edit→Preferences→Grids (Windows) or InDesign → Preferences → Grids (Mac). This opens the Preferences dialog box to the Grids section (Figure 15-2). The options here are divided into two sections: Baseline Grid and Document Grid. The baseline grid determines the position of lines of text within text frames. The document grid determines the position of objects on the page (Figure 15-3). Note that the base-line grid consists of only horizontal lines, since it is used only to aid in the positioning of lines of text. The document grid is a true grid, with both horizontal and vertical lines.

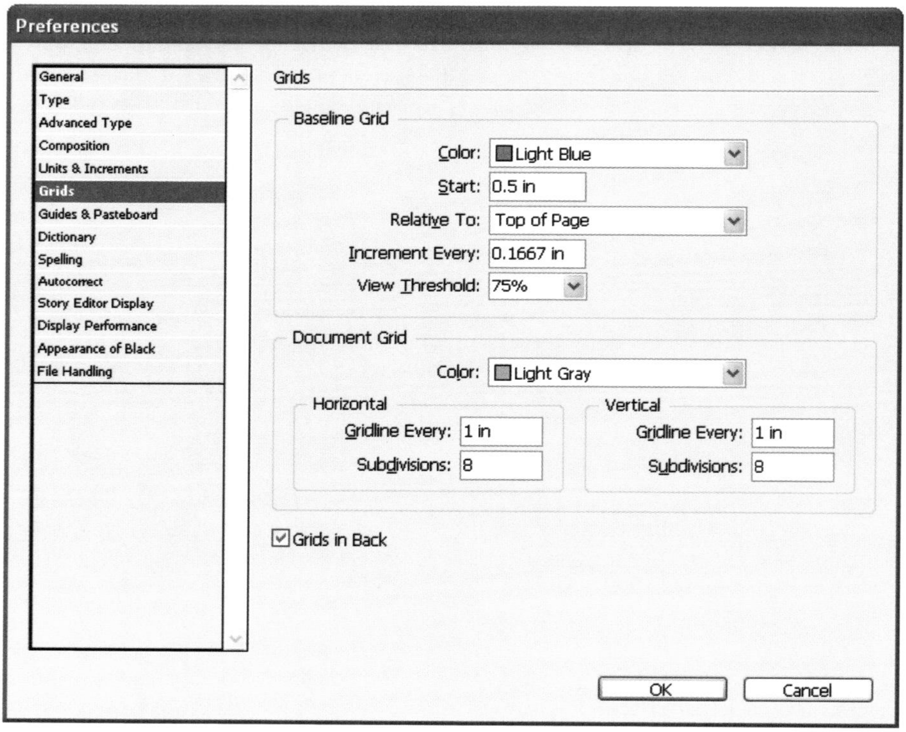

Preferences

General	Grids
Type	
Advanced Type	Baseline Grid
Composition	
Units & Increments	Color: ■ Light Blue
Grids	Start: 0.5 in
Guides & Pasteboard	Relative To: Top of Page
Dictionary	Increment Every: 0.1667 in
Spelling	View Threshold: 75%
Autocorrect	
Story Editor Display	Document Grid
Display Performance	
Appearance of Black	Color: ■ Light Gray
File Handling	

Document Grid

Color: ■ Light Gray

Horizontal — Gridline Every: 1 in   Vertical — Gridline Every: 1 in
Subdivisions: 8   Subdivisions: 8

☑ Grids in Back

[OK] [Cancel]

FIGURE 15-2

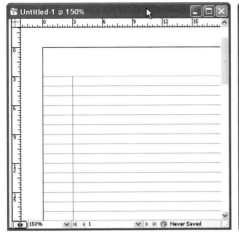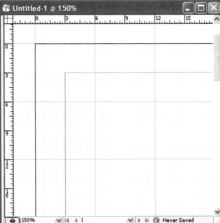

FIGURE 15-3

2. Enter values for the following Baseline Grid options:

COLOR: Choose the color of the gridlines.

START: Indicate how far down the first gridline should appear.

RELATIVE TO: Choose whether the amount specified in the Start field is applied to the top of the page or to the top margin.

INCREMENT EVERY: Specify the distance between gridlines.

VIEW THRESHOLD: Set the magnification level at which the gridlines will become visible. (This applies only if gridlines are being displayed. If gridlines are not being displayed, they don't appear at any magnification.)

3. Enter values for the following Document Grid options:

COLOR: Choose the color of the gridlines.

GRIDLINE EVERY: Specify the distances between the horizontal and vertical gridlines.

SUBDIVISIONS: Indicate how many subdivision lines you want to appear between one gridline and the next. Subdivision lines are thinner than normal gridlines.

4. Click OK.

1. Choose View→Grids & Guides→Show Baseline Grid or Show Document Grid.

2. Choose View→Grids & Guides→Hide Baseline Grid or Hide Document Grid.

1. Choose View→Grids & Guides→Snap to Document Grid.

2. Repeat to turn off this behavior.

Guides are nonprinting lines that appear in the document window to help you position objects. By default, all guides are visible. Some guides, such as margin and column guides, are created automatically when you create a new document (Figure 15-4). Other guides, called *ruler guides*, you can create, move, and delete as needed. Ruler guides are called "ruler guides" because you use the document ruler to create them.

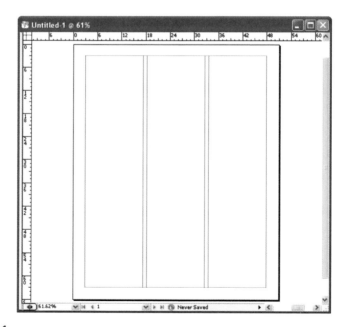

FIGURE 15-4

The document ruler is also helpful in its own right for positioning objects. However, even with the aid of the ruler, it is next to impossible to precisely position objects unless you have them snap to either a guide or the document grid.

1. Choose View→Show Rulers.

2. Choose View→Hide Rulers.

When the ruler is displayed, it shows the location of the cursor as a dotted line that moves along both the horizontal and vertical ruler displays. If you are moving an object, the left and right object boundaries are displayed in the horizontal ruler, and the top and bottom object boundaries are displayed in the vertical ruler.

To create a ruler guide:

1. Place the cursor in either the horizontal ruler or the vertical ruler, and click and drag the mouse into the document area (Figure 15-5). Do not release the mouse button.

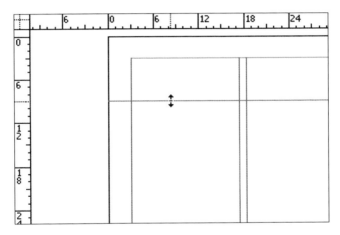

FIGURE 15-5

2. Move the guide to the desired location, keeping an eye on the cursor position indicator in the ruler. Release the mouse button when the guide is properly positioned.

3. To move a guide, place the tip of the Selection tool (the black arrow) on the guide and drag it to a new location.

4. To remove a guide, select it and press Backspace (Delete for Windows).

1. Choose View→Grids & Guides→Hide Guides.

2. Choose View→Grids & Guides→Show Guides.

Because the whole point of guides is to help you align objects, the default behavior is to have objects snap to guides. To turn off this behavior, choose View→Grids & Guides→ Snap to Guides. Repeat this command to reinstate snapping to guides.

PLACING TEXT

As previously mentioned, InDesign is not a content creation application. Very rarely do you compose text or create graphics within InDesign. Instead, you typically take text and graphics created in other applications and place them into InDesign documents. For text, this "other application" is almost always Microsoft Word. InDesign supports many different text formats, including Rich Text and plain text, but Microsoft Word is by far the most common source application for incoming text files.

Bringing text into InDesign involves two steps: placing the text and flowing the text. Placing the text gets it into your publication, although usually with only the first section showing. (Think of the front page of a newspaper, which usually displays only the beginning of an article.) Flowing the text allows you to specify where the remainder of the incoming text appears, such as in another column or on another page.

To bring text into InDesign:

1. Choose File→Place.

2. In the Place dialog box, locate and select the desired text file and click the Open button. This loads the contents of the text file into your cursor (Figure 15-6).

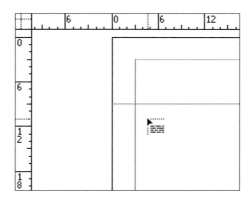

FIGURE 15-6

3. With the loaded text cursor, click on an existing, empty text frame, or click and drag to define a new text frame. The text is placed within the frame, and you get a normal Selection tool cursor. If the frame is not big enough to contain all of the text from the file, a red plus-sign overflow indicator appears in the lower-right corner of the text frame (Figure 15-7).

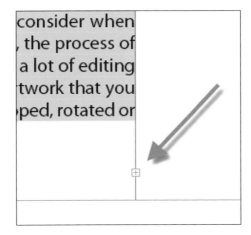

FIGURE 15-7

4. Click on this overflow indicator to load the excess text back into the cursor and then repeat step 3, either flowing the text into another empty text frame or creating a new frame to flow it into by clicking and dragging with the loaded text cursor. Continue this process of loading and placing overflow text until the entire contents of the file are visible.

EDITING AND FORMATTING TEXT

Ideally, the text that you place into your InDesign publication will already have been thoroughly reviewed and won't need any further editing. Realistically, though, there will always be changes that need to be made even after the text has been laid out.

InDesign offers a couple of different ways for you to work with text: you can edit text in the regular layout window, or use InDesign's Story Editor to isolate the text from the rest of the layout.

Editing in the Layout Window

For quick and simple edits, there is no reason not to work in the layout window. Here, in addition to editing the content of the text, you can apply a wide variety of character and paragraph formatting commands—from basic ones such as boldface and italic to advanced formatting such as adjusting the *kerning* (the space between letters) and *leading* (the space between lines of text).

To edit text in the layout window:

1. Select the Type tool in the Toolbox.

2. Position the text editing cursor in any text frame.

3. Click and drag to select a block of text, or click to place an insertion point in your text.

4. Insert, delete, or replace text as you would in any word processing application.

tip

If you like clicking your mouse, you're going to love InDesign's text selection shortcuts:

- Single-click to position your insertion point.
- Double-click to select a word.
- Triple-click to select a line.
- Quadruple-click to select a paragraph.
- Quintuple-click to select an entire story.

You can also Shift-click to extend the selection from the insertion point (or start of the current selection) to any location in the current story.

Editing in the Story Editor

An InDesign "story" is the contents of a text block or a set of linked text blocks, such as one chapter of a book or a single newspaper or magazine article. The Story Editor lets you view and edit an entire story in a separate window, freeing you from having to wait for formatting or text flow to update as you work, or from having to move from one text block to another (and often back again) as you make changes throughout a lengthy story.

To edit text in the Story Editor:

1. Select a text frame that contains text. You cannot use the Story Editor to create new stories.

2. Choose Edit→Edit in Story Editor (Figure 15-8). The Story Editor window appears, with the portion of the story that starts in the selected text frame displayed at the top of the window. Note that the Story Editor is a different way of viewing the text in a story—it is *not* a copy of the text in a separate document.

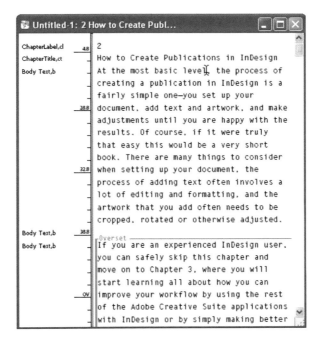

FIGURE 15-8

3. Make any necessary edits. The edits are displayed in both the Story Editor window and in the document window. Close the Story Editor when you're done.

The Story Editor window displays informational features not found in the layout window:

PARAGRAPH STYLES: The style applied to each paragraph of text is displayed in the left pane.

TEXT DEPTH: The location where the text appears is shown on the vertical ruler.

OVERSET TEXT: If there is text that exists in the story but has overflowed the text frame, it will be displayed below the Overset line in the Story Editor.

You can drag the vertical section divider to adjust the relative width of the information and text panes in the Story Editor window.

Text Formatting

Whenever you have text selected, whether in the layout window or the Story Editor, the Control palette at the top of the document window displays a dizzying array of formatting options. At the far left of the options bar are two buttons that let you switch back and forth between character and paragraph formatting controls (Figure 15-9).

FIGURE 15-9

Character formats affect only the selected text. If no text is selected, any new text typed at the current insertion point takes on the specified character formatting. (If you move the insertion point, the character formatting controls will update to reflect the formatting of the text at the new insertion point.)

Character formats include font, size, emphasis (boldface, italics, underline), capitalization, position (subscript and superscript), and several text spacing and scaling options. *Paragraph formats* affect entire paragraphs and are applied to the paragraph that contains the insertion point, or all selected paragraphs. Paragraph formats include alignment and justification, indents, spacing, hyphenation, and column and list options.

PLACING AND MODIFYING ARTWORK

InDesign makes it easy to add artwork (photographs, illustrations, logos, maps, and more) to any publication. Once your artwork is placed, you can resize it, rotate it, crop it, wrap text around it, and even place a drop shadow behind it—all from within InDesign.

Placing Artwork

The procedure for placing artwork is virtually identical to that for placing text. One difference is that when placing text you often define the dimensions of the new text frame by clicking and dragging with the loaded text cursor. Conversely, while placing artwork in a new frame you almost always let the dimensions of the incoming image determine the dimensions of the frame that is created for it. All you have to worry about is where you want the new frame to appear.

However, when laying out a publication, empty frames are often created (using the Frame or Shape tools) for artwork that does not yet exist or has not yet been chosen. This lets the designer place and adjust the text while the artwork is being created or selected. It's also more convenient to do all of the text work without any art, because the page display redraws much faster with text only. After the layout has been completed, the artwork can then be placed.

Artwork initially appears at full size, even if the frame that it is placed into is not big enough to display the entire image. Consequently, placing artwork into an existing frame usually requires one or two additional steps to resize the artwork and possibly center it within the frame.

To place artwork in a new frame:

1. Choose File→Place.

2. In the Place dialog box, locate and select the desired file and click OK. This loads the artwork into your cursor (Figure 15-10).

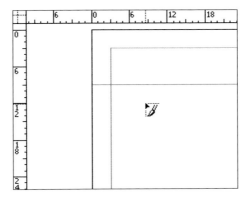

FIGURE 15-10

3. Click in the document window to place the artwork. A frame will be created that matches the dimensions of the artwork.

1. Select the frame you want to use as the destination for the incoming artwork.

2. Choose File→Place.

3. In the Place dialog box, locate and select the desired file. Make sure that the Replace Selected Item checkbox is selected (Figure 15-11).

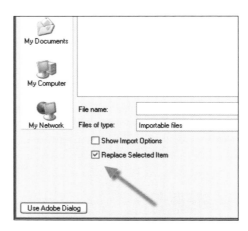

FIGURE 15-11

4. Click OK. The artwork is automatically placed in the selected frame, replacing any image that the frame may have contained.

5. Adjust the image within the frame as desired. Choose from these options:

   • To resize the image to fit the frame, choose Object→Fitting→Fit Content to Frame or Fit Content Proportionally.

   • To resize the frame to fit the image, choose Object→Fitting→Fit Frame to Content.

   • To center the image within the frame, choose Object→Fitting→Center Content.

   • To move the image within the frame, select the Direct Selection tool (Figure 15-12), and click and drag within the frame.

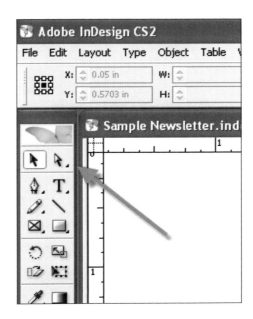

FIGURE 15-12

Rotating and Resizing Artwork

InDesign is not an image editing application, but it does allow you to apply some simple transformations to any placed artwork. Of these, the two most common are rotating and resizing (Figure 15-13).

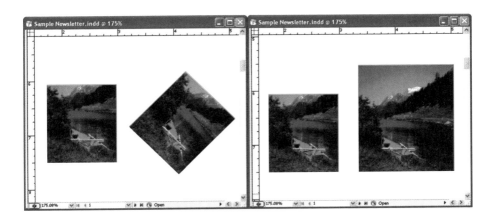

FIGURE 15-13

1. Select the frame that contains the image you want to rotate.

2. Choose Object→Transform→Rotate. Click the Preview checkbox if you want to see the effect of your changes without exiting the dialog box.

3. In the Rotate dialog box, enter an angle of rotation. (Objects are rotated counter-clockwise, so a rotation of 90 will turn the object on its left side.)

4. If you want the frame to remain in place but have the image inside the frame rotate instead, select the Rotate Content option.

5. Click OK. (To create a rotated copy of the object, click Copy instead of OK.)

tip

If you want to preview a different angle of rotation or size for scaling, uncheck the Preview box and then check it again to see your change take effect.

To resize artwork:

1. Select the frame that contains the image you want to resize.

2. Choose Object→Transform→Scale. Click the Preview checkbox if you want to see the effect of your changes without exiting the dialog box.

3. Enter the desired enlargement or reduction percentage in the Scale field.

4. If you want to resize the artwork non-proportionally, select the Non-Uniform option and enter separate percentages in the Horizontal and Vertical fields.

5. If you want to resize the frame only, deselect the Scale Content option.

6. Click OK. (To create a resized copy of the object, click Copy instead of OK.)

WORKING WITH MULTIPLE PAGES

So far in this chapter you have been working with a single-page document, but most InDesign documents consist of multiple pages. Thanks to InDesign's Pages palette (Figure 15-14), adding new pages to a document is remarkably easy.

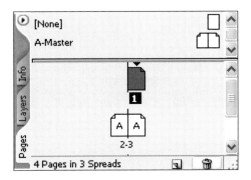

FIGURE 15-14

The Pages palette also makes it easy to delete or rearrange pages:

• To add a new page to your document, click the Create new page icon in the Pages palette.

• To delete a page, either drag the page to the Trash icon in the Pages palette or select the page and click the Trash icon.

• To move a page, drag the page to the desired location in the Pages palette's page display (Figure 15-15).

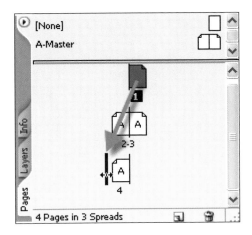

FIGURE 15-15

Controls for navigating in a multipage document are displayed at the bottom of the document window (Figure 15-16). You can click the First Spread, Previous Spread, Next Spread, and Last Spread controls to jump to the desired spread. (A *spread* is a set of two or more pages designed to be viewed together. For example, when you open a book, you always view a two-page spread.) The Page combo box in the middle of the controls can be used to jump to a specific page in two ways: you can either click the arrow to select a page from the drop-down list or type the desired page number in the text area and press Return (Enter for Windows).

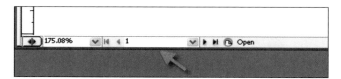

FIGURE 15-16

**Here are the most important things to take away
from this chapter:**

1. Properly setting up your document before you begin placing text and images will save you time. In the New Document dialog box, you can specify the page size and orientation as well as setting up columns and margins.

2. Use the File→Place command to place text created in another application into a text box in your InDesign document. The process of placing text involves loading a text file into the cursor and then using this "loaded text" cursor to select or create text frames for the text to flow into. Overflow text can be reloaded and placed in subsequent text boxes until the entire file has been placed.

3. You can edit text either in the layout window or in a separate Story Editor window. Numerous character and paragraph formats can be applied to text as well (typically in the layout window).

4. Artwork is placed in a similar fashion to text. Once placed, you have numerous options for altering the artwork, including rotating, cropping, and scaling.

5. The Pages palette allows you to easily add, move, and delete pages. The page navigation controls (at the bottom of the document window) let you quickly move from one page to another.

16

How to Use InDesign with the
Other Creative Suite Applications

More than any other Creative Suite 2 application, InDesign benefits from the synergy among these awesome products. Photoshop and Illustrator are self-contained and are often used to great effect with no interaction with other applications. Acrobat absolutely requires a document created in another application, but more often than not, source documents for Acrobat are created in Microsoft Word or Excel (although InDesign is also a popular starting point). Even GoLive, which is closer to InDesign in purpose and workflow than the rest of the Creative Suite, does most of its real work with Photoshop images. InDesign, on the other hand, is often used to combine images from Photoshop and Illustrator for multiple-page layouts and can be used to great effect with both Acrobat and GoLive.

USING PHOTOSHOP IMAGES IN INDESIGN

Probably the most common interaction between InDesign and the other Creative Suite 2 applications involves placing and working with Photoshop images. Most InDesign publications contain photographs and other pixel-based images, and no other product on the planet is better at working with these types of images than Photoshop.

Photoshop lets you export images in a wide variety of file formats, virtually all of which are compatible for use with InDesign. However, you'll want to use Photoshop's native file format (*.psd*) as often as possible, because placing a *.psd* file in an InDesign publication creates a link between the placed image and the Photoshop application. This makes it easy to open the image in Photoshop whenever you need to work with it.

To open a Photoshop file from within InDesign, simply select any placed *.psd* image and choose Edit→Edit Original. After you've edited and saved the original file in Photoshop, the placed image will automatically be updated in InDesign.

Even without opening them in Photoshop, though, there are a couple of ways in which you can control the appearance of *.psd* files in your InDesign publications: you can take advantage of layers and alpha channels, two of Photoshop's most powerful features.

Working with Layers

Layers are used in Photoshop for a staggering number of purposes. Their popularity is due both to their ease of use and to the large number of options and effects that can be applied to individual layers. Although InDesign supports layers in placed Photoshop files, what you can do with those layers is pretty much limited to displaying them or not displaying them. This may seem somewhat limiting at first, but you can use this capability to work with layers to good effect to vary the appearance of an image to fit the context in which it is being used. A good example of this is a cover image for a magazine or brochure that will be published in different languages. A designer can put the image by itself on one layer and create separate layers for the title and other cover text in each language. In InDesign, you can then display each text layer in turn, hiding the others (Figure 16-1).

FIGURE 16-1

To set layer visibility:

1. Select the placed *.psd* object.

2. Choose Object→Object Layer Options.

3. In the Object Layer Options dialog box (Figure 16-2), click the Preview checkbox so that you can see the effects of hiding various layers.

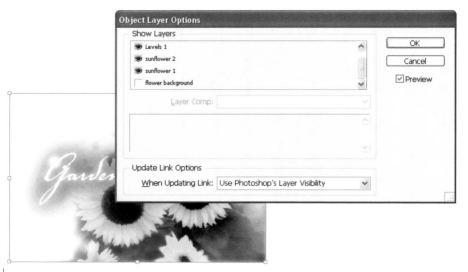

FIGURE 16-2

4. Click the eyeball icon next to each listed layer to hide that layer. Click the empty box next to a hidden layer to reveal it.

5. If you want to keep your custom layer visibility when updating this linked object, select Keep Layer Visibility Overrides from the When Updating Link drop-down menu.

Using Alpha Channels, Clipping Paths, and Masks

Another wonderful feature of Photoshop is its capability to create sophisticated alpha channels. An *alpha channel* is a grayscale image that can be used to define which parts of an image are visible and which are hidden. This process of hiding parts of an image is called *masking*. The advantage of masking is that it allows you to hide portions of an image without deleting any data. For example, you could create an alpha channel from a block of text and use that text as a mask, revealing only the parts of the image that appear within the text (Figure 16-3). A different alpha channel could be used on the same image to create a totally different effect, such as isolating an object from the background (Figure 16-4).

FIGURE 16-3

FIGURE 16-4

In recent versions Photoshop's vector-based drawing tools have become more robust, and you can now create sophisticated *paths* (lines that are used to form shapes) in your pixel-based images. These paths can be used for any number of purposes in Photoshop.

InDesign fully supports alpha channels and paths in placed Photoshop images. InDesign converts them to clipping paths, which serve the exact same purpose in InDesign as masks do in Photoshop: defining which parts of an image should be visible and which should be hidden.

To apply a clipping path to an image:

1. Select a placed *.psd* object that contains masking data (either an alpha channel or a path).

2. Choose Object→Clipping Path.

3. In the Clipping Path dialog box (Figure 16-5), select the Preview checkbox so that you can see the effects of the clipping path.

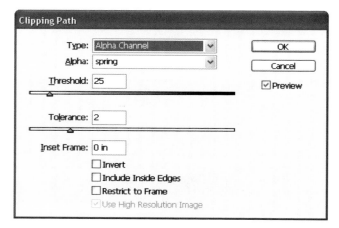

FIGURE 16-5

4. From the Type drop-down menu, select Alpha Channel (or Photoshop Path if your image contains a path that you want to use as a clipping path).

5. If your image contains more than one alpha channel (or path), select the one you want to use from the Alpha (or Path) drop-down menu that appears below the Type drop-down menu.

6. Click OK to apply the clipping path to the image.

USING ILLUSTRATOR ARTWORK IN INDESIGN

Although Illustrator creates a much different style of artwork from Photoshop and the two programs use completely different file formats, the process of placing and working with Illustrator files in InDesign is remarkably similar to that for Photoshop files and other file formats. This ability to work with different types of files using one set of commands and procedures is one of the many great features of InDesign. For example, you can:

- Place an Illustrator file by choosing File→Place, locating and selecting the desired file, and then clicking with the loaded artwork cursor anywhere in your InDesign document.

- Edit a placed Illustrator file in Illustrator by selecting the object and choosing Edit→Edit Original.

One key difference is in the area of layer visibility. InDesign does not allow you to set the layer visibility of placed native Illustrator files (those with an *.ai* extension), but it does allow you to set the layer visibility of layered PDF files. Therefore, if you want to be able to set layer visibility once you have the file in your InDesign document, all you have to do is save your Illustrator file in the PDF format before placing it.

To save an Illustrator file as a layered PDF file:

1. In Illustrator, choose File→Save As.

2. Change the file type from Illustrator to PDF in the File Type (Windows) or Format (Mac) drop-down menu in Illustrator's Save As dialog box (Figure 16-6).

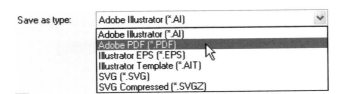

FIGURE 16-6

3. Click the Save button.

4. In the Save Adobe PDF dialog box that appears, choose Acrobat 6 (PDF 1.5) or Acrobat 7 (PDF 1.6) from the Compatibility drop-down menu.

5. Select the Create Acrobat Layers from Top-Level Layers option and click Save PDF.

Once you have done this and placed the file in InDesign, you can set layer visibility the exact same way you do for placed Photoshop images (by selecting the object and choosing Object→Object Layer Options).

Another key difference is that unlinked Illustrator files (those inserted via copying and pasting rather than with the Place command) can be edited to some extent from inside InDesign. This is possible because when you copy and paste, you put all of the file data into your publication—when you use Place, you only put a lower-quality proxy into the publication, with a link back to the original file (Figure 16-7).

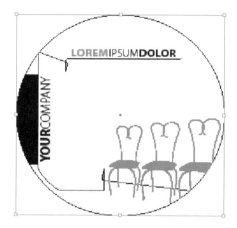

FIGURE 16-7

1. Select the Direct Selection tool (the white, or hollow, arrow tool), as shown in Figure 16-8.

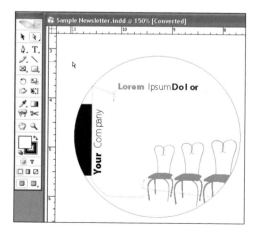

FIGURE 16-8

2. Click on any object within the image to select it. Shift-click to select additional objects.

3. Move, rotate, or scale the object. Change its color, move it forward or backward in the stacking order, or change other properties as desired (Figure 16-9).

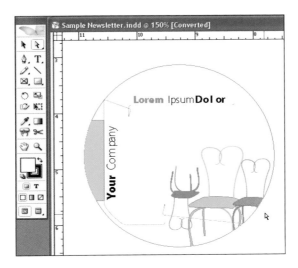

FIGURE 16-9

WORKING WITH COLOR SPACES AND PACKAGING

Regardless of whether your placed images come from Photoshop or from Illustrator (or even from a third-party source), you'll need to keep two things in mind when working with artwork files: color space and packaging.

Understanding Color Spaces

The first consideration when placing images is the color space in which you created your images. Different devices use different methods to reproduce color, and no one method can reproduce all the colors in the visible spectrum. The range of colors that a particular method can reproduce is known as a *color space*. Most InDesign documents are destined for traditional paper-based publishing. This means that they will typically be output with toners and inks using the traditional CMYK (cyan, magenta, yellow, and black) color space. Both Photoshop and Illustrator also let you work in the RGB (red, green, and blue) color space, which is the format used for displaying onscreen images, as well as several other color spaces.

You can switch color spaces as you work, or you can change the color space just before saving or exporting a file. However, if your final output will be CMYK, it is highly recommended that you stick with the CMYK color space throughout the creation and editing of your image. This will avoid potential color-conversion problems.

Packaging Your Publication

Another important point to keep in mind is that placing a file in InDesign does not actually place the file itself into your publication. Instead, a lower-quality preview of the image is placed in the publication. This image contains a link to the original, high-quality file. (This is true of all placed images, not just Photoshop and Illustrator files.) Placing linked proxies to image files instead of the image files themselves keeps the size of the InDesign publication file manageable. However, this can cause problems if you move the publication to a location where it cannot access the placed files, such as when you copy it to disk or email it to a printing company.

For this reason, InDesign has a Package command that finds all linked files and copies them to one "package" folder, which you can then send out as needed.

To package a publication:

1. Choose File→Package. A set of progress bars will appear briefly as InDesign preflights the document, examining your publication for potential printing problems.

2. If any problems are detected, InDesign will present you with a warning dialog box (Figure 16-10). Preflighting is covered in detail in Chapter 17. For now, click the Continue button if this dialog box appears.

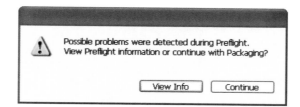

Possible problems were detected during Preflight.
View Preflight information or continue with Packaging?

View Info   Continue

FIGURE 16-10

3. Another dialog box will appear with fields for printing instructions and contact information (Figure 16-11). Fill in the fields in this dialog box as needed, and click Continue.

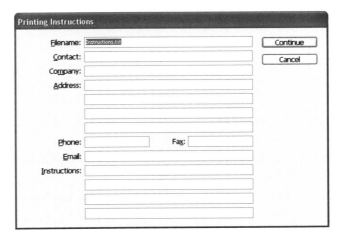

CHAPTER 16

FIGURE 16-11

4. You will then be presented with a final Package Publication (Windows) or Create Package Folder (Mac) dialog box (Figure 16-12). Enter a name for your package and select a destination. Do not close this dialog box.

FIGURE 16-12

5. In the Package Publication (Windows) or Create Package Folder (Mac) dialog box, choose additional package options:

COPY FONTS (EXCEPT CJK): Copies all necessary font files, not the entire typeface.

COPY LINKED GRAPHICS: Copies linked graphics files. Linked text files are always copied.

UPDATE GRAPHIC LINKS IN PACKAGE: Changes the current graphic links to point to the package folder.

USE DOCUMENT HYPHENATION EXCEPTIONS ONLY: Prevents the document from composing with the external user dictionary.

INCLUDE FONTS AND LINKS FROM HIDDEN DOCUMENT LAYERS: Packages objects located on these hidden layers.

VIEW REPORT: Opens the printing instructions report in a text editor immediately after packaging.

6. Click the Package (Windows) or Save (Mac) button to create your package.

USING ACROBAT WITH INDESIGN

Acrobat and InDesign have an interesting relationship. InDesign is used to combine text and images to create newsletters, brochures, magazines, and newspapers, whereas Acrobat is used to convert any type of document file into a document that can be viewed onscreen. (InDesign files are just one of dozens, if not hundreds, of file types that can be converted to PDF.) However, you also can create PDFs of your InDesign documents directly within InDesign. Adobe has even given InDesign a lot of Acrobat-like functionality to allow InDesign users to create interactive PDFs. As you'll see in the next chapter, you can create hyperlinks, bookmarks, and buttons in your InDesign documents, and you can even add sound and video. (Of course, because all of this interactivity doesn't translate well to the printed page, adding these features to your document makes sense only if you are planning to convert the document to PDF.)

So, given InDesign's relatively sophisticated PDF-creation capabilities, why would you want to use Acrobat at all in conjunction with InDesign? As it happens, Acrobat is actually a much better tool for adding interactive features to your PDF documents. Although it's true that InDesign allows you to add interactivity to your documents for when you convert them to PDF, it is a bit easier and you will have more options if you convert them to PDF first (in either InDesign or Acrobat), and then use Acrobat to add any interactive elements. When working on projects in InDesign, you're also likely to find Acrobat's facilities for sending out PDFs for commenting and review invaluable.

USING INDESIGN WITH GOLIVE

The relationship between GoLive and InDesign is also a curious one. Both perform a similar function, in the sense that they are each layout applications where you combine text and graphics together on the page—but whereas InDesign publications consist of traditional printed pages, GoLive web sites consist of multiple onscreen pages. Because both applications are destinations for components created in other applications and neither application creates source components that the other might use, GoLive and InDesign have practically no interaction with each other.

On the other hand, because both applications are used to prepare layouts for publication, there is often some level of redundancy for designers and companies that publish information in both traditional and online formats. Fortunately, InDesign has a feature that lets you repurpose an InDesign publication for use in GoLive. This feature is called Package for GoLive, and it prepares a package for a web designer to use in creating a GoLive web site. This package contains all of the text and images from the InDesign publication, with some very useful changes:

- Graphics are stored in TIFF format for easy conversion to GIF or JPEG format when placed in GoLive.

- Text formatting is translated to Cascading Style Sheets.

- A PDF file representing the original layout of the InDesign document is created.

- An *Assets* folder containing separate folders for each type of asset (text stories, original images, formatted images, multimedia files, etc.) is created, as shown in Figure 16-13.

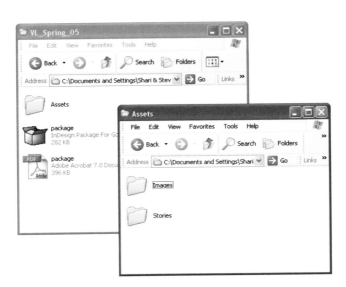

FIGURE 16-13

1. In InDesign, choose File→Package for GoLive.

2. In the Package Publication for GoLive dialog box (Figure 16-14), name the file and choose a location, and then click Package (Windows) or Save (Mac).

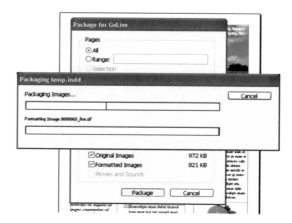

FIGURE 16-14

3. In the Package for GoLive dialog box that appears, choose the desired options for your package:

   • In the Pages section, select which pages you want to include in the package and whether or not you want to include items on hidden layers.

   • In the Options section, choose whether or not you want to view the package when it's complete. If selected, GoLive will automatically launch and will load the package contents for viewing. (You can also change the encoding method used, but it's probably best to leave this on the default setting unless you have a specific need for a different type of encoding.)

   • In the Images, Movies & Sounds section, select which types of graphic and multimedia content you want included in your package. Document text is always included, which is why there are no text-related options.

4. Click the Package button to create your package.

The package folder will contain an XML file that GoLive uses to interpret the contents of the package, including links to all the files, formatting instructions, and more. It will also contain a PDF file that represents the layout of the document (and from which you can simply drag and drop objects into your GoLive pages), as well as an *Assets* folder that contains separate subfolders for each type of asset, such as images, stories, sounds, and movies.

Here are the most important things to take away from this chapter:

1. Using native Photoshop files in your InDesign publications has two advantages over using TIFF and other common formats: you can control which layers from your Photoshop file are visible in InDesign, and if your Photoshop file contains alpha channels or paths, you can use them in InDesign to create a clipping path to hide portions of the image.

2. Illustrator files can be placed and manipulated in InDesign just like Photoshop files, but InDesign cannot read layer information from native Illustrator files. Instead, save layered Illustrator files in the PDF format.

3. Regardless of where your images come from, create them using the CMYK color space if they will be used in an InDesign publication intended for traditional printing. Also, be sure to package all of the files you use in your publication by using the File→ Package command.

4. InDesign has features for adding interactivity to documents that will be converted to the PDF format, but the process isn't as easy or as reliable as adding interactivity using Acrobat after you convert the file.

5. Packaging an InDesign publication for GoLive is a great way to repurpose text and images from InDesign for use in a GoLive web site. Packaging a publication converts graphics and text styles to web-friendly formats and organizes the component pieces for easy access from within GoLive.

Top 15 How Do I...? Indesign Questions

In this chapter, you will find the answers to the top 15 questions designers ask about InDesign. These most commonly asked questions were compiled from questions asked in the InDesign forums and posed to the InDesign product team. If you have a specific problem or are looking to improve your skills, the step-by-step solutions included here should help. You'll find tips that will save you time, strengthen your creativity, and much more.

HOW DO I CREATE AND USE MASTER PAGES?

Most multipage publications have certain elements that appear throughout the publication, such as page numbers, document or section titles, borders, or other graphical elements. Placing these items on each page would be both extremely time-consuming and virtually impossible to do without some errors or inconsistencies. This is where master pages and master spreads come in.

A *master page* is a page that serves as a background template for other pages. Items placed on a master page appear on every page that you associate with that master page. A *master spread* is a set of master pages. Master spreads typically contain one left- and one right-facing master page, but they can contain up to 10 master pages. Together, master pages and master spreads are referred to simply as "masters." A document can contain multiple masters, such as a master page for the publication cover, a master spread for front matter (copyright, table of contents, etc.), and a master spread for the remainder of the document. Masters are created, deleted, and applied using the Pages palette (Figure 17-1).

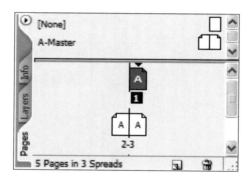

FIGURE 17-1

To create a master page:

1. Open the document to which you want to add master pages.

2. From the Pages palette menu (Figure 17-2), select New Master.

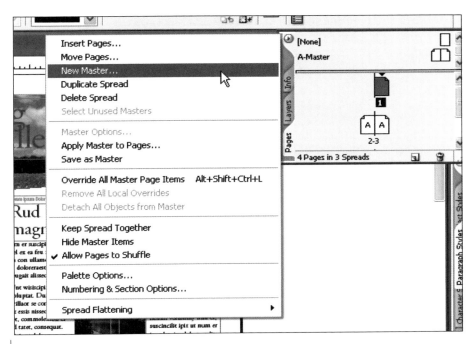

FIGURE 17-2

3. Specify options for your new master:

PREFIX: Defines one to four characters that will be used in the document portion of the Pages palette to identify which master page is applied to a particular document page.

NAME: Defines the name of the master page. This name will show up in drop-down lists in the Master Options and Apply Master dialog boxes.

BASED ON MASTER: Lets you use an existing master as the basis for this new master. All objects and guides on the old master will be copied to the new master and can then be moved, formatted, or deleted as desired.

NUMBER OF PAGES: Indicates the number of pages in the master.

4. Click the OK button to create your new master. The new master page or spread will be added to the master section of the Pages palette.

5. Add guides, text frames, graphic elements, or other objects to your new master. If you based your new master on an existing master, you may want to delete or modify objects carried over from the old master.

To apply a master page to a single document page:

1. Drag the master page icon from the top of the Pages palette onto the desired document page icon in the bottom of the Pages palette.

To apply a master page to multiple document pages:

1. Click the arrow in the upper-right corner of the Pages palette and select Apply Master to Pages from the palette menu.

2. Specify the desired options in the Apply Master dialog box (Figure 17-3):

   APPLY MASTER: Use this drop-down list to choose the master page that you want to use.

   TO PAGES: Enter the pages to which you want the master applied. Use hyphens to indicate page ranges (such as 5-10) and commas to separate pages or page ranges (such as 1, 5, 8-12).

FIGURE 17-3

3. Click OK to apply the master to the specified pages.

To delete a master page:

1. Click the unwanted master page in the top half of the Pages palette. Shift-click or Ctrl-click to select additional master pages.

2. Click the trash can icon at the bottom of the Pages palette, or drag the unwanted master page(s) to the trash can icon.

HOW DO I CREATE AND USE TEXT STYLES?

A style is nothing more than a set of formatting instructions that can be applied to a block of text. InDesign has both *paragraph styles*, which can be applied to one or more paragraphs, and *character styles*, which can be applied to one or more characters of text. Paragraph styles are by far the more commonly used of the two types. Paragraph styles contain both character and paragraph formatting instructions, whereas character styles contain only character formatting instructions.

Styles provide a way to quickly and consistently format an entire document. For example, you can create a paragraph style that consists of instructions to format the text to be 16-point Arial, blue, and bold, with 12 points of blank space above the paragraph and 6 points of blank space below, and to be preceded by a 2-point blue rule (line). You can then quickly apply all of these formatting instructions to a headline paragraph with a single click, repeating this simple step for each headline in your document. Another huge benefit to using styles is that you can edit the style later, and every single paragraph that uses the style will automatically be updated to reflect the changes.

To create a style:

1. Select text to be used as the basis for the new style. For a new paragraph style, click anywhere in a paragraph that uses the formatting that you want to use for the new paragraph style. For a character style, select a word or phrase that has the desired formatting applied to it.

2. In the Paragraph Styles palette or Character Styles palette, choose New Paragraph Style or New Character Style from the palette menu (Figure 17-4).

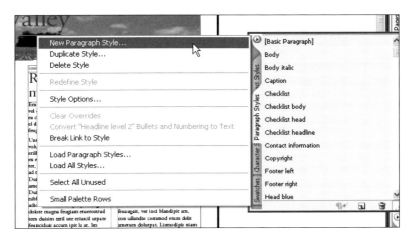

FIGURE 17-4

3. Specify general style parameters in the dialog box:

STYLE NAME: Defines the name of the style. Style names are listed in the style palettes and in any style drop-down lists.

BASED ON: Links the current style to an existing style. If any trait that the two styles share is changed in the "parent" style, that trait will automatically be changed in the "child" style. A good example of this is styles for main and sub-headings.

SHORTCUT: Lets you assign a numeric keypad shortcut to the style. You cannot use letters or non-keypad keys, but you can use any combination of Ctrl, Shift, and Alt keys (Windows) or Command, Shift, and Option keys (Mac) with the numeric keypad keys.

4. Click OK to finish creating your new style. If you want to change formatting or apply advanced formatting, click a new category in the list on the left side of the dialog box and change the settings for that category before clicking OK.

To apply a style:

1. Click in a paragraph or select multiple paragraphs if you want to apply a paragraph style. Select a word or phrase if you want to apply a character style.

2. Activate the Paragraph Styles or Character Styles palette, and click on the desired style.

To edit a style:

1. Select the style that you want to work with in the Paragraph Styles or Character Styles palette.

2. From the palette menu, choose Style Options. (You can also simply double-click the style in the Styles palette list to access style options.)

3. In the Style Options dialog box (Figure 17-5), select which category of formatting options you want to work with. The options for that category will be displayed on the right side of the dialog box.

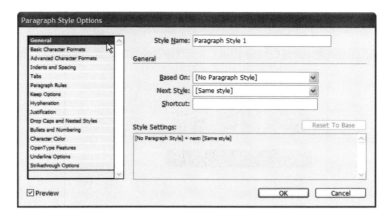

FIGURE 17-5

4. Specify the settings for the displayed options, repeating the process for other categories until the style suits your needs, and then click OK. All text that has this style applied to it will automatically be reformatted to match the new style settings.

HOW DO I CREATE AND FORMAT TABLES?

When it comes to presenting data in a document, nothing beats a good table. Tables have been a powerful feature of word-processing applications such as Microsoft Word for years, but until recently it was difficult to import tables or create them yourself in publishing applications. Fortunately, you can easily create tables in InDesign (or place them from Word) and apply a wide variety of formatting to them.

To create a table:

1. Select the Type tool then press and drag in your document to create a text frame.

2. Choose Table→Insert Table.

3. Enter the table dimensions in the Insert Table dialog box. Enter values for Body Rows, Columns, Header Rows, and Footer Rows.

4. Click OK. InDesign inserts a table into the selected text frame (Figure 17-6).

FIGURE 17-6

5. With the Type tool selected, click in any table cell to enter data.

1. If necessary, reselect the Type tool and click anywhere within the table to select it. Choose Table→Table Options→Table Setup to bring up the Table Options dialog box with the Table Setup tab visible (Figure 17-7).

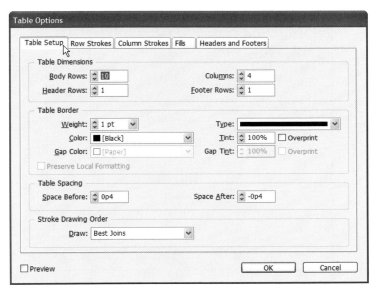

FIGURE 17-7

2. Specify settings for Table Dimensions, Border, Spacing, and Stroke Drawing Order.

3. If necessary, click the Row Strokes, Column Strokes, Fills, or Headers and Footers tabs to change options on those tabs.

4. Click OK.

1. Press and drag with the Text tool across a range of cells and choose Table→Cell Options→Text. This brings up the Cell Options dialog box with the Text tab visible (Figure 17-8).

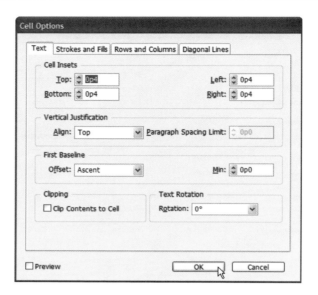

FIGURE 17-8

2. Specify options for text settings, including Cell Insets, Vertical Justification, First Baseline, Clipping, and Text Rotation.

3. If necessary, click the Strokes and Fills, Rows and Columns, or Diagonal Lines tabs to make additional changes.

4. Click OK.

HOW DO I CREATE CUSTOM KEYBOARD SHORTCUTS?

Why use keyboard shortcuts? To speed up the workflow. The big challenge is learning all the different keyboard shortcuts. If you're not familiar with many of the InDesign keyboard shortcuts, you can view them from the Keyboard Shortcuts dialog box.

To display the shortcuts:

1. Choose Edit→Keyboard Shortcuts to open the Keyboard Shortcuts dialog box (Figure 17-9).

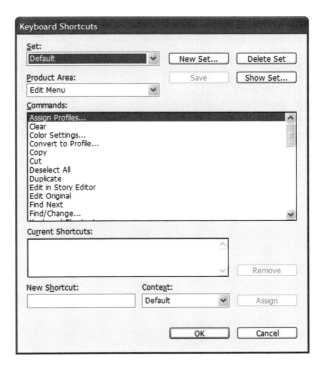

FIGURE 17-9

2. With Set on Default, choose a Product Area from the drop-down menu (Figure 17-10).

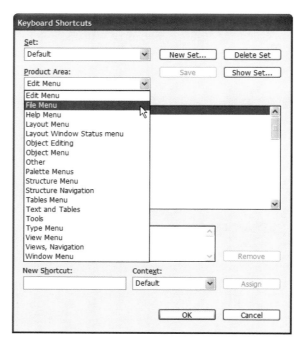

FIGURE 17-10

3. Select a command from the Commands selection area. The current keyboard shortcut assigned to that command is displayed in the Current Shortcuts text box area. If there is no shortcut assigned to that command, the Current Shortcuts text box area remains blank.

[NOTE]

For a quick reference, you can print out a hard copy of all the default keyboard shortcut commands (or the keyboard shortcuts for whatever other set you have selected in the Set drop-down). Click the Show Set button in the Keyboard Shortcuts dialog box. The *Default.txt* (or corresponding) file will automatically open in a text editor, and you can then print it or save it.

1. Choose Edit→Keyboard Shortcuts to open the Keyboard Shortcuts dialog box.

2. Select a Product Area from the drop-down menu.

3. From the Commands selection area, select a command.

4. Click in the New Shortcut text box, and type the desired keystroke shortcut for the command. If the keystroke is already assigned to another command, InDesign lets you know by displaying "Currently Assigned To" and the command that keystroke is assigned to right below the New Shortcut text box. You can then either choose to change the assignation of that keystroke or enter a different keystroke for the command.

5. Click Assign. Click OK to close the Keyboard Shortcuts dialog box.

To modify a keyboard shortcut:

1. Choose Edit→Keyboard Shortcuts to open the Keyboard Shortcuts dialog box.

2. Select a Product Area from the drop-down menu.

3. In the Commands selection area, select the command whose shortcut you wish to modify.

4. In the New Shortcut text box, delete the existing keystroke and type a new keystroke shortcut for the command.

5. From the Context drop-down menu, select when you want the shortcut to apply. This lets you use the same shortcut to perform different actions, depending on what you are doing at the time.

If you're a longtime user of QuarkXPress or PageMaker and are familiar with the keyboard shortcuts from those applications, beware—those shortcuts either will not work in InDesign or will produce different results from what you expect. Fortunately, to make the transition to InDesign easier, you can choose to use QuarkXPress or PageMaker keyboard shortcut sets in InDesign.

1. Choose Edit→Keyboard Shortcuts to open the Keyboard Shortcuts dialog box.

2. From the Set drop-down menu, select either PageMaker 7.0 or QuarkXPress 4.0.

Three keyboard shortcut sets come with InDesign (Default, QuarkXPress, and PageMaker), but you can also add (or delete) other keyboard shortcut sets.

To add a new set:

1. Open the Keyboard Shortcuts dialog box.

2. Click the New Set button to open the New Set dialog box, as shown in Figure 17-11.

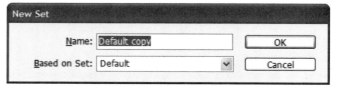

FIGURE 17-11

3. Enter a new set name in the Name text field.

4. Select which set you want your new set based on.

5. Click OK.

You can then add or make changes to the shortcuts in the new set, as described above.

To delete a set:

1. Open the Keyboard Shortcuts dialog box.

2. In the Set drop-down menu, select the set to be deleted.

3. Click Delete Set.

4. An Adobe InDesign warning box will appear, asking if you want to delete the set.
   Click Yes.

HOW DO I ADD DROP SHADOWS AND OTHER EFFECTS TO TEXT AND IMAGES?

You can apply several effects to images in your InDesign documents—you can apply drop shadows, feather the edges, or add corner effects (such as beveled, inset, or rounded corners).

1. Open the InDesign document containing the image.

2. With the Selection tool, select the image frame and choose Object→Drop Shadow. This will bring up the Drop Shadow dialog box (Figure 17-12).

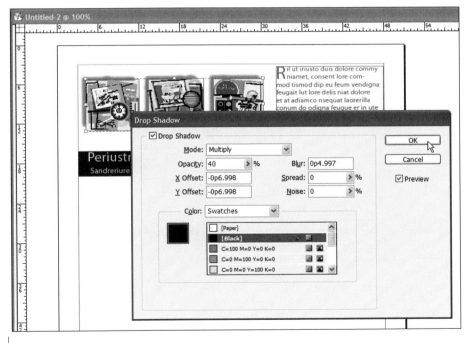

FIGURE 17-12

3. Check the box next to Preview to be able to view the changes in your document.

4. Check the box next to Drop Shadow to enable the drop shadow options.

5. Select a Mode from the drop-down menu, as well as other options such as Opacity, Blur, Offset, and Color.

6. Click OK to save the changes.

1. With the image frame selected, choose Object→Feather to open the Feather dialog box (Figure 17-13).

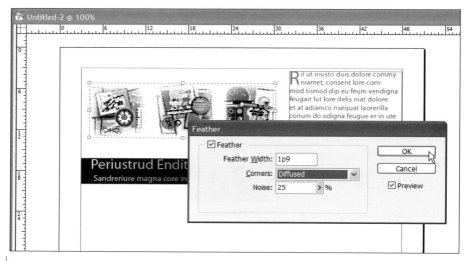

FIGURE 17-13

2. Check the box next to Preview to be able to view the changes made to the image.

3. Check the box next to Feather to enable the feather options.

4. Adjust the width of the feathering by entering a value in the Feather Width text box.

5. Select how you would like the corners displayed from the Corners drop-down menu. Choose from Sharp, Rounded, or Diffused.

6. Select the Noise percentage.

7. Click OK to save the changes.

1. With the image frame selected, choose Object→Corner Effects to open the Corner Effects dialog box (Figure 17-14).

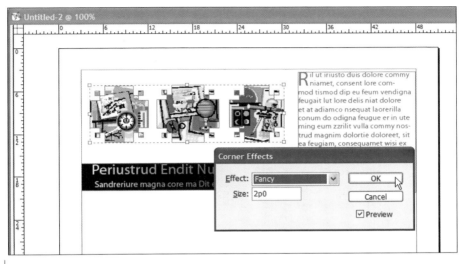

FIGURE 17-14

2. Check the box next to Preview to be able to view the corner effects you're applying to the image.

3. From the Effect drop-down menu, choose a corner effect.

4. Adjust the size of the corner effects in the Size text box.

5. Click OK to save the changes.

HOW DO I CREATE AND USE SNIPPETS?

Snippets are one of the great new features of InDesign CS2. But what exactly is a snippet? From the user's point of view, a snippet is simply a piece of an InDesign page that you can save and reuse in another document. From InDesign's point of view, a snippet is an XML file that contains a full representation of the content of a portion of an InDesign page, including objects, formatting, tags, and document structure information. Snippets are based on the InDesign Interchange file format and have an *.inds* extension.

1. Using the Selection tool, select one or more text frames, graphic frames, or other objects.

2. Choose File→Export to open the Export dialog box (Figure 17-15).

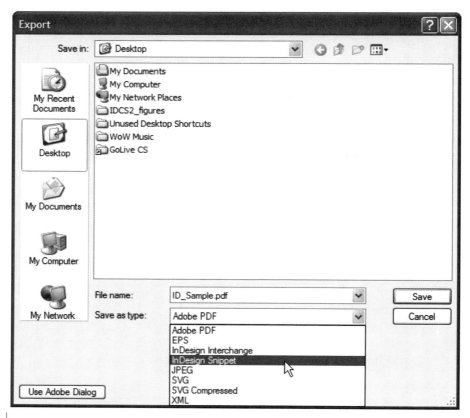

FIGURE 17-15

3. From the Save as type menu (Windows) or the Format menu (Mac), choose InDesign Snippet.

4. Name the file and specify a destination, and then click Save.

1. Choose File→Place.

2. In the Place dialog box, navigate to the location where the snippet is stored, select the snippet, and click Open. The snippet objects are placed in the exact same location in the current document as they were in their original document (Figure 17-16).

FIGURE 17-16

HOW DO I DRAW AND EDIT MY OWN ARTWORK?

Between Photoshop and Illustrator, CS2 users have access to every conceivable tool for creating high-quality artwork. If you want to create sophisticated original artwork, InDesign is definitely not the application to use. However, if all you need to do is create a simple map, diagram, or other line-based (vector) illustration, you can do that within InDesign by using the Pen tool. You can also edit artwork that you have copied and pasted (but not placed using File→Place) using the Direct Selection tool. You can edit placed artwork in the source application with the Edit→Edit Original command.

If you're not familiar with the Pen tool, it can take a little getting used to—but once you get the hang of it, it offers a tremendous amount of control for creating high-quality line art.

The key thing to keep in mind as you use the Pen tool is that it does not function like a real-world pen. Instead of pressing and dragging across the page to define the path of a line (the way you would with a real-world pen or with Photoshop's Paintbrush tool), you click at various locations to set points through which your path travels. If you click three points on the page and then click back on the first point, InDesign draws a path between the three points, creating a triangle (Figure 17-17). If instead of clicking to set a point you press and drag, you create a *curve point*, which your path will travel through with a smooth motion, rather than the sharp angle it takes when going through a *corner point*. By combining corner and curve points, you can create just about any line-based image you can think of (Figure 17-18).

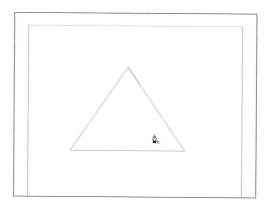

FIGURE 17-17

FIGURE 17-18

To draw shapes using corner and curve points:

1. Select the Pen tool.

2. Position the cursor in an empty area of your document, and click one time to create the first point of the path.

3. Move the mouse (*without* holding down the mouse button) to a new location, and click again to create a second point.

4. Repeat step 2 to create additional points.

5. Move the mouse cursor over your original starting point. A small circle will appear next to the cursor (Figure 17-19). This indicates that you can close the path by clicking again on the original starting point. Closed paths are called *shapes*.

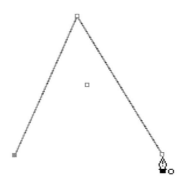

FIGURE 17-19

6. Click to close the path.

7. Start a second path by clicking in a new location.

8. Move the cursor to where you want the second point, but instead of just clicking, press (and hold) the button down.

9. With the mouse button depressed, drag a short distance away from the starting point. As you drag, handles will appear that stretch from the point to the cursor and extend an equal amount in the opposite direction (Figure 17-20).

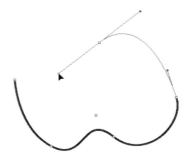

FIGURE 17-20

10. Keeping the mouse button depressed, move the cursor to stretch or rotate the handles of the new point. The rotation of the handle controls the direction the path takes as it passes through the point. The length of the handles controls the curvature of the path as it passes through the point. Shorter handles create sharper curves, while longer handles result in shallower curves.

11. When you are satisfied with the direction and curvature of the path, release the mouse button.

12. Repeat steps 8–11 to create additional curve points.

13. Position the cursor over the original starting point (make sure the circle appears next to the cursor), and click the mouse button to close the path.

To edit the paths you create with the Pen tool, use the Direct Selection tool. The key difference between the Selection and Direct Selection tools is that the Selection tool selects entire objects, whereas the Direct Selection tool selects object components. You might want to think of the Direct Selection tool as the Sub-Selection tool, since it selects parts of a larger object, such as paths or shapes in a piece of artwork, or individual points on a path (Figure 17-21).

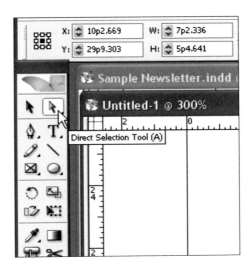

FIGURE 17-21

Once selected, these shapes, paths, or points can be moved or otherwise modified. Shapes can be moved, rotated, scaled, or recolored. Paths can be moved and reformatted, and points can be moved and can have their handles moved to change how the path moves through them.

To modify a shape:

1. Click the Selection tool (the solid black arrow tool).

2. Click on the shape.

3. Use the Color palette to change the object's line and fill colors.

4. Use the Object→Transform submenu to move, rotate, scale, or shear the object, or use the Control palette (between the menus and the document window) to make the same modifications, plus changing the stroke (line) thickness and style.

To edit points and path segments:

1. Click the Direct Selection tool (the hollow white arrow tool).

2. Click on a shape. This selects the shape, but not the frame that it appears within.

3. Position the cursor over a point, and a small square will appear next to the cursor indicating that you can select this point (Figure 17-22).

FIGURE 17-22

4. Click the mouse button to select the point. The point's handles will appear.

5. Press and drag the point to move it, or drag the handles to change the direction and curvature of the path as it passes through the point.

6. To select a segment of the path rather than an individual point, Shift-click to select additional points, or click outside of the object and drag a selection marquee around multiple points.

7. Position the tip of the cursor on the path (between points) and drag to move the sections of the path between the selected points (Figure 17-23).

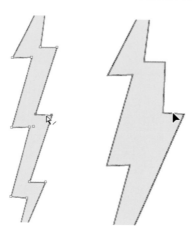

FIGURE 17-23

HOW DO I ADD ANCHORED OBJECTS?

Most objects, such as images, are placed on a page, and the text flows around them. *Anchored* objects, however, are placed inside or next to a block of text and move with that text block, even if the text is reflowed to a new location. The "anchor" in "anchored objects" refers to the object's position relative to a block of text, which is fixed—in other words, the object is "anchored" to the text.

In previous versions of InDesign, anchored objects were referred to as *inline graphics*, but the name has been changed to reflect the expanded nature of anchored objects in the latest version of InDesign. Anchored objects can now include sidebars, callouts, pull quotes, or other blocks of text, as well as figures, icons, and other graphics. Anchored objects can also be positioned with your choice of inline, above line, or custom positioning. Figure 17-24 shows examples of these positions, with inline positioning on top, above line positioning in the middle, and custom positioning on the bottom.

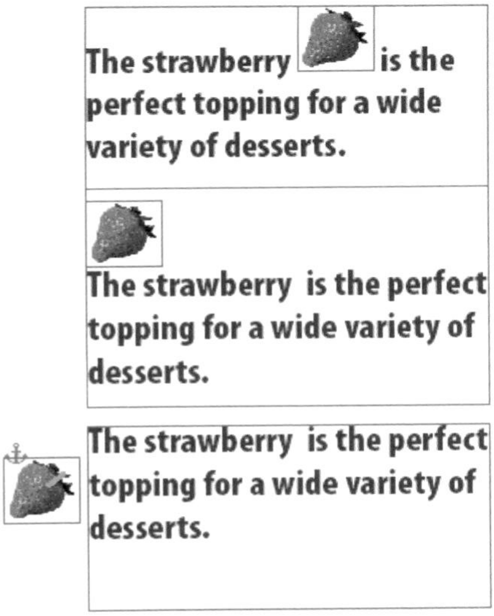

The strawberry is the perfect topping for a wide variety of desserts.

The strawberry is the perfect topping for a wide variety of desserts.

The strawberry is the perfect topping for a wide variety of desserts.

FIGURE 17-24

To create a new anchored object:

1. Select the Type tool and click in your text to position the insertion point where you want the object to be anchored.

2. Choose File→Place. In the Place dialog box that displays, navigate to and select the desired image file, and click Open.

1. With the Selection tool, select the object. Then choose Edit→Cut.

2. Select the Type tool and click in the text frame to which you want the object to be anchored.

3. Choose Edit→Paste.

When you anchor objects in this manner, InDesign uses the default position of inline.

[NOTE]

Anchoring an existing object is the easiest way to create an anchored text object such as a pull quote. This is because placing a text file into a text frame always inserts the contents of the file as additional story text, not as a separate object.

To set inline object position:

1. Select the object with the Selection tool, and choose Object→Anchored Object→Options. InDesign displays the Anchored Object Options dialog box.

2. From the Position pop-up menu, choose Inline or Above Line (see Figure 17-25).

3. Make sure the Inline option button is selected.

4. Set the Y Offset, which controls the object's vertical position relative to the text. In this case, the Y Offset is set to 0.

5. Click OK to apply these settings to your object.

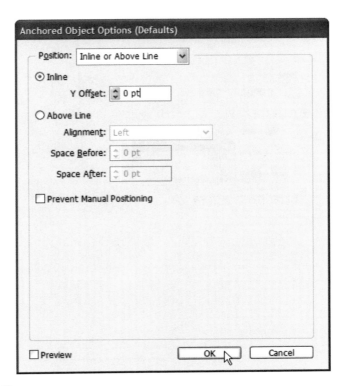

FIGURE 17-25

1. Select the object with the Selection tool, and choose Object→Anchored Object→ Options. InDesign displays the Anchored Object Options dialog box.

2. From the Position pop-up menu, choose Inline or Above Line (see Figure 17-26).

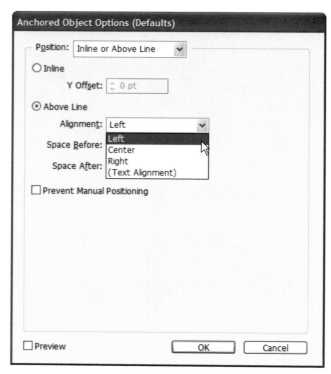

FIGURE 17-26

3. Select the Above Line option button.

4. Specify the following position options:

   ALIGNMENT: Left-, center-, or right-aligns the object within the text column.

   SPACE BEFORE: Positions the object relative to the bottom of the preceding line of text.

   SPACE AFTER: Positions the top of the next line of text relative to the object.

5. Click OK to apply these settings to your object.

To set a custom object position:

1. Select the object with the Selection tool, and choose Object→Anchored Object→ Options. InDesign displays the Anchored Object Options (Defaults) dialog box.

2. From the Position pop-up menu, choose Custom.

3. Set the object's internal reference point and general options in the section just below the Position drop-down menu:

RELATIVE TO SPINE: Interprets the object's position relative to the spine of a two-page spread. If this option is selected, an object along the inside margin of a left-facing page moves to the opposite side of the text frame (so that it remains along the inside margin) when the text flows to a right-facing page.

ANCHORED OBJECT - REFERENCE POINT: Specifies the location on the object that you want to align relative to a location on the page. The small white squares correspond to the top-left corner, top center, top-right corner, etc. Clicking one of these squares sets that location as the reference point.

PREVENT MANUAL POSITIONING: Prevents you from unintentionally moving the object by pressing and dragging it with the mouse.

4. Set the object's position using the options in the Anchored Position section:

REFERENCE POINT: Lets you specify where you want to position the object on the page, relative to the rest of the settings you will be choosing.

X RELATIVE TO: Lets you specify what you want the object's horizontal positioning to be relative to.

X OFFSET: Moves the object left or right, depending on the reference point.

Y RELATIVE TO: Lets you specify what you want the object's vertical positioning to be relative to.

Y OFFSET: Moves the object up or down, depending on the reference point.

KEEP WITHIN TOP/BOTTOM COLUMN BOUNDARIES: Prevents the object from moving so that it does not extend below the bottom boundary or above the top boundary of the text frame.

5. Click OK to apply these settings to your object.

HOW DO I COMBINE MULTIPLE DOCUMENTS INTO A BOOK?

A *book file* is a collection of InDesign documents that share character, paragraph, and graphic styles, as well as color swatches. Documents in a book can be numbered sequentially, as well as easily printed or exported to PDF together. Individual documents can be used in multiple book files. For example, you might have an End-User License Agreement file that you want to include in multiple software user manuals.

When creating a book file, you must designate one document as the style source. The styles and color swatches in this file will replace those in the other documents in the book. By default, the first file in the book is the style source, but you can specify any document you want as the style source at any time.

To combine multiple documents into a book:

1. Choose File→New→Book.

2. In the New Book dialog box that displays, enter a name for the book, select a location, and then click the Save button. The book file is created, and the Book palette appears in your document window.

3. Click the plus button at the bottom of the Book palette, or choose Add Document from the palette menu (Figure 17-27).

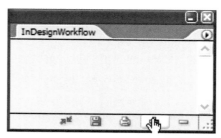

Add documents

FIGURE 17-27

4. In the Add Documents dialog box, select the InDesign document (*.indd*) files that you want to add to the book and click Open.

5. In the Save As dialog box, save each file under a new name (such as *BookName_Chapter1*, *BookName_Chapter2*, etc.). Alternatively, you can keep the original names and save the documents in a new location, such as in a *BookName* folder.

6. If necessary, rearrange the order of the documents in the Book palette by dragging the document names up or down in the list.

7. Designate one document as the style source by clicking the box next to the name of the document (Figure 17-28).

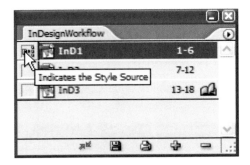

FIGURE 17-28

HOW DO I CREATE A TABLE OF CONTENTS?

The longer your publication is, the more your readers will benefit from a table of contents (TOC) to help them locate information. If you are familiar with creating TOCs in Microsoft Word, you will be right at home with InDesign, because the processes in the two applications are very similar.

Creating a table of contents in InDesign is heavily dependent on the proper use of paragraph styles. InDesign creates the table of contents by searching your document for paragraphs—such as chapter, section, or topic headings—that use a specified style or styles and then adding those paragraphs to the table of contents. This process requires that you apply these styles to your heading paragraphs *before* creating a table of contents and that you do so consistently, so that no paragraphs are missed. Once you have applied paragraph styles to your document (or documents, for a book file), you are ready to create the TOC.

The first step is to create a TOC style. This should not be confused with the paragraph styles that you apply to text in your documents—a *TOC style* determines what paragraph styles get included in the table of contents and how each entry appears. You can have multiple TOC styles in a document to use for other tables, such as tables of figures, tables of advertisers, and so on. These aren't tables of *contents*, but you can apply TOC styles to them as well.

1. Choose Layout→Table of Contents Styles.

2. In the Table of Contents Styles dialog box that displays, click New (Figure 17-29).

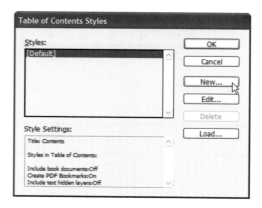

FIGURE 17-29

3. In the New Table of Contents Style dialog box (Figure 17-30), enter a name for your new TOC style. In this case, the name is InDesign Workflow.

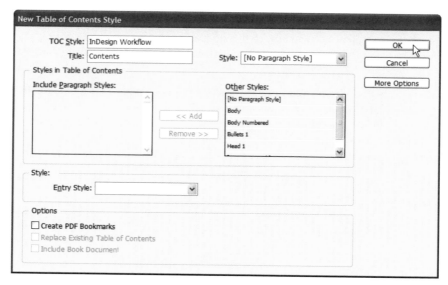

FIGURE 17-30

4. Enter a title for your table (such as Contents, Advertisers, Images, etc.), and apply a paragraph style to the title by selecting one from the Style pop-up menu.

5. Add styles to the Include Paragraph Styles section by selecting them in the Other Styles section and clicking the Add button. For example, you might choose the style Head 1, which is the style used for all of the main headings in a book or article. The order in which you add styles determines their position in the table hierarchy.

6. If necessary, remove unwanted styles by selecting them in the Include Paragraph Styles section and clicking the Remove button.

7. For each style that you add to the Include Paragraph Styles section, you can apply a different paragraph style. To do so, select the style and then choose a style other than [Same style] from the Entry Style pop-up menu.

8. For now, ignore the Options section at the bottom of the dialog box. You will set these options when you generate your TOC, as described below. Click the OK button to finish defining your TOC style, and then click OK again.

Once you've defined the TOC style, you're ready to generate your table of contents.

To generate a table of contents:

1. If you are generating a table of contents for multiple documents in a book file, create or open the document that will contain the table of contents, make sure that it is part of the book, and then open the book file.

2. At or near the beginning of the document, add a new page that will contain the table of contents.

[NOTE]

The table of contents should always be a separate story in its own text frame (or frames, for a lengthy table), because updating a table of contents updates the story that contains the table. If you simply add the table to the beginning of an existing story, the entire story will be replaced when you update the table of contents.

3. Choose Layout→Table of Contents. This brings up the Table of Contents dialog box, which is identical to the Table of Contents Styles dialog box, with one exception: in this dialog box you choose a TOC style from a pop-up menu instead of entering a name for the new TOC style you are creating.

4. From the TOC Style pop-up menu, select a custom style or use [Default] to format the entries in your table of contents exactly as they are formatted in the document (Figure 17-31).

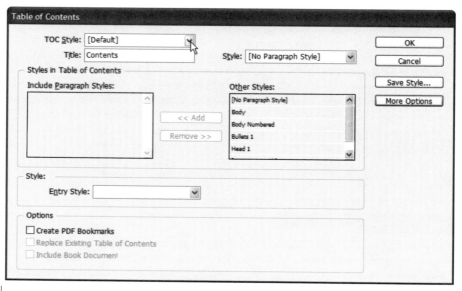

FIGURE 17-31

5. If you want to customize the TOC style, you can do so by adding or removing paragraph styles and modifying entry styles, as described in steps 5–7 of the preceding section.

6. If necessary, in the Options section, select the following options as desired:

   CREATE PDF BOOKMARKS: Generates bookmarks based on your table of contents when you export the document to PDF.

   REPLACE EXISTING TABLE OF CONTENTS: Replaces the entire story that contains the current table of contents with the new table of contents.

   INCLUDE BOOK DOCUMENTS: Creates a table of contents that includes paragraphs in other documents in the book file that use the paragraph styles specified in the TOC style.

7. Click the OK button to generate your table of contents. InDesign will load the text into the cursor. You can then place the TOC by clicking on the page or by clicking and dragging to define a custom text frame.

HOW DO I CREATE AN INDEX?

Like a table of contents, an index is a valuable resource for readers. Although not as common as tables of contents, indexes are just as valuable and can be included in your documents with a moderate amount of effort.

There are two steps to creating an index. The first step is to add index entries to your document. These entries tell InDesign where the index items appear in the document and how you want the items to appear in the index. The second step is to generate the index itself.

To add index entries:

1. Select the Text tool and click in a text frame to place an insertion point. Alternatively, select a word or short phrase. If you select text, this text will be used as the basis for the index reference.

2. Choose Window→Type & Tables→Index to display the Index palette (Figure 17-32).

FIGURE 17-32

3. Make sure the Reference option at the top of the palette is selected. To view index entries for any open documents in a book file, select the Book checkbox.

4. Choose New Page Reference from the palette menu, or click the "Create a new index entry" button at the bottom of the palette. This brings up the New Page Reference dialog box (Figure 17-33).

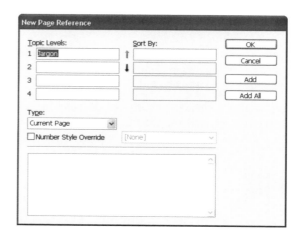

5. Enter text for this index entry:

- If you selected text in step 1 and want this to be a simple index entry (without sub-entries), you do not need to enter any additional text.

- If you did not select any text in step 1, type the text for the entry in the Topic Levels 1 field to create a simple index entry.

- If you want to create a complex index entry, type a main entry in the Topic Levels 1 field. As desired, enter additional subentries in the Topic Levels 2, 3, and 4 fields (Figure 17-34).

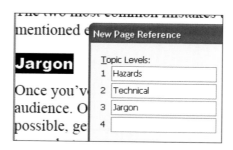

FIGURE 17-34

- To replace the text in any field with text from an existing index entry, select a field and then double-click an entry from the listbox at the bottom of the New Page Reference dialog box.

6. If you want an entry to be sorted in a different manner from the actual entry text, type the new text in the Sort By field to the right of the entry. For example, to sort an index entry about Bob Jones by his last name, type "Jones, Bob" in the Sort By field next to the Bob Jones entry.

7. Choose an entry type from the Type pop-up menu:
   - For a range of pages, choose one of the options to indicate the length of this entry.
   - For an entry without a page reference, choose Suppress Page Range.
   - For a cross-referenced entry, choose one of the cross-reference options (See or See also) and enter the entry to which the reference points in the Referenced field.

8. Click OK to create the entry and close the dialog box. Alternatively, to add this entry without closing the dialog box, click the Add button.

[NOTE]

If you selected text in step 1, you can click the Add All button to create index entries for every instance of the selected text.

To generate an index:

1. If you are generating an index for multiple documents in a book, create or open the document that will contain the index and make sure that it is part of the book. At or near the end of the document, add a new page that will contain the index.

2. If the Index palette isn't visible, display it by choosing Window→Type & Tables→Index.

3. Choose Generate Index from the palette menu, or click the "Generate index" button at the bottom of the palette.

4. In the Generate Index dialog box that appears (Figure 17-35), enter settings for your index:

   TITLE: Specifies the name of the index (usually just "Index"), which will appear at the top of the index.

   TITLE STYLE: Specifies which paragraph style you want to apply to the index title.

REPLACE EXISTING INDEX: Replaces the story that contains the current index with the new index. You should never add an index to a story that contains other text!

INCLUDE BOOK DOCUMENTS: Includes index entries from other documents in the book file.

INCLUDE ENTRIES ON HIDDEN LAYERS: Allows you to create an index that includes entries for text that never appears in the printed document (for example, the text itself may appear on layers that have been hidden). This is often used to point the reader to a page that contains material related to a topic but may never actually mention the index entry topic by name.

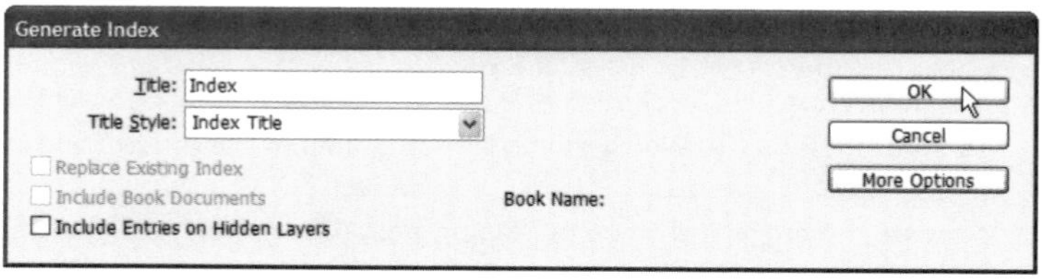

FIGURE 17-35

5. Click the OK button to generate the index and load the text into the cursor. Place the text as you would any story.

HOW DO I CREATE PDF BOOKMARKS?

The PDF format is an increasingly popular destination for documents these days. PDF lets you distribute your documents digitally, whether via email, as an Internet download, or on a shared server (ideal for archiving documents within your company or department). In addition to the convenience of distributing documents digitally, converting your documents to PDF form also allows you to add a navigational structure in the form of bookmarks. By now, most computer users have seen and used bookmarks in PDF documents, so you probably already know that they're a great way to make your documents immediately more accessible to the reader.

If you own Acrobat, you can add bookmarks (and much more) to your PDF within Acrobat. But what most people don't know is that you can also add bookmarks to a document that you intend to output as a PDF right in InDesign.

This section discusses working with individual bookmarks. The most common method for creating a bookmark structure for your document is via a table of contents, as discussed in the sections "How Do I Create a Table of Contents?" and "How Do I Create an Index?"

To add a new bookmark:

1. Select the destination for your new bookmark *before* creating it, by doing one of the following:

   - With the Text tool, click in a block of text to create an insertion point.

   - With the Text tool, highlight a block of text. The highlighted text will be used as the name for the new bookmark.

   - With the Selection tool, select a piece of artwork.

   - In the Pages palette, double-click a page.

2. If necessary, adjust the magnification level and position of the document in the window as desired.

3. Display the Bookmarks palette by choosing Window→Interactive→Bookmarks.

4. Click the bookmark (if any) under which you want the new bookmark to appear. If you do not click a bookmark, your new bookmark will appear at the end of the list.

5. Create your bookmark either by clicking the "Create new bookmark" button at the bottom of the Bookmarks palette or by choosing New Bookmark from the palette menu (Figure 17-36).

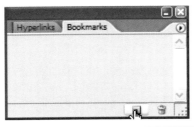

Create new bookmark

FIGURE 17-36

6. To test your bookmarks, export the document to PDF using the File→Export command, set the fileType (Windows) or Format (Mac OS) to Adobe PDF, and then click Save. In the Export Adobe PDF dialog box that appears, be sure to select the Bookmarks option in the Include section.

To rename a bookmark:

1. Click the bookmark in the Bookmarks palette.

2. Choose Rename Bookmark from the palette menu. Alternatively, right-click (Windows) or just click (Mac) the bookmark, and choose Rename from the contextual menu.

3. Type a new name for the bookmark and press Enter/Return.

To delete a bookmark:

1. Click the bookmark in the Bookmarks palette.

2. Choose Delete Bookmark from the palette menu. Alternatively, right-click (Windows) or just click (Mac) the bookmark, and choose Delete Bookmark from the contextual menu.

HOW DO I CREATE PDF HYPERLINKS?

A *hyperlink* is a word or phrase that, when clicked, takes the user to another destination. That destination can be another page in the document (an internal link), a page in a different document (an external link), or a web page (a web link).

Hyperlinks, like bookmarks and buttons, are features that it only makes sense to add to your document if you intend to output it as a PDF. However, if that is your document's final destination, hyperlinks and buttons can greatly increase the appeal and functionality of the document.

The simplest way to create a hyperlink is to use the Hyperlinks palette and point it to a page, a location in a text block, or a URL. However, if you plan on creating a lot of hyperlinks, you may want to define various destinations first, then create your hyperlinks. The advantage of this second method is that once you have defined your destinations, you can link to them by simply selecting them from a list when creating your hyperlinks. This requires more planning ahead of time, but it makes the process of creating a lot of links faster and less prone to error.

To define a hyperlink destination:

1. Define the page or text anchor destination:

   - For a page destination, go to the document and page that you want to use, and adjust the magnification and positioning of the page within the document window as desired.

   - For a text anchor destination, go to the document and page that contain the text that you want to use and either position the insertion point or select a block of text.

2. Choose Window→Interactive→Hyperlinks to display the Hyperlinks palette.

3. Choose New Hyperlink Destination from the palette menu.

4. From the Type pop-up menu, choose Page, Text Anchor, or URL.

5. Specify the setting for your destination:

   - For a page destination, either type a name or click the Name with Page Number checkbox, and then select a page and a zoom setting.

   - For a text anchor destination, name the destination.

   - For a URL destination, name the destination, and then type or paste the URL into the URL field.

6. Click the OK button to create your hyperlink destination.

You will *not* see the destination in the Hyperlinks palette, but it will show up in the Name pop-up list in the New Hyperlink dialog box.

1. Make sure that the destination document is open. You cannot create a hyperlink that points to an unopened document.

2. In the source document, select the text or graphic that you want to use as the hyperlink source (the clickable item that sends the user to the hyperlink destination).

3. If the Hyperlinks palette is not already displayed, choose Window→Interactive→Hyperlinks to display it.

4. Click the "Create new hyperlink" (Windows) or Create Hyperlink (Mac OS) button at the bottom of the Hyperlinks palette, or choose New Hyperlink from the palette menu (Figure 17-37).

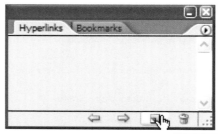

Create new hyperlink

FIGURE 17-37

5. In the New Hyperlink dialog box, rename the hyperlink, if desired (Figure 17-38). Renaming the hyperlink does not change the text (if any) used as the hyperlink source, but it does change the name of the hyperlink in the Hyperlinks palette.

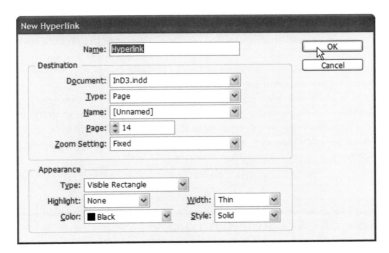

FIGURE 17-38

---

6. In the Destination section, specify settings for your new hyperlink's destination:

DOCUMENT: The name of the document that contains the source to which you want the hyperlink to point. All open documents that have been saved appear in this list.

TYPE: The type of destination for the hyperlink: Page, Text Anchor, or URL.

NAME: The name of the hyperlink destination. To create a hyperlink to an unnamed destination, leave this set to Unnamed. If you're creating a hyperlink to a previously created destination, select the appropriate name from this list. This option is not available for text anchor destinations.

PAGE: The page number of the destination document to which you want to link. If you selected Text Anchor as the destination type, this option will be unavailable. If you selected URL as the destination type, this option will be replaced with a URL field in which you can specify the web address that you want to use as the hyperlink destination.

ZOOM SETTING: The magnification level of the destination page. This option is available only for page destinations.

---

7. In the Appearance section, specify how you want your new hyperlink to look:

TYPE: Set the link type (either Visible Rectangle or Invisible Rectangle).

HIGHLIGHT: Set the appearance of the hyperlink when the user clicks on it.

WIDTH: Set the width of the rectangle surrounding the hyperlink (available only for Visible Rectangle).

COLOR: Set the color of the rectangle (available only for Visible Rectangle).

STYLE: Choose either a solid or dashed rectangle (available only for Visible Rectangle).

8. Click the OK button to create your new hyperlink.

9. To test your hyperlink, export the document to PDF using the File→Export command, set the file Type (Windows) or Format (Mac OS) to Adobe PDF, and then click Save. In the Export Adobe PDF dialog box that appears, be sure to select the Hyperlinks option in the Include section.

HOW DO I CREATE PDF BUTTONS?

One of the great features of online documentation compared with traditional printed documentation is that you can add a high level of interactivity to online (PDF) documents. This interactivity can include bookmarks and hyperlinks, but the pinnacle of interactivity comes in the form of buttons.

Buttons can be placed anywhere you want and can look like anything you want. Although they can't exactly do anything you want them to, they can do quite a lot—for example, buttons can provide navigation for the document, add audio and visual content, and even allow users to open and close files or exit an application.

So that your buttons will be more visually appealing and as easy as possible for you to create in InDesign, it is highly recommended that you use Photoshop or Illustrator to create the graphics for each button, including any graphics for multiple states for rollover effects, ahead of time.

To create a PDF button:

1. Select the Button tool.

2. Click where you want the button to appear, and then enter the desired height and width for your new button in the Button dialog box that appears (Figure 17-39). Alternatively, you can click and drag with the Button tool to define the size and shape of your button.

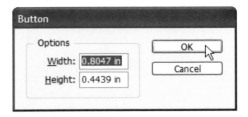

FIGURE 17-39

3. Select the button with the Selection tool, and either double-click it or choose Object→
   Interactive→Button Options.

4. On the General tab of the Button Options dialog box (Figure 17-40), specify settings for
   your button:

   NAME: The name of the button.

   DESCRIPTION: The text that will appear when the user mouses over the button.

   VISIBILITY: Whether the button will be hidden or visible when the document is
   exported to PDF. Most buttons are visible, but you may want to have a button that is
   hidden until activated by a mouse moving over it.

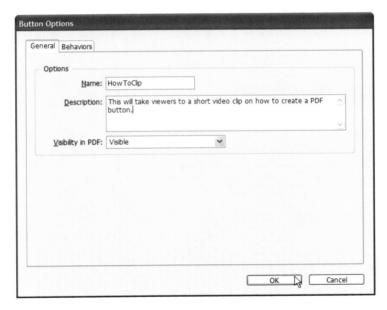

FIGURE 17-40

5. Click the OK button to apply these settings.

6. Add content to the button to identify its purpose to the user. You can do this with text or images:

FOR TEXT: Select the Text tool, click on the button, and type a word or short phrase. Select the text and then format it as desired. You can use the Direct Selection tool to select and move the text block within the button.

FOR IMAGES: Select the button with the Selection tool, choose File→Place, and choose a graphic file to place in the button. You can then use the Object→Fitting commands to adjust how the image fits within the button.

[NOTE]

You can convert any placed image or text frame into a button by selecting the object with the Selection tool and choosing Object→Interactive→Convert to Button.

Due to our exposure to the Internet, most users now look for visual cues as much as textual content to discern interactive elements from static elements. *Rollovers* are visual effects that you can add to a button to help viewers understand that the button is something that they can interact with. Rollovers have three states: Up (when the mouse is not over the button), Rollover (when the mouse is hovering over the button), and Down (when the mouse button is clicked).

To create button rollover effects:

1. Use the Selection tool to select the button to which you want to add a rollover effect, and choose Window→Interactive→States. This brings up the States palette, with the current button states displayed. For a new button, the only state that displays is the Up state (Figure 17-41).

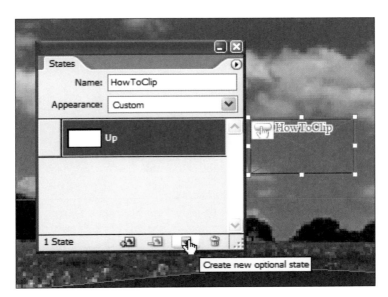

FIGURE 17-41

2. Click the "New optional state" button at the bottom of the palette. This creates a Roll-over state, which will be displayed when the mouse is over the button.

3. Click the "New optional state" button again to create a third state, Down, which will be displayed when the mouse button is clicked or pressed while the mouse is over the button.

4. Click on the Rollover state, and then click the "Place content" button at the bottom of the palette. This brings up the same Place dialog box that you get when you place content into your document using the File→Place command.

5. Locate and select the image or text file that you want to use for the button's Rollover state, and click OK.

6. Repeat steps 4 and 5 for the Down state. When your document is exported to PDF, the button will have a different appearance for each state.

That's all well and good, but creating a button and giving it a cool rollover effect are two pointless exercises unless your button actually does something. These "things" that buttons do—the things that make them useful—are called *behaviors*. Behaviors can include a wide range of effects, such as taking the user to another location, playing sound and video clips, or hiding and displaying other buttons.

To add button behaviors:

1. Select the button with the Selection tool, and double-click it to open the Button Options dialog box.

2. Click the Behaviors tab to display the behavior controls (Figure 17-42).

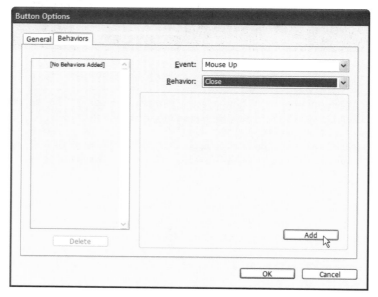

FIGURE 17-42

3. Choose an event from the Event pop-up menu. This event is the trigger for the behavior that you will choose next. The events include:

   MOUSE UP: Occurs when the mouse button is released. This is the typical "click" action.

   MOUSE DOWN: Occurs while the mouse button is down. This is usually a "press" action, because in a click the Mouse Down event is immediately followed by a Mouse Up event.

CHAPTER 17

MOUSE ENTER: Occurs when the mouse cursor moves over the button.

MOUSE EXIT: Occurs when the mouse cursor moves out of the area occupied by the button.

ON FOCUS: Occurs when the visitor tabs to the button (i.e., presses the Tab key to select it).

ON BLUR: Occurs when the visitor tabs to the next button.

4. Choose a behavior from the Behavior pop-up menu. Each behavior will have additional options for you to choose. The possible behaviors include:

CLOSE: Closes the PDF document.

EXIT: Quits the application in which the PDF document is being viewed.

GO TO: Jumps to a specific location, such as a text anchor, page, document, or view.

MOVIE: Lets you play, pause, stop, or resume the specified movie file.

OPEN FILE: Opens a specified file (non-PDF files require an application capable of opening them to be available).

SHOW/HIDE FIELDS: Displays or hides a field in a PDF document.

SOUND: Lets you play, pause, stop, or resume the specified sound file.

VIEW ZOOM: Changes the magnification, layout, and rotation of the PDF document.

5. After you have selected a behavior and set its options, click the Add button to add the event/behavior combination to your button.

6. Add additional event/behavior combinations as needed, or click the OK button to finish the process.

7. To test your buttons, export the document to PDF using the File→Export command, and set the file Type (Windows) or Format (Mac OS) to PDF. Click Save. In the Export Adobe PDF dialog box that appears, be sure to select the Interactive Elements option in the Include section.

HOW DO I PREFLIGHT AND PACKAGE MY DOCUMENT?

You've now created or gathered the text and graphics; designed the document layout; placed all the elements together; and edited, formatted, and proofread every page. You're almost ready to send your publication to the printer. The last topic in this "How Do I..." chapter is appropriately focused on these last steps: preflighting and packaging the document.

Preflighting is the term used in the publishing industry that refers to the process of checking a document for possible printing problems. The term was inspired by the airline industry's thorough preflight checks, and it serves the same function—to detect problems before they become disasters. InDesign's preflight utility checks the document for a number of different potential problems, such as missing graphics files and missing fonts. It also provides information that can help a professional printer diagnose issues specific to their process, such as those related to the inks used, font usage within the document, and other print settings.

Packaging a publication is the last step before sending it off to the printer. The packaging process copies all of the files and fonts used in the publication, organizes them into a simple folder structure, and resets all of the links in the publication to point to the newly copied files. By sending this package to the printer, rather than just the publication file, you ensure that the printer will have access to every file and font used in the publication.

Packaging can be done using the File→Package command, or as part of the preflighting process.

To preflight and package your InDesign document:

1. Choose File→Preflight. InDesign runs a check on your document and opens the Preflight dialog box (Figure 17-43).

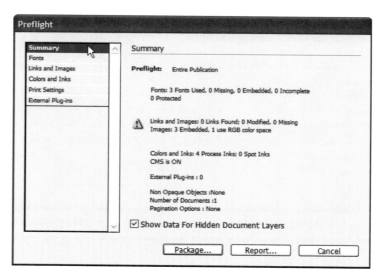

FIGURE 17-43

2. Select a category from the list on the left side of the Preflight dialog box. When you select a category, potential problems and information related to this category display on the right side of the dialog box. The categories include:

SUMMARY: Indicates all the potential problems that InDesign has found in the document and displays special warning icons.

FONTS: Displays more detailed information about font usage, including a list of all the fonts used in the document, the type of each font, the status of each font (i.e., whether it is included in the document), whether the fonts are protected (i.e., cannot be embedded due to licensing restrictions), and even the page on which each font in the document was first used. Choose Show Problems Only to display only the problem fonts. If any fonts are missing from your document, you can choose to either load those fonts on your computer or replace them with different fonts.

To replace a font, click Find Font. In the Find Font dialog box, the missing font will be at the top of the list of fonts, and a warning icon will be displayed next to it. You can now replace it with another font from the same family by selecting the desired font in the Replace With section and clicking Change All. When you're finished, click Done.

LINKS AND IMAGES: Displays a list of all the links and images used in the document. To see only problem links and images, select Show Problems Only. For an image that has been modified outside of InDesign, you will need to update the image by selecting the warning message for that image in the Preflight dialog window and clicking the Update button. For a missing image, select the warning message for that image and click the Relink button. A Find dialog box will appear where you can then navigate to that file, select it, and click Open. If InDesign locates any RGB errors, you will not be able to make any changes from the Preflight dialog box. Instead, you will need to modify the image in Photoshop or another image application.

COLORS AND INKS: Displays a list of all the inks used in the document, including both process colors and spot colors. Spot colors are generally undesirable because they increase both printing costs and complexity. For this reason, you may want to convert spot colors to process colors. If you want to make color changes, you must make them by using the Swatches palette.

PRINT SETTINGS: Displays the print settings that appear in the Print dialog box.

EXTERNAL PLUG-INS: Displays a list of external plug-ins that were used in creating the InDesign document and indicates whether you will need them to output the document.

3. If you would like to save the summary as a text file, click the Report button.

4. Click the Package button. InDesign will prompt you to save any changes made during the Preflight process. Click Save to continue.

5. In the Printing Instructions dialog box, enter information such as the contact name, company name, address, phone number, fax number, email address, and any printing instructions. This information is saved as a text file (the default filename is *instructions.txt*) and is included in the InDesign package. Click Continue.

6. In the Package Publication (Windows) or Create Package Folder (Mac) dialog box that appears, navigate to the location where you would like to save the InDesign package. By default, the package is given the same name as the original document. You can change the name by typing a new name in the Save As text box.

7. At the bottom of the dialog box, select the most common options to include in the In-Design package: Copy Fonts, Copy Linked Graphics, Update Graphic Links in Package, and Use Document Hyphenation Exceptions Only. The Include Fonts and Links from Hidden Document Layers and View Report options are optional and not as crucial to include in the package.

8. Click the Save button. A Font Alert warning box will appear, notifying you of legal information on fonts. Click OK, and InDesign will start to package the document. Note that larger files take a longer time to package.

[NOTE]

You can view or make changes to the instructions.txt file created previously by clicking the Instructions button in the Package Publication (Windows) or Create Package Folder (Mac) dialog box.

THE END

This ends the answers to the Top 15 How Do I...? questions. Should you find yourself with more questions that you need answers to, check out the Adobe InDesign forums at Adobe's web site: *http://www.Adobe.com/support/forums/main.html*.

GoLive as Part of the Creative Suite

As a standalone application, the new Adobe GoLive CS2 is a very easy application to use to create a web site. But when it's used in conjunction with Adobe Photoshop CS2, Adobe Illustrator CS2, and the other Creative Suite 2 applications, it becomes an even more powerful tool that you can use to create an amazing end product. This chapter will cover some of the basics of GoLive, and we'll take this knowledge further in the following chapters.

AN OVERVIEW OF GOLIVE

Of all the applications in the Creative Suite, Adobe GoLive is probably the one least familiar to the average user. Photoshop is practically a household term, and most people have
at least heard of Illustrator and have an idea of what it does. InDesign has the benefit of
a huge installed base of PageMaker fans to work with, and Acrobat, although not really
understood by most people, is at least a recognized product the world over. But what
GoLive lacks in recognition, it more than makes up for in power. GoLive sports a huge
number of truly impressive features and has something to offer any web designer.

Unlike Photoshop, Illustrator, and InDesign (and even Acrobat, to some extent), GoLive
has nothing to do with Adobe's traditional home court: print publishing. Instead, GoL-
ive is focused solely on web publishing. And while some of GoLive's interface will look
familiar to longtime Adobe users, its tools and approach to content creation are totally
different from those of the other CS2 products.

However, just because GoLive's focus is different from the rest of the Creative Suite
doesn't mean that it stands alone. GoLive is tightly integrated with the other Creative
Suite products, especially through Smart Objects and Version Cue. A *Smart Object* is a
web-optimized version of a native Photoshop, Illustrator, or PDF file. Without images created in Photoshop and Illustrator, GoLive's web sites would look empty indeed—and with
Smart Objects, modifying native Adobe files is fast and easy.

Who Uses GoLive

GoLive was designed for web site creation and management, and like all of its CS2 siblings, it does what it was designed for extremely well. For the most part, GoLive web sites
are created and managed by web designers, but "web designer" is a hat that can be worn
by anyone from a trained and experienced "real" web designer to a high school student
who is creating a personal weblog (or blog) to share with her friends. Here are just a few
examples of how GoLive is used:

- A teenager who loves his video games uses GoLive's weblog objects to keep his gaming site up to date with the latest tips, tricks, and screenshots. He also uses the weblog
  calendaring object to keep his friends posted on any upcoming gaming events.

- A young woman who was recently hired at a start-up company to create and maintain
  its internal and public sites uses the full Creative Suite for her work. She creates logos
  and buttons in Illustrator, prepares photos and other images in Photoshop, and converts white papers and other internal documents to PDF format with Acrobat. All of this
  content is then placed in GoLive as Smart Objects so that she can quickly and easily
  edit the files as needed.

- A senior web designer who works for a large retail chain is expanding its online store-front. The designer is responsible for maintaining the integrity of hundreds of images and other files for the store's online catalog. He uses GoLive's site window to track online assets and the In & Out Links palette to find and fix any broken links.

CREATING A WEB SITE WITH GOLIVE

When you first launch GoLive, a Welcome screen appears, like the Welcome screen in the other Creative Suite 2 applications (Figure 18-1). You can select from one of the many options on the Welcome screen (What's New in GoLive, Tutorials, and Cool Extras), or you can choose New Document or Open Document to create a new document or open an existing document, respectively.

FIGURE 18-1

To create a new web site from the Welcome screen, select New Document. The New dialog box appears, and the Site Creation Wizard walks you step by step through several screens to set up your new web site. (If you have disabled the Welcome screen, another way to bring up the Site Creation Wizard is to choose File→New from the menu bar.) If the Site Creation Wizard is not displayed after you have selected to create a new document, click on the Site icon on the left and make sure the Create Site option is selected in the middle panel.

If you intend to publish your site to a live server, you will need the server address, the name of the directory to which you will be uploading your site, and your username and password (which you can get from either your Internet service provider or your system administrator). If you do not have this information handy when creating your web site, you can always enter it at a later date.

Now that you have created a new, blank web page, familiarize yourself with the GoLive work area (Figure 18-2) before you start your development.

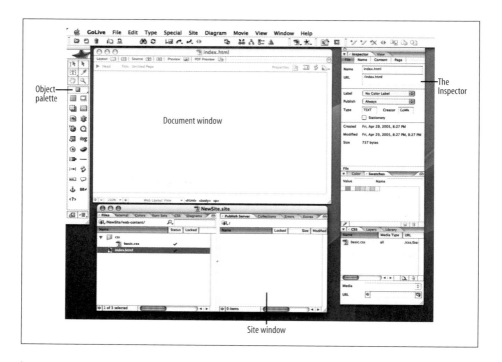

Site window

FIGURE 18-2

The GoLive work area contains these main components:

SITE WINDOW: This window is the control center of your web site. All file maintenance should be performed here.

DOCUMENT WINDOW: This window displays the content within your web page, either in a graphical layout format or as source code. You'll have one document window for each open page.

THE INSPECTOR: This feature displays information about the selected file or object and is also used to create links.

OBJECTS PALETTE: This palette displays tools and objects used to create your web site.

OTHER PALETTES: Other palettes that you'll use in creating your web site include the Color, Swatches, CSS, Layers, and Library palettes. If a particular palette is not visible, from the GoLive menu bar, choose Window and select the palette you wish to display.

EXPLORING THE GOLIVE SITE WINDOW

The site window is one of the most important features in GoLive CS2. Using the site window is imperative for any type of file management. If you need to add, delete, or move a file or image, always use the site window. Although you can perform all these functions manually directly in the *web-content*, *web-data*, or *web-settings* folders, you run the risk of possibly breaking links and creating *orphan files*, which are files that have not been saved to the site's *Root* folder and will cause broken links when you upload your site to a live server. The *web-content*, *web-data*, and *web-settings* folders are located in your site folder and are automatically generated when you create a new web site. Figure 18-3 shows an example of a site window.

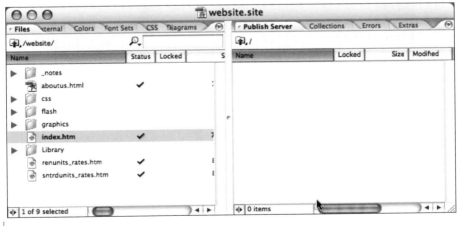

FIGURE 18-3

The site window is divided into two tab sets. The tabs on the left display your site assets, such as HTML files, images, CSS files, and color and font sets:

FILES: Displays the structure of your web site, including all HTML/XHTML files, images, JavaScripts, PDFs, and CSS files you are currently using.

EXTERNAL: Contains all external URLs that are used within your site. If you need to change a URL link that appears on several pages, simply make the changes to the URL in the External tab, and the relevant links on all the web pages will be updated with the changes.

COLORS: Shows all of the colors currently in use in your site. When you select a color from the Colors tab, the In & Out Links palette displays all the pages on which that particular color is being used.

FONT SETS: Displays all the font sets currently used in your site. Not all computers have the same fonts installed, so if the viewer's computer does not have the same fonts available that you used to create your site, different fonts will be substituted. A *font set* is a list of acceptable font substitutions.

CSS: Lists all CSS external files, classes, and identifiers used in your web site. The CSS tab displays how many times a CSS file, class, or identifier is used within the site.

DIAGRAMS: Displays a list of user-created site diagrams. A *site diagram* is a graphical representation of a site's organizational structure.

On the right side of the site window are tabs used for site management:

PUBLISH SERVER: Lists all of the files that are currently on your live server. This file list should be an exact mirror of the list in the Files tab.

COLLECTIONS: Displays a list of collections. A *collection* is a set of files defined either by a user or as the result of a query.

ERRORS: Lists any errors in your local site, which you should fix before uploading it to a live server. This is helpful for checking for broken links to images, other files, or external URLs.

EXTRAS: Contains information about your site and other files that you would not necessarily upload to a live server, such as templates or Smart Objects in their native formats.

The In & Out Links Palette

The In & Out Links palette is another very powerful tool that can be used in conjunction with the site window. To open the In & Out Links palette, choose Window→Site→In & Out Links. You can also use the keyboard shortcut Command-5 (Mac) or Ctrl-5 (Windows) to open the palette.

The Links tab of the In & Out Links palette displays a graphical representation of links and file references to and from the selected file in your site window. To the left are all the files that contain links to the selected file. To the right are all the files that the selected file links to. The In & Out Links palette also indicates any broken links, which is especially useful when troubleshooting link errors. Figure 18-4 is an example of the In & Out Links palette, displaying the *index.html* page and all the images associated with that particular page.

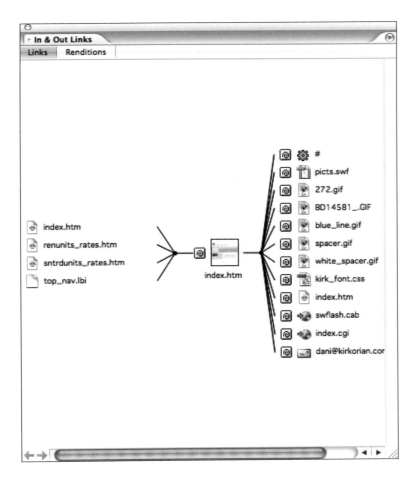

FIGURE 18-4

You can also use this palette to view which of your web site's pages use a particular CSS file or font set, or even a certain color. The Renditions tab shows implied links between files, such as a native Photoshop source image and its web-optimized target image.

The amount of information displayed in the In & Out Links palette can sometimes be overwhelming. You can control what is displayed in the palette by changing the palette options. To access the palette options, click the Palette Options button in the upper-right corner of the In & Out Links palette. From the Palette Options window, select or deselect the information you want displayed.

New Search Functionality in GoLive CS2

A new feature of the GoLive CS2 site window is the capability to search for files directly in the site window itself. While in the Files tab, click and hold the magnifying glass to bring up the drop-down menu shown in Figure 18-5, and select from one of the following: Contains, Is, Begins With, or Ends With. Then type the keyword in the blank text box, and press Enter (Mac) or Return (Windows). The results will be displayed in the Files tab of the site window. To close the file search window, click on the X just to the right of the search text box.

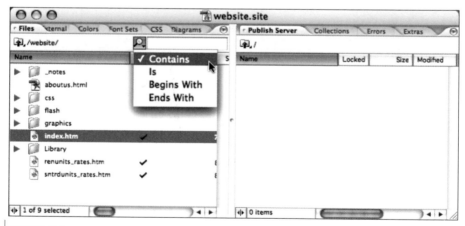

FIGURE 18-5

CHAPTER 18

USING THE OBJECTS PALETTE

The Objects palette in GoLive CS2 may look similar to the Toolboxes in Illustrator, Photoshop, and the other Creative Suite 2 applications, but it is in fact quite different. Because Photoshop and Illustrator (and, to a lesser extent, InDesign) are applications for creating and manipulating graphics, they share a similar set of tools. The GoLive Objects palette, on the other hand, consists primarily of objects that can be placed on a web page, rather than a set of editing tools—GoLive does provide some editing tools, but not nearly as many as are found in the other Creative Suite 2 applications.

GoLive's Objects palette is shown in Figure 18-6. The top section of the Objects palette contains some traditional editing tools: Standard Editing, Object Selection, Layer, Eyedropper, Hand, and Zoom. The bottom section contains the various types of objects that you can add to your web site, such as tables, images, and QuickTime movies (included in the Basic objects set).

FIGURE 18-6

The following sets of objects are also available, via the pull-down menu immediately beneath the editing tools:

SMART: You can use various Smart Object elements in your web site, such as Smart Photoshop, Smart PDF, and Smart Illustrator Objects.

CSS: Different table layouts—such as a three-column table with a scaling center cell, a two-column table with a fixed left cell, and a vertical navigation bar—are available for your use.

FORM: Several form elements (Submit Button, Text Field, Radio Button, etc.) can be used when creating a form on your web site.

HEAD: These tools are for items that go in the Head section of your web site, such as keywords for web searches, comments you might want to add about your web site, or a script to run a particular action.

FRAME: These tools create frames within your web site. There are several different frame sets to choose from, such as two columns with a variable right or three rows with a variable middle.

SITE: These tools can be used in your site window, to add a generic page, add a URL or email address, set a new font group, and more.

DIAGRAM: Use this set of tools when creating a site map. Open a new diagram window by choosing Diagram→New Diagram, and click and drag the appropriate objects onto your diagram window to create your new site diagram.

QUICKTIME: This set of objects contains several QuickTime elements you can use to add a QuickTime movie to your web site, such as Movie, Video, Color, and even SWF Tracks.

MOVEABLE TYPE 3.X: Drag and drop these objects (calendar, comments section, archive link, and more) onto your web page to create an online weblog. For more information about Moveable Type, visit *http://www.movabletype.org*.

SMIL: The Synchronized Multimedia Integration Language objects are used to create interactive presentations.

TYPEPAD BLOG: This set of objects is also used in creating an online blog. For more information about TypePad, visit *http://www.typepad.com*.

If you've used a previous version of GoLive and want to change the Objects palette to look more like a palette than a toolbox (as it did in previous versions of GoLive), click the "Separate tools and objects" button in the lower-left corner of the palette.

USING THE INSPECTOR

As its name implies, the Inspector contains information about the object that is currently selected in the document window. When you select an HTML file, a table, an image, or even a form object, its properties are displayed in the Basic tab in the Inspector (see Figure 18-7). For example, if you select an image, its width, height, and alignment are displayed in the Inspector. If you click on a different object within your web page, such as a table, the table's details are displayed (how many rows and columns the table contains, the height of the table, and more). If the Inspector is not visible, you can display it by choosing Windows→Inspector or using the keyboard shortcut Command-1 (Mac) or Ctrl-1 (Windows).

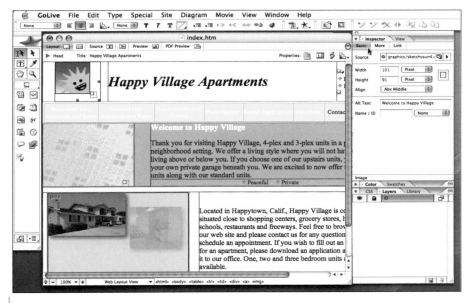

FIGURE 18-7

In addition to obtaining information about an object, you can use the Inspector to replace an existing image.

To replace an existing image using the Inspector:

1. Drag a line from the Fetch URL tool (the squiggly icon to the left of the Source field in the Basic tab) to the image file in the Files tab of your site window. The Fetch URL tool is also known as the *pick whip*.

2. Release the pick whip, and GoLive will update the image.

. . . .

Setting a Link

Another function of the Inspector is to assign links to images and selected text, so that users can click on an image or text block to navigate to a different spot on the page, or to a new page or web site.

To create a link:

1. Select the image or block of text you want to turn into a link.

2. In the Inspector, click the Create Link button.

3. Do one of the following:

   - In the Link field in the Inspector, manually type in the URL.

   - Point and shoot with the Fetch URL tool to select a file to link to in the Files tab of the site window.

   - Browse to a specific file by clicking the Browse button located to the right of the Link field.

   - Click on the arrow next to the Browse button to display a list of recent files to choose from.

WORKING WITH THE CSS EDITOR

Cascading Style Sheets (CSS) are a web designer's dream come true. You can easily control font attributes (such as color, size, style, and weight), page layouts, and even tables using CSS—simply modify a style in one location, and the entire look of your web site changes. This combination of formatting efficiency and consistency is the true power of CSS.

To add CSS styles to your web site, use the GoLive CSS Editor. To open the CSS Editor, click the Open CSS Editor icon in the upper-right corner of the document window, as shown in Figure 18-8. On the left side of the CSS Editor are the internal and external styles associated with the web site. (An *internal style* is directly written into the Head section of the web page. An *external style* is stored in a separate style sheet.) On the right side is a menu of icons that help you create the various styles, as depicted in Figure 18-9. You can also choose to display these icons at the top of the CSS Editor by selecting the Show These Buttons at Top checkbox.

FIGURE 18-8

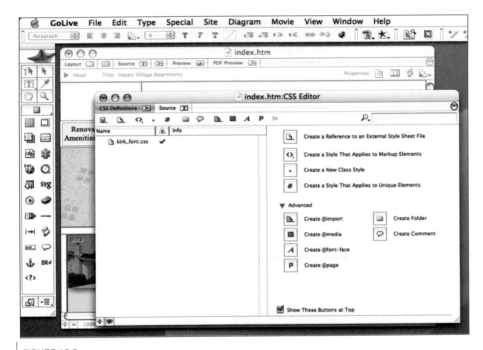

FIGURE 18-9

Creating a Style

Three different types of CSS style can be applied to a web site (note: to return the CSS Editor to its default state, make sure no style is selected on the left side):

ELEMENT STYLES: These styles are associated with markup elements (such as an HTML/XHTML tag) and are assigned to all occurrences of that tag. To add an element style to a specific HTML tag, choose the Create a Style That Applies to Markup Elements button in the CSS Editor, drag the cursor to display the menu, and select the tag (see Figure 18-10).

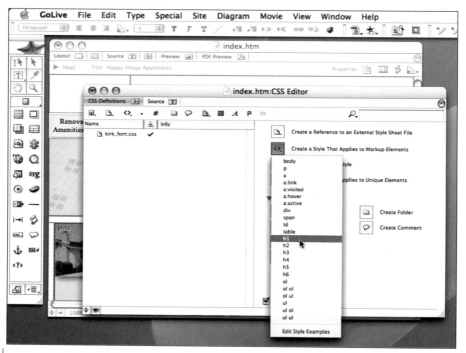

FIGURE 18-10

ID STYLES: You can assign ID styles to only one element in a document, and that element must be unique in order for the style to be applied. The ID style name must be preceded by a pound sign (#). To create an ID style from the CSS Editor, click the Create a Style That Applies to Unique Elements button. Then click on the Selector and Properties button in the CSS Editor menu bar, and add style properties.

CLASS STYLES: Class styles are similar to element styles, but they are more flexible in that they can be applied to any type of content within your web site, such as a block of text, an image, or even a cell in a table. They can also be applied multiple times. Class style names must begin with a period (.). To create a class style, click the Create a New Class Style button in the CSS Editor.

More advanced CSS users can view and make changes to the CSS script source code by clicking on the Source tab in the upper-left side of the CSS Editor. The source code is color-coded for your convenience, as shown in Figure 18-11. To return to the regular viewing of the CSS Editor, click the CSS Definition tab just to the left of the Source tab.

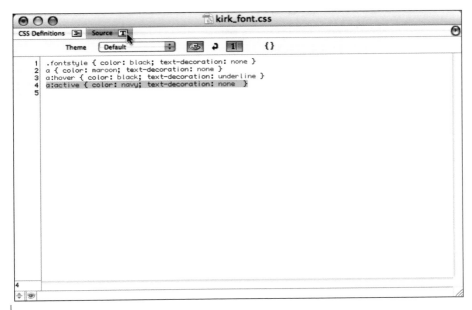

FIGURE 18-11

Determining When to Use External and Internal Style Sheets

An external style sheet is ideal if you want to be able to change the look of multiple web pages or an entire web site but only have to change the styles in one location. An external style sheet resides outside of the web site itself, in its own document.

To create an external style sheet:

1. Click the Create a Reference to an External Style Sheet File button, located on the right side panel of the CSS Editor. This will create an empty placeholder.

2. Click the Create button (Figure 18-12). The Save As dialog box will open, and you'll be prompted for a filename. Click the Save button when you're done.

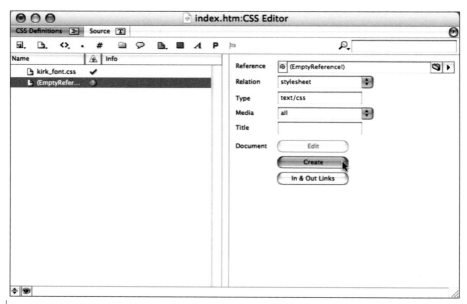

FIGURE 18-12

3. Click the Edit button in the CSS Editor to begin adding styles to your external style sheet.

An internal style sheet is usually used when only one web page requires a specific formatting. Internal styles reside within the actual web page itself, either in the Head section or inside the individual HTML tags. If a conflict occurs between styles, the internal style will take precedence over the styles specified in the external style sheet.

Applying Styles

After you've created your Cascading Style Sheets, you need to apply ID and class styles to your web site. There are several ways you can add class styles to a web page. After selecting the text or item to which you wish to apply the style, choose one of the following ways of adding the style:

• Choose a style from the CSS palette (Figure 18-13), which lists all the available internal and external styles.

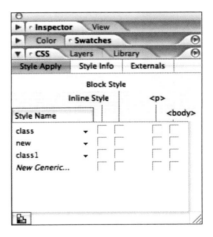

FIGURE 18-13

• Click the "Apply CSS style" icon in the toolbar (Figure 18-14), and then select a formatting option from the CSS Style preview that appears.

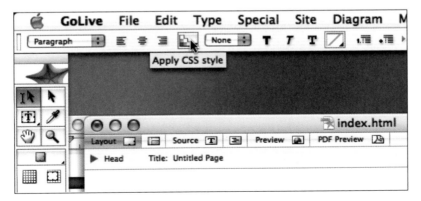

FIGURE 18-14

- Choose Type→CSS Style from the menu bar (Figure 18-15), and then select a formatting option from the CSS Style preview.

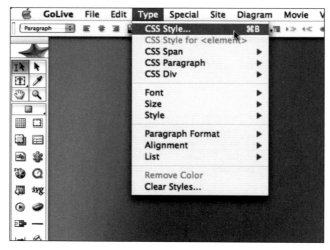

To apply an ID style, you have to manually add CSS tags to your HTML code. Select the appropriate text or item, and then add the style using either the Source Code Editor or the Visual Tag Editor (which allows you to edit the source code of a single element without having to open the Source Code Editor):

- To open the Visual Tag Editor, choose Special→Visual Tag Editor from the menu bar. Then enter the code to assign the ID within the brackets.

- To access the Source Code Editor, select the Source tab in the document window. The source code for the selected item will be highlighted. Once you've located it, add the ID style name as an attribute to the item's start tag, omitting the pound sign at the beginning of the style name (i.e., ID="*stylename*").

**Here are the most important things to take away
from this chapter:**

1. Site window, site window, site window. Did I mention the site window? That's how important it is to always use the site window when doing any type of file maintenance to your site.

2. The In & Out Links palette is an extremely useful tool. Used together with the site window, it can save you hours of frustration when trying to find and fix broken links.

3. The Inspector not only displays information about the selected file or object but also can be used to replace images and create links.

4. Cascading Style Sheets are your friends! They ensure that your formatting remains consistent from one page to the next, and they make reformatting a fast and easy process.

5. When using external and internal style sheets, always remember that the internal styles override any external styles applied to a web page.

19

Web Site Design with GoLive

In the past year alone, designing a web site has become increasingly easy. The primary reason for this was the release of Adobe's GoLive CS2. Long gone are the days when you needed to learn HTML to put together a web site—GoLive does all the behind-the-scenes work for you, allowing you to create your site in several different ways. You can use GoLive's tables, frames, layout grid, layers, or even predefined templates. In this chapter, you will learn how to create a site using layers. You can do many amazing things with layers, such as creating drop-down menus and overlapping images.

CREATING A WEB SITE USING LAYERS

GoLive layers are similar in some ways to layers in Photoshop and Illustrator. In all three applications, layers are containers for text and images. Layers allow you to group certain images or blocks of text and then display or manipulate them independently from the text and images in other layers. Where GoLive layers differ is that they can be different sizes.

What Are Layers?

GoLive layers are adjustable boxes that you add to your web page. These boxes can contain text and/or images. Unlike tables, which are difficult to resize or reposition, you can drag and drop a layer almost anywhere on the page, change the size of a layer at will, hide or show a layer, and even overlap layers. The biggest disadvantage to using layers is that you cannot scale them, meaning that you cannot set a layer to span a certain percentage of a browser window, as you can with a table. Still, you will find many occasions for which you will want to use GoLive layers instead tables—for example, the hide/show feature for layers allows you to create those really cool drop-down menus you see on so many web sites today.

Adding Layers to Your Web Page

When you add a layer to your document, it will automatically appear in the Layers palette. To add a layer to your document or page, select from any one of these three methods:

- Drag the Layer icon from the Draggable Basic Objects section of the Objects palette onto your document. To resize the layer, make sure the layer is selected and then hold your cursor over one of the blue markers (resize handles) until it turns into a double-sided arrow, as shown Figure 19-1. Press and drag to resize the layer, and then release.

- Select the Layer tool from the top section of the Objects palette. On your document, click and drag with the cursor until you have created a layer of the desired size, and then release.

- Click within the page to place your cursor and then, in the lower-right corner of the Layers palette, select the "Create new layer" button. GoLive creates a new layer at the location of the cursor. Resize the layer as described above.

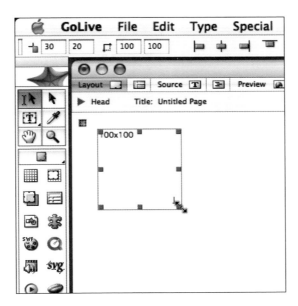

FIGURE 19-1

[NOTE]

If you find yourself having a difficult time getting a layer to be a specific size, you can also resize the layer from the Inspector. Select the layer and then, in the Layer tab in the Inspector, specify the desired width and height in the Width and Height fields.

Naming Layers

After you create a layer, naming that layer is extremely important. As the image on the left in Figure 19-2 shows, if you don't name your layers you won't be able to distinguish between them in the Layers palette. The layers in the Layers palette on the right, in contrast, have been given descriptive names. When it's 3:00 a.m. and you're faced with a deadline that can't be pushed back, which palette would you want to be working with?

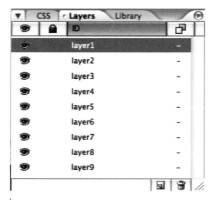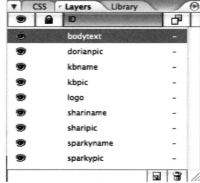

FIGURE 19-2

Just as there is more than one way to create a layer, there is more than one way to name a layer. To begin, select the layer you want to name, and then choose from either of these methods:

- In the Layer tab in the Inspector, enter the layer's name in the Name field. Click outside of the Inspector to deselect the Name field.

- In the Layers palette, enter the layer's name in the ID field by clicking once on the name to change it to an editable field and entering the name. Click on a different layer to deselect the newly named layer.

Selecting and Moving Layers

Now that you've created a layer, you might need to move it around to position it just right. When working with a single layer or layers that are spaced out, it's easy to simply click on a particular layer to select it. However, when you are working with multiple layers that either are stacked on top of each other or are too close to select easily, you'll need to use one of the following methods:

- With either the Object Selection tool or the Standard Editing tool, click on the little yellow square marker icon that was automatically created at the original insertion point of the layer, as shown in Figure 19-3. When you click on the marker, it not only selects the layer, but the Inspector also displays information for that layer. This yellow marker icon comes in quite handy when you're working with multiple layers that are stacked on top of each other or are hidden.

- Select a layer in the Layers palette. Click on the layer's name in the ID column, and you'll see that the appropriate layer within your document is now selected.

- With your layer selected, you can now move it to its new location.

FIGURE 19-3

To move a layer:

1. Move the cursor over the border of the layer until it turns into a sideways hand.

2. Press and drag, and notice that the open hand turns into a closed fist, indicating that it has "grabbed" the layer and that it's now ready to be moved to its new location (Figure 19-4).

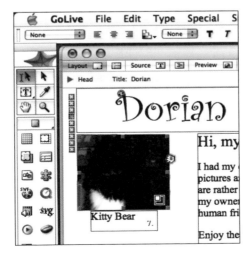

FIGURE 19-4

3. Move the layer around. As you do, you'll notice that a temporary layout grid appears in the background. Release the layer, and the grid disappears! When you're working with multiple layers a crosshair will appear, indicating when the layer is aligned with another layer.

[NOTE]

If you know exactly where you want to move the layer within your document, you can enter the position in the Left and Top fields of the Layer tab in the Inspector. The position coordinates must be measured in pixels, from the upper-left corner of the document window.

If you have layers stacked on top of each other, you can turn off (hide) the top layer to access the layer(s) beneath it. To do so, click on the visibility icon (the eyeball) to the left of the layer name in the Layers palette. To turn a layer back on, click on the empty space where the visibility icon was previously displayed.

[NOTE]

Hiding the content of a layer in GoLive does not make the layer invisible when viewing it in a browser. To do that, you will need to change the layer's visibility status in the Inspector.

Assigning Order to Multiple Layers

When you're working with multiple layers—especially ones that are stacked on top of each other or overlap—it's a good idea to assign each layer a *z-index*. A layer's z-index determines its position in regard to other layers. For example, a layer with a higher z-index number will appear closer to the top of the layer stack than a layer that has a lower or negative z-index number.

To add a z-index to a layer:

1. Select the layer by clicking on its corresponding yellow marker icon or selecting the layer name from the Layers palette.

2. In the Layer tab in the Inspector, add the desired z-index number in the Z-index field (Figure 19-5).

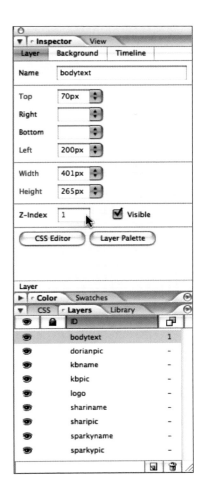

FIGURE 19-5

ADDING TEXT AND GRAPHICS TO A LAYER

Just when you thought creating a web site was all work and no play, this is where the fun
begins. You can truly see your web site come together when you start adding text and
images. To add text to a layer, click in the layer, select the Standard Editing tool (if it's not
already selected), and type the new text. To add a regular image to a layer, such as a GIF,
JPEG, or BMP file, drag the image from the file listing in the site window into the layer.
You can even add color or a background image to a layer, just as you would in a table—
but the true magic happens when you add text styles and Smart Objects to your web site.

Applying Styles and Formatting

- It's easy to just type in text and leave it as it is, but where's the creativeness in that? With the CSS Editor, you can add styles to text, or even to a layer. When you open the CSS Editor, all the layers are listed in the panel on the left. When you click on a layer, the properties of the style applied to that layer display on the panel on the right, as shown in Figure 19-6.

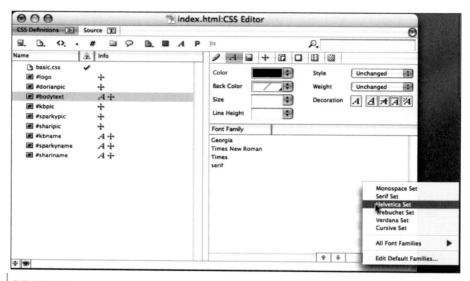

FIGURE 19-6

To jazz up the text, you can change its color or size; add decoration such as an underline, strikethrough, or overline; or even make it blink. To access the CSS Editor, do one of the following:

- Choose Special→CSS→Open Editor.

- Click the Open CSS Editor button located in the upper-right corner of an open web page.

- Press Option-Command-C (Mac) or Alt-Shift-Ctrl-C (Windows).

Using Smart Objects

So what's all this talk about Smart Objects, and why would you want to use them when creating your web site? If you are a longtime user of GoLive and the other Creative Suite applications, you know that when working with images, Smart Objects are better than aspirin because they stop headaches before they even begin. If you are new to GoLive and the Creative Suite, you will be blown away by how easy Adobe has made your web workflow by creating Smart Objects.

In the pre–Creative Suite era, you needed to know the exact size of an image before bringing it into your web site. After you'd placed an image in your site, resizing the image damaged its integrity, causing distortion and pixelated edges. Instead, you had to go back to the application that the image was created in and resize the original image to the specific dimensions required for your web site. It was sometimes necessary to go back and forth several times to get an image to just the right size.

Then along came Adobe's Creative Suite Smart Objects. With Smart Objects, resizing an image that you've placed in your web site is no longer a problem. GoLive allows you to drag and drop native Photoshop, Illustrator, EPS, and even PDF files directly onto your web site and then converts the files into web-compatible formats, such as JPEG and GIF, that can then be used in the site.

To add an image to a layer:

1. Select the layer to which you want to add the image.

2. From the Objects palette, under the Smart set, drag a Smart Photoshop, Smart Illustrator, or any of the other Smart Object icons into the layer.

3. In the Basic tab in the Inspector, select the file by either dragging a line from the Fetch URL tool (the squiggly line icon to the left of the Source field) to the destination in the site window or browsing to the file by clicking the icon to the right of the Source field.

4. After you have selected the file, the Save For Web – Powered By ImageReady window appears, as shown in Figure 19-7. Under the Optimize tab, decide whether you want to save your image as a JPEG or a GIF. A big deciding factor is the size of the final file, which is displayed in the lower-left corner of the Optimized tab. Click the Save button.

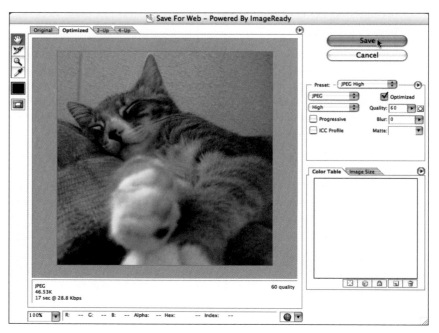

FIGURE 19-7

---

5. The Save dialog box appears, and GoLive prompts you to save the Smart Object target file. When saving the file, always be sure to save it to your site's *web-content* folder. To make sure you are saving the file to the correct location, click the folder icon next to Site Folder in the lower-left corner of the Save dialog box and select the *Root* folder. If you choose not to save the file to the site folder, a warning window will appear. GoLive automatically gives the newly converted file the same name as the original image but saves it in the previously specified JPEG or GIF format. Click Save.

---

6. If your newly created Smart Object image is a little bigger than you would have liked, or doesn't quite fill up enough space, simply select the image and drag one of the resize handles. When you release the mouse button, GoLive will regenerate the image.

Give yourself a big hand. You've just created your first Smart Object and added it to a layer! Chapter 20 goes into more detail on the various types of Smart Objects that are available to use when creating your web site.

[NOTE]

If you do not save the Smart Object target file to the *Root* folder of your site, you could create missing links when it comes time to upload your site to a live server, because any files saved outside of the *web-content* folder will not be uploaded. Of course, there are ways to fix these missing links later, but why create more work for yourself when it's just as easy to save the file in the proper folder?

Adding a Background Color or Image

If, after you have added the desired content to a layer, the layer still looks a little dull, you can add a background color or image to that layer to give it a little pizzazz. Keep in mind, however, that you do not want the background color or image to detract from the content in the layer. Make sure that the background color blends in with the overall color scheme of your web site and that the background image is light enough so that the text remains legible.

To add a background color to a layer:

1. Select the layer.

2. From the Background tab in the Inspector, choose the checkbox next to Color.

3. To change the color, click the lower-right corner of the color field to display a menu of color choices, or click in the color field and change the color in the Color palette (Figure 19-8).

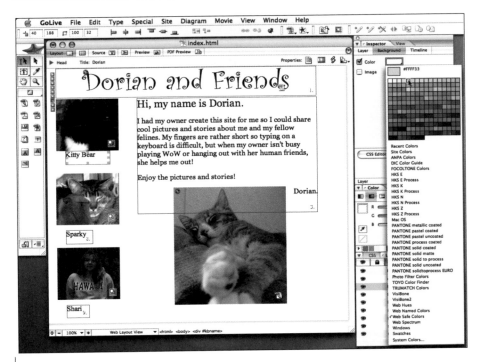

FIGURE 19-8

1. Select the layer.

2. From the Background tab in the Inspector, choose the checkbox next to Image.

3. Select an image by either using the Fetch URL tool, browsing to where the image is located, or using the flyout menu to the right of the Browse icon and then selecting from the list of recently used files.

PREFLIGHTING YOUR SITE FOR THE WEB

Preflighting? And you thought you were creating a web site, not an Acrobat PDF! Although preflighting is a word most commonly used in the context of Acrobat and printing, it can also be applied to a web site in GoLive. After all the hard work and time you have put into your web site, you want others to be able to view it. But before presenting your creation to the public, you will want to make sure your site is free from errors. You have several ways to ensure a properly functioning web site: checking for broken links, removing unused files, and checking to see if you're uploading the latest version of your site.

Checking for Errors

Whether you're working with a small or large web site, overlooking missing files and broken links is quite easy. Of course, if you have been using the site window to do all your file maintenance (moving, adding, and deleting files), your site should be error-free and ready to upload to a live server. But if errors have occurred due to either moving or deleting files manually, the In & Out Links palette and the Files and Errors tabs in the site window will locate those errors for you.

You can access the In & Out Links palette by using either of these methods:

• Select Window→Site→In & Out Links.

• Press Command-5 (Mac) or Ctrl-5 (Windows).

Figure 19-9 shows the possible error icons that might appear in the site window or the In & Out Links palette.

FIGURE 19-9

From left to right, the error icons are:

BUG ICON: Indicates broken links in a web page. As cute as this little icon is, you won't want many of these popping up in your site window.

STOP ICON: Indicates a missing file.

ALERT ICON: Refers to Smart Objects and indicates that a target file was not created when copying a Smart Object.

EMPTY PAGE ICON: Indicates a blank page.

QUESTION MARK ICON: Indicates a file that cannot be opened by GoLive.

ORPHAN FILE ICON: Indicates a link was created to a file that was not found in the *web-content* folder and will not be uploaded.

[NOTE]

If your site window displays several errors the first time you check it, don't panic. Instead, refresh the site window by choosing Site→Update→Refresh All. Likely, these errors will disappear. Magic? No. It's possible that filenames were changed or files were moved, but GoLive did not reflect these changes.

Correcting Errors

In the old days, when web designers had to hand-code HTML to create a web site, they had to search line after line of code to find what was causing each little error. Today, debugging has become much easier. For the most part, GoLive finds all of your site errors for you. This section will show you how to fix those errors.

Figure 19-10 shows an example of a web site that has several errors, including missing and orphan files. On the left side of the site window, in the Files tab, the bug icon displays to the right of the *index.html* file, indicating a broken link on that page. On the right side of the site window, the Errors tab lists all the orphan and missing files.

Under the Files tab in the Inspector, information on the orphan file is displayed, including the location of that file. Orphan files that are not added to the *web-content* folder will not be uploaded to the server, resulting in broken links.

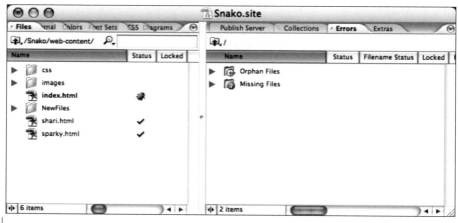

FIGURE 19-10

1. Select the orphan file located in the Errors tab in the site window.

2. Drag the selected orphan file onto the Files tab in the site window. The Copy Files dialog box appears, informing you of which files will be updated due to the relocation of the orphan file. Click OK. GoLive will copy the orphan file from its current location to your web site's *web-content* folder.

3. The once-orphaned file is now listed in the Files tab, but don't be surprised if it doesn't immediately disappear from the Errors tab. Close the site window, and when you reopen it, the orphaned file will be gone.

Missing files are also listed in the Errors tab, but unfortunately, fixing a missing file error is not as easy as dragging and dropping it to a new location. Here are some of the methods you can use to correct missing file errors:

• In the Files tab in the site window, select the file with the broken link indicator. In the In & Out Links palette, the selected page will be displayed along with all files linked to it, including the missing links, indicated by the missing link bug icon. Drag a line from the Fetch URL tool to the correct file, and GoLive will update and correct the missing link error.

• From the Errors tab in the site window, select the missing file. In the Inspector, drag a line from the Fetch URL tool to the correct file. The URL field will be updated with the correct location of the once-missing file.

- Select the missing file in the Errors tab. In the In & Out Links palette, drag a line from the Fetch URL tool to the correct file. Release the tool, and GoLive will update the link with the correct file location.

Setting Options to Clean Up Your Site

You're almost ready to put your site up on a live server! Now comes the cleanup part, which, once again, GoLive makes as painless as possible. If you're wondering why you would want to clean up your site, there are several good reasons. If you have limited server space for your web site, cleaning it up will remove any unused files and reduce the overall size of your site. Also, GoLive will remove any unused external links, colors, and font sets, so if you go back and edit your site later you'll be sure to use consistent font and color sets. Finally, any files that are referenced from within your site but exist outside of the *web-content* folder will be added to the *web-content* folder, preventing any orphan links.

To set cleanup options and start cleaning:

1. From the GoLive menu bar, choose Site→Update→Clean Up Site. The Clean Up Site Options dialog box will appear (Figure 19-11). Make sure that any open documents are closed before you do a site cleanup.

FIGURE 19-11

2. In the Add Used section, choose which options you wish to add, such as Files (files located outside of the *web-content* folder), External Links, Colors, or Font Sets.

3. In the Remove section, choose which options you wish to have GoLive remove from your site, such as Files Not Linked, Unused External Links, Unused Colors, and Unused Font Sets. After you have made your selections, click OK.

4. If there are any files that will be added, the Clean Up Site window will appear, listing those files. Click OK. Next, the Copy Files dialog box will appear, informing you that the files listed will be updated with the change. Click OK.

5. If there are any files that will be deleted from your site, the Clean Up Site window will again appear, listing all the files to be discarded. Click OK.

Could cleaning up your site be any easier? Well, probably, but only if someone else was doing it for you!

PUBLISHING YOUR SITE

Now that you have created your web site, checked it for errors, and done a little spring-cleaning, you're probably itching to upload it to a live server. But before you can upload your site, you will need to have purchased a domain name and opened an account with a web-hosting provider. You can find many reputable domain registrars and web-hosting providers by doing a Google search.

> **[NOTE]**
>
> Many web-hosting providers either offer package deals at a discount price or include a free domain name. When shopping for a web-hosting provider, there are three things to consider: price, storage space, and number of email addresses.

After registering your domain name and setting up your account, you will need to get the following information from your web-hosting provider in order to upload your site:

- Server address
- Directory
- Username
- Password

Setting Up Your Server

As intimidating as this may sound, as long as you have the necessary information at hand GoLive makes it easy to set up your server.

To set up your server:

1. From the GoLive menu bar, choose Site→Publish Server→Set Up Server. This will display your site's Settings dialog box (Figure 19-12).

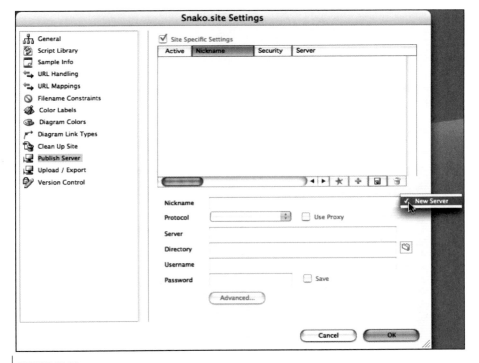

FIGURE 19-12

2. Click on the double arrows located on the right side of the Nickname field to add a new server. Enter a name for this new server connection.

3. Select FTP from the Protocol pop-up menu. FTP is the recommended method of uploading files to a server.

4. Enter the Server address, directory, username, and password information in the fields provided. Click OK.

After you have entered your server information, you are ready to begin uploading your site. If you are not already connected to the server, you can do so by going to Site→ Publish Server→Connect. You can upload files simply by selecting them in the Files tab in the site window and dragging them to the Publish Server tab, but this is an error-prone method—you might accidentally drag an image into the wrong folder or replace a newer version of a file on the server with an older version. To prevent these types of errors, there are three upload options available to you:

- Select the files you want to upload, and choose Site→Publish Server→Upload Selection to upload them to the server.

- Choose Site→Publish Server→Upload Modified Files to upload only those files that have been modified and are newer than the files on the server.

- Choose Site→Publish Server→Upload All to upload all the site files from your hard drive to your server.

After you have chosen an upload option, the Upload dialog box appears, displaying all the files and the folder structure that will be uploaded to the server (Figure 19-13). Verify that the correct files are selected, and click OK. Congratulations—you've just uploaded your site!

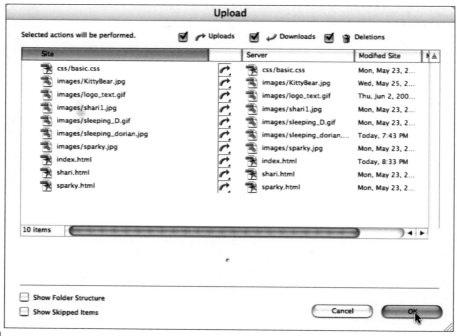

FIGURE 19-13

TOP FIVE THINGS TO TAKE AWAY FROM THIS CHAPTER

**Here are the most important things to take away
from this chapter:**

1. Always name your layers. When working with multiple layers, it will be much easier for you to keep track of which layer is which if you give each layer a descriptive name.

2. Smart Objects are a web designer's best friend. When working with images, always be sure to use Smart Objects whenever possible.

3. Preflighting your site is very important. There is nothing worse than uploading your site to a live server, only to find that some of the links are broken and that you have missing files.

4. Be sure to have your server address, directory, username, and password information handy when setting up your server. If you do not have this information, contact your web-hosting provider.

5. When uploading files to the server, let GoLive do the work for you. Choose from uploading all files, a selection of files, or only the modified files to your server.

20

How to Use GoLive with the Other
Creative Suite Applications

In the previous two chapters, you learned about the different tools available to create a web site using GoLive, the various palettes that help you design your site, and even how to create a web site using layers. In this chapter, we'll go a step further by examining how to add Smart Objects from Photoshop, Illustrator, and Acrobat to your web site. You'll also learn how to take an InDesign file, package it, and bring it into GoLive. There's a lot to learn about the various Smart Objects and how they're integrated into GoLive, but you'll be grateful you've taken the time. Knowing how to work with Smart Objects will make creating top-notch web sites much easier.

WHY GET THE CREATIVE SUITE INSTEAD OF JUST GOLIVE?

Why use Photoshop, Illustrator, and the rest of the Creative Suite 2 products together with GoLive? Because of Smart Objects. Smart Objects make a web designer's life easier, in many different ways. For example, when you have to resize an image in your web site, GoLive can automatically reoptimize that image so that it remains crisp and clear. Smart Objects allow GoLive and the other Creative Suite 2 products to work together, forming the perfect partnership for creating amazing web sites.

Smart Objects will soon become a household name, as common as Kleenex® and TiVo®. Well, okay, maybe only in geek households—but nonetheless, Smart Objects will be around for a long time to come.

GoLive users will find many reasons to own the entire Creative Suite. Here are just a few of those reasons:

- You can easily create and modify your own images in Photoshop and then bring them into GoLive as Smart Objects, so that your web images look as good as the originals.

- You won't find a better tool than Illustrator for making buttons and other web site elements that are scalable.

- If you use InDesign to create newsletters, brochures, or other publications, you can package your InDesign files and then select either all the items or certain components for reuse in your GoLive web site. This prevents the need to recreate text and images.

- You'll be able to keep track of all the files used for your web site, such as image files, PDFs, and text files, with CS2's Version Cue and Bridge.

INTEGRATING PHOTOSHOP IMAGES THAT CONTAIN TEXT INTO GOLIVE

How many times have you added text to a photo and then placed it into your web site, only to realize you made a mistake in the text and you have to redo the entire image? Well, when you use Smart Photoshop Objects in GoLive, you can take advantage of GoLive's amazing variable text layer feature and keep the text and the underlying image separate. What does this mean to you as a web designer? When the topmost layer of your Photoshop image contains text, GoLive will automatically ask you if you would like to turn that layer into a variable text layer. You won't have to flip-flop between applications to modify text in your image; you can edit it right in GoLive.

Creating a Text Layer in Photoshop

Even if you're not a regular user of Photoshop, if you're designing web sites with GoLive and have the rest of the Creative Suite at your disposal, at some point you're sure to want to bring a Photoshop image with a text element into your web site. To make this experience as painless as possible, follow these simple instructions to prepare the image in Photoshop.

To add a text layer to an image in Photoshop:

1. Open Photoshop and then open the image you want to modify.

2. After you have modified the image to your liking (adjusting the color balance, or resizing or even rotating the image), you need to create a new layer for the text. You can use any of these methods:

   - From the Layer menu in Photoshop, choose New→Layer.

   - Click the "Create a new layer" button in the Layers palette.

   - Use the keyboard shortcut Shift-Command-N (Mac) or Shift-Ctrl-N (Windows).

3. In the New Layer dialog box, enter a name for the new layer and click OK.

4. With the new layer active, select a Text tool from the Toolbox. (Choices include the Horizontal Type, Vertical Type, Horizontal Type Mask, and Vertical Type Mask tools.)

5. Click the cursor at the location where you wish to insert the text, and start typing. The text that you add to the image will be replaced when you bring it into GoLive, so for now, just type in any text as a placeholder.

6. Although the text will be replaced, you can format it as you would like it to appear in your web site—you can specify a favorite font, a color, or even effects.

7. Save the file as a native Photoshop (*.psd*) file.

Now you're ready to place your newly created Photoshop image into GoLive.

Adding a Smart Photoshop Object in GoLive

Now that you have added a text layer to your image, you can add the image to your web site.

1. In GoLive, select the Draggable Smart Objects set in the Objects palette. Drag a Smart Photoshop icon onto the web page.

2. With the Smart Photoshop icon selected, go to the Basic tab of the Inspector and either browse to the location of your recently created Photoshop file (by clicking the Browse icon next to the Source text field) or use the Fetch URL tool to retrieve it.

3. Once you've selected the native Photoshop file, a Variable Settings dialog box will appear. Select the Topmost Textlayer checkbox to enable the variable settings. A blank text input field will appear. Type in the text you wish to use on your image (Figure 20-1), and click OK.

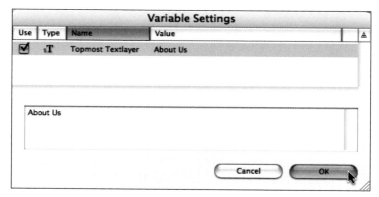

FIGURE 20-1

4. The Save For Web – Powered By ImageReady dialog box will appear, displaying the image and your newly added text (which will have replaced the placeholder text you entered in Photoshop). Select the format in which you wish to save the file—GIF, JPEG, PNG-8, PNG-24, or WBMP—and click Save. Be sure to save the file to your site's web-content folder (see Figure 20-2).

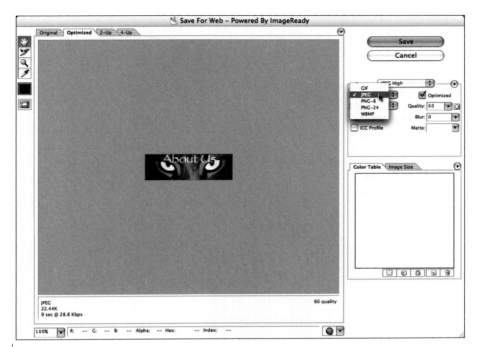

CHAPTER 20

FIGURE 20-2

When you select the Smart Photoshop Object, the Settings and Variables buttons will be available in the Basic tab of the Inspector. If you need to make a simple text correction, select the Variables button. This will open the Variable Settings dialog box, where you can make any corrections or changes to the text. Select the Settings button to save any changes you've made to the text.

tip	When you're only changing the text on an image created from a Photoshop file, you are not prompted to resave the image under a new name.

To create multiple versions of an image that has varying text:

1. Drag a new Smart Photoshop icon from the Draggable Smart Objects palette onto the web page.

2. In the Basic tab of the Inspector, once again browse or use the Fetch URL tool to select the original native Photoshop file.

3. When the Variable Settings dialog box appears, select the Topmost Text layer checkbox and add the new text into the blank text input field. Click OK.

4. The Save For Web – Powered By ImageReady dialog box will appear. Select the file format in which you wish to save the image, and then click Save.

You now have two versions of the same image in your page, but with different text—and you didn't even have to open Photoshop! Figure 20-3 is an example of how you can use this technique to create multiple menu buttons using the same image.

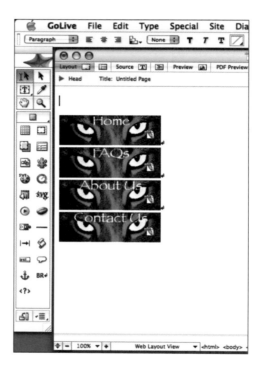

FIGURE 20-3

INTEGRATING ILLUSTRATOR FILES INTO GOLIVE

Need to create a logo or some menu buttons for your web site, but aren't sure which application to use? Both Illustrator and Photoshop are good tools to use to create buttons, logos, backgrounds, and other graphical content, but Illustrator has one big advantage over Photoshop: namely, objects created in Illustrator can easily be resized or otherwise modified. This is because Illustrator creates vector-based (line-based) objects, while Photoshop creates pixel-based images. When you scale up a pixel-based image to better fit in a particular area of your web page, you resize the individual pixels, which leaves your image with a jagged and boxy look. Vector-based images, on the other hand, can be scaled up or down with no loss of quality.

GoLive's Smart Illustrator Objects work the same way that all other Smart Objects do—that is, you can access the original file in Illustrator while in GoLive. This lets you take advantage of Illustrator's capability to easily resize, reshape, and otherwise alter the image. Using Smart Illustrator Objects, your images can remain crisp and clear, regardless of how you resize them.

Using Smart Illustrator Objects

By now, you have been bombarded with information about Smart Objects, how easy they are to use, why you might want to use them in your web site, and how simple they can make your life (as a designer, that is). All of this applies to Smart Illustrator Objects as well. Take a native Illustrator *.ai* or *.svg* file, and GoLive will convert it into a Smart Object that can be used throughout your web site.

To add a Smart Illustrator Object to your web site:

1. From the Draggable Smart Objects set in the Objects palette, drag the Smart Illustrator icon onto your web page.

2. With the Smart Illustrator icon selected, in the Basic tab of the Inspector, either browse or use the Fetch URL tool to select the native Illustrator file. (Alternatively, you can drag and drop the native file directly onto your web page and get the same results.)

3. If you are using an Illustrator *.ai* file, a Conversion Settings dialog box will appear, as shown in Figure 20-4. (See step 4 if you are using an *.svg* file.)

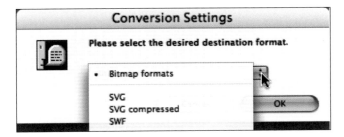

FIGURE 20-4

Select from Bitmap Format, SVG, SVG Compressed, or SWF:

- If you choose a bitmap format, the *Save For Web – Powered By ImageReady* window will appear, and you can then save the file as either a GIF, JPEG, PNG-8, PNG-24, or WBMP file.

- If you choose to save the file as an *SVG* or *SVG Compressed file*, the *SVG Options* dialog box will appear. Click *OK* to continue, and then save the file.

- If you choose to save the file as an SWF file, the Macromedia Flash (SWF) Format Options dialog box will appear. Click OK to continue, then save the file.

4. If you use an Illustrator *.svg* file, the Save For Web – Powered By ImageReady window will appear, and you can then save the file as either a GIF, JPEG, PNG-8, PNG-24, or WBMP file. Click Save to continue.

Understanding SVG

Here's the 4-1-1 on SVG. SVG stands for *Scalable Vector Graphics*, which is a graphics file format originally created by Adobe, but later turned over to the World Wide Web Consortium (also known as W3C). SVG is now an open file format for creating scalable vector-based graphics.

Adobe Illustrator fully supports the creation and editing of SVG files. Up until now Illustrator was the only Adobe application that let you work with SVG files, but with the introduction of Creative Suite 2 you can now work with SVG files in GoLive. Although you must use Illustrator to create the SVG file and to edit the artwork, after you have brought the SVG file into GoLive, you can resize it and add simple animation and interactivity to the image.

Going Mobile with GoLive and SVG

People always seem to be on the go these days—and thanks to GoLive and Illustrator SVG files, web sites are no longer restricted to just desktop viewing. People can now surf the Web with their cell phones, PDAs, or any other type of mobile device.

When designing a web site to be viewed on a mobile device, you'll need to bear in mind that the viewable screen area of a cell phone or PDA is significantly smaller than that of a desktop monitor or laptop. Thus, you will want to use fewer images and keep the detail down to a minimum. But fear not! You don't have to completely give up using graphics in your mobile-friendly web site. Let's take a look at how to design graphics for mobile web sites.

Before you begin, you will need an Illustrator SVG file, an animation application such as Ikivo (*http://www.ikivo.com*), and GoLive.

1. Save your Illustrator file in the SVG file format.

2. Import the SVG file into Ikivo (or whichever animation application you are using).

3. Move, scale, rotate, or change any other object attributes, and resave the file in the *SVG-t* (SVG-tiny) format.

4. Import the SVG-t file in the site window and double-click to open the file in the SVG Editor.

5. Use the SVG Editor to view or edit existing SVG animation and interactivity, such as increasing the size of a text label when you mouse over it.

You can also add additional animation effects in the SVG Editor. For more information, check out *http://www.adobe.com* and *http://www.ikivo.com*.

INTEGRATING INDESIGN PACKAGES INTO GOLIVE

Entire books have been written about InDesign, what it is, how it is used, and what it can do. In a nutshell, InDesign is a desktop publishing application that allows you to combine text and artwork to produce magazines, newsletters, and full-color brochures, to name just a few of the endless possibilities. This section will cover packaging an InDesign document and bringing it into GoLive—a very small but very useful feature in InDesign that can make creating web sites based on InDesign content vastly easier.

So what do we mean by integrating InDesign packages into GoLive? Well, if you have an existing InDesign document, such as a full-color brochure complete with images and text, you can move that content from the InDesign document straight into your GoLive web site. Why recreate that content when you can simply drag and drop the various components from an InDesign document into your web site?

Creating an InDesign Package for GoLive

Before doing anything in GoLive, you will need to package the InDesign document so that you can bring it into GoLive. An InDesign *package* is a specific type of file that contains the various objects used in the InDesign document, such as the images and blocks of text (known as "stories").

1. In InDesign, choose the Package for GoLive command from the File menu (Figure 20-5).

2. The Package Publication for GoLive dialog box appears, prompting you for a Save As name and location. Click Save.

3. The Package for GoLive dialog box appears, as shown in Figure 20-6. You'll need to specify the page range. If you would like to see a preview of the document, select the View Package When Complete option. Finally, choose to copy over original or format-ted images to the subfolder that is included in the InDesign package.

4. When you have selected your desired options, click Package.

Now that the content has been packaged, you can start using it in your web site.

FIGURE 20-5

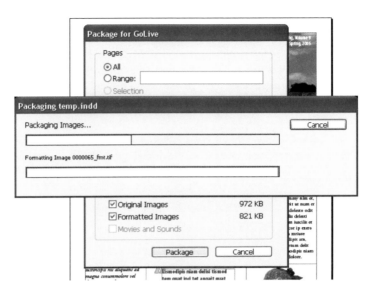

FIGURE 20-6

. . . .

Using Content from an InDesign Package

It's a good habit to save any files you use in your web site to your site's *web-content* folder. This includes any InDesign packages you use in GoLive. The InDesign package you created in the previous section should now be listed in the Extras tab in the site window of your web site. If the InDesign package is not listed there, follow the instructions below.

To add an InDesign package to the site window:

1. From GoLive's File menu, choose Import→From InDesign.

2. In the Select InDesign Package File dialog box, navigate to the location where the InDesign package is saved and click Open.

3. A dialog box will appear, asking if you would like to copy the package into your site. Click Yes.

4. The Copy Files dialog box will appear, confirming the package to be copied to your site. Click OK to copy.

Now when you look at the Extras tab in your site window, your newly created InDesign package will be listed under InDesignPackages.

Of course, this is only the beginning. You can open the InDesign package and start dragging and dropping images and text from your InDesign document directly into your GoLive web site. To view the InDesign document in GoLive, double-click on the package in the Extras tab in the site window. A small preview window will open, displaying the document. When your mouse passes over an item that you can use in your web site, that item will change color to indicate that you can use it. You can then drag and drop that item onto your web page.

By now, you've probably noticed that there are three tabs at the top of the small preview window: InDesign Layout, Assets, and HTML Preview (Figure 20-7).

Here's what these tabs are for:

INDESIGN LAYOUT: Lets you view the InDesign document and drag items from it to your web site.

ASSETS: Lists all of the Stories and Images used in the document (stories are blocks of text used in your document). If you double-click on a story, it will be displayed in the InDesign layout window.

HTML PREVIEW: Gives you a preview of the file in straight HTML.

FIGURE 20-7

To get a closer look at the contents of a particular story, you can zoom in by either double-clicking on the story or using the Zoom In icon located at the bottom of the preview window. To zoom out of a story once you've zoomed in, either double-click on the story again or use the Zoom Out icon, also located at the bottom of the preview window.

Selecting InDesign Text Options

Before actually moving any stories (blocks of text) from the InDesign document over to your web page, decide if you would like to make the story Editable Text, a Smart Component, or a Snapshot Image. These options can be found in the Inspector, as shown in Figure 20-8.

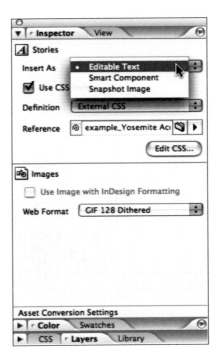

FIGURE 20-8

Here's the lowdown on each of these options:

EDITABLE TEXT: Editable text is just that—editable. You'll be able to edit this text once you have moved it over to your web page.

SMART COMPONENT: If you make the text a Smart Component, it will automatically be updated when you make any changes to the original InDesign file and repackage it for GoLive.

SNAPSHOT IMAGE: This option takes a snapshot of an item (such as a story or image) to use in your web page, which is useful for when you want the exact style used in the In-Design file and GoLive will not be able to duplicate the formatting and style. This is great if your InDesign document contains detailed images, special fonts, or specific formatting.

INTEGRATING ACROBAT SMART PDF OBJECTS INTO GOLIVE

Ever wish there were a way to use an image of a document—say, a page from a Word document or a slide from a PowerPoint presentation—to represent a link to that document, instead of just a plain text link? With Adobe Acrobat's PDFs and GoLive, you can do just that. You can even choose which page to use as the thumbnail. Following is a quick and easy way to create a PDF from Word, PowerPoint, or Excel. After you have created the PDF, you can then place a Smart PDF Object into GoLive to use as a link to that document.

Creating a PDF

Creating a PDF isn't as difficult as you might think. In fact, it's just a few clicks away. Adobe Acrobat 7.0 Professional works in conjunction with Microsoft applications such as Word, providing you with the Adobe Acrobat PDFMaker buttons shown in Figure 20-9. These buttons will convert any Word, PowerPoint, or Excel document into a PDF.

FIGURE 20-9

To convert a Word document into a PDF:

1. Open the source document in Microsoft Word (or PowerPoint or Excel).

2. In the main toolbar, click the Convert to Adobe PDF button.

3. The Save Adobe PDF File As dialog box appears. Give the file a new name and specify a location to save the PDF. Click OK.

4. After the original document is converted to a PDF, Acrobat will launch and display the newly created PDF file.

With just a few quick clicks, you can easily create a PDF. Now that you have the PDF, you can add a Smart PDF Object to your web site.

Adding a Smart PDF Object

Using Smart PDF Objects is a creative way to add links and images to your web site. Sure, you can use regular old text links, but these thumbnails will definitely draw more attention to your document links than just plain text. Plus, you can use them to give visitors a little preview of what is in the documents themselves. To add a Smart PDF Object to your web site, choose one of the following methods:

- In GoLive, select the Draggable Smart Objects set in the Objects palette and drag a Smart PDF icon onto the web page. This creates a placeholder for the Smart PDF Object. From the Basic tab in the Inspector, browse to the location of the PDF and select the file, or use the Fetch URL tool to select the PDF from the site window. This will launch the PDF Options dialog box.

- From the Files tab in the site window, drag the PDF onto your web page and release it. The PDF Options dialog box will appear.

From this point, the instructions for saving the PDF thumbnail and creating a link to it are the same.

To add a Smart PDF Object:

1. In the PDF Options dialog box (see the preceding list for directions on launching this dialog), scroll up or down to select the page you wish to use as the thumbnail display. Click OK.

2. The Save For Web – Powered By ImageReady dialog box appears, displaying the page you chose to use as the thumbnail. Choose a file format and click Save. The standard Save dialog box appears, where you can browse for a location to save the file to. Click Save.

3. You will need to do a little image resizing after GoLive adds the Smart PDF Object to your web site. To maintain the same constraint proportions, hold down the Shift key while clicking and dragging the blue resize markers to resize the image.

4. In the Link tab of the Inspector, browse or use the Fetch URL tool to select the target PDF file.

If, after you have added the Smart PDF Object and set the link, you decide you don't like the page you used as a thumbnail, don't worry. You don't have to delete the link and start all over again—simply select the Smart PDF Object and, in the Basic tab of the Inspector, click the Settings button. This will open the PDF Options dialog box, where you can select a new page to use as your thumbnail.

Here are the most important things to take away from this chapter:

1. Using Adobe Smart Objects can make your life much easier, because it streamlines your workflow.

2. You no longer have to recreate a button just to change a line of text. When using Photoshop images, use GoLive's variable text layer feature to adjust the topmost text layer while still in GoLive.

3. Use Smart Illustrator Objects to create logos, menu buttons, or even backgrounds for your web site.

4. If you have an existing InDesign document, such as a newsletter or full-color brochure, save time and creative juices by packaging up the InDesign document and reusing its contents in your GoLive web site.

5. Use an Acrobat PDF as a thumbnail to indicate a link to the document. Why use just a plain text link when you can show an actual page from your PDF?

21

Top 15 How Do I...? GoLive Questions

In this chapter, you will find the answers to the top 15 questions designers ask about GoLive. These most commonly asked questions were compiled from questions asked in the GoLive forums and posed to the GoLive product team. If you have a specific problem or are looking to improve your skills, the step-by-step solutions included here should help. You'll find tips that will save you time, strengthen your creativity, and much more.

HOW DO I CHANGE THE COLOR
OF A TEXT LINK ROLLOVER?

Don't have the time to jazz up your web site? One quick and easy way to add a little animation to your site is to change the color of hyperlinks when viewers mouse over them: when the cursor is moved over a link it changes color, and when the cursor moves off the text it reverts to its original color.

To create a text link rollover in GoLive:

1. Open the CSS Editor by clicking the Open CSS Editor button found in the upper-right corner of the document window (Figure 21-1), and open the *basic.css* file. (Alternatively, you can double-click the *basic.css* file in the CSS tab of the site window or in the *CSS* folder in the Files tab of the site window to open it in the CSS Editor.)

FIGURE 21-1

2. On the left side of the CSS Editor window is a list of the different internal styles cur-rently applied to the document (Figure 21-2). There are four styles that you can alter to create a text link rollover, corresponding to the four states of a hyperlink:

A:LINK: Indicates that the selected text (or block of text) is an unvisited hyperlink.

A:VISITED: Indicates that the hyperlink has previously been clicked and visited.

A:HOVER: When you move the cursor over a hyperlink, indicates that whatever action is assigned to that link will occur if you click on it.

A:ACTIVE: Indicates that the hyperlink is in the active state (i.e., is being clicked).

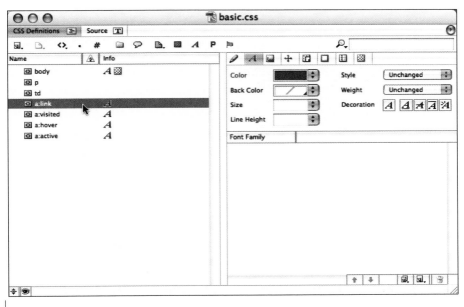

FIGURE 21-2

3. To change the color of a hyperlink when the viewer's cursor is moved over the link, select the a:hover style. On the right side of the CSS Editor window, under the A tab (the Font Properties tab), select a new color from the Color pop-up menu, as shown in Figure 21-3. Be sure to select a color that will be easy to read—the last thing you want is for your new hyperlink color to blend in with the background and be illegible.

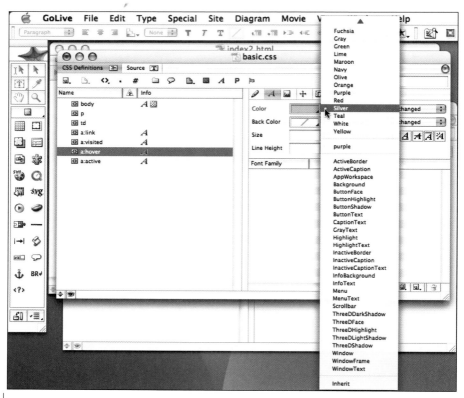

FIGURE 21-3

4. To change the color of the remaining hyperlink states, repeat step 3 with a:link, a:visited, and a:active.

While changing the color of a hyperlink, you can also set the Decoration style. For example, you can set hyperlinks to never display an underline, even when the cursor is moved over them. This is a nice change from the usual underlined hyperlink text. Additionally, you can set the text decoration to strikethrough, overline, or even have it blink. (Although this may sound fun, many viewers quickly tire of having text blinking at them, so use this decoration wisely.)

1. Select a hyperlink state, such as the one shown in Figure 21-4.

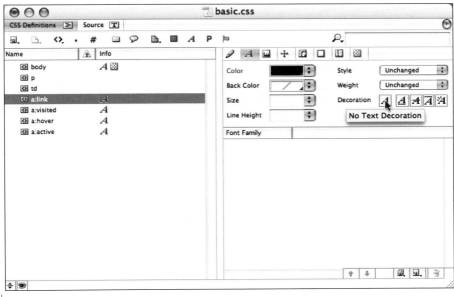

FIGURE 21-4

2. Next to the Decorations option, select from (from left to right) No Text Decoration, Text Decoration Underline, Text Decoration Strike Through, Text Decoration Overline, or Text Decoration Blink.

HOW DO I CREATE A ROLLOVER IMAGE?

So, you've seen rollovers on other web sites and you'd like to put one on your own, but you're worried that you'll have to spend so much time learning and writing code that you won't have any left to do the things you enjoy doing. Never fear—GoLive will write the code for you! All you need are the images you would like to use for your rollover.

1. Add an image to the page. This image represents the Normal state of the rollover.

2. With the image selected, in the Links tab of the Inspector, use the Fetch URL tool, browse to another HTML page within your site, or manually type in a URL to create a link.

3. Choose Window→Rollovers to open the Rollovers palette. The Name/ID text field should automatically populate with the name of the image used in the Normal state. If it doesn't, you will need to manually enter a unique name in that field.

4. Select the Over state and click the "Create new rollover image" button (Figure 21-5).

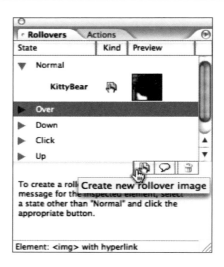

FIGURE 21-5

5. Browse or use the Fetch URL tool to assign a new image to the Over state (Figure 21-6). If you select the Preload checkbox, GoLive will automatically load rollover images when the web page loads into the web browser. If the Preload checkbox is left unchecked, viewers will have to wait for the rollover images to download, which (depending on their Internet connection speeds and the size of the rollover images) could take some time.

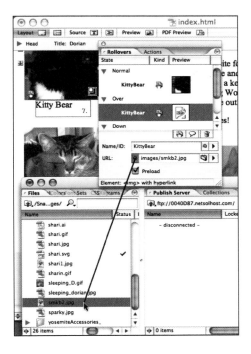

FIGURE 21-6

[NOTE]

You can also assign images to the other rollover states. Repeat steps 3 and 4, selecting the Down, Click, Up, or Out state in step 3 and adding a new image in step 4.

6. To preview the rollover, click the Preview tab. Figure 21-7 shows the image in its normal state, before the cursor passes over it. Figure 21-8 shows the new rollover image as the cursor passes over the image.

FIGURE 21-7

FIGURE 21-8

Figure 21-9 shows all the hard work you didn't have to do to create the rollover. GoLive
wrote all that code, while pretty much all you had to do was drag and drop images onto
the web page!

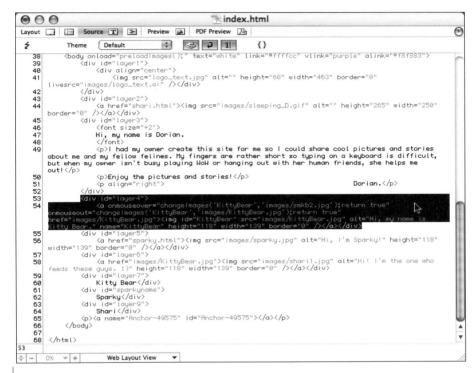

FIGURE 21-9

As a final touch, you can add a status message to your rollover image. Select the Normal state of the image, click the "Create new message" button, and type a status message in the text box provided in the Rollovers palette (Figure 21-10). When the image is rolled over, the status message will display in the lower-left corner of the browser window.

FIGURE 21-10

[NOTE]

One great feature of GoLive is that if you name the different versions of your images according to standard rollover naming conventions, such as _over or _down, GoLive will use those different versions to automatically create rollover buttons. For example, if you have one button image called *home.jpg* and another called *home_over.jpg*, GoLive will use the *home.jpg* image as the Normal state for your home button and the *home_over.jpg* image as the Over state of your home button.

HOW DO I CREATE A REMOTE ROLLOVER?

In a previous "How Do I…" question, you learned how to create a simple rollover. Here, you'll learn how to create a remote rollover. You're probably wondering what exactly a remote rollover is. In a normal rollover, the viewer moves the cursor over an image, and that image is replaced with a different image. In a *remote* rollover, the viewer interacts with an image (or other item, such as a text link), triggering a change in a separate image located somewhere else on the page.

Before creating a remote rollover, you will need two images: one to be displayed before the rollover event occurs and a second image that will appear during or after the rollover event. Both pictures should be about the same size; otherwise, the second picture could become distorted. If you're using an image as the trigger for the remote rollover, you'll also need a separate image for that purpose.

To create a remote rollover:

1. Add the image that will trigger the remote rollover action (Figure 21-11). You can also use a text link to trigger a remote rollover.

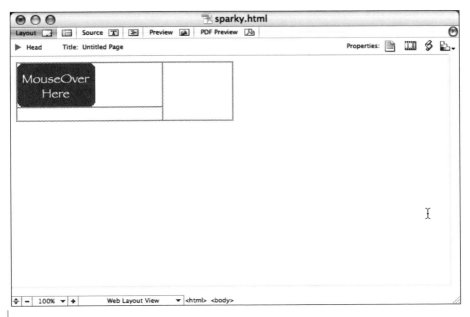

FIGURE 21-11

2. Place the image that will be used as the original image in the remote rollover (Figure 21-12). Give this image a name in the Name/ID text field in the Basic tab of the Inspector, as shown in Figure 21-13.

FIGURE 21-12

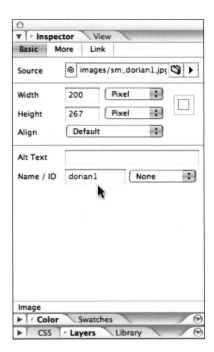

FIGURE 21-13

You will select the replacement image for the rollover momentarily. First, you need to set the rollover action to trigger when the viewer moves the cursor over the triggering image (or text link).

To set the rollover action:

1. Select the image/text that will be used as the remote rollover trigger, and choose Window→Actions from the menu bar to display the Actions palette.

2. Select Mouse Enter in the Events column on the left side of the Actions palette.

3. Click the "Create new action" button under the Actions section in the Actions palette to create a new action (Figure 21-14). This will enable the Action drop-down menu below the Events column.

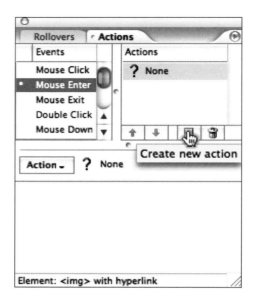

FIGURE 21-14

---

4. From the Action drop-down menu, choose Image→Set Image URL (Figure 21-15).

---

5. From the Image drop-down menu, select the name you previously assigned to the original image used in the remote rollover.

---

6. Browse or use the Fetch URL tool in the Inspector to choose the image you wish to use as the secondary image in the rollover.

---

7. To reset the image after the cursor has moved off the trigger image, select Mouse Exit in the Events column of the Actions palette.

---

8. Click the "Create new action" button again to re-enable the Action drop-down menu. From the Action menu, choose Image→Set Image URL.

FIGURE 21-15

9. From the Image drop-down menu, select the name you previously assigned to the original image used in the remote rollover.

10. Browse or use the Fetch URL tool to choose the original image you used as the primary image in the rollover.

11. Click the Preview tab in the document window to preview your handiwork. Figure 21-16 shows the remote image before the cursor moves onto the trigger image, and Figure 21-17 shows the new image after the cursor has triggered the remote rollover.

FIGURE 21-16

FIGURE 21-17

HOW DO I ADD A FAVICON TO THE ADDRESS BAR IN A BROWSER WINDOW?

As you surf the Web, you'll notice that more and more web sites are displaying small icons next to their URLs in the address bar. These are called *favorite icons*, or *favicons* as they're more commonly known. As shown in Figure 21-18, favicons may also display in the Bookmarks/Favorites menus in the browser window.

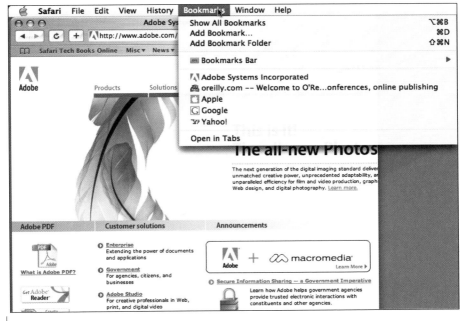

FIGURE 21-18

Before GoLive CS2, if you wanted to add a favicon to your web site, you had to convert your image file into a special file recognized by browsers as a favorite icon, known as an *.ico* file, before adding it to your web page. This usually meant having to purchase a separate application that would take your native Photoshop or Illustrator file and turn it into this special file type. With GoLive CS2, creating these favicons just got a little easier—thanks to Smart Objects, all you need is the native image file, and GoLive will work its magic to convert it into an *.ico* file for you!

1. Design or find an image to use as your favicon. If you're creating your own favicon in Photoshop or Illustrator, bear in mind that the size of the image must be 16 x 16 pixels. You can create a larger image and scale it down to 16 x 16 pixels, but if you do, try to keep the dimensions divisible by 16 (e.g., 32 x 32 or 64 x 64 pixels). Also, because the image is so small, you will want to keep it simple.

[NOTE]

To find favicons, do a Google search. You can find many companies that either will have premade favicons available for you to purchase or will custom-design one for you.

---

2. From the Draggable Smart Objects set in the Objects palette, drag and drop the Smart Favorite Icon anywhere on your web page. GoLive will automatically put it in the Head section, as shown in Figure 21-19.

FIGURE 21-19

3. With the Smart Favorite Icon selected in your web page, browse or use the Fetch URL tool in the Inspector to select the image file. This image can be a regular GIF, JPEG, or BMP file, or even a native Photoshop or Illustrator file. GoLive will change it into an *.ico* file for you.

4. After you have selected your image file, the Settings dialog box will appear (Figure 21-20). This displays different color depths and qualities, which allows a browser to use the image quality settings most appropriate for the favicon. Select which image quality or qualities you wish to use. If you're not sure which image quality settings to use, leave all four options checked. If you're savvier with the color lingo and know that your image needs true colors or an alpha channel, you can select or deselect the lower or higher quality settings.

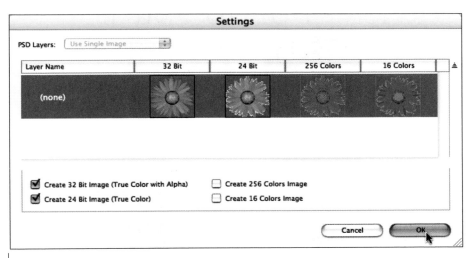

FIGURE 21-20

5. Click OK, then specify a filename and location for the newly created favicon. GoLive will automatically save it as an *.ico* file.

6. In the layout document window, the Smart Favorite Icon in the Head section now displays the image you are using as your favicon (Figure 21-21).

FIGURE 21-21

7. To preview how your favicon looks in most browsers, you will need to upload your site to a live server. If you have the Firefox browser, available at *http://www.mozilla. org*, you can see how your favicon looks on your site by opening a browser window, choosing File→Open, and then navigating to the location of your *index.html* page. The favicon should appear next to the URL in the address bar, as shown in Figure 21-22.

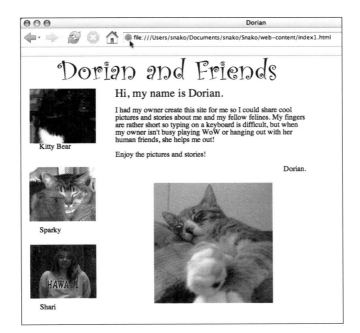

FIGURE 21-22

HOW DO I CREATE A STATIC BACKGROUND?

Ever visit a web site and notice that when you scroll up or down (or left or right), the background image doesn't move? In fact, no matter how much you scroll around the web page, that image just won't budge? That's because the web designer used a fixed background image, also known as a "non-moving background" or "static wallpaper." With GoLive's CSS Editor, you can create this same effect throughout your entire web site, or on a single page.

1. Open the CSS Editor by clicking the Open CSS Editor button in the upper-right corner of the document window. In the CSS Editor, select the *basic.css* style sheet and double-click on it, or click the Edit button next to Document to open this style sheet (Figure 21-23).

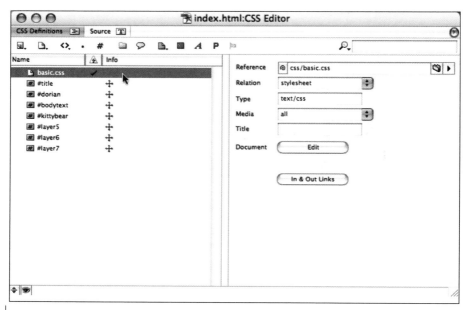

FIGURE 21-23

2. Select the body style on the left to view the style properties currently set for the back-ground image. If the background properties are not displayed, click the Background Properties tab, as shown in Figure 21-24.

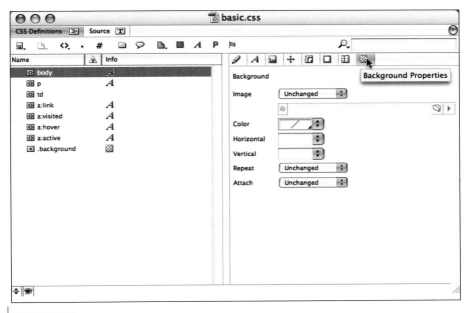

FIGURE 21-24

3. Choose URL from the Image drop-down menu and either browse or use the Fetch URL tool in the Inspector to select the background image.

4. To set the background image so that only one instance of the image displays in the background, select Once from the Repeat drop-down menu (Figure 21-25).

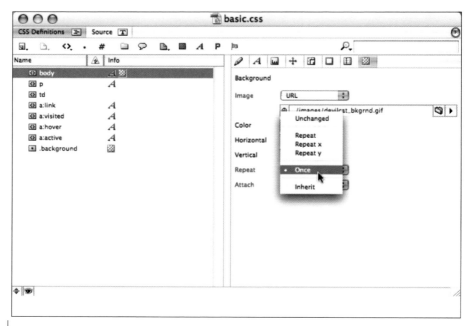

FIGURE 21-25

If you prefer to tile your image, you can also select from one of the other Image options:

REPEAT: Tiles the background image both horizontally and vertically.

REPEAT X: Tiles the background image horizontally.

REPEAT Y: Tiles the background image vertically.

5. You also have the option to set the background to scroll or not to scroll with the other objects on the web page. To create a static background, select Fixed from the Attach menu.

6. Save the changes to the *basic.css* file. Now when you add content to your web pages, the background will not tile or scroll.

1. Click the "Show page properties" button, located in the upper-right corner of the document window (Figure 21-26). In the Background section of the Page tab in the Inspector, select the Image checkbox. Browse or use the Fetch URL tool to select the desired background image.

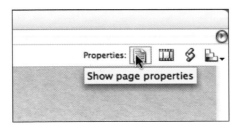

FIGURE 21-26

2. Select the body style in the CSS Editor to view the style properties currently set for the background image.

3. Repeat steps 4–6 from the preceding set of steps for setting a background for an entire site.

Voilà! You have just created a web page with a static background. Now you can add text and other images as desired.

HOW DO I CREATE A DROP-DOWN MENU?

Anyone who can create a web site can create a basic set of navigation buttons. If you have some artistic ability, you can even create some pretty nice buttons—but they're still just buttons. And why settle for buttons when you can create your own custom drop-down menus using GoLive layers? Drop-down menus give your web site a far more professional appearance. They also have the added advantage of saving a lot of space, because they appear only when needed.

1. Set up the main menu buttons as shown in Figure 21-27. You will be creating your drop-down menus off of this main menu. (This is the more common way of using a drop-down menu, but you also can create an image or button anywhere on your web page and turn it into a drop-down menu. Be creative.)

FIGURE 21-27

2. From the Draggable Basic Objects set in the Objects palette, click and drag the Layer icon onto the web page and position it under the menu item you wish to turn into a drop-down menu. Make sure to position the layer so that it just slightly overlaps with the main menu image, as shown in Figure 21-28. You'll see why it's important to over-lap the layer with the main menu button in an upcoming step.

FIGURE 21-28

3. Give the layer a unique name. This is especially important if your web page contains multiple layers. You can also change the width and height of the layer, but this is not as crucial as giving the layer a specific name.

4. Add the submenu buttons. Click and drag the button images into the layer to create the drop-down section of the menu (Figure 21-29). The layer will expand to accommodate larger images.

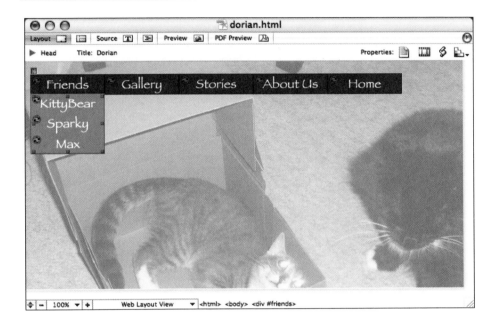

FIGURE 21-29

5. After you have added the button images to the layer, create the links to the appropriate pages by either browsing or using the Fetch URL tool in the Links tab of the Inspector to select new pages.

Now that you have the submenu set up, you need to add the action that enables the drop-down menu to appear and disappear.

1. Select the main menu image and choose Window→Actions. This will open the Actions palette. From the Events menu in the Actions palette, select Mouse Enter (Figure 21-30). This means that when the viewer's mouse passes over the main menu button area, the action associated with the Mouse Enter event will be triggered. In this case, the drop-down menu will appear.

FIGURE 21-30

2. Click the "Create new action" button under the Actions section in the Actions palette. This will enable the Action drop-down menu, located below the Events section.

3. To set up the drop-down menu so that it will display when the cursor enters the main menu button area, from the Action drop-down menu choose Multimedia→ShowHide.

4. From the Layer drop-down menu in the Actions palette, choose the layer you wish to show or hide. From the Mode drop-down menu in the Actions palette, select Show. Figure 21-31 shows an example of what the Actions palette should look like after you have selected the event, action, and layers to show the drop-down menu.

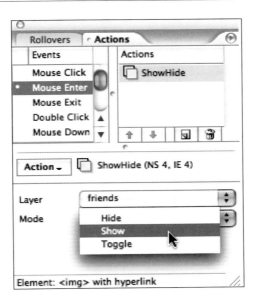

FIGURE 21-31

5. From the Events menu in the Actions palette, select Mouse Exit. This creates the action that will hide the drop-down menu when the viewer moves the cursor out of the main menu button area.

6. Click the "Create new action" button under the Actions section to enable the Action drop-down menu. Click and hold the Action button, and select ShowHide from the pop-up menu. (Because you've previously selected the ShowHide option, it is now available in the actions list without you having to navigate down to it.)

7. From the Layer drop-down menu, choose the same layer you selected in step 4, but this time select the Hide option from the Mode drop-down instead of selecting Show. This will hide the layer when the cursor is moved out of the main menu button area. When you're done selecting the event, action, and layer, the Actions palette should look similar to Figure 21-32.

FIGURE 21-32

8. Now select the drop-down layer, and repeat steps 2–7 to set the mouse event, action, layer name (which is the layer itself), and mode.

You're getting close, but you're still not quite finished. Remember in the beginning, when you slightly overlapped the drop-down menu layer with the main menu button area? Well, there is a very good reason for that. The way the main menu button is set up, the drop-down menu layer will hide when the user moves the cursor off the main menu button. To keep the drop-down menu visible, the cursor must enter the drop-down menu layer before it exits the main menu button. Therefore, the drop-down menu layer must overlap the main menu button.

To enable this behavior, you need to change the initial visibility of the drop-down menu layer. If you were to preview the web page at this time, the drop-down menu would not behave appropriately—it would be visible when the web page loaded and would not disappear until you moved your cursor over and out of the main menu button and drop-down menu area.

1. Select the drop-down menu layer. In the Layer tab of the Inspector, uncheck the box next to Visible (Figure 21-33). The layer will completely disappear from your document window. It's okay—this is supposed to happen.

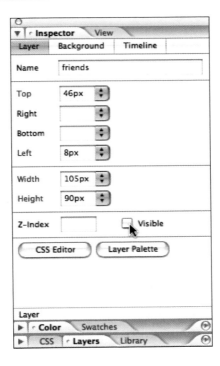

FIGURE 21-33

2. Now it's time to see the results of all your hard work. Preview the web page, moving your cursor over the main menu buttons, down the drop-down menu and back up.

Repeat this exercise to add drop-down menus to other main menu buttons.

HOW DO I ADD A DATE AND TIME STAMP TO MY WEB SITE?

Say you have a web page that requires constant updates—such as an online catalog, a work schedule, or even a daily planner—and you would like others to know when you last updated the page. You could manually change the date and time each time you make changes, or you could let GoLive do the work for you. If you use a Smart Modified Date Object in your web page, every time you make a change to the page, GoLive will automatically update the date and time stamp for you.

To add a time stamp to your web page:

1. From the Draggable Smart Objects set in the Objects palette, drag the Modified Date icon onto your web page (Figure 21-34).

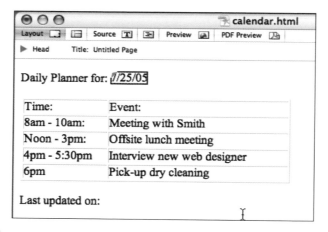

FIGURE 21-34

2. In the Inspector, select your region from the Format drop-down menu. The region you select will determine the type of time stamp available to use on your web page. For example, Figure 21-35 shows the time and date stamp for the United States, and Figure 21-36 shows the time and date stamp for France.

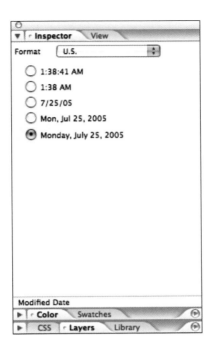

FIGURE 21-35

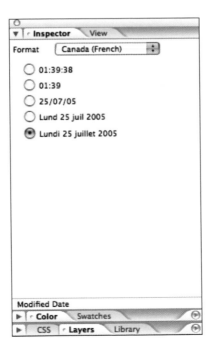

FIGURE 21-36

3. Select the radio button next to the date or time format you wish to use on your web page.

The Smart Modified Date Object displays only the date or only the time, but you can always add a second Smart Modified Date Object so that you can display both the date and the time, as shown in Figure 21-37. Now when you make any changes or updates to your web page, GoLive will automatically update the Smart Modified Date Object date and time stamps.

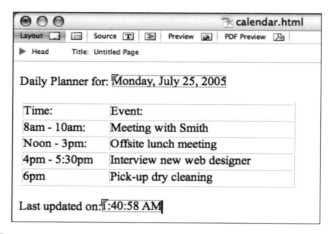

FIGURE 21-37

HOW DO I SPELLCHECK MY WEB SITE?

When submitting a resume for a potential job, you would never turn in a resume with misspelled words—you would check it over several times to make sure you've dotted all your i's and crossed all your t's. The same should go for your web site. You want to make a good impression on your viewers, and even a single misspelled word can look unprofessional. Spend the extra few minutes it takes to run a spellcheck to ensure that your site is free of any misspellings.

1. Open the web page you wish to spellcheck. To open the Check Spelling dialog box, choose Edit→Check Spelling or use the keyboard shortcut Option-Command-U (Mac) or Shift-Ctrl-U (Windows).

2. Before checking your document for any misspelled words, make sure the correct language is selected in the Language menu. (See Figure 21-38 for the complete list of available languages.)

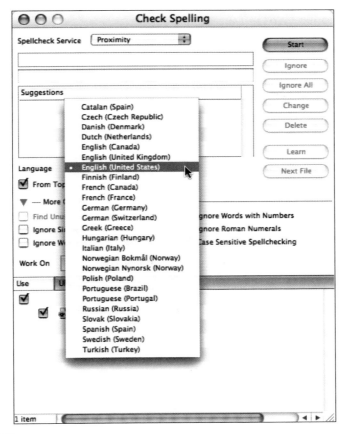

FIGURE 21-38

3. Other spellchecking options are available in the More Options section of the Check Spelling dialog box. As necessary, select from any combination of these options:

FIND UNUSUAL CAPITALIZATION: Looks for any words that have a capital letter in the middle or contain more than one capital letter. This option is usually grayed out, because the spell-checker automatically looks for this type of error.

IGNORE SINGLE CHARACTERS: Ignores any single character, such as when you use an initial to refer to a person instead of an entire name.

IGNORE WORDS WITH ONLY UPPERCASE: Ignores any words that are all upper-case, such as CIA or UFO.

IGNORE WORDS WITH NUMBERS: Ignores any words that contain numbers, such as those used in the very popular "l33t" (also known as "d00d") speak among gaming enthusiasts.

IGNORE ROMAN NUMERALS: Ignores numbers such as IV or iii.

CASE SENSITIVE SPELLCHECKING: Treats different capitalizations of the same word as different words. For example, Check Spelling considers "Home" to be different from "home," even though they are spelled the same way. This option is checked by default.

4. From the Work On menu, you can choose to work on the current open document from the top of the document, select other HTML files to spell-check, or check the entire site. Figure 21-39 shows all the options available in the Work On menu. The bottom portion of the Check Spelling dialog box shows which files GoLive is currently running a spellcheck on.

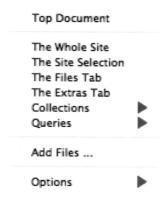

FIGURE 21-39

5. Click the Start button. GoLive will start at the top of the document and look for any misspelled words, according to the options you set. When the spellchecker comes across a word it does not recognize, the misspelled word will be displayed in the text field, as shown in Figure 21-40.

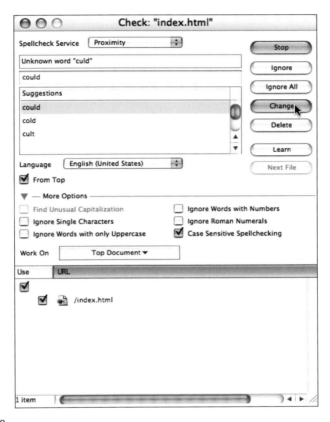

FIGURE 21-40

At this point, you can click one of these buttons:

IGNORE: Ignores that particular instance of the misspelled word and moves on to the next misspelled word.

IGNORE ALL: Ignores all instances of this word. Use this option when you know that the word is spelled correctly yet is not recognized by the spellchecker.

CHANGE: Allows you to choose from a list of suggested words when the spell-checker finds a misspelled word. You can also manually type in your own changes in the text field instead of using one of the words suggested by the GoLive dictionary.

DELETE: Deletes this instance of the word completely.

LEARN: Adds the word to the GoLive dictionary. Use this option when you know that the misspelled word is in fact correct but is not recognized by the spellchecker.

6. When the spellchecker is finished, the message "No more misspellings found" will be displayed in the text field (Figure 21-41).

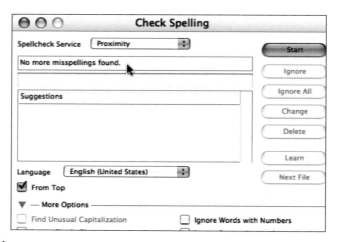

FIGURE 21-41

[NOTE]

You can also select documents from the site window and drag them onto the lower section of the Check Spelling dialog box to start spellchecking. If the spellchecker finds any misspelled words in a document, it will open that document.

HOW DO I ADD AN INTERACTIVE QUICKTIME MOVIE TO MY WEB SITE?

Now that most computer users, both at home and in the workplace, have DSL, T1–T3 lines, or high-speed dial-up connections, streaming video over the Web has become increasingly popular. With QuickTime movies, you can share family vacation trips, how-to videos, or anything else you can capture on video via your web site. Adding a QuickTime movie to your web site in GoLive is quick and easy. If you'd like, you can even add a decorative frame around your QuickTime movie to give it a little pizzazz.

There are two ways to add an interactive QuickTime movie to a web page:

- From the Draggable Basic Objects set in the Objects palette, drag the QuickTime icon onto the web page. From the Basic tab in the Inspector, browse or use the Fetch URL tool to select the QuickTime movie.

- Drag the QuickTime movie directly onto the web page from the site window.

By default, GoLive displays the first frame of the movie (Figure 21-42). If you were to preview this web page in a browser, the QuickTime movie would play automatically. Viewers would have no way of interacting with it except to pause and play the movie by double-clicking on it. However, you can set up your movie so that visitors can start, pause, or end the movie, and more.

FIGURE 21-42

To add a controller for your QuickTime movie:

1. With the QuickTime movie selected, go to the QuickTime tab in the Inspector.

2. In the Standard tab, choose Show Controller. This adds a controller that allows the viewer to start and pause the movie, move forward and backward through the movie, and even adjust the volume (Figure 21-43).

FIGURE 21-43

3. If desired, enable any of the following attributes:

   CACHE: Causes the browser to store the movie in its memory so that the next time the viewer plays the movie, it will play immediately, instead of having to be down-loaded again.

   AUTOPLAY: Sets the QuickTime movie so that it automatically plays when a viewer visits your site. By default, GoLive enables this attribute.

   LOOP: Sets the movie to play continuously.

[NOTE]

An attribute you might not want to enable is the Play Every Frame attribute. Just as its name implies, Play Every Frame causes every single frame of the movie to be played. This can bog down older brows-ers and result in the QuickTime movie slowing down.

---

4. Disable Autoplay so that the QuickTime movie will not play unless the viewer clicks the Play button on the controller.

5. Preview the QuickTime movie you've just added to your web page.

When you preview the web page in a browser now, you'll notice that GoLive has placed a controller right under the movie (see Figure 21-43). Now the viewer can play and pause the movie, adjust the volume, forward to the next scene, or replay a scene.

HOW DO I ORGANIZE HYPERLINKS INTO A DROP-DOWN LIST?

Another space-saving object and organizer is the URL pop-up menu. Unlike drop-down menus, where you have to create buttons and then set the hyperlinks, URL pop-up menus are simply hyperlinks listed in a drop-down list. If you notice that you have a lot of hyperlinks on your web page and they're not well organized, a URL pop-up menu is the thing to use. Although these URL pop-up menus look very similar to the drop-down list menus used in forms, URL pop-up menus have an action attached to them, such as opening a document once the viewer has selected that hyperlink from the URL pop-up menu.

To add a URL pop-up menu to a web page:

1. From the Draggable Smart Objects set in the Objects palette, click and drag the URL Popup icon onto the web page (Figure 21-44).

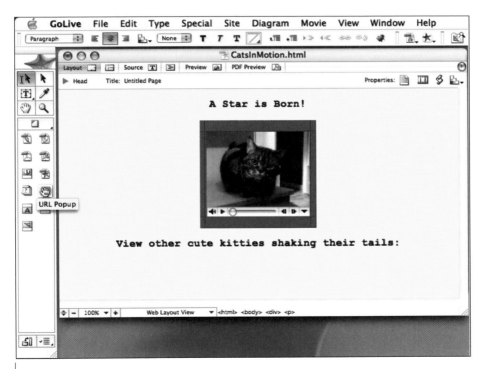

FIGURE 21-44

2. Open the Inspector. You'll notice that there are already two links listed in the Inspector ("Choose" and a link to the Adobe site). You can easily delete one or both of these links by selecting the link and clicking the trash can icon.

3. Click the "Create new item" button in the Inspector to add a new hyperlink to the list (Figure 21-45).

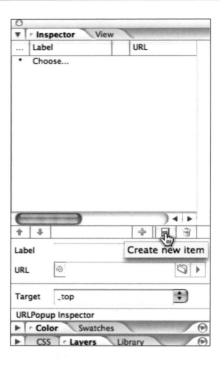

FIGURE 21-45

4. The Label text field will be visible in the URL pop-up menu, so enter a short label. For example, use "Home" if the hyperlink will take the viewer back to the home page.

5. Select the target for the URL by either browsing or using the Fetch URL tool to point to it.

6. Select where you would like the browser to open the hyperlink. From the Target menu, select one of these options:

_TOP: Loads the new page into the main browser window

_PARENT: Loads the new page into the immediate parent of the current document

_SELF: Loads the new page into the current browser window

_BLANK: Loads the new page into a new browser window

7. Click the Preview tab in your document window to preview the URL pop-up menu.

If you're entering the hyperlinks in a specific order and you notice that you've forgotten to add one, don't worry. You won't need to delete all the hyperlinks up to the point where you forgot to enter that hyperlink—simply add the forgotten link and use the up arrow (Figure 21-46) to move it to the correct location. You can also move hyperlinks down in the list if you need to rearrange them.

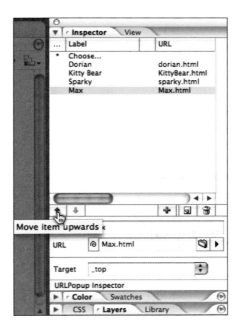

FIGURE 21-46

HOW DO I CREATE A KEYWORD META TAG?

Ever looked on the Internet for information on a particular topic? Or maybe you wanted to buy a product online but weren't sure where to look? If so, you've probably used a search engine to find it. Internet search engines such as Google use a variety of methods to locate web sites that match your search criteria. One strategy is to look at keyword meta tags. A *keyword meta tag* is a word or phrase that reflects the content of the web site. For example, a web site dedicated to cats may never actually use the word "feline," but someone doing a search on "feline" may still be interested in such a web site. To make this site appear in the listing of search results for that term, the site's creator could include "feline" as a keyword.

To create a keyword meta tag:

1. From the Draggable Head Objects set in the Objects palette, drag the Keywords icon onto the Head section of your web site (Figure 21-47).

FIGURE 21-47

2. With the Keywords icon selected, in the Inspector you can add keywords using either of these methods:

   • In the blank text box located at the bottom of the Inspector, type in the keyword and press Return (Mac) or Enter (Windows). This will add the keyword to the keywords list (Figure 21-48).

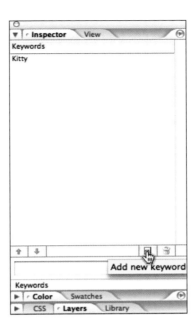

FIGURE 21-48

- Click the "Add new keyword" button, replace the New Keyword text with the new keyword, and press Return (Mac) or Enter (Windows).

You won't be able to see the keywords displayed anywhere in your web page unless you view the source code. If you would like to see how GoLive writes the keyword meta tags, click the "Keyword meta tag" button in the Head section of your web page in the Layout tab in the document window, and then click the Source tab. The highlighted source code is the meta tag command that GoLive has written, including the keywords.

If you've added a keyword to the list and notice that you've misspelled it, you can edit the keyword by selecting it from the keywords list, making the necessary changes in the text box, and then pressing Return (Mac) or Enter (Windows) to save the changes. If you need to delete a keyword, select it in the keywords list and click the "Remove selected keywords" button (the trash can).

HOW DO I IMPORT DATA INTO A TABLE?

Do you have data in a spreadsheet that you would like to display on your web site so that others can view it? You can add this data to your web site in any number of ways, all while maintaining the table layout of the spreadsheet. You can type it in manually or copy and paste it into the web page—or you can let GoLive do the majority of the work for you and import the data directly into a table in your web page.

GoLive can import data in the form of a tab-delimited text file from a number of different applications, such as Microsoft Excel or Microsoft Word. Before importing any data into the web page, however, you need to save the spreadsheet or document in the appropriate format. In this example, an Excel spreadsheet will be used.

To set up the data:

1. Open the spreadsheet in Excel.

2. Choose File→Save As. In the Save As dialog box, from the Format drop-down menu, choose Text (Tab delimited), as shown in Figure 21-49. This will create a *.txt* file that you will use to import the data into GoLive.

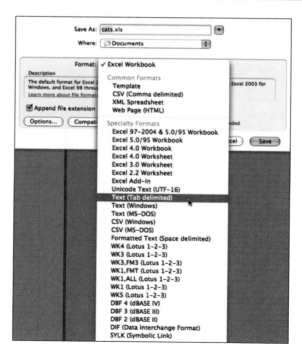

FIGURE 21-49

3. Click Save and close Excel.

To import the data into a table:

1. In GoLive, create a new web page or open an existing web page. Drag the Table icon from Draggable Basic Objects set in the Objects palette onto the web page. Don't worry about the table's dimensions.

2. Select the table into which you wish to import the data. From the Table tab in the Inspector, click the Import button next to Tab-Text (Figure 21-50).

FIGURE 21-50

3. In the Open dialog box that displays, navigate to the *.txt* file and click Open. GoLive imports the data in the *.txt* file into the table on your web page, automatically adding the correct number of rows and columns. Figure 21-51 shows a table in GoLive after it has been populated with data from an Excel spreadsheet.

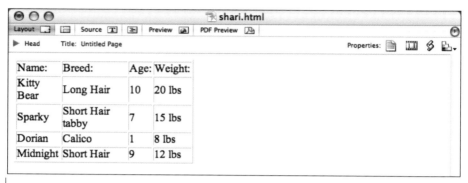

FIGURE 21-51

Just as you can add data to a table in a GoLive web page, you can also export data from a table to a spreadsheet or Word document.

To export data from a table:

1. In GoLive, select the table with the data you wish to export.

2. From the Table tab in the Inspector, click the Export button next to Tab-Text (see Figure 21-52).

3. The Export Tab-Text window will appear. Navigate to the location where you wish to save the file, name the file, and click Save. The file will be saved as a *.txt* file, which you can then import into Excel or any other application that recognizes tab-delimited data.

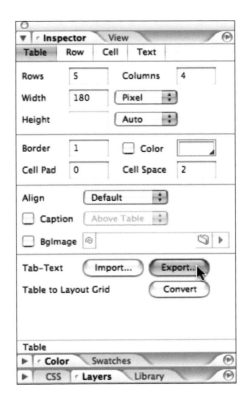

FIGURE 21-52

HOW DO I CREATE A TEMPLATE?

If you're creating a large site with multiple pages and you want to maintain a consistent look throughout the site, or if you have a team of designers working on your site, templates are the way to go. You can create a template and lock down certain areas that you do not want modified, such as logos and navigation buttons, while leaving other areas editable so that content can be added or modified as needed.

GoLive remembers the connection between a template and the pages created from that template, so when you make changes to the template, GoLive updates the content on all the pages that were created from the template. Being able to make changes to one page and let GoLive do the work for you on all the others almost sounds too good to be true!

1. Create a basic web page or open an existing page that you are going to use as the template.

2. Choose File→Save As to create the template. In the Save As dialog box, click the Site Folder icon located in the lower-left corner and select Templates. This will take you directly to the *Templates* folder in your site's *web-content* folder (Figure 21-53). Give the new template a name, and click Save.

FIGURE 21-53

3. Set the areas that can be edited. Choose Special→Template→New Editable Paragraph Region (Figure 21-54), and GoLive will change the region to green to indicate that it is now editable. Any region that is not green is not editable (Figure 21-55).

FIGURE 21-54

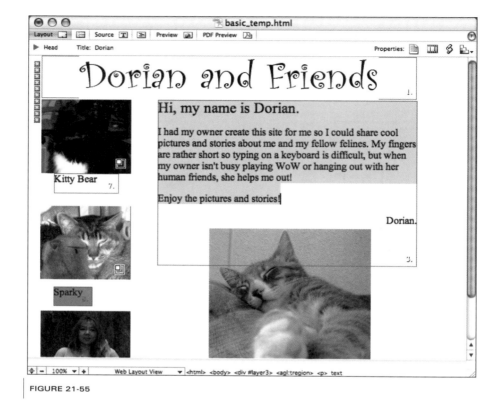

FIGURE 21-55

---

4. Repeat step 3 with any other areas you would like to be editable, then save the template.

After you've created the template, you can use it to create other pages for your web site. Templates are located in the Extras tab in the site window. There are three ways you can create a new page based on a template.

1. Choose File→New. From the New window, choose Web→Pages→Template Page, and select the template you created in the steps outlined above (Figure 21-56).

FIGURE 21-56

2. Right-click (PC) or Ctrl-click (Mac) in the site window, and choose New Page from Template from the pop-up menu, as shown in Figure 21-57.

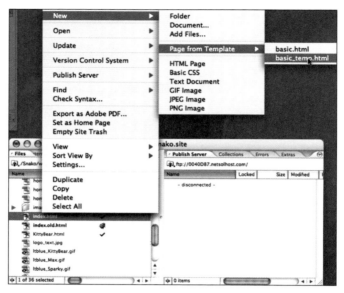

FIGURE 21-57

3. Double-click the Template icon itself in the *Templates* folder in the site window. GoLive will ask whether you want to modify the template or create a new page. Select Create (see Figure 21-58).

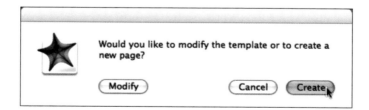

FIGURE 21-58

When the new web page is created from the template, you'll notice that it contains several areas of purple (Figure 21-59). These purple areas indicate the regions that cannot be modified. Save the file after you have made the necessary changes. Pages created from a template will have a special icon next to them in the site window (Figure 21-60).

FIGURE 21-59

FIGURE 21-60

1. Open the template by double-clicking on it in the *Templates* folder located in the Extras tab of the site window. GoLive will ask whether you would like to modify the template or create a new page. Select Modify.

2. Make the necessary changes to the template (for example, making changes to an image or text that is in a noneditable region).

3. When you save the changes you've made to the template, GoLive remembers that other pages are based on the template and lists them in the Updating Template window (Figure 21-61). Click OK. GoLive then displays a progress window. Click OK again.

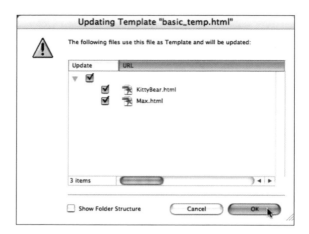

Updating Template "basic_temp.html"

The following files use this file as Template and will be updated:

Update	URL
☑	
☑	KittyBear.html
☑	Max.html

3 items

☐ Show Folder Structure   Cancel   OK

FIGURE 21-61

If you open the page created from the template, you'll see that GoLive has updated that page with the changes made in the template. Aren't templates wonderful?

[NOTE]

You can also disable the connection between a template and a page created from that template by detaching it. This turns the page into just a regular page, which is completely editable. To sever the connection between a page and its template, choose Special→Template→Detach From Template. You might want to do this if you wanted to use the template for the basis of a page but weren't worried about maintaining perfect consistency with other pages. You may also want to consider using stationery files rather than templates for this kind of purpose (see "How Do I Use Stationery and Snippets?," later in this chapter.)

HOW DO I USE COMPONENTS?

A *component* is an object that you place on your page that serves as a placeholder for an item stored in a source file. You can use the same component on multiple web pages, and each will point to the same source file. For example, you might add a component to each page of your web site that points to a source file that contains a navigation bar.

The advantage to this technique is that if you want to edit the navigation bar, you'll only have to make the changes in one place—any changes that you make to the source file are automatically reflected on each page that uses that component.

To create a component source file:

1. Choose File→New. In the New window, select the Web tab and choose Pages→Component Page to create a new component page, which is also known as the component source file (Figure 21-62). Click OK.

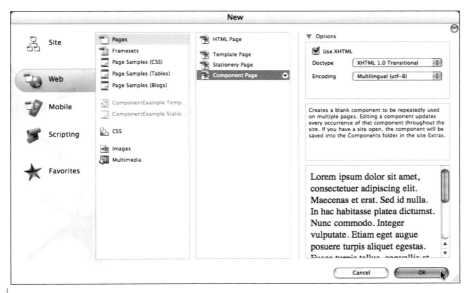

FIGURE 21-62

2. Add the desired content (e.g., tables, layers, text, or images) to the component source file.

3. When you are done adding content, choose File→Save As. Give the component a name, choose Components from the Site Folder pop-up menu, and click Save (Figure 21-63). This will ensure that the component source file is saved in the site's *web-data* folder and that GoLive will recognize it as a component page.

FIGURE 21-63

Now you're ready to add a component box to your web page, along with a component source file.

To use a component:

1. Create a new web page or open an existing web page to which you want to add a component.

2. From the Draggable Smart Objects set in the Objects palette, drag a Component icon onto the web page. A blank box will be created on the page, as shown in Figure 21-64.

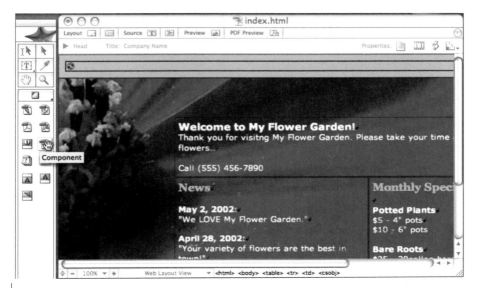

FIGURE 21-64

3. With the component object still selected, browse or use the Fetch URL tool in the Inspector to select the component source file you created in the previous steps (Figure 21-65).

The component box now contains the component source file.

FIGURE 21-65

1. You can open the component source file in two ways:

   - Double-click on the component source file in a web page that contains the source file.

   - Double-click on the component source file, located in the *Components* folder under the Extras tab in the site window.

2. Make the desired changes and save the component source file.

3. The Updating Component dialog box appears (Figure 21-66), listing all the web pages that contain this component source file. Click OK to update the components on each of these pages.

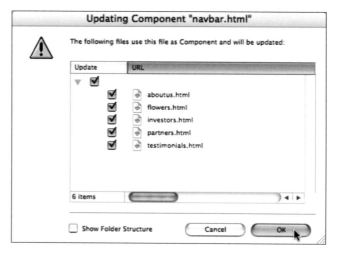

FIGURE 21-66

You can also permanently detach a component from the source file, if you want to be able to edit that version of the component separately from the source file.

1. Open the web page that contains the component you wish to detach from the source file.

2. Select the component box in the web page. To detach it, choose Special→Component→Detach Selected Component.

3. Figure 21-67 shows the warning box that will appear, asking if you are sure you want to detach this component from its source file. Click OK. If you look at the web page, you'll see that the component box is gone. You can now update this area independently of the other web pages.

Would you like to detach this page from its component(s)?

This cannot be undone.

Cancel   OK

FIGURE 21-67

HOW DO I USE STATIONERY AND SNIPPETS?

If you have a web page that you would like to use as a template for another web page but don't want the dependency that comes along with using an actual template, consider using stationery and snippets. Web pages created from stationery and snippets are not linked in any way, which means that any changes made to the original stationery or snippet file will not affect the web pages generated from those files.

Stationery files are templates used to create other web pages—but unlike with a normal template file, the connection stops there. Stationery files are ideal when you want to base a page or group of pages on a template but be able to customize them independently.

1. Open the web page you want to use as the stationery file.

2. Choose File→Save As to open the Save As dialog box. Name and save the file in the *Stationery* folder located in the web site's *web-data* folder (Figure 21-68).

FIGURE 21-68

[NOTE]

To be sure you are in the correct folder, click the Site Folder button located at the bottom of the Save As dialog box, and choose Stationery from the pop-up menu that appears. Always be sure to save files in the correct folder, because it does make a difference which folder you save files to. For example, if you save a file to the *Templates* folder, GoLive will treat it as a template file, complete with template options. The same goes for files saved to the *Components*, *Snippets*, and *Stationery* folders.

1. From the Extras tab in the site window, double-click on the newly created stationery file. GoLive will ask if you would like to modify the stationery or create a new page, as shown in Figure 21-69. Select Create.

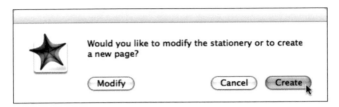

Would you like to modify the stationery or to create a new page?

Modify Cancel Create

FIGURE 21-69

2. Make the necessary changes to the web page. You can add and delete elements and modify all areas of this web page. Give the file a different name and save it.

Snippets are very similar to components. They both contain items such as text and/or images such as logos, navigation bars, or copyright notices that can be reused on other web pages. But unlike components, snippets are not linked to their original source files, so any changes made to an original snippet file will not affect the snippet after it has been added to a web page.

To create a snippet:

1. Open the Snippets tab in the Library palette, as shown in Figure 21-70. (Choose Window→Site→Library to open the Library palette.)

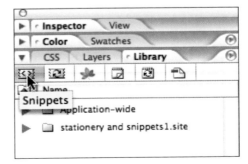

FIGURE 21-70

2. Using the Standard Editing tool or the Object Selection tool, select the text and/or images you wish to use in your snippet.

3. Drag the highlighted section down to the Snippets tab of the Library palette and drop it into the site folder, as shown in Figure 21-71. GoLive creates a *snippet.agls* file. (If you're wondering what the *.agls* stands for, it's a GoLive-specific file extension that is the abbreviation of Adobe GoLive Snippets.)

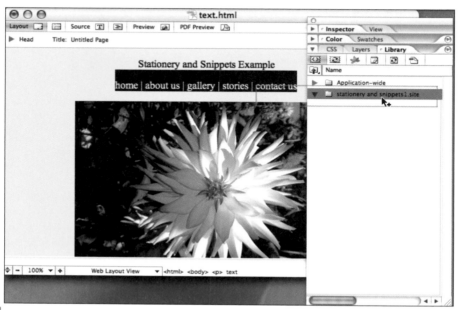

FIGURE 21-71

4. To change the name of the snippet file, select the *snippet.agls* file in the Snippets tab and click once on the name. Then enter a new name for the snippet.

To add a snippet to a web page, select the snippet file in the Snippets tab of the Library palette and drag and drop it onto the web page. If you make any changes to the original snippet, any instances of that snippet will not be updated.

THE END

This ends the answers to the Top 15 How Do I...? questions. Should you find yourself with more questions that you need answers to, check out the Adobe GoLive forums at Adobe's web site: *http://www.Adobe.com/support/forums/main.html*.

INDEX

Better than e-books

Try it Free! Sign up today
and get your first 14 days free.
Go to *safari.oreilly.com*

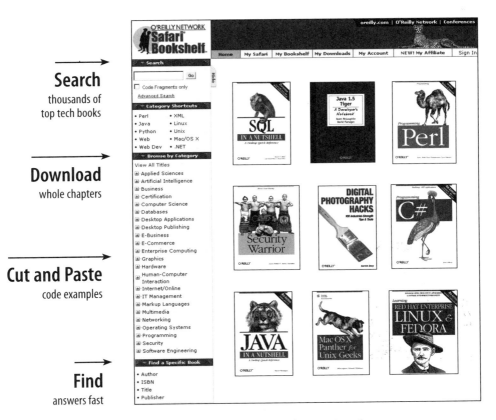

Search thousands of top tech books

Download whole chapters

Cut and Paste code examples

Find answers fast

Search Safari! The premier electronic reference library for programmers and IT professionals.

Related Titles from O'Reilly

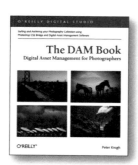

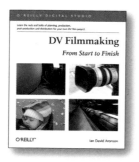

Digital Media

Adobe InDesign CS2
One-on-One

Adobe Encore DVD:
In the Studio

The DAM Book: Digital
Asset Management for
Photographers

Digital Audio Essentials

Digital Photography:
Expert Techniques

Digital Photography Hacks

Digital Photography Pocket
Guide, *3rd Edition*

Digital Video Hacks

Digital Video Pocket Guide

Digital Video Production
Cookbook

DV Filmmaking: From Start
to Finish

DVD Studio Pro 3:
In the Studio

GarageBand 2: The Missing
Manual, *2nd Edition*

Home Theater Hacks

iLife '05: The Missing Manual

iMovie HD & iDVD 5:
The Missing Manual

InDesign Production
Cookbook

iPhoto 5: The Missing
Manual, *4th Edition*

iPod & iTunes Hacks

iPod & iTunes: The Missing
Manual, *3rd Edition*

iPod Fan Book

iPod Playlists

iPod Shuffle Fan Book

PDF Hacks

O'REILLY®

Our books are available at most retail and online bookstores.

To order direct: 1-800-998-9938 • *order@oreilly.com* • *www.oreilly.com*

Online editions of most O'Reilly titles are available by subscription at *safari.oreilly.com*